Robert Knox

The Races of Men

A Philosophical Enquiry into the Influence of Race over the Destinies of Nations

I0592415

Robert Knox

The Races of Men
A Philosophical Enquiry into the Influence of Race over the Destinies of Nations

ISBN/EAN: 9783741163487

Manufactured in Europe, USA, Canada, Australia, Japa

Cover: Foto ©Thomas Meinert / pixelio.de

Manufactured and distributed by brebook publishing software
(www.brebook.com)

Robert Knox

The Races of Men

THE

RACES OF MEN:

A PHILOSOPHICAL ENQUIRY

INTO THE

Influence of Race over the Destinies of Nations.

BY

ROBERT KNOX, M.D.,

LECTURER ON ANATOMY,
CORRESPONDING MEMBER OF THE IMPERIAL ACADEMY OF MEDICINE OF
FRANCE,
HONORARY MEMBER OF THE ETHNOLOGICAL SOCIETY OF LONDON,
AND
REIGN ASSOCIATE OF THE ANTHROPOLOGICAL SOCIETY OF PARIS,
ETC. ETC.

SECOND EDITION, WITH SUPPLEMENTARY CHAPTERS.

"THE PROPER STUDY OF MANKIND IS MAN."—POPE.

PREFACE.

THE work I here present to the world has cost me much thought and anxiety, the views it contains being wholly at variance with long-received doctrines, stereotyped prejudices, national delusions, and a physiology and a cosmogony based on a fantastic myth as old at least as the Hebrew record.

That human character, individual and national, is traceable solely to the nature of that race to which the individual or nation belongs, is a statement which I know must meet with the sternest opposition. It runs counter to nearly all the chronicles of events called histories: it overturns the theories of statesmen, of theologians, of philanthropists of all shades—from the dreamy Essayist, whose remedy for every ill that flesh is heir to, is summed up in " the coming man," to the " whitened sepulchres of England," the hard-handed, spatula-fingered Saxon utilitarian, whose best plea for religion and sound morals, and philanthropy, is " the profitableness thereof "—imposters all! to such the truths in this little work must ever be most unpalatable. Nevertheless, that race in human affairs is everything, is simply a fact, the most remarkable, the most comprehensive, which philosophy has ever announced. Race is everything: literature, science, art—in a word, civilization, depends on it.

Each race treated of in this little work will complain of my *not* having done *them* justice; of all others they will admit that I have spoken the truth. The placing the Slavonian and Gothic races foremost amongst men, first and greatest in philosophy, will much, I believe, astonish the men of other races; the Saxon and Celt; the Italian and Sarmatian; the inordinate self-esteem of the Saxon will be especially shocked thereby, nor will he listen with composure to a theory which tells him, proves to him, that his race cannot domineer over the earth—cannot even exist permanently on any continent to which he is not indigenous —cannot ever become native, true-born Americans—cannot hold in permanency any portion of any continent but the one on which he *first* originated. Physiologists will dispute with me the great laws I have endeavoured to substitute for the effete common-place of the schools; geologists will think me hasty in declaring the æra of Cuvier at an end; theologians——but here I stop; a reply shall not be wanting. As to the hack compilers, their course is simple: they will first deny the doctrine to be true; when this becomes clearly untenable, they will deny that it is new; and they will finish by engrossing the whole in their next compilations, omitting carefully the name of the author.

Lest my readers feel surprise at the repetition of so many of the woodcuts, I have to observe that this was rendered necessary by the nature of the work. These woodcuts are from drawings made expressly for this work by my friend, Dr. Westmacott, an accomplished artist, in whose praise I need say nothing. They are much more expressive of the true character of race than will at first appear to the careless observer.

R. K.

London, 1st July, 1850.

————

PREFACE TO THE SECOND EDITION.

This new edition differs from the first only in having attached to it a Supplement, in which many important philosophical questions are treated of, all having reference, more or less directly, to the great question of race.

London, Jan. 1862.

CONTENTS.

SUPPLEMENT.

INTRODUCTION.

THE outlines of Lectures now presented to the Public, I have designated " A Fragment." I disclaim all pretensions of attempting a complete history of mankind, even from the single point of view from which I contemplate Human history. No materials exist for such a history. Of man's origin we know nothing correctly; we know not when he first appeared in space; his place in time, then, is unknown. Still thought to have been coeval with the existing order of things, this theory will require revision, now that the dawn of the present organic world, even as it now stands, can be shown to have an antiquity agreeing ill with human chronologies. In the meantime how worthless are these chronologies! How replete with error human history has been proved to be.

The basis of the view I take of man is his Physical structure; if I may so say, his Zoological history. To know this must be the first step in all inquiries into man's history: all abstractions, neglecting or despising this great element, the physical character and constitution of man,

B

his mental and corporeal attributes must, of necessity, be at the least Utopian, if not erroneous. Men are of various Races; call them Species, if you will; call them permanent Varieties; it matters not. The fact, the simple fact, remains just as it was: men are of different races. Now, the object of these lectures is to show that in human history race is everything.

Of the minute physical structure of most of the races of men we know nothing, anatomical inquiries having as yet been confined to the investigation of a very few European races; I may almost say, merely to the Saxon and Celtic. When some superficial observer has made a few remarks on the skeleton of a race, he fancies he knows its anatomy! But from my own, I admit very limited, observations, I feel disposed to affirm, that the races of men, when carefully examined, will be found to show remarkable organic differences. In a dark or coloured person, whose structure I had an opportunity of observing, the nerves of the limbs were at least a third less than those of the Saxon man of the same height. M. Tiedemann, of Heidelberg, informed me that he had every reason to believe that the native Australian race differed in an extraordinary manner from the European: that this is the case with the Hottentot and Bosjeman race has been long known.

The mind of the race, instinctive and reasoning,

naturally differs in correspondence with the organization. What wild, Utopian theories have been
advanced—what misstatements, respecting civilization! The most important of man's intellectual
faculties, the surest, the best,—the instinctive,
namely,—has even been declared to be wanting
to human nature! What wild and fanciful theories of human progress, of human civilization!
Look at Europe; at either bank of the Danube;
at Northern Africa; at Egypt; at the shores of
the Mediterranean, generally, and say what progress civilization has made in these countries
since the decline of the Roman Empire. Is Ireland civilized? In Cicero's time the Island of
Rhodes presented a civilization which no part of
Britain can pretend to: what is its state at this
moment?

But, it may be said, Christianity has done much.
This I doubt; but admitting it to be the case, its
progress is not evident: to me it seems to lose
ground. It presents also a variety of forms
essentially distinct: with each race its character
is altered; Celtic, Saxon, Sarmatian, express in
so many words, the Greek, Roman, Lutheran
forms of worship. M. Daubigny has expended
many words in explaining the rejection of the
Reformation by certain nations, its adoption by
others; let him look to the map, and he will find
that, with a slight exception, if it *really be one*,
the Celtic race universally rejected the Refor-

mation of Luther; the Saxon race as certainly
adopted it. There need be no mystery in stating
so simple a fact.

The *morale* of a race has little or nothing to do
with its religion: I offer the English invasion
of Hindostan in proof—the invasion of Scinde
and Affghan, the plunder of China. A profitable war is a pleasant thing for a Saxon nation;
and a crusade against the heathen has always
been declared praiseworthy.

The study of the races of men—the tracing, at
least, some of those great events, distinguishing
their national histories, to their physical and moral
natures—has ever been with me a favourite pur-
suit. I early examined the work of Blumenbach, of
which the laborious writings of Dr. Prichard were
an extension—an imperfect work, leading to no
results; teaching a physiology as old as Herodotus
and Hippocrates. More than thirty years ago,
observation taught me that the great question of
race—the most important, unquestionably, to man
—had been for the most part scrupulously, shall
we say purposely, avoided—by the statesman, the
historian, the theologian; by journalists of nearly
all countries. Unpalatable doctrines, no doubt, to
dynasties lording it over nations composed of
different races.

Empires, monarchies, nations, are human contrivances; often held together by fraud and violence: Ireland, for example, and England; Prussia

and Posen; Austria and Hungary. Does an
emeute take place in Canada? See with what
anxiety it is attempted to be shown in Parliament
that it is not a fight of race against race! All in
vain! The terrible question cannot be concealed
any longer. The savage rule of the Tedeschi will
no longer be endured in Italy; the Saxon-German
detests the Slavonian, who repays his hatred
with defiance. Long-headed statesmen, like
Metternich and Guizot, who knew so well the
nature of the races they governed, would fain
mystify the question, ascribing the war of race to
a wild spirit of democracy—to peripatetic agita-
tors; in Ireland, to the smallness of the holdings;
and perhaps, in Canada, to the largeness of the
holdings! Profound observers, who could pass
their lives amongst a race of men without discovering their nature! Let the Norman government of England look to it. Its views and policy
are antagonistic to the Saxon race it governs;
1888 may complete what 1088 left imperfect,
and an Anglo-Saxon republic, looking again towards Scandinavia, may found a European con-
federacy, against which the dynasty-loving Celt
and the swinish, abject Cossaque, may strike in
vain. Then, and not till then, will terminate the
evil effects of the conquest of England by the
Normans.

Human history cannot be a mere chapter of
accidents. The fate of nations cannot always be

regulated by chance; its literature, science, art, wealth, religion, language, laws, and morals, cannot surely be the result of merely accidental circumstances. If any one insists with me that a Negro or a Tasmanian accidentally born in England becomes thereby an Englishman, I yield the point; but should he further insist that he, the said Negro or Tasmanian, may become also a Saxon or Scandinavian, I must contend against so ludicrous an error. And yet errors like this are committed daily by well-educated and well-informed persons. With me, race, or hereditary descent, is everything; it stamps the man. Setting aside all theories, I have endeavoured to view mankind as they now exist, divided as they are, and seem always to have been, into distinct races. As the origin of these races is lost in the past, I trace them from the present towards the past; from the partially known to the totally unknown. Well-meaning, timid persons dread the question of race; they wish it left where Prichard did, that is, where Hippocrates left it.' But this cannot be : the human mind is free to think, if not on the Rhine or on the Thames, at least on the Ohio and the Missouri.

The greatest difficulty I have experienced in the drawing up these lectures, whether as lectures delivered to public audiences, or written, as they now are, for publication, has been, to decide on the arrangement best calculated to submit my views briefly, yet intelligibly, to the public. After various trials I have decided on the following; it may not be the best: it is not systematic; it is not methodical; but it seems to me adapted to a very numerous class of readers, who, though highly educated, are yet not scientific. To place the great physiological principles regulating human and other living beings before them in an intelligible form, has been of course my main difficulty. This, I trust, I have now overcome.

The races of men as they now exist on the globe constitute a fact which cannot be overlooked. They differ from each other widely—most widely:—but that such differences exist, and important ones too, has not been denied; the word, *race*, is of daily use, applied even to man: since the war of race commenced in continental Europe and in Ireland, no expression is of more frequent occurrence than the term race. It is not, then, a new phrase I use, but I use it in a new sense; for whilst the statesman, the historian, the theologian, the universalist, and the mere scholar, either attached no special meaning to the term, for reasons best known to themselves; or refused to follow out the principle to its consequences; or ascribed the moral difference in the races of men to fanciful causes, such as edu-

cation, religion, climate, &c.—and their physical
distinctions sometimes to the same hap-hazard influences—sometimes to climate alone—sometimes
to climate aided by a mysterious law—such as that
imagined by Prichard, that the fair individuals
of any family separating themselves from the
darker branches would with each successive generation become fairer, and the darker become
darker, forgetting that this theory was refuted by
the very first fact from which he starts, and which
actually forms the basis of his whole theory—
namely, that individuals having a specific tendency towards different races are constantly being
born in every family;—or, lastly, ascribing to
mere chance and hap-hazard, as in the story of
the short-legged American sheep, the production
of the permanent varieties of man:—I, in opposition to these views, am prepared to assert that race
is everything in human history; that the races of
men are not the result of accident; that they are
not convertible into each other by any contrivance whatever.   The eternal laws of nature
must prevail over protocols and dynasties: fraud,
—that is, the law; and brute force—that is, the
bayonet, may effect much; have effected much;
but they cannot alter nature.

The reader, no doubt, will already have an
idea of the plan I intend following in the publishing of these lectures: certain great physical

or physiological principles will be discussed when speaking of each particular race; the principle may apply, no doubt, to all, but I leave its application to my readers: the chief applications will be made, in order to avoid repetition, to the race whose history I at the moment discuss.

I have also very carefully considered the question as to "the race" with which I should commence the history of man. Here, again, great difficulties presented themselves. We know not the history of any one race on the earth. All is conjecture, pretension, error, obscurity. The most illustrious name applied to any race has been the Roman, and yet it does not appear that there ever was any distinct *race* to which this name could be applied! This is human history! Abstract terms have been invented to express relations which do not exist: such, for example, as the term Teuton, used by Dr. Arnold in a sense which all history, ancient and modern, refutes.

But I need not further enlarge on the course laid down, it will unfold itself as I proceed. Nor even at this moment, whilst I write this Introduction, have I fully made up my mind as to the race with whose history I shall commence this work. No race interests us so much as the Saxon, or as I prefer calling him, for reasons to be afterwards explained, the Scandinavian. He

is about to be the dominant race on the earth; a
section of the race, the Anglo-Saxon, has for nearly
a century been all-powerful on the ocean; the grand
tyrants by sea, the British; as the Muscovite has
been the grand tyrant by land: so said Napoleon,
that mighty intellect, an over-match for the world.
I may probably, then, commence with the Physiological history of the Saxon, tracing the moral
and physical characteristics which distinguish
him from all other races of men—his religious
formulas, his literature, his contempt for art, his
abhorrence for theory—that is, for science and
scientific men, his acquisitive and applicative
genius, tracing all to the eternal, unalterable
qualities of race. It will be my endeavour to show
him in all climes, and under all circumstances;
how he modifies for the time being his natural
but unalterable character to suit the existing
order of things; to prove to you how the Hippocratic theory of man is, like most other medical theories, wholly untrue; inapplicable to the
Saxon, and, indeed, to every other race. Forget
for a time the word *nation*, and ask yourselves
whence come the people composing any ancient
assemblage called a nation. a state, a republic, a
monarchy, an empire? Ask yourselves this plain
question, are they indigenous to the soil, or have
they migrated from somewhere else? and if so,
have they altered in structure, in character?

How perfectly does the modern Scandinavian or Saxon resemble the original tribes as they started from the woods of Germany to meet Cæsar on the Rhine! Whether, under Pretorius, in Southern Africa, he throws out a defiance to the military despot, the irresponsible agent of a dynasty, ruling a Saxon race by laws hateful to their nature, antagonistic of their feelings; or, demanding in Upper Canada free institutions; or driving that same dynasty, with its sham constitution, from the mighty continent of America for ever; establishing in the place of its hateful and paltry thraldom, a republican empire, destined some future day to rule the world; everywhere is he the same; nature's democrat—the respecter of law when the law is made *by himself*; —but I anticipate my first lecture. Let me conclude, therefore, without delay, an Introduction already too long.

As a living and material being, the history of man is included in the history of the organic world. He is of this world; he did not create it, he creates nothing; you cannot separate his history from the organic world. Apart no doubt he stands; but all species stand apart from each other quite as much as he does from them. He has his specific laws regulating his form, but these are in perfect accordance with all nature's works. By the unity of organization is he connected with all life —past, present, and to come. Other animals

have but one history, their zoological; man has
two, the zoological and the intellectual.   The
latter must ever, to a certain extent, be regulated
by the former.   Like other animals, he is found
to occupy only a portion of space and a fraction
of time—that is, of the continuous succession of
events.   It seems as if there was a period when
he existed not, and, to believe Geologists, a long
period too.   I do not hold this to be quite proved
in any sense; but grant it at present, he holds in
this respect the identical relation to time and
space which we find all other animals do.   This
is their history.   There was a period when they
existed not in space, or cannot now be discovered; they next appear to run their determined
course, they then cease to be.   Judging by the
past, this must also be the fate of man.   But now
my reader will readily perceive that I again
digress from the business in hand, which is to
bring this Introduction to a close; this I shall do
by a few remarks on the history of the lectures
themselves.

The obvious differences in the races of men
attracted my attention, as I have already observed, from my earliest years.   In my native
country, Britain, there have been, from the earliest
recorded times, at the least *two* distinct races of
men; I am disposed to think *three*.   I do not
allude to the sprinkling of gipsy, Jew, and

Phœnician races, who still hold their ground in various parts of the island, nor to some traces of others, as of the Huns, visible amongst the hop-gatherers of Kent; but to three large bodies of men, of sufficient numerical strength to maintain, if not political power and unity, at least their integrity as a race distinct from others, in sufficient numbers to resist the aggressive action of the admixture of race by intermarriage; to neutralize, to a great extent, such intermarriages, and to render that admixture comparatively unimportant. These races are the Celtic, Saxon, and Belgian or Flemish. They inhabited, in the remotest period, different parts of the country, as they still do, from a period, in fact, beyond the historical era. I cannot find any era in history when the Celtic races occupied the lowlands of England and of Scotland; I believe this theory to be completely erroneous—a dream, a fable. The story of the arrival of the Saxons in England, of the Jutes and Angles, Danes, Swedes, Holsteinians—let us say at once Saxons or Scandinavians—is a very pretty story, true enough as regards that horde and that date, but altogether false if it be pretended that this was the first advent of the Scandinavian into Britain. Again, it was not the barbarous Celt whom Cæsar met in Kent; nor did he meet the Germans, whom he knew well; he met the Flemings, deeply inter-

mingled with the Phœnicians. When had the
Celtic races war-chariots? Did the Dictator encounter any such in Gaul?

These and other reflections occurred to me
early in life; that is, so soon as, in 1814, I looked
attentively at the population of Southern England. I have been ever anxious to get at elementary knowledge, knowing its vital importance;
by this I do not mean the sort of information
given to children, consisting wholly of words,
without a meaning, but to the great elements
of knowledge on which human thoughts and
reflections are to be engaged. Now here is
one of these elementary, all-important facts,
which is either true or not; if true, its consequences are without a limit; if not true, it
ought to be distinctly refuted. To me the Caledonian Celt of *Scotland* appears a race as
distinct from the Lowland Saxon of the same
country, as any two races can possibly be: as
negro from American; Hottentot from Caffre;
Esquimaux from Saxon. But statesmen, historians, theologians, have not only refused to
acknowledge the importance of this fact; they
have gone further; they have denied its existence
and purposely falsified history: the fact has been
carefully excluded from the high educational
institutions of the country. An English clergyman, an Oxonian, a gentleman, and a scholar,

remarked to me, about two years ago, "So, then, it really does appear that there are two distinct races of men in Scotland!" I was confounded; but allowing him to proceed, I found that he had just made this notable discovery in the columns of *The Times!* The journalist had also just discovered the fact, and had actually had the courage to hint that there might also be two races in Ireland! The proprietors sent a reporter to Ireland who made out this fact: nothing additional that I am aware of, unless it be that he ascertained that the middlemen and landlords were mostly Celtic also! Profound observer! Why did he pass St. Giles's? Marylebone? Whitechapel? Yet, true to his trade, within a year the editor throws this fact and all its consequences overboard; describes the Celtic rebellion of Scotland as a national rebellion of Scotland against England; knowing at the same time that there was scarcely a Scottish man, properly speaking, in the Stuart army. The Caledonian Celtic race, not Scotland, fell at Culloden, never more to rise; the Boyne was the Waterloo of Celtic Ireland. If the French Celt recovers from the terrible disaster of 1815 it will cause me surprise. Napoleon, whom he betrayed, whom he sold to England and to Russia, is dead: the Celt now reaps the fruits of his treachery.

Whilst still young I readily perceived that the

philosophic formula of Blumenbach led to no results: explained nothing: investigated no causes. It was the external-character naturalist trying " his method " on man. It left every great physiological question unanswered; nor was it until certain great philosophic and original minds returned to the grand principles already sketched for them by Leibnitz, Newton, and others, that philosophy once more recovered its hold of physiology. This movement I trace, not to the Scandinavian or North German, but to the Slavonian, or to the south and middle German; to Oken and Goethe, Spix, Von Martius, and a host of others: but not to Berlin, nor to Heidelberg; nor to any section of the Scandinavian or true German race. In a word, transcendental anatomy, which alone, of all systems, affords us a glimpse and a hope of a true " theory of nature," seems to me of Slavonian origin strictly; no Saxon could ever have imagined it; scarcely comprehend it: the low transcendentalists of England are a diverting crew, who nibble at a question they cannot refute, yet dare not adopt.

Whilst tracing the progress of events all over the world since the period I mention, I have seen the question of race tested in a great variety of ways; its strength especially; its endurance. The evidence in its favour, up to 1844, enabled me to predict the coming war of race against race, which has convulsed Europe during the last two years. This I did in various courses of lectures delivered in 1844-45-46 and 47, as I shall presently explain. So early as 1830, I asked the persons who called themselves Germans to point out *Germany* to me on the map; to tell me who are the Germans? I asked them if the Viennese and the Bohemians were Germans? If they thought they would ever become so? If the inhabitants of Posen were Germans? If the Dutch, Danes, Swedes, Norwegians, were Germans? To these questions I could never get a rational reply. The educated men to whom I spoke were quite aware that, strictly speaking, there was no such place as Germany, and no single race to which the word German could apply? They knew that the countries which at various times have figured on the map as the German Empire, Germany, Prussia, Saxony, &c., contain within them various races of men; the Saxon or classic German of Roman writers; the Slavonian, the Sarmatian, and another race, not yet well described; they were quite aware of this; they knew well that such conflicting elements could never agree. Accordingly, in 1845, I foretold the breaking down of the iron despotisms of Hapsburg and Brandenburg as a necessary result of a war of race: it came in '47. The gold of England, and the sword of Russia, either thought invincible,

c

could not amalgamate the dark-haired Fleming
with the Saxon-Dutchman: 700 years of absolute
possession has not advanced by a single step the
amalgamation of the Irish Celt with the Saxon-
English: the Cymbri of Wales remain as they
were: the Caledonian still lingers in diminished
numbers, but unaltered, on the wild shores of his
lochs and friths, scraping a miserable subsistence
from the narrow patch of soil left him by the
stern climate of his native land.   Transplant him
to another climate, a brighter sky, a greater field,
free from the trammels of artificial life, the harnessed routine of European civilization; carry
him to Canada, *he is still the same;* mysterious
fact. I beseech you, you great essayists, Utopians,
universalists, and shrewd fatalist statesmen, to
explain the facts if you can; if not, why not admit them to exist. The habitans, le bas Canadian,
is a being of the age of Louis Quatorze. Seigno-
ries, monkeries, jesuits, grand domains; idle-
ness, indolence, slavery; a mental slavery, the
most dreadful of all human conditions. See him
cling to the banks of rivers, fearing to plunge into
the forest; without self-reliance; without self-confidence. If you seek an explanation, go back to
France; go back to Ireland, and you will find it
there: it is the race. Even in the states, the free
United States, where if a man remain a slave
in mind it is his own affair, the Celt is distinct

from the Saxon to this day. The progress of the question of race cannot be for a moment mistaken : the question will some day test the strength of the " Declaration of Independence ;" for the Celt does not understand what we Saxons mean by independence : a military leader he understands ; a faction-fight ; a fortified camp, for a Capital is his delight. But I again forget that I am busy, or ought to be, with the introduction to my lectures, and not with the lectures themselves.

As my opinions became more matured, strengthened by daily observation and research, I resolved to submit them to the public in one form or other. It is true that I should have greatly preferred examining still further into the history of the races composing the heterogeneous empire of Austria, and more especially the actual position of the Slavonian race, using the term in its most extensive signification.' This journey across Europe I could not, however, accomplish, and hence I remained, with most others, I presume, but little acquainted with the actual position of the Slavonian race. But I at least avoided the errors into which most of my countrymen have fallen ; I never mistook them for Germans ; neither did I suppose that they would be transformed into Germans by merely living under a German dynasty and breathing German air : I never mistook the Florentines or Milanese for Tedeschi, merely because they had been for some centuries under the abhorred dominion of Austria. With me the Anglo-Saxon in America is a Saxon, and not a *native:* the Celt will prove a Celt wherever he is born, wherever he is found. The possible conversion of one race into another I hold to be a statement contradicted by all history.

In making my opinions known I resorted first to the method most familiar to me—namely, by public lectures; and accordingly the sum and substance of these lectures were delivered, about five years ago, to many of the Philosophical and Popular Educational Institutions of England; in Newcastle, Birmingham, Manchester, &c.

My first course was delivered before the Philosophical Society of Newcastle—an institution remarkable for the number of distinguished men it includes. The lectures were briefly reported at the time by the public press. They were soon after repeated at Birmingham and Manchester, before the members of the Royal Institution, and at the Athenæum. Here ample reports were made of my lectures, and published in the newspaper press of Manchester. This was fully two years before the occurrence of any of the extraordinary events which, during the last two years, have shaken the stability of the artificial governmental arrangements of men and families, dynasties and protocols. At that time I had the great question of race, the all-absorbing question of the day, wholly to myself. Europe was tranquil!' Highly-educated men asked me if the French were Celts!—if there were *two* races of men in Britain and in Ireland! —and supposing there were two races, how it was that they could not agree!—who were the Slavonians! and such other questions as satisfied me that they and I viewed human history from two different points; they, as a chapter of accidents, and I, as tracing human character, individual, social, national, to the all-pervading, unalterable, physical character of race.

Of the brief reports of my lectures thus made known by the provincial press, the London press took no notice. I scarcely at first expected this. The nations, it is true, were, according to their views, tranquil, consolidated, happy, free, contented, flourishing, under the treaties of Vienna and the Quadruple Alliance! Still I expected to have met with, on all hands, a stout denial of the premises on which my conclusions were founded, and an attempt, at least, at a refutation of the conclusions themselves. Did the neglect to notice my lectures arise from their having some doubts themselves of the future tranquillity of Europe? Or, seeing the matter perhaps in the same light with myself, they had yet thought it prudent to avoid all such dangerous topics, opinions, predictions of events which might not occur for centuries?

I know not; but such was the case. For two years
at least I had the whole question of race to myself. In a kingdom composed of disunited races,
the press adopted, no doubt, the more prudent
course; and they were bound, moreover, to consult
the feelings of their contributors and readers—the
English people, strong in their *nationality*, despising alike all other nations and races; some for
their race, others for those very qualities of race
which they most prize in themselves. Then burst
forth the mighty convulsion of the Celtic race of
France; the Italian races rose against the barbarous
savage Tedeschi, who, under the assumed name of
Germans, to which they have not the most distant
claim, lorded it over Italy; then arose the Saxon
element of the German race in Austria, demanding
freedom, and a division from the barbarous
Slavonian; then fell that miserable drum-head
monarchy of Prussia, and the grand duchy of
Posen furnished the field of contest between the
German and Slavonian races.

The views I had so long adopted of human
nature, human history, and the future, had led me
long ago to foresee the approaching struggle of
race against race. The evidence appeared to me
so clear that I felt greatly disappointed on finding
so few disposed to acquiesce in the views I
had adopted. But now that the question can
be no longer concealed, the London press has

honoured me with a notice I did not, I confess, aspire to. One leading journal, at least, has fairly reprinted nearly all my views in the form of leaders, to which, of course, no name was attached. As these views had been delivered in public lectures at least three years previously; as they had been reprinted in the provincial press; and as they were then reporting in the *Medical Times* journal,—I scarcely expected in an English newspaper so barefaced a piracy. My friends have complained of it to me frequently; they have called on me to denounce and expose the parties. I leave the matter in the hands of the public.

In presenting this first complete edition of my *Lectures on the Races of Men* to public criticism, I have weighed most anxiously the form of the publication, and the order or method to be followed in arranging the lectures. It has indeed been my great difficulty. Materials for a systematic history of the races of men are wholly wanting; the great problem of human nature has scarcely been touched on in any previous history of race. The illustrious Prichard, with the best intentions in the world, has succeeded in misdirecting the English mind as to all the great questions of race. This misdirection has told, as we have seen, even on the scholar and on the scientific man. As a consequence of its misdirection, on the mere mention of the word race, the popular mind flies off to Tasmania, the polar circle, or the land of the Hottentot. Englishmen cannot be made to believe, can scarcely be made to comprehend, that races of men, differing as widely from each other as races can possibly do, inhabit, not merely continental Europe, but portions of Great Britain and Ireland. And next to the difficulty of getting this great fact admitted to be one, has been an unwillingness to admit the full importance of *race*, militating as it does against the thousand-and-one prejudices of the so-called civilized state of man; opposed as it is to the Utopian views based on education, religion, government. Two courses were open to me; the first, and that I should have preferred, was to commence the history of race by inquiring into the history of man as he stands related to the organic world; thus attempting at once the solution of the great problem—man's existence on the earth. But the failure of Alexander von Humboldt, in his *Cosmos*, and the obscurity of the Slavonian transcendentalism of Oken and his school, even admitting, as I do, that its basis is in truth, finally deterred me from this course, even after I had arranged my lectures in accordance with it.

A word or two more, and I have done with this introductory matter. The timid, of all sects, as well as the members of the primitive catholic church, have thought my views of the Jewish race open to doubt: some have thought them not orthodox. It is difficult in the present day to ascertain precisely what is orthodox and what is not. Some of my views, and those the more important, coincide strictly with those of some eminent divines.* Of this I was not aware at the time I published my lectures. On the other hand, I have been assured that this does not avail, as the same objection, heterodoxy, lies against their opinions as against mine. Here I must leave the matter in the hands of the theologian, upon whose province I neither must nor mean to intrude.

2. Many have thought and said that the character I have given the Celt was overdrawn and exaggerated. I wish I could think with them. For the Celtic race I have the highest regard and esteem; but as an inquirer into truth, I have of necessity been compelled to adhere to facts. In my first lecture, delivered five years ago, I said that the Celtic race does not, and never could be made to comprehend the meaning of the word liberty. My readers will have the goodness to recollect that the opinion I gave had no reference to recent events, but was deduced from past history: the histories of '92, of '15, of '32; add now the events of '48 and '40, and say, have I erred in the estimate I formed of this race? On four

* M'Neile and others.

eventful occasions the supreme power has returned into the hands of the Celtic men of France:
never was the destruction of a dynasty more complete. What use have they made of this power?
Have the conscript laws been abolished? Have
the passport laws for Frenchmen ceased to exist?
Is the press free? Paris open, and unfortified?
The population peaceably armed? Or is it true
that they have turned their capital into a fortified
camp?—elected as a military leader the nephew of
the greatest of men, whom they betrayed?—con-
scription, passports, all in force. I appeal to the
Saxon men of all countries whether I am right
or not in my estimate of the Celtic character.
Furious fanaticism; a love of war and disorder; a
hatred for order and patient industry; no accumulative habits; restless, treacherous, uncertain:
look at Ireland. This is the dark side of the character. But there is a bright and brilliant view
which my readers will find I have not failed to
observe. What race has done such glorious
deeds? Still it is never to be forgotten that the
continental Celt deserted and betrayed the greatest
of men, Napoleon, thus losing the sovereignty
of the world: here the fatal blow was struck from
which the continental Celt cannot hope to recover.
Culloden decided the fate, not of Scotland, as the
Times has it, but of the Caledonian Celt: the
Lowland Saxon Scotch took part against them:

Celtic Ireland fell at the Boyne; this was their Waterloo. Sir Robert Peel's Encumbered Estate Bill aims simply at the quiet and gradual extinction of tho Celtic race in Ireland: this is its sole aim, and it will prove successful. A similar bill is wanted for Caledonia, or may be required shortly: the Celtic race cannot too soon escape from under Saxon rule. As a Saxon, I abhor all dynasties, monarchies and bayonet governments, but this latter seems to be the only one suitable for the Celtic man.

A short time ago a psendo-philosophical work excited much conversation and prejudice against the transcendental theories of the origin of man; the theory of development in time. It jumbled up the theory of human progress with the theory of development; its critics, the church and colleges, compelled its anonymous compiler to seek a refuge in the doctrine of final cause; a doctrine which tho whole scope of the work repudiated. The doctrines of Geoffroy were in this work*, misstated, to serve a purpose; those of Humboldt and others withheld. But the public mind has now been disabused in respect of this work, and of its power to do mischief, so that further criticism seems unnecessary.

I doubt all theories of human progress in time:

---

* Vestiges of Creation.

they are refuted by history: I question the theories of progress in time, if by progress be meant
improvement as regards all animals; some at
least of the extinct organic world were equal, if
not superior, to that now existing. Man was
probably there also; it is these and other such
questions which Jesuits of all denominations—for
they are not confined to the Roman-catholic
world—declaim against. Hence, also, their dislike to the geologist and the anatomist.' Science
has nothing to do with such persons; and but for
the frequency of their open and insidious attacks,
I should deem it lost time the giving to them
even a passing thought. The history of the ter-
restrial globe, and of all that it contains, perhaps
even of the universe, points to a past, a present, and a future. "If we look into space with
a telescope, we may perceive a star so distant
that light from it would require a million of
years to reach this globe; thus showing a past
as regards that star, of at least a million of
years." How is it with the globe itself? "If we
dissect and examine the strata of this earth,
science shows the fossil remains of former organic
worlds imbedded in these strata; of countless
races of animals now extinct; but it shows us
more than this. It displays strata requiring for
their formation countless thousands of years.

The earth, then, is old, very old. Here there is a past and a present, and a probable future. What a mass of idle, wild, visionary speculation did not Hutton overthrow! See what a single anatomist did!—one shrewd truth-loving observer! Before Hutton appeared, what were the theories of the schools? Before the anatomist spoke out, what was geology? He (Cuvier) showed the past and the present. Lastly; and this discovery exceeds all others;—"When we look into animal structure, say the human embryo, or of any other mammal, we discover a past and a present; and we conjecture a physical future." We discover structures in the embryo not persistent but transitory, evanescent; we see that the individual is in fact passing through a series of metamorphoses, expressed briefly by the term development; passing through forms which represent the permanent forms of other adult beings belonging to the organic world, not human, but bestial; of whom some belong to the existing world, whilst others may represent forms which once existed, but are now extinct; or, finally, forms which may be destined some day to appear, running their destined course, then to perish as their predecessors. Thus in the embryonic changes or metamorphoses of man and other animals, are shadowed forth, more or less completely, all other organic forms; the fully developed, or grown-up brute forms of birds and fishes, of reptiles and mammals, are represented in the organic structures of the human embryo; whilst this again, in its short and fleeting course from a simple vesicle or cell, as it may be, to birth, represents in its ever-varying types the history of all organic existences from the beginning of time to the present day. Thus is man linked by structure and by plan to all that has lived or may yet live. One plan, one grand scheme of nature; unity of organization; unity in time and space; hence, here also we see the past and the present, and we conjecture a future. This discovery, the unity of the organization, the laws of development, the laws of formation and deformation, we owe entirely to the south German, or perhaps I should say, to the Bohemian or Slavonian race. France contributed a little towards its history; England, not at all. Even in philosophic Paris, where the transcendental theory was first mooted by Geoffroy, following in the steps of Oken and Spix, of Goethe and Leibnitz, it was extinguished at once by the sarcasms of Cuvier and his adherents. The history of this affair merits a place in the annals of science: we shall speak of it shortly: in the meantime let me explain, by a few examples and illustrations, the real nature of that transcendental theory which first gave thinking, reasoning man a glimpse of the great system of nature. A few

illustrations must suffice: this is a mere fragment
I write, and not a systematic work: time and
materials are wholly wanting to attempt so great
an undertaking as tho zoological history of man.

Place yourself in the midst of any considerable
assemblage of people, and a little careful observation will convince you, that although a general
resemblance pervades all, provided they be of
one race, there is yet in each an individuality
not to bo mistaken: or that, in short, he or she
differs in a hundred ways from all around. If
men of other races be present, tho differences
aro at once striking, and not to bo overlooked.
In what these differences consist wo shall afterwards consider. They have been described with
a painfully fastidious detail of petty circumstances
by zoological formulists; the causes of theso
differences have been as carefully avoided, as if
man, all-important man, were not a fit object of
inquiry—man, the only really important animal
to man, was to be let alone; Providence or chance
had been pleased to make men as they are; from
white she had turned some to black, others to
brown; some olive, others yellow; "call it
climate, or anything you like, but do not inquire
into the cause:" the inquiry, in fact, is not a
legitimate one.' But why, in that case, inquire
into any science? What signifies truth? Water
will not rise higher in a pump-well, whether we

know the philosophy of atmospheric pressure or not. According to these persons it is sufficient for us to know that it will rise to a certain height in a pump-well. It is to universities, colleges, and schools that we owe the perpetuation of error; of neatly-formuled untruths. I was taught that the round head of the Turk depended on his wearing a turban: it was repeated, on the authority of Blumenbach, that the small hands of the Hottentots as compared with the Caffres was caused by a scarcity of food! And but lately I read, in one of those miserable, trashy, popular physiologies,* that the Dutch owe their dulness and phlegm to their living amongst marshes? And to this day, I verily believe, this is the physiology of the schools. The spindle form of the English legs, so slender, ill made, disproportioned to the torso, I have repeatedly heard ascribed, by Sir Charles Bell, to the early use of heavy shoes or clogs: the vigorous calf of the French woman's leg ascribed to there being no side pavements in Paris: and in a country where, at any hour of the day, you may meet with numbers of persons of all ranks in whom the facial angle equals the best of the antique, the same excellent man not only persisted in overlooking the fact, but denied its possibility.

* Combe.

I return to my first proposition. If the assemblage observed be composed of different races, tho differences will bo still more striking; explained away they may be, but they cannot be overlooked. And now, should an opportunity occur, to look more narrowly into the differences characterizing the individuals forming this motley group, other extraordinary circumstances will be discovered. It will be found, that somo cannot extend their arms or limbs to the due degree or to full extension: that some have two or more fingers and toes webbed: that some have no arms, but merely hands: others, no legs, but merely feet: or the thighs are too short: or the arms: and in some the back is perfectly straight, instead of being arched and curved: some have the nails round, others have them pointed like claws: harelip with cleft palato may be seen among the crowd: on the finest necks of tho adult man or woman may occasionally be seen somo exceedingly small openings, marking tho vestiges of branchial arches or gills, which all animals, man as well, have in their fœtal state: these, and others to be mentioned, are so many illustrations of ono great law—the law of unity of organization, as exhibited in the embryo: tho existence of this unity proved by the various arrests of developments named above. For all, or nearly all, the varieties bere mentioned, are simply fœtal or embryonic condi-

tions, which ought to have been evanescent, had
the law of perfect formation or of species prevailed; but from circumstances not rightly understood, these embryonic forms had persisted in the
individual, and grown up with him to the adult
state.   For every mammal embryo, human or
otherwise, in passing through the various developments, part of the great scheme of nature, no
doubt, exhibits such forms as I have spoken of.
Cleft palate, webbed fingers, absence of arms and
legs, straight spine ; at a later period, semi-flexed
arms and legs, branchial openings in the neck,
leading to vessels arranged in tufts, a structure belonging to the adult state of fishes ; temporary in
man, permanent in the fish: one type then for both
—for all; not two types, but one. The mechanical
utilitarian cannot comprehend this—his mind is
so full of animal mechanics; the carpenter, the
watch and clock-maker, comes out on all occasions.   Socrates and his followers, from Philo
Judæus and Galen, to Derham and Paley, knew
nothing of the great law of unity of the organization; they seemed to fancy every animal made
for itself, and on a separate type; by final causes,
in which the uneducated mind sees the explanation
of every doubt.   But why should there be two or
more types of organized beings ? Cuvier thought
that there must at least be two—the vertebrate
and the avertebrate. Newton seemed to think

that there existed but one kind of matter; he was amongst the earliest to announce the doctrine of unity of the organization. His vast mind foresaw the truth, to be afterwards more fully brought out: Divine mind! in advance of his age by a century at least.

Certain varieties then, in human form, are produced by the law of unity of the organization; for every individual living form grows up influenced, regulated by two contending principles. The law of unity of organization, ever present, ever active, ever ready to retain the embryonic forms: the law, in fact, of deformation as we naturally view it; for, as the human faculties are constituted to look for and to admire the perfect form, so every deviation from this perfect form, the standard and type of which exists in every rightly formed mind, is regarded with a certain dislike. It is to this type that nature as constantly leans in carrying out the development of every individual; the law in fact of individuality; of species. Without it we should have no distinct species of men or animals on the earth; the law of deformation or unity would perpetually alter every form. Nothing could be recognised. Hence, as a part of the great scheme of Nature, arises the law of speculization leading to the perfection of the individual: in the human race, to the absolutely perfect and the beautiful, as we naturally esteem the human form—woman's form, the only absolutely beautiful object on earth.

To be brief, and so conclude.—What is race, and what is species? These terms are easier understood than defined. That the idea of distinct species and of race is fast passing away from the human mind, may, or may not be true; the old doctrine has been deeply shaken; still species and race exist for us; for man, at least; in space, though not in time. In time there is probably no such thing as species: no absolutely new creations ever took place; but, as viewed by the limited mind of man, the question takes another aspect. As regards his individual existence, time is a short span; a few centuries, or a few thousand years, more or less: this is all he can grasp. Now, for that period at least, organic forms seem not to have changed. So far back as history goes, the species of animals as we call them have not changed; the races of men have been absolutely the same. They were distinct then for that period as at present. Are they commutable into each other? Are these causes in constant operation, slowly yet surely altering and changing everything? Or does this happen by sudden cataclasms or geological epochs? Of one thing we are certain, entire races of animals have disappeared from the surface of the globe; other seemingly new creations occupy their place.

But is it really a new creation? This question we shall also discuss.

Look more narrowly into the races of men, and you will find them to be subject to diseases peculiar to each; that the very essence of their language is distinct; their civilization also, if they have any. Trace the matter further, and you will find that transcendental anatomy can alone explain these mysterious circumstances: how all embryos should resemble each other; how they should resemble the primitive forms of life when the world was yet young; how deviations in form or varieties, not intended to be permanent, should repeat primitive forms, as proved by fossil remains; or present human or bestial forms; or take unknown shapes, referring, no doubt, to the future: lastly, and that is the most difficult question, how specializations should ever appear at all, and be, for a time at least, permanent. Two questions remain, beyond, I fear, human enquiry:—1st, The origin of life on the globe; 2nd, The secondary laws, for they must be so, and can be nothing else, which create out of primitive forms, the past, the present, and the future organic worlds, clothing them with beauteous scenery. Endless, but defined variety of forms, adorn the earth, the air, the waters; the scheme of creation, in fact, in so far as man's feeble reason can judge; not the object of creation; not the object of man's creation, which, though won-

derful, is not more so than that of any other form;
not then the object of man's creation as an intellectual being; this has been revealed to us by divine
minds. But I must view this last question also
as an anatomist and physiologist, confining my
remarks to man merely as a material being; the
most perfect, no doubt, that exists. In woman's
form I see the perfection of Nature's works: the
absolutely perfect; the beautiful, the highest manifestation of abstract life, clothed in a physical
form, adapted to the corresponding minds of her
race and species.

LECTURES

THE RACES OF MEN.

LECTURE I.

HISTORY OF THE SAXON OR SCANDINAVIAN RACE.

IT was Columbus, I think, who said to Ferdinand and Isabella, "The world is not so vast as
people suppose." How full of meaning are these
expressions! How comprehensive, how universal
the genius of the man who uttered them! To
grasp the universal is unquestionably the attribute
of genius; it is a god-like quality, even when it
leads to error.

Columbus thought that the world is not so
large as most people suppose it to be. This limitation of the globe's extent to the mind's eye
we owe to science — not, however, to modern
science. The words " *orbis terrarum*," used by
Horace, cannot well be misunderstood. But small
though it be, comparatively, it is yet large enough
to meet the wants of all organic beings which

have hitherto figured on or in it. At no period does the world seem ever to have been overloaded with life, overpeopled with human beings. The production of life is no doubt inconceivably great, but so also is its destruction, or rather its restoration to primitive forms, for it is questionable how far life can be destroyed, in the strict sense of the term. *Why* animals are made to prey on each other — the devouring and the devoured — is a question I leave for a future section; at present our business is with man. St. Cyril, who wrote, I think, about the fifth or sixth century of the Christian æra, defends the institution of nunneries and monasteries on this special ground, that, even in his time, the world (meaning, I have no doubt,

[*A Saxon House: standing always apart, if possible, from all others.*]

the town and district he lived in) was already too
densely populated!   Ingenious priest and Jesuit!
subtle casuist!   In modern times, a descendant
of your craft* has proved to the faithful that the
over-production of life, the destruction of the
young, man himself included, by famine, pestilence, and disease; the savage warfare of the de-
vourer against the devoured all over the world;
the multiplication of the flesh-eating animals, and
of the grass-eating animals to feed them,—was a
grand stroke of nature's polity, to increase pleasure by multiplying life.   Diverting casuist! who
can extract any meaning from any text! You
undertook to fix the æra of the Mosaic deluge,
and you wrote a quarto volume about troops of
antediluvian hyænas, which never existed but in
your own imagination.   Where are your theories
now?   Ignorant of Hebrew, you tamper with the
books of the Hebrews! Had you not better leave
the Jews to themselves, it being but fair to suppose
that they best understand their own writings?

Although man be antagonistic to the organic and
living world in all forms which serve not immediately his own ends, he has not yet succeeded in
destroying all nature's works, although he labours
hard to effect this.   His existence seems to depend
on his success in the war of extinction he carries
on against the *wilde*.   By superior cunning and

* Buckland, Dean of Westminster.

powers of combination, he soon disposes of the
animal world. The vegetable world is more ob-
durate, more difficult to be overcome : the heath,
the bog, the forest, are ever ready to return upon
him, should his incessant labour cease but for an
instant. Hence it is that certain regions of the
earth are more desirable for human residence than
others. Unprofitable, untillable seas cover the
greater part of the globe's surface ; hence may
arise a struggle for certain regions in preference
to others. But, be this as it may, I cannot find
that the earth was ever, as St. Cyril has it, over-
populated. When Babylon was, London was
not; the banks of the Euphrates and Tigris,
which were equal to the support of millions, are
no longer cultivated; the plains of Troy are desert, Mongolia a wilderness. This is human history. Successive races of men appear on the
globe; the space they occupy is of course too
small for them, whether it be England or France,
New York or Calcutta, Moscow or Rome (I mean
ancient Rome)—they find the space always too
narrow for them ; from Point de Galle to the
Himalah, from the Bay of Bengal to the Persian
Gulf, it is always too confined. At times the
plea is commerce, legitimate commerce; Hindostan and China are grasped at; it is quite legitimate—we do not want their territory, we only
want to trade with them. At other times the pre-

meditated robbery is glossed over with a religious pretence—the conversion of the heathen—a noble theme for declamation. A national insult will also serve the purpose, as at Algiers. A wish to serve Africa forms the excuse for an expedition to the Niger, the real object being the enslaving the unhappy Negro, dispossessing him of his lands and freedom. I prefer the manly robber to this sneaking, canting hypocrisy, peculiar to modern civilization and to Christian Europe.

Now, whether the earth be over-populated or not, one thing is certain—the strong will always grasp at the property and lands of the weak. I have been assured that this conduct is not at all incompatible with the highest moral and even Christian feeling. I had fancied that it was, but I have been assured of the contrary. The doctrine which teaches us to love our neighbours as ourselves is admirable, no doubt; but a difficulty lies somehow or other in the way. What is that difficulty, which all seem to know and feel, yet do not like to avow? It is the difference of race. Ask the Dutch Boor whence comes his contempt and inward dislike to the Hottentot, the Negro, the Caffre; ask him for his warrant to reduce these unhappy races to bondage and to slavery; to rob them of their lands, and to enslave their children; to deny them the inalienable right of man to a portion of the earth on which he was born? If he be an

honest and straightforward man, he will point to
the fire-arms suspended over the mantelpiece—
" There is my right !"   The statesmen of modern
Europe manage such matters differently ; they
arrive, it is true, at the same result—robbery,
plunder, seizure of the lands of others—but they
do it by treaties, protocols, alliances, and first
principles.

[*The modern Greek and the Muscovite, or Sarmatian; both of the Caucasian race ! Mark their
resemblance !*]

When the word race, as applied to man, is
spoken of, the English mind wanders immediately
to distant countries ; to Negroes and Hottentots,
Red Indians and savages.   He admits that there
are people who differ a good deal from us, but not
in Europe ; there, mankind are clearly of one
family.   It is the Caucasian race, says one ; it is
the primitive race, says another.   But the object
of this work is to show that the European races, so
called, differ from each other as widely as the
Negro does from the Bushman ; the Caffre from

the Hottentot; the Red Indian of America from
the Esquimaux; the Esquimaux from the Basque.
Blumenbach and Prichard have misled the public
mind so much in this respect, that a century may
elapse before it be disabused. I need not repeat
here the antiquated division of mankind by Blumenbach, nor its modification by Prichard : it
leads to no results. With the history of the
Saxon or Scandinavian race, I shall commence
the physiological history of man.

SAXON OR SCANDINAVIAN RACE.

Of the origin of the Saxon race we know just
as much as we do of the origin of man; that is,
nothing. History, such as it is, shows us that in
remote times a race of men, differing from all
others physically and mentally, dwelt in Scandinavia—say, in Norway, Denmark, Sweden, Holstein—on the shores of the Baltic, in fact; by the
mouths of the Rhine, and on its northern and
eastern bank. Cæsar met Ariovistus at the head
of a German army on the Rhine. The Germans,
as the Scandinavian and other transrhenal races
were then called, had crossed the river, making
excursions into the territories of their Celtic
neighbours, inhabiting Old Gaul. The dictator
defeated them, compelling them to recross the
Rhine into their own territories. But he did not
follow them into their native woods: the Romans

never had any real power beyond the Rhine. At no period did they conquer the Saxon or true German, that is, Scandinavian, race.

What had induced the ancient Scandinavians to cross the Rhine in Cæsar's time? What had led them long before into Italy, where they encountered Marius? Ask the South-African Saxon Boor what induces him to spread himself over a land, one twentieth part of which could easily maintain him in comfort and affluence. What urges him against Caffraria—against Natal? It has been said, that the Scandinavian or Saxon tribes were pressed for space; that more numerous barbarous tribes pushed them on. The over-populousness of their woods and their retiring before another force do not well agree; there is some contradiction here. But the Cape Boor of Saxon origin has no such excuse for spreading himself in a few years over a vast region, which he leaves uncultivated; neither has the Anglo-Saxon American. To me it seems referrible simply to the qualities of the race; to their inordinate self-esteem; to their love of independence, which makes them dislike the proximity of a neighbour; to their hatred for dynasties and governments; democrats by their nature, the only democrats on the earth, the only race which truly comprehends the meaning of the word liberty.

The Scandinavian or Saxon (I avoid the words

German and Teuton, as liable to equivoque) was
early in Greece, say 3500 years ago. This race
still exists in Switzerland, forming its protestant
portion; whilst in Greece, it contributed mainly,
no doubt, to the formation of the noblest of all men
—the statesmen, poets, sculptors, mathematicians,
metaphysicians, historians of ancient Greece.
But from that land nearly all traces of it have
disappeared; so also from Italy. It is gradually
becoming extinct in France and Spain, returning
and confined once more to those countries in
which it was originally found—namely, Holland,
West Prussia, Holstein, the northern states of the
ancient Rhenish Confederation, Saxony Proper,
Norway, Sweden, and Denmark. The Saxon of
England is deemed a colonist from Jutland, Holstein, and Denmark. I feel disposed to view the
question differently. He must have occupied
eastern Scotland and eastern England as far
south as the Humber, long prior to the historic
period, when the German Ocean was scarcely a
sea. The Saxons of these northern coasts of
Scotland and England, resemble very closely tho
natives of the opposite shores; but the Danes
and Angles who attacked South England, already
occupied by a Flemish race, did not make the
same impression on the population. They merely
mingled with it; the country, that is, South
England, remains in the hands of the original in-

habitants to this day.   South England is mainly
occupied by a Belgian race, and were it not for the
centralization of London, it is by no means improbable that much of the true Saxon blood would
have disappeared from south Britain, by that physiological law which extinguishes mixed races (a
people composed of two or more races) and causes
the originally more numerous one to predominate,

[*Contrast the Cherokee head with that of the Apollo
(Frontispiece), the noblest of all human heads;
and belonging to a Scandinavian race, with a
dash of oriental blood.*]

unless supplies be continually drawn from the primitive pure breeds. This important law we shall consider presently. Following out the geographical position of the Saxon race, we find him in Europe, intersected but not amalgamated with the Sarmatian and Slavonian, in eastern Europe; with the Celtic in Switzerland; deeply with the Slavonian and Flaming in Austria and on the Rhine; thinly spread throughout Wales; in possession, as occupants of the soil, of northern and eastern Ireland; lastly, carrying out the destinies of his race, obeying his physical and moral nature, the Anglo-Saxon, aided by his insular position, takes possession of the ocean, becomes the great tyrant at sea; ships, colonies, commerce—these are his wealth, therefore his strength. A nation of shopkeepers grasps at universal power; founds a colony (the States of America) such as the world never saw before; loses it, as a result of the principle of race. Nothing daunted, founds others, to lose them all in succession, and for the same reasons — race: a handful of large-handed spatula-fingered Saxon traders holds military possession of India. Meantime, though divided by nationalities, into different groupes, as English, Dutch, German, United States man, cordially hating each other, the race still hopes ultimately to be masters of the world.

E

But I have not yet spoken of the physical and mental qualities of the Saxon race; these words include all, for " the Chronicle of Events" which have happened to them, whether in England or elsewhere, is a mere chapter of accidents, influenced deeply by the qualities of the average men of the race.   So soon as I shall briefly have described these, it will be proper to consider the import of two great physiological laws already mooted—namely, Can a mixed race be produced and supported by the intermingling of two races? Can any race occupy, colonize, and people a region of the earth to which they are *not* indigenous?

In all climes, and under all circumstances, the Saxons are a tall, powerful, athletic race of men; the strongest, as a race, on the face of the earth. They have fair hair, with blue eyes, and so fine a complexion, that they may almost be considered the only absolutely fair race on the face of the globe.   Generally speaking, they are not a well made or proportioned race, falling off most in the limbs; the torso being large, vast, and disproportioned.   They are so described by Livy, and have never altered; the mistake of Prichard, and the difficulty experienced by the illustrious Niebuhr, the greatest of all historians, respecting the complexion of the *modern German* differing from the ancient, arises simply from this, that

the middle and south German belong to another
race of men. They are not Scandinavians or
Saxons at all, and never were. The mistake
centres in the abuse of the word German; it has
been applied to two or three different races: so also
has the word Teuton; hence my objections to these
terms. The true Germans or Saxons of modern
times resemble, or rather are identical, with
those of antiquity; they follow the law of hereditary descent; climate exercises no influence over
them. Two hundred years of Java, three hundred
years of southern Africa, affect them not. Alter
their health it may, and does, withering up the
frame; rendering the body thin and juiceless;
wasting the adipose cellular tissue; relaxing the
muscles and injuring the complexion, by altering
the condition of the blood and secretions; all
this may be admitted, but they produce no permanent results.

Under the influence of climate, the Saxon
decays in northern America and in Australia,
and he rears his offspring with difficulty. He
has changed his continental locality; a physiological law, I shall shortly explain, is against his
naturalization there. Were the supplies from
Europe not incessant, he could not stand his
ground in these new continents. A *real native* permanent American, or Australian race of pure Saxon
blood, is a dream which can never be realized.

E 2

The Saxon is fair, not because he lives in a temperate or cold climate, but because he is a Saxon. The Esquimaux are nearly black, yet they live amidst eternal snows; the Tasmanian

[*A Celtic groupe; such may be seen at any time in Marylebone, London.*]

is, if possible, darker than the negro, under a climate as mild as England. Climate has no influence in permanently altering the varieties or races of men; destroy them, it may and does, but it cannot convert them into any other race; nor can this be done even by act of parliament, which, to a thorough-going Englishman, with all his amusing nationalities, will appear as something amazing. It has been tried in Wales, in Ireland, in Caledonia — and failed. Explain it, ye Utopians, as you choose; I merely mention the fact. When I lectured in Liverpool, a gentleman, of the name of Martineau, put forth a discourse, in which he maintained, that we had forced Saxon laws upon the Irish too hurriedly; that we had not given them time enough to become good Saxons, into which they would be metamorphosed at last. In what time, Mr. Martineau, do you expect this notable change? The experiment has been going on already for 700 years; I will concede you seven times 700 more, but this will not alter the Celt: no more will it change the Saxon, to whom I return.

Thoughtful, plodding, industrious beyond all other races, a lover of labour for labour's sake; he cares not its amount if it be but profitable; large handed, mechanical, a lover of order, of punctuality in business, of neatness and cleanliness. In those qualities no race approaches him; the wealthy with him is the sole respectable, the respectable the sole good; the word comfort is never out of his mouth—it is the beau ideal of the Saxon.

His genius is wholly applicative, for he invents nothing. In the fine arts, and in music, taste cannot go lower. The race in general has no musical ear, and they mistake noise for music. The marrow-bones and cleaver belong to them. Prize fights, bull-baiting with dogs; sparring matches; rowing, horse racing, gymnastics: the Boor is peculiar to the Saxon race. When young they cannot sit still an instant, so powerful is the desire for work, labour, excitement, muscular exertion. The self-esteem is so great, the self-confidence so matchless, that they cannot possibly imagine any man or set of men to be superior to themselves. Accumulative beyond all others, the wealth of the world collects in their hands.

Our good qualities when in excess become foibles and even vices. I need not dwell on this: my notes to this Lecture will supply the deficiency. The social condition of the Saxon can only be seen in the free States of America, which I have not yet visited. In Britain he was enslaved by a Norman dynasty, antagonistic of his race. His efforts to throw it off have not yet succeeded, though oft repeated. On the Con-

tinent, the Saxon race, broken up into petty
monarchies, without wealth or power; miserably
enslaved and crushed down by the dynasties of
Hapsburgh, Brandenburgh, and a host of others,
presents a condition seemingly hopeless. In
their last struggle for liberty, or in other words
for institutions suited to their race, they were
not joined by the Scandinavian nations, the very
best of their blood. Holland, too, would have
risen, but she remembered the Celtic treachery;
the betrayal of the cause of liberty by the French
Celt in '92; the plunder of Europe by a body of
disciplined savages under Napoleon; so she re-
sponded not to the Celt. The cap of liberty was
raised in vain in Paris; the cautious Hollander
was not again to be deceived. He knew also
that England, commercial England, was sure to
betray him into the hands of the brutal Pruss
and Russ. Thus the noblest blood of the race
is in abeyance: sunk into political insignificance.
Sweden, Denmark, Norway, Holstein, Holland,
commercial England, have overshadowed you. A
colony of your own (England), your first, your
greatest colony, has exercised over your fortunes
that fatal influence which England's first and
greatest colony may some day exercise over hers:
we are to you, what America seems destined to be
to us. Of the same race, commercial, naval, the
only really good sailors in the world, our American

colony already disputes with us the empire of the
seas; a future Paul Jones may yet repay Britain
the affair of Copenhagen; but it must come from
a Saxon race, for the Saxons alone are sailors.

The results of the physical and mental qualities
of a race are naturally manifested in its civilization, for every race has its own form of civilization. The historian, the talented statesman,
Guizot, for example, who failed in forty years to
learn the character of the race amongst whom he
lived and ruled, he of all others, (always excepting the Prince of Bunglers, Metternich,) the most
outrageously mistaken, has written a work about
European civilization; about an abstraction which

[*An Anglo-Saxon house; it always, if possible,
stands detached.*]

does not exist. Each race has its own form of civilization, as it has its own language and arts; I would almost venture to say, science; for although exact science, as being based on eternal and indisputable truths, must ever be the same under all circumstances and under all climes, it does not follow that its truths should even be formuled after the same fashion. Civilization, or the social condition of man, is the result and test of the qualities of every race; but it would be unfair to judge the European Saxon by this standard, seeing that the entire race, insular and continental, is crushed down by dynasties antagonistic of their race. What is effected at Berlin and Vienna by the bayonet, is usually accomplished in London by the law. Hence, notwithstanding the wealth of the Anglo-Saxon, no nation presents such a frightful mass of squalid poverty and wretchedness, rendering it doubtful whether such a form of civilization be a blessing or a curse to humanity. I lean with Tacitus to the latter opinion.

No race perhaps (for I must make allowances for my Saxon descent,) no race perhaps exceeds them in an abstract sense of justice, and a love of fair play; *but only to Saxons.* This of course they do not extend to other races. Aware of his strength of chest and arms, he uses them in self-defence: the Celt flies uniformly to the sword.

To-day and to-morrow is all the Saxon looks to; yesterday he cares not for; it is past and gone. He is the man of circumstances, of expediency without method; "try all things, but do not theorize." Give me "constants," a book of constants; this is his cry. Hence his contempt for men of science: his hatred for genius arises from another cause; he cannot endure the idea that any man is really superior in anything to himself. The absence of genius in his race he feels; he dislikes to be told it: he attempts to crush it wherever it appears. Men of genius he calls humbugs, impostors. His literature is peculiar to himself, and must not be confounded with modern German literature: this latter is chiefly of Slavonian origin, mingled with the race occupying central Europe and stretching into Flanders. Uncertain as to their nature, I have called this race Flemish or Belgian; but the modern Belgians do not well represent them. I believe them peculiar; an off-set perhaps of the Slavonian race; at all events not Saxon or Scandinavian. The word German, and the equivoque it admits of, has greatly confused a very simple matter. It misled Arnold; it misled Niebuhr, and a host of others: my countrymen have confounded the literature of the middle, south German, and Slavonian races with the Scandinavian or north German; nothing was ever more distinct.

All that is free in Saxon countries they, the Saxons, owe to themselves; their laws, manners, institutions, they brought with them from the woods of Germany, and they have transferred them to the woods of America. They owe nothing to any kings or princes or chiefs: originally, they had neither chief nor king; a general in war was *elected* when required. In their ideas of " property in land " they differ also from other races ; they do not admit that any class or family, dynasty or individual, can appropriate to himself and to his hereditary heirs, any portion of the earth's surface. Hence their abhorrence for feudality, tenures, hereditary rights, and laws of primogeniture. Soldiers and soldiering they despise as being unworthy of free men : the difficulty of teaching them military discipline and tactics, arises from the awkwardness of their forms and slowness of movement, and from their inordinate self-esteem. But when disciplined, their infantry, owing to the strength of the men, becomes the first in the world. In the chapter on Germany, I shall examine more carefully into some of these points, characteristic of the race ; concluding this section with some observations on the present position and future prospects, that is, destiny of the race. The failure of the Continental Saxon during the late struggle for liberty, I ventured to foretel at the commencement. They desired to be united, free; disenthralled from the hideous iron despotism which crushes them down: in a German unity, a race mustering at least sixty millions, they hoped to find a counterpoise to Celtic France, and Swinish Russia; that is, to the two *dominant races* of Europe, the Celt and the Sarmatian. But true to their selfish nature, they had not the soul to offer the same freedom to the Slavonian, whom they neglected and despised. They fought with the Slavonians in Posen; they resisted them in Bohemia; they contended with them in Austria; liberty for the German was the war-cry; slavery for all the rest. They now reap the fruits of their selfish nature ; hopeless slavery for centuries: the dynasties are in the ascendant: they have alarmed the holders of *property*, always timid, always cowardly: as a class, the property men are sure to back any dynasty if well supported by the bayonet. No sympathies can be extended to a selfish grasping race, without feelings for others. To their eternal dishonour, they suffered an infamous coward, the first who fled from Potsdam to Windsor, to return and butcher their brethren in Baden and Saxony. When the imbecile House of Hapsburgh fled from Vienna, then was the time to have said to the Slavonian race,—"Arise, and form a nation." But *self* prevailed with the Saxon, and ruin followed. The words of Napoleon have now been verified; Europe is "all Cossaque." All fear of a *Celtic Re-*

public has vanished: the character of the Celt is now fully understood. Rome has settled the question for a time. Celtic liberty is now well comprehended by all Europe. The world thought Celtic France a great and free people; but the world was wrong if they did, for the world forgot the element of race in its calculation on the probable destinies of the French Celt; that element, duly weighed, would have shown them, that a race being composed of individuals resembling each other must, even in its greatest efforts, merely shadow forth the character of the individual. When the French Celt drove out the insupportable and paltry Orleans dynasty, they were merely a fighting clan without a chief; having no self-esteem, how could they act without a leader? That leader had not then, and has not yet, appeared.

The introduction of the Saxon element of mind into civilized Europe is, no doubt, a remarkable event in history: the literature and arts of the Roman world had been already influenced by the Celtic mind; the Gothic or Slavonian followed next; then came the Saxon. Its first result was to produce the dark ages. What the race had been doing since the beginning of time it is impossible to say, but being without inventive genius, I see not how they could originate any but the lowest forms of civilization, such as I have seen in Southern Africa amongst the Dutch, that is, Saxon,

Boors, and such as I have heard prevails in " the far west." Man sinks rapidly in the scale of civilization when removed from the great stream. They are wrong who fancy otherwise. At the third generation the Saxon Boor, in a remote land, sinks nearly to the barbarian; active and energetic, no doubt: still a Saxon, but not the less a boor and a vulgar barbarian.

The remarkable, and almost prophetic, saying of Gibbon, seems about to be verified. As a statesman and a historian, a chronicler of the social and political histories of nations, he applies his remark to England; but it is strictly applicable to the European Saxon, wherever found; insular or continental; applicable to the descendants of those free and bold men who originally brought with them, in all their migrations from Scandinavia, those free institutions under which freemen alone can live, namely, that of trial by jury, and equality before the law, protection of life and property; a race who obeyed no king nor chief; who resisted oppression in every shape, and to whom the most abhorred of all despotisms, a feudal nobility with laws of primogeniture, were unknown: amongst whom all were equal; all noble alike. Such were the ancient Scandinavian or Saxon, called Germans occasionally by some Roman writers—and confounded in later times, even by the immortal Niebuhr, with the middle

German or Upper Danubian race: occasionally, even with the Slavonians.

To all this race, now crushed down by the Sarmatian and Celtic races of Europe: broken up, dispersed, enslaved: their lives and properties placed at the mercy of some five or six brutal families or dynasties: the very best blood of all the race, the Jutlander, the Saxon, the free man of Baden and of Wirtemberg, lorded it over by a few paltry families, unknown to fortune or renown; to all this race Gibbon's remarks apply; to Celtic republican (!) France they now know they need not look for aid in their next struggle for liberty; let Rome be a lesson to them; to all this race, and not to England alone, does this prophetic passage in Gibbon's works apply.

" Should it ever happen," says the immortal historian, whom I quote from recollection, " that in Europe brutal military despots should succeed in extinguishing the liberties of men, threatening with the same unhappy fate the inhabitants of this island (England), they, mindful of their Saxon origin, would doubtless escape across the ocean, carrying to a new world their institutions, religion, and laws."

PHYSIOLOGICAL QUESTION.

SECTION I.—*Do races ever amalgamate? What are the obstacles to a race changing its original locality?*

I have heard persons assert, a few years ago, men of education too, and of observation, that the amalgamation of races into a third or new product, partaking of the qualities of the two primitive ones from which they spring, was not only possible, but that it was the best mode of improving the breed. The whole of this theory has turned out to be false :—1st. As regards the lower animals; 2nd. As regards man. Of the first I shall say but little: man is the great object of human research; the philosophy of Zoology is not indeed wrapt up in him; he is not the end, neither was he the beginning: still, as he is, a knowledge of man is to him all-important.

The theories put forth from time to time, of the production of a new variety, permanent and self-supporting, independent of any draughts or supplies from the pure breeds, have been distinctly disproved. It holds neither in sheep nor cattle: and an author, whose name I cannot recollect, has refuted the whole theory as to the pheasant and to the domestic fowl. He has shown that the artificial breeds so produced are never self-supporting. Man can create nothing: no new species have appeared, apparently, for some thousand years; but this is another question I mean not to discuss here, although it is obvious that if a hybrid could be produced, self-supporting, the elaborate works of Cuvier would fall to the ground. The theory of Aristotle, who explained the variety and strangeness of the animal forms in Africa, on the grounds that a scarcity of water brought to the wells and springs animals of various kinds from whose intercourse sprung the singularly varied African Zoology, has been long known to be a mere fable.

[*Dosjeman, or Yellow African Race.*]

Nature produces no mules; no hybrids, neither in man nor animals. When they accidentally appear they soon cease to be, for they are either non-productive, or one or other of the pure breeds

F

speedily predominates, and the weaker disappears. This weakness may either be numerical or innate.

That this law applies strictly to man himself, all history proves: I once said to a gentleman born in Mexico,—Who are the Mexicans? I put the same question to a gentleman from Peru, as I had done before, to persons calling themselves Germans—neither could give a distinct reply to the question. The fact turns out to be, that there really are no such persons; no such *race.*

When the best blood of Spain migrated to America, they killed as many of the natives, that is, the copper-coloured Indians, indigenous to the soil, as they could. But this could not go on, labourers to till the soil being required. The old Spaniard was found unequal to this; *he could not colonize the conquered country;* he required other aid, native or imported. Then came the admixture with the Indian blood and the Celt-Iberian blood; the produce being the mulatto. But now that the supplies of Spanish blood have ceased, the mulatto must cease, too, for as a hybrid he becomes non-productive after a time, if he intermarries only with the mulatto: he can no longer go back to the Spanish blood: that stock has ceased; of necessity then he is forced upon the Indian breed. Thus, year by year, the Spanish blood disappears, and with it the mulatto, and the population re-

trograding towards the indigenous inhabitants,
returns to that Indian population, the hereditary
descendants of those whom Cortes found there;
whom nature seemingly placed there; not aliens,
nor foreigners, but aboriginal. As it is with
Mexico, so it is with Peru.

When Mr. Canning made his celebrated boast
in Parliament, that he had created the republics
of Mexico and Peru, Columbia, Bolivia, and
Argentine, I made, to some friends, the remark,
that to create races of men was beyond his power,
and that the result of his measure would merely
be to precipitate that return, sure to come at last,
the return to the aboriginal Indian population, from
whom no good could come, from whom nothing
could be expected; a race whose vital energies
were wound up; expiring: hastening onwards
also to ultimate extinction.

If we look to the period of Rome's conquests,
we shall find that no amalgamation of races ever
happened; in Greece it was the same. It would
seem, indeed, that happen what will, no race,
however victorious they may be, has ever succeeded in utterly destroying a native population
and occupying their place. Two laws seem to
me the cause of this. Should the conquering
party be numerous there is still the climate against
them; and if few, the native race, antagonistic of
the conquerors, again predominates; so that after

most conquests the country remains in the hands
of the original race.

Let us turn now to the ancient world, to
Europe, and Asia, and Africa, and inquire into
the history of the pretended amalgamation of
races; the extinction of one race and the substitution of another; for these two questions may
be considered together.

[*The Welsh Celt, or Kymraig.*]

There has been no amalgamation of the Celtic
and Saxon races in Ireland. They abhor each
other cordially. When I publicly asserted this

some years ago, I was as publicly contradicted.
I call on those persons now to say whose opinion
was the correct one; the Irish Celt is as distinct
from the Saxon as he was seven hundred years ago.
There is no mistaking the question now. Mr.
Macaulay, in his Chronicles of the English People,
will have it that the pitiable state of the Irish is
owing to their religion; but the Caledonian Celt
is an Evangelical Protestant, and so also is the
Cymbrii, or Welsh: now I ask this plain question: Is the Caledonian Celt better off than the
Hibernian? is he more industrious? more orderly,
cleanly, temperate? has he accumulated wealth?
does he look forward to to-morrow? Though a
seeming Protestant, can you compare his religious
formula with the Saxon? It is the race, then, and
not the religion; that elastic robe, modern Christianity, adapts itself with wonderful facility to all
races and nations. It has little or no influence
that I can perceive over human affairs, further
than a great state engine serving political purposes; a tub for the whale. The great broad
principles of the morality of man have nothing to
do with any religion. The races of men still remain
distinct—the gipsies mingle not, neither do the
Jews. In Swedish and Russian Lapland, the
Lappes remain apart; the Fins are Slavonians,
they mingle not with the adjoining Saxon race;
the Saxons remain distinct from the Slavonians

in the Grand Duchy of Posen, and in all eastern Prussia. An attempt was made by the Germans to destroy the Slavonian race in Bohemia; it was a thirty years war, conducted by the savage and imbecile House of Hapsburgh against the Bohemians. It utterly failed, and the inhabitants are still Slavonian. The Muscovite has grasped all northern Asia, yet he has not succeeded in destroying any race, neither do they amalgamate with the Russ. The French Celt has never yet been able to live and thrive in Corsica; Algeria, he can, I fear, hold only as a military possession: a colonist, in the proper sense of the term, he never can become. On the banks of the Nilo still wander in considerable numbers the descendants of the men who built the pyramids, and carved the Memnon and the Sphynx. Yet Egypt is in other hands, as if the destinies of the Coptic race had been decided. No one has yet clearly explained to the world the precise nature of the dominant race in Egypt; I mean here, the character of the great bulk of the population. They do not seem to increase in numbers; if this, then, be the case, their ultimate possession of Egypt may be doubted: the Coptic blood still lingers in the land, waiting the return of an Amenoph, a Sesostris, a Leader.

Let us attend now to the greatest of all experiments ever made in respect of the transfer of a

population indigenous to one continent, and attempting by emigration to take possession of
another; to cultivate it with their own hands; to
colonize it; to persuade the world, in time, that
they are *the natives* of the newly occupied land.
Northern America and Australia furnished the
fields for this, the greatest of experiments; already has the horse, the sheep, the ox, become as
it were indigenous to these lands. Nature did
not place them there at first, yet they seem to
thrive, and flourish, and multiply exceedingly.
Yet, even as regards these domestic animals, we
cannot be quite certain; will they eventually be
self-supporting? will they supplant the llama, the
kangaroo, the buffalo, the deer? or, in order to
effect this, will they require to be constantly renovated from Europe? If this be the contin-
gency, then the acclimatation is not perfect. How
is it with man himself? The man planted there
by nature, the Red Indian, differs from all others
on the face of the earth; he gives way before the
European races, the Saxon and the Celtic: the
Celt-Iberian and Lusitanian in the south; the Celt
and Saxon in the north. Of the tropical regions
of the new world I need not speak; every one
knows that none but those whom Nature placed
there can live there: that no Europeans can
colonize a tropical country. But may there not
be some doubts of their self-support in milder

regions? take the Northern States themselves.
There the Saxon and the Celt seem to thrive beyond
all that is recorded in history.   But are we quite
sure that this success is fated to be permanent?
Annually from Europe is poured a hundred thousand men and women of the best blood of the Scandinavian, and twice that number of the pure Celt;
and so long as this continues he is sure to thrive.

[*Cherokee Head—that is, Native American.   Barton Smith foretold that the United States men
would ultimately come to this.   But it can never
be: extinction is the word—not conversion.*]

But check it; arrest it suddenly, as in the case of
Mexico and Peru; throw the *onus* of reproduction
upon the population, no longer European, but
native, or born on the spot; then will come the
struggle between the European alien and his
adopted father-land. The climate; the forests; the
remains of the aborigines not yet extinct; last, not
least, that unknown and mysterious degradation of
life and energy which in ancient times seems to
have decided the fate of all the Phœnician, Grecian,
and Coptic colonies. Cut off from their original
stock they gradually withered and faded, and
finally died away. The Phœnician never became
acclimatized in Africa, nor in Cornwall, nor in
Wales; vestiges of his race, it is true, still remain,
but they are mere vestiges. Peru and Mexico
are fast retrograding to their primitive condition;
may not the Northern States, under similar circumstances, do the same? Already the United
States man differs in appearance from the European: the ladies early lose their teeth; in both
sexes the adipose cellular cushion interposed
between the skin and the aponeuroses and
muscles disappears, or, at least, loses its adipose
portion; the muscles become stringy, and show
themselves; the tendons appear on the surface;
symptoms of premature decay manifest themselves. Now what do these signs, added to the
uncertainty of infant life in the Southern States,

and the smallness of their families in the Northern, indicate? Not the conversion of the Anglo-Saxon into the Red Indian, but warnings, that the climate has not been made for him, nor he for the climate. See what even a small amount of insulation has done for the French Celt in Lower Canada. Look at the race there! small men; small horses; small cattle; still smaller carts; ideas smallest of all; he is not even the Celt of modern France! He is the French Celt of the Regency; the thing of Louis XIII. Stationary, absolutely stationary, his numbers, I believe, depend on the occasional admixture of fresh blood from Europe. He has increased to about a million since his first settlement in Canada; but much of this has come from Britain, and not from France. Give us the statistics of the original families who keep themselves apart from the fresh blood imported into the province; let us have the real and solid increase of the original habitans, as they are pleased to call themselves, and then we may calculate on the result. Had the colony been left to itself, cut off from Europe for a century or two, it is my belief that the forest, the buffalo, the *wilde*, and the Red Indian, would have pushed him into the St. Lawrence, from the banks of which he never had the courage to wander far; amalgamating readily with the Red Indian by intermarriage, (for

the Celt has not that antipathy to the dark races
which so peculiarly characterize the Saxon);—
amalgamating with the Red Indian, the population would speedily have assumed the appearance
it has in Mexico and Peru; to follow the same
fate, perish or return to the original Indian;
and finally, to terminate in the all but utter
destruction of the original race itself.

LECTURE II.

PHYSIOLOGICAL LAWS REGULATING HUMAN LIFE.

In the rapid sketch of the dominant races of
men I am about to submit to you (of the Saxon I
have already spoken), I have endeavoured to
comprise an outline of their history, viewed, as I
have long been in the habit of viewing them, not
as *nations*, but as *races*. I am well aware that
when these lectures were first delivered, about
five years ago, the opinions they contained were
opposed to all the received opinions of the day.
The world was so *national*, and *race* had been so
utterly forgotten, that for at least two years after
delivering my first course of lectures at Newcastle
I had the whole question to myself. But *now*
the press, even in insular England, has been,
most reluctantly I believe, forced to take it up; to
make admissions which I never supposed could
have been wrung from them; to confess it to be
possible that man, after all, may be subject to
some physiological laws hitherto not well understood; that *race*, as well as "democracy,"* or

* Guizot.

socialism,* or bands of peripatetic demagogues,†
or evil spirits,‡ may have had something to do with
the history of nations, and more especially with
the last revolutions in Europe. It is true that
Englishmen will not admit its application to Ireland
or to our *colonies.* "Persons," say they, "situated
as the Irish, so favoured by Divine Providence
as to be permitted to live under our glorious institutions in church and state, should dismiss from
their minds all questions of race ; such questions
may and do apply to the continental people, but
we happy islanders have nothing to do with
them." Of the various ways in which, with a view
to suit the English palate, the great question of
the day, the question of race, has been touched on
by ponderous quarterlies and sprightly weeklies,
some admitting most of my views as already proven,
others qualifying them in a variety of ways, they
are yet unanimous, I think, on this one point, that
the physiological laws proposed by me are not applicable to the Irish nor to the Jews—tabooed races,
which must not be touched. But the question
with me is simply, What is truth ? Man, Celtic
or Judean, is either subject to physiological laws
or he is not. By a happy conceit, the Jew has
been withdrawn from the influence of these laws ;

* English aristocracy. † Russell.
‡ Metternich.

and English statesmen and English men cherish
the fond belief that the Celtic natives of Ireland,
Scotland, and Wales, may yet be converted into
good Saxons, by means of the "Estates Encumbered Bill," aided by Divine Providence. The
latter, no doubt, is an all-powerful auxiliary, could
they but calculate on it; the former is also a
powerful measure, and may do much. The extent
of soil in Celtic Ireland to be converted from
Romanism (Paganism?) is limited, measured. It
is not a continent; it is an island. Sell the
island to Saxon men. It is a powerful measure.
It has succeeded seemingly against some of the
dark races of men, whom it has brought to the
verge of destruction. Caffre and Hottentot, Tasmanian and American: why not against a fair
race—the Celtic natives of Ireland, Wales, and
Caledonia, for they must be classed together?
They are one; the same fate, whatever it be,
awaits all. Placed front to front, antagonistic in
fact with a stronger race, our reason, aided, as it
would at first appear, by past history, might
hastily decide in foretelling their extermination
and ruin. On the other hand, the more I inquire into the history of race, the more I doubt
all theorists who neglect or despise this grand
element; who speak of "European civilization
and a Caucasian race;" of all nature's works
being unalterable, excepting man, who is ever

changing.* But man is also a part of nature;
he must obey certain laws. The object of the
present inquiry is to discover these laws. They
have never been honestly sought for, but conjecture offered instead; from the climatic theory of
Hippocrates to the Caucasian dream of Blumenbach — wild hypotheses have been assumed as
truths. Instinctive, animal man, a part and parcel
of nature's great scheme, has been lost sight of;
because he has built ships and cities, it has been
surmised that his nature changes with circumstances!—that under a wise and liberal government his mind and frame expand! Look at
France; look at Ireland; look at Canada; at
Southern Africa. Ask Pretorius and his bold
Saxon boors how they like the mild and free
government of our "best light-cavalry officer!"
Ask the United States men, who forces them
already to introduce an oppressive and cruel tariff
into their laws? A few years ago they were clamorous against England's restrictive laws; they
blamed the English government. "See," said
they, "the British, the selfish British, refuse to
modify their navigation laws!" Knowing well
the race, I ventured, even then, to declare the whole
to be a false pretence, a delusion, and a mockery.
They were Saxons; that was enough — they

* Quarterly, Nov. 1849.

wanted no free tariff. A commercial war against
the world is what they aim and aimed at; but it
served their purpose to declaim against England;
hypocrisy and unscrupulous selfishness are ble-
mishes, no doubt, in the Saxon element of mind;
they lead to sharp practices in manufactures,
which have, somehow or other, a strange con-
nexion with dishonesty; they give to Saxon commerce a peculiar character, and to Saxon war a
vulgar, low, and mercenary spirit, cold and calculating; profitable wars, keenly taken up, unscru-
pulously followed out. The plains of Hindostan
have been the grand field for Saxon plunder: the
doings there are said to be without a parallel in
history.

[*The Cherokee Head. Men with crania similarly
formed were said by Hippocrates to inhabit the
shores of the Black Sea.*]

Scarcely five years have elapsed since I announced the general principle, that he who would

not or could not see, in the dominant races of
Europe, distinct elements of mind, could never
read aright the history of the past, understand the
present, nor rightly guess the future. And now
the truth of this principle, so stoutly denied by
the chronicler of the *Times*, is already fully admitted. There is still an unwillingness to admit
some other laws announced at the same time:
the physiological laws which regulate the destinies of mankind and of race. Let me here consider some of these laws.

PHYSIOLOGICAL LAWS.

It was Hippocrates who wrote that pleasing
fiction, which, embodying the scattered notions of
his day (for he was a compiler, and a most extensive one, too), gave to theories, based on no proofs,
a *quasi* philosophic character. He assumed
that external circumstances modified human
structure and human character. His actual observations were few, and made on a narrow field
— Greece, I presume, and a portion of Asia
Minor. Like most medical men, he was a great
theorist, and has the credit of having first separated medicine from philosophy. And so I think
he did, much to its disadvantage. What it was
before this unlucky event can scarcely now be
known; since then it has almost rivalled theology

G

in the wildness of its conjectures, its contradictory
views, its conflicting theories.   Let us return to
Hippocrates.

That the minds and bodies of men are influenced, *to a certain extent*, by external circumstances, I see no reason to deny.   But this is not
the real question: the question is, *to what extent?*
Let us first consider the effects of climate.   Hippocrates was enough of a philosopher to see that
it was not merely to the atmosphere that was to
be assigned the supposed influence exercised by
external circumstances over man's form and
mind.   Accordingly, he entitles his work, Περι
υδατων, αερον, και τοπον—which may bo thus translated, On the Influence of the Atmosphere, the
Waters and the *Locality*, over Man.   These
heads were meant to include all possible physical
elements affecting man.   Man's mind he traces
to his bodily frame; if he believed in a heaven
and a future state, he had no faith in Olympus,
nor in a thundering, material Jove, nor Styx, nor
Pluto.   He was a sort of anatomist, and had probably seen the brain—a sight of which tends no
doubt to remove many prejudices.

That the hypotheses sanctioned by his great
name existed long before his period we need not
doubt; it is sufficient for our present purpose to
trace them to him.   In his writings we find hypotheses — 1st, That climate or external circum-

stances make men brave or cowardly, freemen or
slaves; in other words, that man's *mind* was the
result of *climate*. 2ndly, That to climate and to
other external circumstances, summed up in the
expression, "Air, Water, and Place," (Hippocrates!) might be traced all differences in the
form, complexion, and mental qualifications of
men; the varieties, in short, observable everywhere
in their physical structure and mental dispositions; that race, in short, depends on climate.
And 3rdly, That such alterations in form and
mind, the result of external influences, thus constituting a race, become in time permanent, transmissible by hereditary descent, and so independent of their original producing causes;
and lastly, that the head itself, the very brain, by
means of which we lay claim to the character and
title of intellectual beings, might be so altered

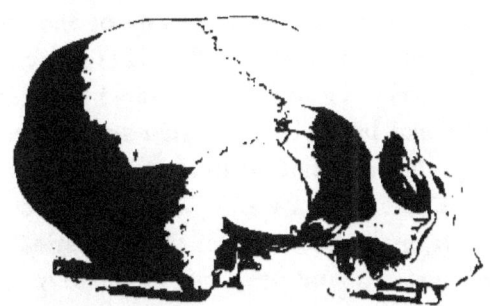

[*The Cherokee cranium. Men with crania similarly
formed were said by Hippocrates to inhabit the
shores of the Black Sea.*]

G 2

by mechanical means, by external pressure, as
scarcely to be recognisable for a human head;
and that this most extraordinary of all forms,
once produced, becomes transmissible by hereditary descent, requiring no longer the influence
of the mechanical cause producing it.

To Hippocrates was ascribed the honour of
having first separated medicine from philosophy;
these are some of the results of this disunion—
hypothesis heaped on hypothesis, unsupported
by observation, based on no truths.   To him, or
at least to those from whose works he compiled,
we owe some, at least, of these conjectures.   He
is supposed (for in ancient history all is suppo-
sition) to have flourished some 470, say 500 years
before the present æra, that is, at the least, 2300
years ago: he has been usually called a physician
—to me he seems to have been a surgeon, and his
success was probably equal to any of the present
day. The opinions he has collected are much older
than the period he lived in; medical theories and
theorists had been already tested and appreciated
by the philosophers of his times—Thucydides, the
historian, knew them well. But Hippocrates, at
all events, embodied some of these theories into a
sort of system, handing them down to posterity
in classic language, bestowing on error immortality.   That his mind was philosophic on the
whole, cannot be questioned; but so was that of

Descartes, of Pythagoras, of Voltaire; all philosophic minds, all impatient of the calm investigation of physical truths. Like many great and
good men, some modern fanatics have accused
him of atheism; those, in fact, and they belong
to all denominations, who accuse of atheism all
who refuse joining their outrageously ridiculous
anthropomorphical notions of a First Cause. He
denied the discrepancy of divine and physical
causes, merging them in one; he treated all phenomena as at once divine and scientifically deter-
minable. This doctrine he applied to disease:
my object is to apply it to all living nature—to
man, the most important of all—to man, the antagonistic animal of nature's works; to that animal who wages perpetual war with nature's fairest
productions. It is in vain that theologians endeavour to divert the attention of men's minds from
this great question, How are the races of men
produced? whence come they? whither tend
they? Already a learned divine* has stretched
the link between the 2nd and 3rd verses of the
Mosaic record to a coil so extended, so elastic,
as to leave on the part of the scientific nothing
to desire; and whilst I write this passage, a friend
has pointed out to me that a learned theologian,
if not an orthodox divine,† who writes on a sub-

* Buckland.
† British Quarterly, for Nov.—Editor, Rev. Dr. Vaughan.

ject of which I fear he does not know much,—
" the Unity of Man"—cautions his readers not to
mistake the chronology of Bishop Usher for the
true chronology of man, which he candidly admits
has never yet been discovered: he prepares his
readers for a lengthening of the *period* to account
for the different races!   I knew it must come to
this—another version of the Mosaic record to the
hundreds already existing. For the present, I
leave the chronological part in their hands, proceeding with the inquiry into the physiological
laws regulating human life.

[*Bosjeman playing on the gourah.*]

That by mere climate, giving to the expression
its utmost range of meaning, a new race of men
can be established in perpetuity, is an assertion

which for the present is contradicted by every
well-ascertained physiological law, and by all
authentic history. On the limited habitable territory of the Cape of Good Hope, shut in by
deserts and by the sea, lived, when the Saxon
Hollander first landed there, two races of men,
as distinct from each other as can be well imagined, the Hottentot, or Bosjeman, and the
Amakoso Caffre. To these was added a third,
the Saxon Hollander. What time the Bosjeman
child of the desert had hunted these desert and
arid regions, for what period the Hottentot had
listlessly tended his flocks of fat-tailed sheep,
how long the bold Caffre had herded his droves
of cattle, cannot now be ascertained: the Saxon
Hollander found them there 300 years ago, as
they are now in respect of physical structure and
mental qualifications, inferior races, whom he
drove before him, exterminating and enslaving
the coloured man; destroying mercilessly the *wilde*
which nature had placed there; and with the *wilde*,
ultimately the coloured *man*, in harmony with all
around him—antagonistic, it is true, but still in
harmony to a certain extent; non-progressive;
races which mysteriously had run their course,
reaching the time appointed for their destruction.

To assert that a race like the Bosjeman, marked
by so many peculiarities, is convertible, by any
process, into an Amakoso Caffre or Saxon Hol-

lander, is at once to set all physical science at
defiance. If by time, I ask what time? The
influence of this element I mean to refute presently: the Dutch families who settled in Southern
Africa three hundred years ago, are now as fair, and
as pure in Saxon blood, as the native Hollander;
the slightest change in structure or colour can at
once be traced to intermarriage. By intermarriage
an individual is produced, intermediate generally,
and partaking of each parent; but this mulatto
man or woman is a monstrosity of nature—there
is no place for such a family: no such race exists
on the earth, however closely affiliated the parents
may be. To maintain it would require a systematic
course of intermarriage, with constant draughts
from the pure races whence the mixed race derives
its origin. Now, such an arrangement is impossible. Since the earliest recorded times, such

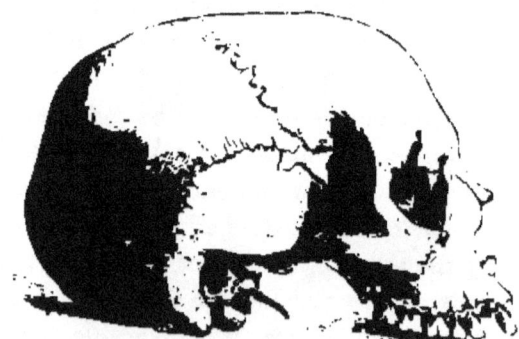

[*Caffre Skull.*]

mixtures have been attempted and always failed;
with Celt and Saxon it is the same as with Hottentot and Saxon, Caffre and Hottentot. The
Slavonian race or races have been deeply intercalated for more than twice ten centuries with the
South German, the pure Scandinavian, the Sarmatian, and even somewhat with the Celt, and with
the Italian as conquerors: have they intermingled?
Do you know of any mixed race the result of such
admixture? Is it in Bohemia? or Saxony? or
Prussia? or Finland?

[*Caffre Race.*]

This seems to be the law. By intermarriage a
new product arises, which cannot stand its ground;
1st, By reason of the innate dislike of race to race,
preventing a renewal of such intermarriages;
2nd, Because the descendants will of necessity
fall back upon the stronger race, and all traces, or
nearly so, of the weaker race must in time be

obliterated. In what time, we shall afterwards
consider. If a pure race has appeared to undergo
a permanent change when transferred to a climate
materially differing from their own, such changes
will be found, on a closer inquiry, to be delusive.
It has been asserted of the West-Indian Creole ;
of the Mexican, Peruvian, and Chilian Creole;
and of the North-American or Saxon Creole, now
called a United States man; but the pretended
changes we shall find are either trifling, or not
permanent, or do not exist. When speaking of
the races so located, that is, dislocated from the
climate and land of their origin, and from the
pure race which sent them forth, swarms of
living beings, in search of new lands, I shall
endeavour to apply those laws practically which
are here merely announced, discussing also, in
separate sections, some of the leading doctrines
applicable to all men. Of other animals I speak
not here, for this obvious reason—the species of
animals as they now exist, have their specific
laws regulating their existence. What is true of
one may or may not be true of another. Sheep
have their specific laws; so have cattle and horses,
pigs and elephants. Some of the laws regulating
their existence are applicable to man in a general
way—others, and the greater part, are not. When
I am told that there is a short-legged race of sheep
somewhere in America, the product of accident,

my reply is simply—I do not believe it, even
although, to make the story look better, it has
been also added, that from among the few short-
legged sheep *accidentally* produced in the flock,
the owner was careful to extrude the long-legged
ones, and so at last his whole flock became short-
legged, and he *had no more trouble with it*. It is the
old fable of Hippocrates and the Macrocephali
reduced to something like a scientific formula;
transferred from sheep, it has been made the basis
of a theory of race, of mankind—reducing all to
accident. By accident, a child darker than the rest
of the family is born; when this happens in the
present day, it is also, by courtesy, called an
accident, but its nature is well understood; not

[*The savage Bosjemen :—Troglodytes; who build no
house or hut; children of the desert.*]

so in former times. This dark child, a little
darker than the others, separates, with a few more,
from the rest of the family, and sojourns in a land
where a hot sun enbrowns them with a still deeper
hue. In time they become blacker and blacker,
or browner and browner. Should they travel
north instead of south, it is all the same, for extreme cold produces the same effect as extreme
heat! This is ancient and modern physiology!
it is the old fable of Hippocrates revived. Men's
minds seem to move in circles, ever reverting to
ancient errors; it is as the struggle of a small body
of men against the gloomy forest, the bog, the
spreading desert; lovers of truth vainly endeavouring to clear away the accumulated ignorance
of fifty centuries.

For my own part, I do not think such theories
worthy a serious refutation. Man is not a rumi-
nant; he has his own physiological laws, which
ought long since to have been traced. But the
statement in question is not even true of sheep,
for by no effort, saving that of a *constant* never-
ceasing intermixture, or draught on the pure
breeds, can a mixed breed be maintained. Leave
it to itself, and it ceases to be. It is the same
with man; with fowls; with cattle; with horses.
Distinct breeds, when not interfered with, mark
them all. Man can create nothing permanent;

modify, he may for a time, but he can create no
new living element. It is said that the cattle fed
on the pampas of South America have assumed
three distinct forms; be it so—the fact proves
nothing, for they are constantly interfered with
by man. I have been assured that our domestic
cattle, imported into New Zealand and New Holland, return after a generation or two to the
primitive breeds—nothing more likely, this, in
fact, being the physiological law. In Britain we
have a white breed of cattle, confined within the
domains of two wealthy families; they remain
white, merely because all calves which show other
colours are destroyed. See how difficult the
simplest physiological question becomes. We
talk freely of men's destiny and races, and their
laws, as if we knew them, whilst as yet no one
has solved so simple a question as the origin of
the white cattle of Britain and of Wales. But to
return to man.

Add to the hypothesis of *accidental* origin of
a variety in family, its separation from its tribe,
yet even this explanation will fail; for the family
so separated, by the very law which produced
the variety, will be fertile in other varieties; they
therefore must also appear in numbers at least
equal to the others. In the history of the Jewish
and Gipsy races I shall consider this question at

greater length, and endeavour to show that the
application of the doctrines of transcendental
anatomy made in this direction is also false.

"Time and development change all things;"
this is my own belief: but what is the time required? when was man different from what we
find him now? Development is positive: time
has no existence. The existing order of things
we see, though imperfectly; of the past, but little
has been preserved in human records—that little
is not understood. One thing, however, is certain—the Pyramids exist, and the ancient tombs
of Egypt; the ruins of Karnác; the paintings on
the walls of these tombs; some Etruscan remains;
the Egyptian mummies; the Cyclopean walls—

[*Egyptian Pyramid.*]

these are nearly all the sure data which man has
to depend on whilst tracing back his history, and
the history of the existing order of life, towards
that unknown past from which he sprung. Now
what do these amount to? What do they prove?
They are but as yesterday, compared with the
period through which the globe has rolled in
space; through which life has undergone its ever
succeeding developments; yet they announce one
fact at least, that man, up to the earliest recorded
time, did not differ *materially* from what he is
now; that there were races then as now; that
they seemed to be identical (but of this we are
not quite certain) with those now existing, and
that neither over them, nor over the living world
around, has climate or external circumstances
effected any serious changes, produced any new
species, any new groups of animal or vegetable
life, any new varieties of mankind. To the important fact, if it really be one, thus made out,
the illustrious and cautious Cuvier first drew
men's attention; but his reserve, his position, his
habitual caution, induced him to omit all mention
of man. So long as he excluded him from his
line of observation, the Sorbonne, he was aware,
cared not what he did with the rest. It was his
practice to leave untouched whatever he thought
speculative, unsafe, transcendental—whatever ho
fancied shocked too much the present feelings.

Satisfied with the refutation of St. Fond and the
geologists of his day, he desired to proceed no
further. " He had formed an æra—he constituted
an æra:" to his positive opinions and well-ascer-

[*Bust of the young Memnon : British Museum.*]

tained facts were tacked theories by the theolo-
gico-geological school of England, which he never
acknowledged, which he never admitted, which
he never sanctioned by word or writing. We
shall consider these matters in a future section;
in the meantime one thing remains certain, which
he either did not notice or avoided mentioning—
man has changed no more than other animals:
as they were in Egypt when the pyramids were
built, so are they now, men and animals: man
seems different, it is true: at first it would appear
as if a race had become extinct; we shall find it is
not so. The Coptic race is no more extinct than
is the ancient Mexican, and even now it is questionable whether the mixed barbarian and savage
race of slaves, now called Egyptians, will ultimately stand their ground, fed though they be by
imports from Nubia and the White Nile—from
Greece and Asia Minor. They are not Arabs: a
motley crew, as I understand, destined to cease
when the imports are withdrawn, and to assume
a form traceable to the dominant blood now
circulating, be it Copt or Arab, Nubian or Negro.

But in claiming for the races of men an antiquity coeval with the historic period, and with
man's earliest appearance on the earth, I venture
to caution you from accepting of this deduction
or that of M. Cuvier in respect of animals, as
being rigorously accurate. Neither men nor

animals seem to have changed; as regards the
latter, Cuvier asserted that they had not in the
slightest degree.   Admitting the expression to be
sufficiently accurate for his and our purpose, yet
I think it strong, perhaps too strong.   Data sufficiently accurate and extensive are wanting to
enable us to institute a very rigorous comparison.
I do not mean to cavil at the expression: the
changes undergone in five or six thousand years
are so small as to escape notice; but it does not
absolutely follow that no changes whatever have
taken place.   On the tombs of Egypt, the most
valuable of all existing records, there stands the

[*A Persian Lady; from an original drawing,
presented to me by Dr. Charles Bell.*]

Negro, the Jew and Copt, the Persian, the Sarmatian, nearly as we find them now; this is
enough for our purpose. Herodotus says that
the Egyptians of his days were black men: very
possibly; but neither before nor since his period
has this remark been found to be true. The
paintings on the tombs and the mummies entombed alike refute his assertion, if extended
beyond his period. He gossiped, I am afraid,
like some other travellers, and talked a good deal
about what he did not understand. Was he ever
in Egypt? I feel disposed to doubt it. His
story about the Persian skull reminds me of
the next assertion of ancient and modern physiologists, of the supposed influence of external,
even mechanical, means over the human form.

It is to Hippocrates we owe the story of the
Macrocephali, inhabiting at that time the shores
of the Euxine. They were a race with narrow,
elongated, elevated heads and depressed fore-
heads, like the American Indians, or copper-
coloured race, and more especially like the Carib
and the Chenook. This variety in form the illustrious Greek explains in this way—for of the unity
of mankind he never doubted any more than any
other strictly scientific man: he fancied, for it
was more fancy, that this extraordinary form of
head was at first produced by pressure, but that
in time this pressure became unnecessary, the

malformation becoming permanent by hereditary descent. Two hypotheses in a breath, both opposed to well-ascertained physiological laws. That the Carib and Chenook, and the ancient Macrocephali, fancied that by pressure they could give to the human head what form they chose, is certain enough; but does it follow that they could do so? The form of the head I speak of is peculiar to the race; it may be exaggerated somewhat by such means, but cannot be so produced: neither will such deformation become hereditary. For four thousand years have the Chinese been endeavouring to disfigure the feet of their women: have they succeeded in making the deformation permanent? Corsets have been worn time out of mind: Galen complains of them; he ascribes to them all sorts of bad results, deformities of spine and chest. Have such become hereditary? All

The Cherokee Skull.]

matrons still produce virgin daughters. For
how long have the Jews, with most African and
Eastern nations, practised circumcision? Has
the deformation become hereditary? Is there
any instance of such accidental or mechanical
deformities becoming transmissible by hereditary
descent?

[*Foot of a Chinese Woman; from the Collection
in King's College, London.*]

The varieties of form classed under the law of
deformation, and dependent on the operation of
the great law of unity of organization, belong to
a different category, as will be explained in a
distinct chapter on that head; but even they are
kept in constant check by the laws of specialization, restoring man and animals to their specific

shapes, else what would life terminate in?
Varieties in form proceed only to a certain
length — they are constantly checked by two
laws, the laws maintaining *species as they exist*—
1, the tendency to reproduce the specific form
instead of the variety; 2, non-viability or non-
reproduction, that is, extinction.   This it is
which checks deformations of all kinds, and I
even think I have observed varieties in form to
be more common in those who die young than
in those reaching adult years, as if the very
circumstance of these internal deformations or
varieties, however unimportant they may seem,
coincided at least, if they were not the efficient
cause of early decay of the vital powers and of
premature death.   Had the heads of the Macrocephali of ancient times, and of the Carib and
Chenook and Peruvian of modern, owed their
forms to mechanical means, that form would and
must have ceased with their immediate descendants, or the race would have perished.   How
much more singular is the *fact*, that there should
exist naturally men with heads and brains so
singularly shaped; that it should be in their
nature; that the form should still persist—unalterable, dependent on no climate, Asiatic—
American; ancient and modern.   This curious
question we shall discuss when speaking of the
American race; let us in the meantime bring

this lecture to a close: the great laws announced
in it will fall to be examined again in their
application to race and to human history.

It was Herodotus who said, that on a field of
battle it was easy to distinguish the Egyptian
from the Persian skull, the former being hard,
the latter soft. Herodotus must, I think, have
studied medicine; he gives a reason in such a
pleasant, off-hand way for all natural phenomena.
The reason he assigns for this difference is, that
the Persians covered the head—the Egyptians
used no head-dress. Admitting both facts to be
true, and I doubt them both, the reason given
explains nothing; if there was a difference, it
depended on race. The Copt was African; the
Persian, Asiatic: they were different races of
men—that is all. The *black* Egyptians of Herodotus have not been seen since his time.

The theories and the errors of Hippocrates
and Herodotus linger in the physiological schools
to this day. M. Foville, for example, ascribes to
mechanical pressure on the head of the infant,
the wide hollow groove occasionally traversing
it over the region of the vertex, and so frequently
persisting to the adult state — a deformation
wholly independent of such a cause, and occurring in all countries. The late Mr. Key persisted in blaming tight and short shoes for the
most common deformity of the feet; and Dr.

Combe,* still lingering on the gossip of Herodotus, finds a Bœotia in Holland, with all its
presumed results — a marshy, foggy, wet, and
heavy land, giving rise to phlegm and dulness—
the grave and witless, plodding Dutchman.   I
put these three observations, but not the writers,
under the same category; the last is refuted by
every observation, and is below notice.   But to
return.

To Hippocrates, then, as representing the
entire class of physiologists, we owe most of the
medical, philosophical, and theo-philosophical
notions of the present day; the theories which
teach that cities looking to the west differ very
materially from cities looking to the east, as
also their inhabitants; the reason why Asiatics
differ from Europeans—not one word of which
is true; how in a country where the seasons and
climates differ much, the inhabitants also must
differ much, the reverse of which is nearer the
truth: to him we owe the theory, that people
living under a monarchy are servile and cowardly,
whilst republicans are bold and brave—a doctrine
which certainly has some little show of truth, and
which we may afterwards discuss.   His theories
he transmitted to the scholars of Greece; they
affected even Aristotle, a master mind, who ought

* Combe on Digestion.

to have known better; but it is difficult to shake off the prejudices of ceuturies and of education· Aristotle assigns as a cause for the variety of strange and fantastic forms of animal life with

[*The young Memnon; representing the Coptic Race.*]

which Africa abounds, and abounded also in his
time, the scarcity of water, which, bringing to the
same wells and springs all sorts of animals, gave
rise to an endless variety of offspring! And this
reminds me of a mysterious law in nature, not
yet fully investigated, to which I next beg to call
your attention. I know that I have little or no
occasion now to tell you, that climate in no way
influences man's form or colour permanently;
some of the exceptions to this statement, which
will no doubt occur to you, fall to be explained
in the next section.

SECTION II. *Can a race of men permanently change
their locality—say Continental, or rather Ter-
restrial Zone? Can a Saxon become an American? or an African? Can an Asiatic become a
European? Can any race live and thrive in all
climates?*

The earth was made for man, and man was
made for the earth. The one proposition is quite
as intelligible as the other. That it was not
always so we now know, thanks to anatomical
research and true science. The necessary conditions of his existence were not always present;
his tenancy of the globe, according to the most
orthodox and best received doctrines, has been
but of short duration. This is not my opinion;

but I promised to consider first, in as far as I could, man as he is now, tracing him back into the unknown past as far as truth and science enable us to go.

Can any race of men live and thrive in any climate? Need I discuss this question seriously? Will any one venture to affirm it of man? Travel to the Antilles, and see the European struggling with existence, a prey to fever and dysentery, unequal to all labour, wasted and wan, finally perishing, and becoming rapidly extinct as a race, but for the constant influx of fresh European blood. European inhabitants of Jamaica, of Cuba, of Hispaniola, and of the Windward and Lee-ward Isles, what progress have you made since your first establishment there? Can you say you are established? Cease importing fresh European blood, and watch the results. Labour you can-not, hence the necessity for a black population; your pale, wan, and sickly offspring would in half a century be non-productive; face to face with the energetic negro race, your colour must alter—first brown, then black; look at Hayti: with a deepening colour vanishes civilization, the arts of peace, science, literature, abstract justice; Chris-tianity becomes a mere name, or puts on a feti-chian robe—why not? The Roman robe was, and is, Pagan; the Byzantine, misnamed Greek, has an outrageous oriental look; the Protestant

is a calculating, sober, drab-coloured cloak; why
may not the fetiche be attached to the cloak as well
as the mitre and the incense-box? Is the one
superior to the other? The European, then, cannot
colonize a tropical country; he cannot identify
himself with it; hold it he may, with the sword,
as we hold India, and as Spain once held Central
America, but inhabitants of it, in the strict sense
of the term, they cannot become. It never can
absolutely become theirs; nature gave it not to
them as an inheritance; they seized it by fraud
and violence, holding it by deeds of blood and
infamy, as we hold India; still it may be for a
short tenure, nay, it may even be at any time
measured. Withdraw from a tropical country
the annual fresh influx of European blood, and
in a century its European inhabitants cease to
exist.

Mr. Canning made his celebrated boast in
the English Parliament, that if he had lost the
influence and support of Old Spain, he had
created the South American Republics — free
states, whose traffic (it is always traffic with an
English statesman)—whose traffic with England
would amply supply the loss of that influence!
But where are these free states now? Mr. Canning
was too high a statesman to take into calculation
the element of race. When the boast was made,
I put this plain question to myself and others—

Who are the Mexicans? the Peruvians? the
Chilians? the Argentines? the Brazilians?
Whence do they spring, and what are the vital
forces supplying their population? Applying the
physiological laws, which seemed to me sufficiently well ascertained, I had little difficulty in
arriving at the following results. Man has found
it difficult to destroy a race of man, nor do I
think that he has yet succeeded even in this;
still it is a possible event apparently, but he
has not yet succeeded in effecting it To *create*
a race of men or animals is entirely beyond his
power. A Mexican nation may be formed by a
protocol, a treaty, a victory; an illustrious robber
may found a nation; an iron despot may chain
together the free Saxon and the slavish Pruss;
another may yoke in common chains the Slavonian and the German, the Italian and the Hun;
but will such things have a permanence? Consult history, and you will find that it cannot be.
Still less can any power create a Mexican or
Peruvian people, or race. Look at the elements
of Mr. Canning's free states; analyse them; try
them by any of the physiological laws I have
spoken of, and observe the result. A Celt-Iberian
and Lusitanian population make a descent on
America; Old Spain and Portugal send forth
their emigrants—men of a race already decaying,
men of a province of Rome, an off-set of Car-

thage — a combination of races themselves in
decay, and tottering to their fall. These, under
some bold leaders, seize on Southern and Central
America, consolidate their power as masters, and
enter on absolute possession of the soil; one-half
a vast continent becomes thus a mere province of
two paltry European states. During this period of
300 years, all things were favourable for an absolute consolidation with Spain and Portugal—
undisturbed possession, peace, continual emigration, wealth. Where are they now? When the
act of separation from the so-called mother
country took place, the population of Mexico and
Peru consisted of—1, pure Spaniards, whether
European or Creole it matters not; 2, pure
Indians, that is, the original and only true American—the native; 3, a motley crew, composed
of a mixture of these, more or less tinged; 4, a
sprinkling of Negro blood, pure, or mixed with the
Indian and the European. By the act of disunion, the influx of European blood, by which
alone the pure race could be maintained against
climate, and against the continual aggression of
the other more numerous races, was suddenly
withdrawn; even now it rapidly disappears, and
in a century it will have become extinct, for in
these climates a European race cannot labour,
cannot appropriate the soil to themselves, cannot
multiply their offspring. But, secondly, with the

cessation of the supply of European blood, the
mulatto of all shades must also cease; he cannot
extend his race, for he is of no race; there is no
place for him in nature. So soon as he has no longer
the pure blood of some other race to intermingle
with, he ceases to be, receding towards the black,
or advancing to the white, as the case may be;
thus the population I speak of lost by Mr. Canning's act, or will lose in time, the main-spring
of their population, falling back on the *native*,
that is, the American Indian—the race implanted
there by nature—the race in unison with the
forest and the climate, the soil, the air, the place
—the race of whose origin man knows nothing,
any more than he does of the lama and the tapir,
the cavia and the condor—the vegetable and
animal world of that continent on which Columbus gazed with such delight. All these he
found distinct from the rest of the world; and so
was the American man from his fellow man, as
different as is the nandu from the ostrich, the
lama from the camel.

But this last element of population, on which
the Mexican and Peruvian and Chilian no doubt
were thus thrown back, had already mysteriously
run its course; they were on the decline when
Cortes landed; they had passed through their
determined eras and civilization; on the curved
line indicating their course they seemed to have

passed the zenith; their population then, as it is
now, was on the wane—was gradually becoming
extinct. This the motley group called Mexicans and Peruvians now feel—they are instinctively conscious that the period approaches when
all again must become desert or Indian—a moral
or a physical desert; absence of life or absence
of mind. But for the Saxon invasion from the
north, it might have happened in Mexico and
Peru, and in Chili, that the desolation of these

[*Cherokee.*]

countries—say a hundred years hence—would have burst on Europe as an astounding and inexplicable fact. The man of the United States, who as yet delights in no name, might have walked into the land without any interruption or hindrance from any race. Penetrating to the centre of the so called Empire, he might have once more seen the sacrificial fires kindled on the pyramids of Cholula. A native population of nearly pure Iudian would once more have regained its ascendancy, to perish ultimately—to return to that nothing out of which they came.

But now the Saxon, grasping at more wealth, more land, comes in as a new element upon the already effete creations of Canning. Will he fare better? Will he be able to extinguish a race—the Indian of South America—and put himself in its place? I believe not, in that climate at least. Will he succeed even in North America? Is the boasted Union to be permanent? The pettifogging politicians of the day say, seriously and gravely, that in their opinions it must come to a monarchy at last! Profound politicians! A half-dozen monarchies at last—a king of New York, a Leopold installed in Kentucky, an Otho in Michigan, a liberal despotism under a prince of the noble house of Brunswick or Brandenburg. But you forget that these people are Saxons—democrats by their nature. Look at the Dutch Saxon at

I

the Cape, a handful of Boors—yes, a mere handful of Boors—bearding your best cavalry officer
at the head of six regiments. You have yet to discover the true nature of the *Saxon*; you will not
yet understand it, and yet you received a sharp
lesson at Boston and at New Orleans, losing
the mightiest colony ever founded by any race
or nation. Australia comes next; then South
Africa; your Norman government cannot profit
by experience. But to return.

As the Southern States of America become
depopulated by the operation of the physiological laws laid down, that vast land will fall an
easy prey to the Saxon and Celtic races now
occupying the northern States. That they will
ultimately seize on them there cannot be a
doubt, driving before them the expiring remains
of native and Lusitanian, Celt-Iberian and Mulatto
—a worthless race—effete, exhausted, before even
Hannibal and a handful of Carthaginians held
the country from which they sprung as a mere
appendage of Carthage. A single Roman legion
was enough for Old Spain; it could hold it yet.
The United States men, the descendants of Anglo-
Saxon, the Fleming and Celt, with a sprinkling of
South and Middle German, are now in possession
of Northern America—it seems to be absolutely
theirs: they form a union—they begin to talk of
natives and foreigners—they have forgotten who

they are, and fancy themselves *Americans* because
they choose to call themselves so; just as our
West India planters might have assumed the
name and title of native true-born Caribs. The
" United States man" believes himself to be independent of Europe, by which, if he means anything, he must mean independent of the *race* or
races from which he sprung.

Now, before I apply this great question to the
present United States men, trace back with me the
narrative, the chronicle of events called history.
If history be philosophy (which I doubt) teaching
by examples, it should enlighten us somewhat on
such questions as these—the extinction of one race
by another, and the substitution of one race for
another. The world, with man on it, is said to be
not old; and yet the end of the world we are told
approaches; the millennium is at hand; the Jews
are becoming Christians; the Celtic Irish abandoning pagan Rome, and adopting the Saxon
ritual, as by law established! Do not believe
those who tell you so. Nature alters, no doubt;
but *physical* changes must precede the *moral*,
and I see no symptoms of such.

The chronicles called histories tell us that the
Roman empire extended from the Clyde and
Forth to the Tigris and Euphrates. Northern,
extra-tropical Africa was said to be thoroughly
Roman; Italy, of course, was Roman to the core.

Where are the Romans now ?   What races have
they destroyed?   What races have they supplanted ?   For fourteen centuries they lorded it
over the semi-civilized world ; and now they are
of no more note than the ancient Scythians or
Mongols, Copts or Tartars.   They established
themselves nowhere as Romans.   Perhaps they
never were a race at all.   But be this as it may,
they destroyed no other race, supplanted no other
race : and now look over the map of their empire,
and tell me where you find a physical vestige of
the race ; on the Thames or Danube, Rhine or
Guadalquivir, Rhone or Nile.   Italy itself seems
all but clear of them.   Southern Italy was Græcia
Magna before they invaded it ; and Sicily is even
now more Greek than Italian.   Byzantium was a
Roman city, and so was York.   And so it is with
other conquering races.   Northern Africa never
was Phœnician, properly speaking, any more
than Algiers is Celtic now, or India English.
Even in Corsica the Celtic race of France have
failed to establish themselves, though, from its
proximity to France and presumed analogy of
climate, and, as has been erroneously asserted, of
races, there seems no reason why Corsica should
not become Celtic or French.   But it is not so.
The Corsicans are not Celts, they are not
Frenchmen ; nor are the Sardinians Italians,
properly speaking.   It is not merely the empires

of Rome and Carthage which have become extinct
in Northern Africa; it is the races which founded
these empires that are no longer to be found
there.   It may perhaps be urged, that Northern
Africa never really was either Carthaginian or
Roman; but this does not affect the question,
which is, Can one race supplant another on a soil
foreign to their nature; foreign to their origin?

The Greeks, who, under Alexander, marched
victorious to the Indus, supplanted no other race.
Rome and Carthage failed.   Attila and his Huns
also failed; and so did the Mongol.   The rem-
nant of Huns in Hungary now struggle for existence; they are interlopers seemingly amongst the
Slavonian race, and will probably perish.   But
neither have the Slavonians succeeded in supplanting the Italian, though masters, under the
name of Austrian and German, of Italy for nearly
ten centuries.   For at least two thousand years
have the Scandinavian and South Germans made
war on the Celtic race in the west, and made
head against the Sarmatian and Slavonian races
in the east, without advancing a single step, in so
far as I can discover.   These races hold the same
position to each other which they did in the remotest period of authentic history.

The whole force of the so-called German Empire,
headed by Austria, could not dislodge the Slavonian from Bohemia; the Norman, though he met

in South England a kindred race, could not destroy the *Saxon race* of North England.   To this
day the country seems to be divided between
them, notwithstanding the centralizing influence
of Flemish London.   The Celts still hold the
western limits of Britain and Ireland, just as they
did before the period of authentic history.

*The Mongolian, travelling to this day on the
Steppes of Asia, with his tent on a cart; precisely as in the days of Herodotus: the race has
never altered in any way.]*

But it may be said, England is a colony from
Scandinavia, from Holstein, and Jutland; Ireland
seemingly of Spain; the Celtic colony has not
been prosperous; nevertheless, numerically it has
thriven; the Saxon colony has succeeded to admiration.   The parent country of the Anglo-
Saxon, ancient Scandinavia, has withered in presence of the blighting influence of the abhorred
Sarmatian (Russ and Pruss) and Slavonian (Haps-

burg—Gotho-Austrian) governments. Why may
not, then, the Celt prosper in Africa—the Saxon
in Australia, in Southern Africa, in Northern America? Do we not see how the Saxon thrives in
these countries? Look at the population of the
States! Mark its progress; and then admit the fact
that man was made to thrive everywhere." Should
this argument fail, the Utopian falls back on a
final cause: " Vast regions are deserted; why not
occupy them? Is it not clear that they were intended to be occupied by man ?" Lastly, they go
ack on the humanities, and claim for a suffering,
over-stocked population, the sad privilege de-
signed them by a wise Providence, to quit the
land of their birth, and seize on the soil of any
other race who promise the richest spoils with
the least resistance. This is the Utopian, the
man of final causes, of necessities, humanities, and
expediencies. What has science to do with such
notions ?

The question of the destruction of one race by
another—that is, by violence—is distinct from
that of natural causes, leading to the supplanting
one race by another; and, of consequence, the
successful transplanting of a race of men from one
continent to another, from one zone of the earth
to its opposite, or even to one seemingly analogous, is one merely of *fact*, and has nothing whatever to do with moral, metaphysical, or theological

theories; it is an inquiry into the physical or physiological laws regulating man's existence on the
globe.

"All nature is fixed but man, who is for ever
changing."* In this effective passage there are
more errors than words. For if by *nature* the writer
meant the living world, then we have the evidence
of Cuvier and all anatomists that it has not
changed since *that period* to which the writer
assigns "the creation of all things;" and 2ndly,
man never changes any more than other living
beings, belonging, as he evidently does, to the
same category with them. The existing order of
things did not always exist; this is now a *fact*
which the "effective writers" just quoted resisted
to the very last. Nature changes, no doubt: the
era of the Saurians is gone and past; and the
semi-barbarous modern Celt and money-loving
Saxon deems the descendants of ancient Rome
unworthy the treatment of men! Still I hold that
neither Celt nor Roman is essentially changed
from what he was, as time will show.

The isothermal lines of the northern and
southern hemispheres may be analogous, but they
are not identical. When first discovered, each
continent and large island was found to have its
own zoology and botany—its fauna and its flora.
What Britain was prior to the historic period we

* Quarterly for Nov. 1849.

know not; but there is no reason for viewing
it otherwise than a portion of continental
Europe, perhaps united to it, or separated by
shallow water-basins, of muddy water, of brackish
pools, not affecting greatly the climate of the
country; not more at least than Northern Holland
and large portions of Denmark are to be viewed
as distinct from the present continental atmospheric constitution. Of Ireland and Wales it
may be said that their relation with Spain must
have been most direct; Cornwall also. But
the relations of South England must have been
with Flanders and Northern and Western France.
That colonies from the opposite shores, crossing
merely an inland sea, should succeed in establishing themselves on its margins or coasts,
need not excite any surprise. But when the
same or other races attempt the colonization
of another and a different region—a zone of the
earth distinct from theirs, a group of land and

[*Arm and hand of the fossil Saurian, which Sir C.
Bell and the "final cause" philosophers imagine to be formed on a plan or scheme distinct
from all existing forms of life. But this opinion
is erroneous in the highest degree.*]

water on which originated a distinct group of life, animal and vegetable—the case is widely different, as all history proves.   I have already alluded to Corsica and to Sardinia.   These countries seem not to have belonged originally to the European or African continents, but to a Mediterranean group distinct from all others.   Hence the failure of the Celt and Italian in Sardinia.   The Maltese are not Italians; and the races of the Spanish Isles have yet to be examined.

But be this as it may, the invasion of Africa by the Celtic race, and their attempt on Algiers, although a momentous question, is not a new one, as modern journalists would have you to suppose: it is a question older than Rome.   Its solution was tried by the Phœnician and the Roman; next poured in the barbarous tribes of Gaul and Germany; they wrought with their Christianity, St. Cyril and the "humanities;" yet all would not do.   Then followed other invasions of Africa, European and Asiatic.   Still the Levantine remains; the man of the Mediterranean group, who is neither Arab nor Turk, Roman nor Celt, Goth nor Visigoth.   So soon, indeed, as the emigrant supplies were withdrawn which fed the original colony, the race expired, or became so feeble as scarcely to claim an existence.   It must be the same with Algiers: a Celtic population may be supported there by a constant influx of fresh

emigrants from old France; fresh Celtic blood
will supply the waste of life, maintain a Celtic
ascendancy in a seeming French civilization; or
prudence may suggest the transfer of negro
labourers to the soil, and France may then for
a few centuries govern Northern Africa, as we do
India and Ceylon. But in the absence of this
alternative, not likely to occur, the Celt, forced to
depend on his own resources, must fail in time;
the period may be long or short, but come it will.
A war on the Rhine might hasten it by a century;
for the continental Celt could not, single-handed,
maintain a war against a European race and an
African at the same time; more especially as, in
the latter case, the war must of necessity be carried on against climate and race.

Turn for a moment to the position of the
Turcoman in Europe; his decreasing influence
and population gradually expiring or going back
to the original races. Turn to Spain and Portugal: their population does not exceed nor equal
what it did in the time of the Romans. Is it
luxury which destroys the population of Old
Spain? the luxury to live on chestnuts and
mouldy cheese? When was the Spaniard an in-
temperate and luxurious man? A week's supplies
of our beef-loving army would have fed Madrid
for a month! Yet the population does not increase. Of the Slavonian race I have already

spoken; they occupy their original ground, nor has any other race been able to supplant them. Trodden down by the Sarmatian, the German, the Roman, the Turcoman, the Hun, they occupy still the same ground they did before all history. Their eastern origin is a fable. Twice I think did the Hun and the Turcoman penetrate to Vienna, across and through the great mass of the Slavonian race, and twice has the Crescent returned from the Slavonian native land, leaving no traces of their passage.

Now this great race, the most intellectual of all, occupy, as I have said, as nearly as may be, at the present day, the same countries as in the remotest periods; at times advancing, at times receding; assailed by Roman power; overrun by the terrible Attila and his Cossaques; crushed down by the Mongol; oppressed by the Turcoman; cruelly butchered in Bohemia, and Posen, and Prussia, by the Sarmatian and German races; decimated by the Russ in Poland,—there they still remain, aboriginal occupiers of the soil; no change in features or form, but always recognisable by the surrounding races: Gothic, no doubt; high-minded, original, inventive, mystical, transcendental. The Turcoman left in Hungary a portion of his race, the Magyars, but they cannot hold their ground, noble though they be; nor can there be a doubt that their existence depends on the admixture by marriage with Slavonian families.

Napoleon, at the head of his Celtic army, swept over their land: what impressions remain? Could a Celt thrive on the banks of the Theiss, even had he retained their country? I do not believe it; but even if he could, a Celtic colony on the banks of the Danube or Theiss must in time become extinct; its success would be merely individual, or confined to a few generations; gradually the race would lose its energies, " the form " its distinctive element of youth; in the face of a more numerous race, the less numerous must give way, until nearly all traces would disappear. Thus, happen what may, it would seem that a race cannot be changed, cannot be extinguished; or at least certain races; neither by metamorphosis, nor by conquest and the sword, nor by intermarriage, so long as they occupy the soil on which nature first placed them.

That the southern hemisphere of this globe should differ in many respects from the northern in its fauna and its flora, will cause no surprise to men in quest of truth; but that it differs so widely as it really does, is not generally known, and still less believed. When I describe the Bosjeman and Hottentot, the Australian and Tasmanian, then will be the proper time to unfold this great fact: that the races of everything living, from man to the whale; from the whale, to the zoophyte, to the entomostraca, which serve as food to the so-called herring of the Bay of Islands, differ from the northern.   And yet not always, if we trust fossil geology.   But it is sufficient for us that it differs now, and has differed for thousands of years: that is enough for man. Of the exceptions, real or only seeming, I shall speak hereafter; the most remarkable being the asserted identity of the Red Indian

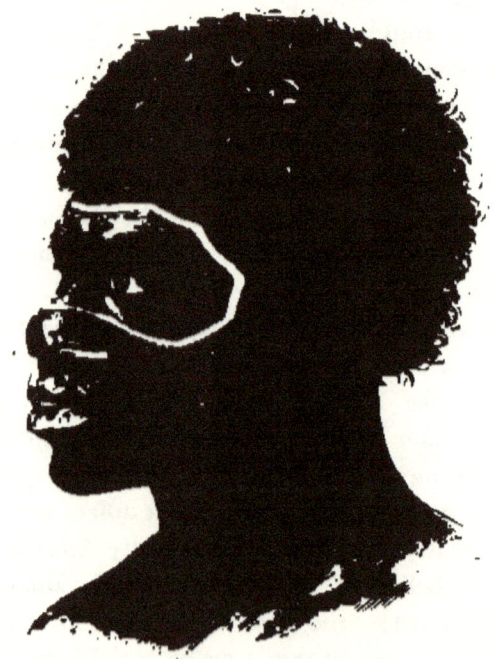

[*The aboriginal native of Australia : from Peron.*]

throughout the entire range of continental America : this I doubt, but avoid discussing the doubt here. Sufficient for our purpose is the fact, that nature placed in the southern hemisphere another form of life, not perhaps altogether dependent on its being a southern hemisphere, but with other geographical arrangements, of which we know but

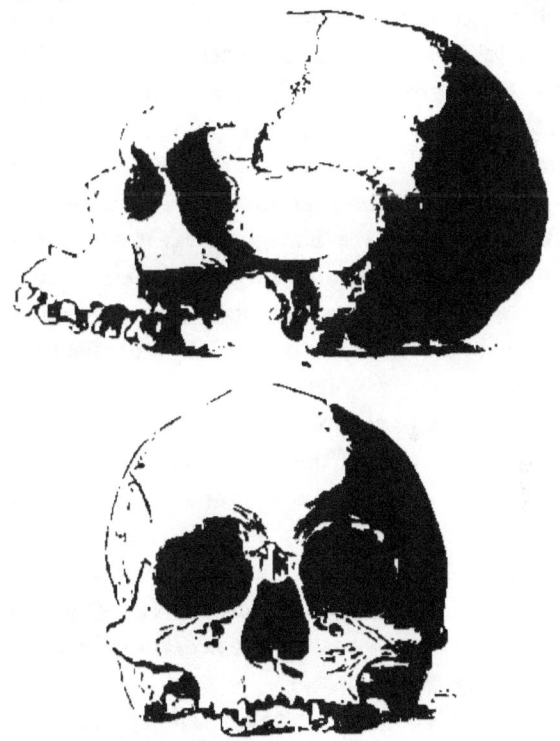

[*Australian Cranium ; from the Collection in King's College, London.*]

little. Now, it is into this southern hemisphere
that the European has penetrated at last; he
tried Northern Africa, but it would not do; next
he tried Central or Tropical Africa—the failure
here was disastrous and decided.   Of India we
need say nothing; nobody, not even Lord Russell,
proposes colonizing India. In the Antilles the
Celtic race failed : Napoleon himself never ventured to renew the hopeless struggle with climate
and the Negro race.   *Spanish* America is at an
end ; and the Canning's Republics foresee their
fate.   Our West Indian colonies are no colonies
—every one knows this now ; and if there be any
who believe that the European races now occupying Florida and the countries bordering on the
Gulf of Mexico can colonize and supplant the
coloured races, they will, I think, find themselves
in error.

Hitherto I have spoken, for the most part, of
the transplanting of the European races to countries which, if not tropical, are at least unhealthy
or inimical to European life.   It is something to
get this fact admitted.   Let me now discuss with
you events of more recent occurrence—migrations
of modern times—testing the present delusions by
the history of the past.

Lower Canada was colonized by France; a
Celtic race, a highly civilized people ; the most
highly civilized people on the earth, transferred

to a vast country, a boundless land, a portion of their people. This was no helter-skelter, pell-mell, go-ahead, Saxon rush ; no Californian rout ; it was an emigration of a portion of a Celtic race, with all their household gods, their monkeries and mummeries, their nunneries and seigniories, feudality and primogeniture ; with every other law and influence which feudalism and religion could devise to enslave the souls and bodies of men. It was to be old France on a small scale ; and so it became very speedily, with this difference, that,

[*The Cymrais, or Welsh Celt.*]

K

being withdrawn from the vast body of their race,
and being composed of men whoso nature is of
the slowest progressive character, they remained
nearly agricultural, as France was when they
migrated, so that a traveller on landing might
fancy himself suddenly translated back in time to
the period of Louis Quatorze or even of the
Regency itself: little men with sky-blue coats,
like dreamy half-crazed fiddlers; little women;
little horses and cattle; little carts; still smaller
ideas.   To clear them out of " New France," *le
bas Canada,* all that was wanted was to repeal the
laws of primogeniture and entail; break up the
seigniories; and let in the large-armed, large-
handed Saxon race upon them.

There is a result of the most curious kind
flowing from this great experiment; the transfer
of a portion of civilized France to America—
temperate America—and its total failure as a
colony. It would appear that, but for fresh supplies of emigrants from the parent stock living on
the parent soil of France, the Canadian Frenchman must gradually have become extinct.   Had
they been placed face to face with a more energetic race than the Red Indian, then rapid extinction was most certain. That several physiological
laws contribute to such a result is no doubt true,
but the word *race* embraces all.   The race degenerated; the *habitans* submitted to a mere handful

of English troops; they could not strike one blow
for their country. They had sunk so low that
when the glorious name of Liberty inscribed on
her colours enabled Old France, in a period so
brief as to appear incredible, to strike down, for a
time at least, the monstrous dynasties of Europe,
the Canadian Celt remained quiescent, with the
noblest republic for his next neighbour the world
ever saw. Race is everything. Seigniories and
monkeries, nunneries and feudality, do not form,
neither do they modify, the character of any
people; they are an *effect*, not a *cause*, let *chroniclers** say what they will. They indicate the
character of a race — they do not make that
character.

Thus it would seem that in 4000 years the
Celt, under no climate, has been able to substitute
himself for any other race: Syria, Egypt, Greece,
Corsica, Algiers, Canada, St. Domingo—all have
been tried and failed.

Let me conclude this section by an examination
of the pretensions of another race, of all others
the most outrageously boasting, arrogant, self-
sufficient beyond endurance, holding in utter
contempt all other races and all other men—the
Saxon.

In remote times the Scandinavian or Saxon

---

* Macaulay, and the " effective" journalists of the day.

attempted Gaul, Sarmatia, and Slavonia. They
have been constantly defeated. The Austrian
empire is not Saxon — it is not even German.
They next attempted Italy and Greece, with no
better success. Malta is not English, any more
than Cephalonia. In western tropical Africa, the
"season" generally reduces England's efforts at
colonization to a dozen or two white men,
the result of a century's exertions on the part
of England. Mighty England, with her fast-
growing race, cannot colonize a single acre of
a tropical African country; her flag, however,
still waves over it, no African seemingly thinking
it worth while to pull it down. The experiments
on this head are not altogether before the public ;
the springs and causes of action seldom reach
the surface so as to be visible. Two bold
attempts at least were made in my own time to
convert Central Africa into another India; to
discover in Central Africa a "mine of patronage ;"
but it would not do. The first attempt, in my
own recollection, was to fill the country with
troops; commerce would have answered better,
but our Norman government always prefers
the bayonet to any other form of progress.
They first tried the bayonet; troops were sent in
large numbers, composed of men who, having
deserted, had commuted their sentence of punishment into enlisting into what was called a con-

demned regiment—that is, a regiment serving
on the west coast of Africa. Condemned they
were, no doubt, for few escaped the effects of the
deadly climate. Nearly all perished, and the experiment was a failure.

The second attempt was made by that profound
statesman, Lord Russell. The open bayonet
having failed, it was covered with bales of goods,
and sent up the Niger; the bayonet was still
there, but concealed. A central fort, high up the
Niger or Quorra, was wanted in the centre of
tropical Africa — a Fort Vittoria — to enslave
countless nations, hitherto free. But the second
experiment failed, like the first, to be repeated
again, no doubt, at some future period. This is
not the first time the Saxon has attempted to
extend his race to Africa; he tried it during the
dark ages, but the natives beat *him*. With gunpowder and wealth, the sinews of war, he made
his last attempt: climate defeated it. So at least
it seemed; but I partly doubt this. The affair
might have gone off better under able leaders.

Let us next examine the question from a point
of view, new, I believe, and it may be startling, to
most of my readers. Taught to believe that man,
and especially Saxon man, may live anywhere, he
has been taught that vast regions of the earth have
been depeopled by " the mysterious arrangements of
Providence, to facilitate the extension of the Saxon

race ;" that the coloured races die out before him for the same reason—wither at his mere approach, and perish ; that, peculiarly favoured by Providence and its divine dispensations, aided by gunpowder and the art of printing, the globe itself must ultimately be his.   He cannot imagine the bare possibility of the race being found unequal to the colonizing a country enjoying a temperate climate. Ho is the man of to-day ; yesterday is nothing to him ; he forgets, he despises, he denies its existence.   Ho is the man of this day.   Onward ! is the cry.   The adage of Horace was written for him.   Here is a picture of the man.

Requested by a friend to revisit Paris, on matters important to him, I proceeded to Folkestone, an ancient sea-side, fishing, and smuggling town on the southern coast of England, the nearest point, I believe, to Boulogne-sur-Mer.   We were to embark for " beautiful France" next morning. A night perfectly calm, mild, clear, a moonlight night, though cold, tempted me from the great hotel complete with English comforts, to the closely-adjoining beach, where wandering alone, by the margin of the rippling tide, listening to its hollow murmur, and gazing on the placid waters trembling under the ineffectual beams of the silvery orb, my mind reverted to times and events long past.   At no great distance from the shore where I stood, I had myself embarked for France,

when hopes and years were fresh and young:
along these shores had I brought to England the
first of the wounded of Mont St. Jean. But the
scene shifted to the past. Memory, ever active,
ever restless, unfolded visions of historic recollections. At a short distance, nay, perhaps on
this very spot, Harold surveyed his troops; at no
great distance, I knew, lay Hastings; that bloody
field, surpassing far in its terrible results the unhappy day of Waterloo. From this the Celt has
recovered, but not so the Saxon. To this day he
feels, and feels deeply, the most disastrous day
that ever befel his race; here he was trodden down
by the Norman—whose iron-heel is on him yet.
Here William found a congenial race, driving
with them into northern England the Saxon
race; and here was all but annihilated the liberties of mankind: the question which transcends
all others—whether man is to be a free man or a
slave—was nearly settled at Hastings. To this
day the Saxon race in England have never recovered a tithe of their rights: and, probably, never
will.

As I thought over these great events, (great, not
from the handful of men, who boldly cut each other's
throats at Hastings, like stout yeomen and good
Christians; but great, beyond all expression, when
viewed as a contest of principle, of race; freedom
against slavery; the reign of the law against the

reign of the sword; whose most terrible evils still
subsist in England, untouched and unassailed,)
I bethought me of visiting the bee-hive looking
village, not altered, I believe, since Harold's time,
clustered on the slope of those white cliffs so
celebrated in English song. A vulgar, filthy
mechanical wall and rail crossed the village, but
clearing its low, ill-shaped arch, the sea-beach
was once more before me, with ships high and dry
on the strand in no ways larger than what accompanied William on that grand voyage when, true
to his race, he singled out England as his antagonist—Saxon England, freed at the time from
continental despotism; continental slavery; continental dynasties. Here, on this strand, I heard

[*The Anglo-Saxon House.*]

the sound of revelry, proceeding from a small inn
or ale-house, frequented, no doubt, by tradesmen
and fishermen. Music it was not; it would be a
profanation of the term to call it so: a body of
jolly companions were roaring the ditty called
" Rule Britannia;" and how Britons would never
be slaves—on that very spot where these Britons
were beaten to a stand-still by the single force of
an adventurer, and their country subjected to the
most abject slavery: an enduring slavery, never
to be overcome.

Now revert we to the primitive colony of the
Anglo-Saxon; the Jutlander, the Dane, the Holsteiner, the Swede, the Norwegian, the Saxon in
fact, who founded an Anglo-Saxon colony in
Britain, and tell me, have you yet succeeded in
substituting yourselves for another race? In south
England you overthrew the Fleming and the
Norman at first; but William drove you back
again into northern and central England: your
government is strictly Norman; your dynasty
continental; your peasantry slaves. Had a bridge
connected Normandy with south England, your
race would then have been driven still further to
the north by an antagonistic race, numerically as
strong as you are. In Wales you have made no
progress; your very language being rejected by
the Cymri; in Ireland your existence seems to
me to depend on the Orange lodges, composed,

no doubt, mostly of Saxon men. Eastern and
Southern Scotland is no doubt yours, but the
Caledonian Celt still holds his country.

Thus it would appear that, after all, Britain is
not so thoroughly a Saxon colony as was thought;
a repetition of *Hastings* under Napoleon would
have closed its career as a *Saxon country*, and
free men of true Saxon blood must have sped
their way in ships and boats across the Atlantic,
there to make their last stand for civil and religious liberty. These you have not in Britain nor
in Ireland, but in their stead, a mighty sham
which suits the age and times.

Let us follow the Saxon across the Atlantic;
trace him to northern America, to the Cape, to
Australia; first to northern America, where Celt
and Saxon, for both assisted, have, no doubt,
founded a colony to which the annals of mankind afford no parallel.

A mighty forest, extending from sea to sea, to
man seemingly boundless; a new vegetable and
animal world; another climate, another continent; another soil. These suffice for the existence of the native red Indian, the man of the
woods; the American, in fact; he perishes from
famine and wars, but seemingly not from disease;
yet, when the Saxon and Celt first located themselves there, even then this race seemed to be on the
wane, following in the sad round of fate others who

had preceded them. Beyond them all is mystery, yet they seem to have succeeded others, now mouldering into dust or long since become a portion of that soil from which they drew their support—to which they have returned—perishing, and for ever extinct, without a name, without a history. In this land, the Celt and Saxon, with different fortunes and different views, located themselves; the Celtic colony (Canada) remained as it was; the Saxon-Celtic, impelled by Saxon energy, rapidly progressed to an astounding magnitude, threatening to overtop the world. Already the Saxon democrat raises the cry—America is ours, from the land of fire to the icy shores, where Englishmen have sought a western passage; from the Arctic to the Antarctic Circle. We are the natives, shout the Saxon! Such was the language, no doubt, of the Roman, when, calmly reposing on the banks of the gently flowing Ouse, he transmitted, by post, letters to his friends at Rome or Antioch, Rhodes or Carthage, Syracuse or Byzantium, surer to reach him then than now; and such, no doubt, was the language of Cortes when he unfurled the Spanish flag in Mexico; so thought Attila, when, penetrating into Europe, he scarcely saw an enemy worthy his arms. Sesostris (if there was ever such a person) had dreams like these; and Tamerlane, Zengis Khan, and Napoleon, at Moscow. But all these reckoned without their host;

that is, Nature! whose laws are not human laws,
who consults no man: who bids you look on and
chronicle events, but predict not. The scheme of
nature was never revealed to them nor to you.

It was Barton Smith, I think, who foretold
that in time the European races located in
Northern America would gradually degenerate(?)
into the red Indian! This incredible nonsense
passed in my younger days for sound physiology
—sound orthodox philosophy. In defiance of

[*The Esquimaux: representing the circum-polar races
of the American Continent.*]

all history, this nonsense was listened to. But
why did Barton Smith stop there? Why not
extend it to all animals and plants? Why should
man alone be the subject of such a metamorphosis? But we have already discussed this
point; let us keep to man himself.

The Saxon and Celt migrate to America; they
multiply, or seem to multiply, exceedingly, in
many parts of the territory; they are equal to
labour in the field—that field has, in consequence,
become theirs. In the Southern States, the
labourer is the negro—that field therefore is not
theirs, and that they must lose in time. Hindoos
and Chinese will work as slaves for ten centuries
or more, but not negroes. In the Northern States,
the Saxon is a labourer; his health and strength
seem unimpaired; the statistics of population
seem to be in his favour as to the extension of
his race; but this is still doubtful: no sweeping
epidemic, such as formerly destroyed his settlements, seem now to affect him — at least
not seriously; to avoid them, he migrates or
oscillates northward and southward, as the case
may be; finally, and that to any race is the
most important of all, he confronts no other
energetic or numerically stronger race in which
his race might and would merge, becoming annihilated and lost even to the recollections of men.
And yet, with all this, I doubt the fact of his

ultimately making good his boast, of his ultimately becoming a race of native true born
Americans.   For, 1st, Spain thought so, and
where is she now? Where is the boasted Empire
of the Indies? 2. The native races are not yet
extinct; in the Southern States there is a negro
population, who may one day be masters — remember St. Domingo. 3. Year after year, day
almost by day, the best blood of England and
Ireland is poured into the great American colony,
from Nouvelle Orleans to Montreal; infused into
the mass to leaven and uphold it, not in a
niggard stream, as from Spain and Portugal, but
in a vast tide, equal annually to the founding a
mighty empire. Whilst this goes on, no statistics
of population in America are worthy a moment's
consideration. But when this stream shall stop,
as stop it must, when the colony comes to be
thrown on its own resources, when fresh blood is
no longer infused into it, and that, too, from the
very sources whence they originally sprung;
when the separation of Celt, Saxon, and South
German shall have taken place in America itself
—an event sure to happen—then will come the
time to calculate the probable result of this
great experiment on man. All previous ones of
this nature have failed; why should this succeed?
Already I imagine I can perceive in the early loss
of the subcutaneous adipose cushion which marks

the Saxon and Celtic American — proofs of a
climate telling against the very principle of life—
against the very emblem of youth, and marking
with a premature appearance of age the race whose
sojourn in any land can never be eternal under
circumstances striking at the essence of life itself.
Symptoms of a premature decay, as the early
loss of teeth, have a similar signification; the
notion that the races become taller in America I
have shown to be false; statistics, sound statistics,
have yet to be found; we want the history of a
thousand families, and of their descendants, who
have been located in America 200 years ago, and
who have not intermingled with blood fresh from
Europe. The population returns offered us now
are worthless, on a question of this kind. The
colonization, then, of Northern America by Celt
and Saxon, and South or Middle German, is a
problem, whose success cannot be foretold, cannot reasonably be believed. All such experiments have hitherto failed.

The physiological laws just laid down, apply,
mutatis mutandis, to the Saxon colony of southern
Africa. The Dutch boer never laboured there.
He lived a wandering nomad life, the cruel oppressor of the native dark races, whom he nearly
extinguished. The Anglo-Saxon assisted him
bravely in the extermination of the Caffre: when
the Dutch boer could no longer lord it over the

dark races, he quitted the colony. Of all countries
known, the Cape of Good Hope and Australia,
that is, extra-tropical Africa and Australia, are
esteemed the healthiest, and if anywhere, it is
here that an European race might hope to live
and thrive; let us hope for the best. In Australia
it can scarcely be said that an antagonistic race
faces them, so miserably sunk is the native population. A ready way too of extinguishing them
has been discovered; the Anglo-Saxon has al-

[*The Red Indian, or Native American.*]

ready cleared out Tasmania. It was a cruel, cold-blooded, heartless deed. Australia is too large to attempt the same plan there; but by shooting the natives as freely as we do crows in other countries, the population must become thin and scarce in time. But I touch the history of the dark races of men which must not be entered on here. The so-called ancient races first merit our attention; some of these called white or fair, Caucasian by courtesy, the Jew, the Gipsy, the Copt, the Hindoo. These first require our attention: in briefly describing these races we shall touch on the physiological laws embraced in this question: Have any races of men become extinct? Or any races of animals? Have the doctrines ascribed to Cuvier any foundation in truth? "The elucidation of the direct and indirect antagonism of man to nature's works" belongs to the chapter on the Dark Races.

L.

LECTURE III.

HISTORY OF THE GIPSY, COPT, AND JEW.

SECTION I.—In drawing up the following lectures, embracing most of my views respecting the physical and psychological history of man, I have never had in view the composing a systematic, laboured treatise on man's natural history. Those who attempt this seem to me to have mistaken

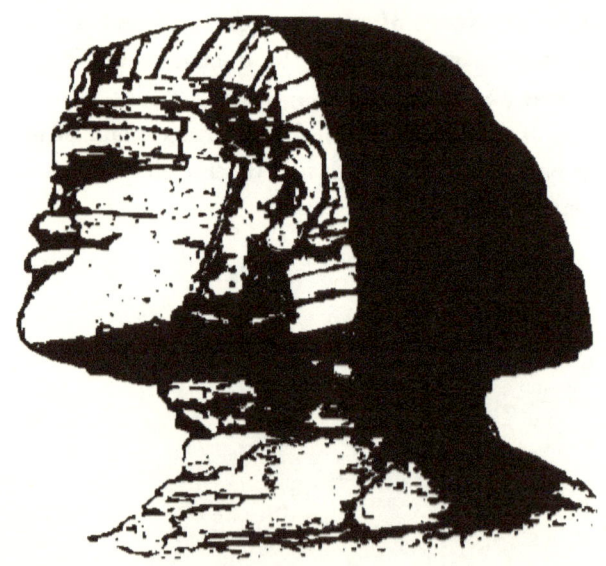

[*The Egyptian Sphynx.*]

man's true nature, and to have further committed
this great error—namely, the attempting that for
which no correct data exist. The labours of man's
mind are too vast to be embraced, compared, and
described in generalities; the " average man,"* of
the illustrious Quetelet has led to no important
results. " European civilization" seems a philosophic enough term, but to me at least it conveys
no clear ideas; and when I am told that of two
nations closely adjoining each other, equally
civilized, equally favoured by climate and external circumstances, living under regular governments for many hundred years, the one uniformly
respects and advocates the law, the other as
uniformly despises and violates it; that the one
loves war, the other peace; that the one fences
in and fortifies its towns, converting its metro-
polis into a vast fortress, bristling with cannon
and bayonets; the other runs the streets of its
wealthiest town quite into the open country,
fills up the fosse of its remaining bastile (the
Tower of London), converting the horrid excava-
tion into a pleasant garden; that the one nation
is Protestant and tolerant, the other Catholic,
fanatical, and persecuting; then I must not be
told that distinctions so wide as these, differences
seemingly insurmountable, are the mere effects

* " Quetelet sur l'Homme," French and English editions.

of accidental circumstances; that these races may
be spoken of in the abstract as the branches of
one great family; of some ideal Indo-Germanic
stock; of some fabulous Caucasian family, who
would never have differed had no seas divided
them.   Views like these have no practical bearing; and, moreover, they are substantially untrue;
they misdirect and mislead men's minds.   Many
years ago, when I first asked who are the Germans? and where is Germany, their fatherland?
I was advised to look into history and at Vienna.
It was to no purpose that I called attention to
the fact that the Slavonian races had not united
with the true German race, and that Austria was
essentially a Slavonian empire located in Europe;
that its paternal government was a frightful despotism, almost unequalled in history; it was even
urged repeatedly, as a proof against my views and
those of my esteemed friend, Dr. Edwards, who
held similar ones, that the Celtic and Saxon races
were so united in Great Britain and Ireland that
they now form but one *united race!*

Let the journalists and historians of the day, who
thus argued three years ago, come forth now; and
let us hear what they think of the *amalgamation
of races,* of which they boasted so much; let them
condescend to fix the lapse of years required for
the amalgamation of two or more races. For more
than seven hundred years have the Slavonians

held imperial dominion over South Germany and
Northern Italy; have they fraternized with the
other races? If so, what means this Slavonian
confederation now sitting at Prague? Whence
the alarm of the Germans that they be driven from
Vienna and South Germany? Have we not been
told* that they are all the sons of Teutonia? of
the South-Germanic race? Nonsensical generalities and abstractions like these have contributed largely to mystify the plainest truths.

SECTION II.—Systematic writers on the natural
history of man have composed treatises respecting numerous races of men of whom little or
nothing is known; hence the meagreness and
dryness of their details—the poverty of their conclusions. Of man's origin we know nothing, yet
the subject is unquestionably of the highest interest; of the comparative antiquity of races we
can merely offer a conjecture; the extinction of a
race or races is a problem still unsolved; man's
relation with the existing animal world and to
those Faunas which once lived, but which are
now no more, may be considered as well in speaking of any one race as another; why should his
transcendental anatomy then precede all other

* Letters of " T. T." (a Jew), in the *Manchester Examiner*,
in reply to my observations on the Jews. This respectable
Hebrew person describes himself in these letters as an Englishman of the Jewish belief; and a son of Teutonia, having been
born in Hamburg? This defies all reasoning.

topics; or why should the history of man's intellectual capabilities, his amount of progress, his
position in art, science, and literature, which
merely means his civilization, be discussed as a
general question, instead of forming a part of the
history of that race—with whom seemingly originated all true civilization—the Greek? Why
invent terms such as Teutonic, South Germanic,
Caucasian, calculated only to mislead, to confound things diametrically opposed? Long reflection has taught me that misdirection is sure to
follow the adoption of such terms; and such
ideas have strengthened me in adhering to the
present form, in which I beg leave to present
these lectures to the scientific and general public.

History offers us no guide, no data, for the composition of a systematic work on man; chrono-
logics are mere fables. Let us examine man and
his races as they are *now* distributed over the
globe; inquire into the present and the past, and
so conjecture the future.

THE GIPSY RACE.

On the southern border of Scotland, not far
from the sources of the Beaumont Water, and in
a secluded valley communicating with that vast
range of mountain country, of which the Great
Cheviot may be considered the centre, there stands
a village inhabited by at least two distinct races

of men:—1. The common Saxon race of the
south of Scotland; 2. The race of gipsies. These,
the gipsy people, reside during the winter months
in this village, decamping, like the Arabs, I presume, as the summer advances, late in April or
early in May, like migratory birds or quadrupeds
seeking other lands, to return again with the first
snows to their winter dormitory. They neither
toil nor think; theirs is the life of the wild animal,
unaltered and unalterable; confine them, limit
their range, and they perish. Their ancient history is utterly unknown: in the meantime, the climate of Britain has had much less effect on them
than on surrounding Cheviot; swarthy in complexion, with dark long eyes, black hair, a somewhat oval face, an Eastern physiognomy, neither
Jewish, nor Coptic, nor Arab; mouth larger than
in the European; nostrils somewhat expanded;
stature moderate. Their history is unknown;
they prefer the tent to the hut, and, but for our
climate, would probably never settle down anywhere; in England, I understand, they never do
so, even during winter. Their modern position
in Spain has been sketched by a vigorous but
somewhat romantic pen. Let me state to you
calmly the facts I have myself witnessed, the few
observations I have made on this race, which we
in ignorance call singular, merely because their
animal nature, their instincts, their whole views

of life and its objects, differ essentially and eter-
nally from ours.   That they remain as they are in
physical form, is simply because climate and the
other external agencies to which Hippocrates
assigned such importance really have no permanent effects on man nor on any other animal, so
long as the existing media and order of things
prevail.   They do not intermarry with other races;
this is the grand secret.   To Saxon and white
races they have the same horror that the Saxon
has for the Negro; the singularity, then, applies
as well to one as the other; in fact, there is
nothing singular in it, seeing that it merely
amounts to the dislike which one race bears to
another.

But if the gipsy woman will not intermarry
with the Saxon, the gipsy male has no such dislike to the Saxon fair, as is proved, I think, by
the following anecdote.   Early in May, or late in
April, our academic seminary closes, and I promised a friend that we should, for the sake of
fresh air and relaxation, visit the gipsy country.
Town Yetholm is the name of a village occupied
in part as a winter habitation of the race, and to
this we repaired.   Crossing the Tweed at Kelso,
and entering the valleys leading southwards towards the border and to the Great Cheviot, we
were in hopes that we should still be in time to
see the great gipsy family in their winter encamp-

ment, and these hopes were increased by my
seeing on the roadside, about a mile from the
village, a young girl, some ten or twelve years of
age, tending cattle. I pointed her out to my
friend as a *gipsy* girl, but not a good specimen of
the race: there was a something in her colour
which made me doubtful; I offered nor attempted
any explanation of this, but assured him we
should find much better specimens of the race,
which, you perceive, I do not call singular any
longer, seeing that they are not more so than the
Saxon, Celt, or any other race of mankind. On
reaching the inn of Kirk Yetholm, our first care
was to inquire for the gipsies, but the landlord
assured us that some three days ago, like a flight
of cranes or storks, they had collected together,
and, taking their departure from the village, scattered themselves over the country. He further
told us that, on such occasions, they *never leave a
single individual of their race in the village.* I now
informed him, that about a mile from the village
I met a young girl tending cattle, whose race on
oath, if required, I should have maintained to be
gipsy. He then related to me the following
curious history.

The girl we had seen was an illegitimate child,
and had given rise to an action against the reputed
father. The mother of the girl was a Saxon
woman, the presumed father was of the gipsy

race. He refused to acknowledge it as his; but
of this there could not be a shadow of doubt.
Saxon women do not carry gipsy children, nor
Jewish-looking sons and daughters, to Saxon
fathers; persons who believe in such things must
have a strength of belief in the doctrine of chances
which passes all comprehension.

Foiled in this endeavour to see the gipsies collected, I returned, on a subsequent occasion, with
my brother. We were now more fortunate; the
gipsies were at home, if home it could be called;
but on walking through their street, scarcely any
showed themselves at the doors of their hovels.
Timid and sensitive, like wild animals, they shun
the contact of the Saxon. The expedient I fell
on, to see at least one of them, was this:—Knock-
ing at the door of one of the gipsy hovels, a young
and extremely beautiful woman came out; she
might be about sixteen or seventeen; her features
admirably regular, eyes and hair dark, and her
whole form seemingly corresponding. She was,
I think, the finest of the race I ever saw; for
even in the best specimens the mouth is too
large, and the upper jaw, as in the Jewess, quite
disproportioned to the lower jaw, and to the rest
of the features. The lips also of the gipsy are
large, partaking, in fact, of the African character.
But in this young person age had not driven
away the beauty of youth, nor decomposed the

features and disturbed their proportions; nor had
the features as yet sympathized with the respi-
ratory, digestive, and reproductive systems.

To detain her at the door, I inquired our way
to the sources of the College Water; she raised
her fine arm to point out the mountain path
which led to it, exposing the part above the
elbow. On the inner side of the arm there stood
a circular leprous spot, not to be mistaken. Quick
as thought she observed, by a look I gave my
friend, that the spot had been noticed by me, and
as suddenly withdrew her arm, retiring within the
hovel immediately.

To what extent the dreadful lepra afflicts the
race I know not; the Jew is, I think, also subject
to it; races, no doubt, have their peculiar diseases, which, although they may not afflict them
exclusively, are yet of more frequent occurrence
than in other races.

Strange to say, the leader of the gipsy tribe
here seemed to me not pure—I fancied him an
impostor as a gipsy. Their own feelings connect
them with the *dark races*, as is evident from the
following brief narrative:—

On the banks of the Yarrow, a mountain
stream much celebrated in Scottish song, at the
base of that bleak and desolate range of mountain country called Minch Moor, there is a small
colony of mulattoes. This swarthy colony origi-

nated in this way. A gentleman to whom a portion of this valley belonged, returning from India,
as I was informed, brought with him two servant-
men of a dark race; not Negroes, but of a meek
African look, and bronze colour. These men
settled in this valley, and they married two Saxon
women. Of these two, one only had a family,
who, marrying other Scotch Saxons, gave rise to
several families of mulattoes, more or less deeply
coloured. In one instance, two mulattoes had
married, and they also had a family; but I do
not believe that any mulatto race can be maintained beyond the third or fourth generation by
mulattoes merely; they must intermarry with the
pure races, or perish. Nature creates no mules,
nor will she tolerate them. This point we shall
illustrate when speaking of the Peruvians and
Mexicans.

Now, these persons informed me that when
gipsies came into the valley, they uniformly en-
camped near the dark colony, and spoke of them
as " our people."

But to return to the gipsies. They are found
all over Europe, or at least in France, in the
Peninsula, in Germany, and Russia. Their history and origin could, I think, be discovered,
were a few practical scholars and scientific men
to proceed eastward, tracing them from one
country to another. My own opinion is, that

they are of vast antiquity, and are dying out. I
never heard of their being considered any of the
ten lost tribes, who, no doubt, must have gone
into the interior of the globe by the opening which
Captain Symmes discovered near the Southern
Pole. There let them remain, whether gipsy or
Jew. Of races which cultivate not the earth,
which manufacture nothing, which progress not
in art nor in science, we have already enough
upon the surface: their absence or their presence
must in the history of man go for little. The inhabitants, for example, of Central Africa, have no
history any more than if they had been so many
bales of cotton, or spinning-jennies, or spindles,
or spindle-drivers. " Nati consumere fruges" was
the expressive phrase of Horace: it were vain to
attempt one more apt. Regret them not. Athens,
and Corinth, and Syracuse, and Rome, live within
our remembrance; their fame must endure whilst
men having pure reason inhabit the earth; but
were Central Africa, from the edge of the Sahara to
the Cape of Storms, sunk under the ocean wave,
and with it the gipsy race, what should we lose?
—nothing which can or ever will adorn humanity;
no inventions nor discoveries, no fine arts, no
sublime thoughts, nothing to distinguish man
from the brute.

In the autumn of 1846, I resided for a considerable time in Derbyshire, which I found to be a

county, I was about to say, occasionally, or rather
pretty frequently, infested with the gipsy gangs,
and with them other lawless gangs, composed of
persons evidently of Saxon and of Celtic origins.
These gangs, or families, remain distinct in so
far as I could discover; and it was curious to
observe, independent of a difference in physical
structure, the different characters of the races;
the gipsy has made up his mind, like the Jews, to
do no work, but to live by the industry of others.
The tramping, vagabondizing Saxon makes a show
of work. The gipsies as a race, and seemingly from
instinctive feelings, have sworn as a race that
they never will do any work whatever; and that,
in so far as they are concerned, the great curse
on mankind is to be wholly inoperative. I do
most solemnly believe that, rather than labour,
they would willingly starve—a character not uncommon amongst the Celtic race; the money
they get by begging and telling fortunes they
seemingly conceal; back from their hands again
it never seems to return into society;—at least, I
never heard of an instance of their purchasing
anything. They have discovered the grand secret,
that they can live by the labour of others. I
suppose they look on the Saxon as some Celts
do—the Saxon, to whom the soul-consuming,
body-wasting labour is a natural instinct; him
they look on as a mean-spirited, low-minded

scoundrel, who would work the soul out of himself for a few shillings, instead of acting as they do—I mean the gipsy and the Celt—never doing any labour which they can get another to do for them; thus living a fine, dashing, do-nothing life, like a true-born gentleman. This is the gipsy—a race without a redeeming quality. Their men are well enough made, small and active; the women look well for a short time, but they have not the elements of beauty, or at least very few of them; they will not bear a close inspection. Dirty and coarse in language beyond belief, they are yet seemingly chaste; never well dressed—they and their children are in rags; the middle-aged men, on the contrary, are generally well dressed, well shod, comfortably arranged in all their apparel. During the day they (the men) seemingly rest at full length in their tents, ever ready for a start at a moment's notice. They steal, no doubt, at night, and at a great distance from their then locality: the fox, it is said, has this sagacity in common with the gipsy. One thing is certain, they commit no depredations in their immediate vicinity; but, as they must live, they beg and steal. With unshaken faith in a kind and over-ruling Providence, superior to savings-banks, and stronger than the constable's baton, they trust to be fed and clothed like the beasts and birds of the field, taking no heed of

to-morrow. In their language may be traced the
roots of many Hindostanee words, and they are
obviously an Eastern race; but this is all which
is known of them.

When the gipsies first appeared in England is
not perhaps well ascertained; but one thing is
certain, they early attracted the attention of a
Legislature, half Saxon, half Norman: a race
with whom property had its rights; a race perpetually called to perform duties and services to
the state; hence, no doubt, originated some of
the severe laws which have appeared from time
to time for the suppression of the gipsy race; but
all to no purpose, seeing that they are still in
Britain in considerable numbers.

A most respectable and kind-hearted English
clergyman told me that, during a whole winter,
he had much intercourse with a gipsy family who
had located themselves in his parish; he had
formed a favourable opinion of them, and, having
baptized a number of their children, had taken
up the strange notion that by doing so they had
become Christians: now, as circumcision does
not make a Jew, neither will baptism make a
Christian: an idea of this kind seems to me
merely a vestige of Romanism. He told me,
moreover, that they went occasionally to church,
and were a very quiet kind of persons. I have
no doubt that they are; the strength of the law

is well known to them now. The gang was called
Boswell, which must have been an assumed name;
St. Boswell's Green, in Scotland, is a favourite
haunt of the border gipsies. But to these notions
of this well-meaning gentleman, I reply—will the
leopard change his spots, or the Ethiopian change
his dye? When that happens, I shall then believe
that the gipsy may become a labouring, industrious Christian man; supporting his family de-
cently and quietly; taking his share of trouble as
a parish constable, churchwarden, and vestryman;
paying his rates, general and local; duly attending divine worship, and clamorous in support of
high church or low church, free church or church
and state! What mighty changes must have
passed over the globe before all this happens! I
will not pretend even to guess at it; but conclude
my remarks on the gipsy race by the brief discussion of a philosophic question.

Section II.—*Intermarriage of the Gipsy Woman
with the Saxon.*—The chastity of the gipsy woman
is well known, and her dislike to every other race
is, I believe, fully admitted. Nevertheless, as I
have already said, gipsy blood appears occasionally amongst Saxon families, which may be
explained in this way. I attended a family composed of the father, mother, one son, and two
daughters. The mother was an exceedingly
beautiful woman, not fair absolutely, but yet of

M

the Saxon race: her husband had all the features
of the gipsy race — dark eyes and hair, large
mouth and lips, oval face, nose prominent, eyes
full and long, root of the nose extremely narrow,
nostrils enlarged and full, colour of the skin
darker than in the European. Of the two
daughters of this most worthy family, the eldest
had all the gipsy features, but the skin was fair;
the youngest had also gipsy features, but less
marked—the skin was also fair; the son had well-
marked gipsy features, with a dark skin, much
darker than in the European. .

The only facts I could ascertain were that the
husband's *mother* was of the gipsy race; she was
remarkably dark-coloured when aged. When or
why she had quitted her tribe I could not ascertain.

Queen Elizabeth passed some severe laws
against those above fourteen who consorted with
the gipsies—it compelled both to quit the kingdom.

———

Amongst the gipsies I observed in Derbyshire
were some children with fair hair and blue eyes,
characteristics, no doubt, of the Saxon blood. I
spoke of this to the mother of the children, who
took no offence at my remarks, but assured me,
first, that the fair hair would ultimately darken;

aud that those with blue eyes rosembled her own sister; who, though a true gipsy, had blue eyes; and that such occurrences were not uncommon. Let me here dispose of this physiological question.

1. It is a fact admitted that children occasionally do not at all rcsemble the parents, but rather the aunt, uncle, grand-uncle, grandfather, great-grandmother, &c.; this has been proved over and over again. Thus the influence of one parent extends to an unknown number of successive generations, crossing from one branch of the family to another, reappearing occasionally after the lapse of a century.*

Thus, the dark or fair blood, as the case may be, will extend for centuries, though no further admixture may in the interval have occurred. When mulattoes intermarry, they seem to die out in two or three generations, whether as being in direct violation of that specific law as yet so little understood by us, which determined the species

* In one of the noblest families in Britain there is an admixture of dark blood, which reappears from time to time, although there have been no misalliances of this sort since the first, which must have been about 120 years ago. Yet even now the dark blood appears from time to time in one shape or another; and occasionally with a fair complexion Negro features may be distinctly observed. 1 have also met with a family in Berwickshire in whom the dark blood shows itself from time to time, after more than a hundred years.

of all things—the law of specialization, the law of hereditary descent; or that, having come within the tide of the *law of deformation*, forms and structures are produced by the marriage of mulattoes which are not viable.   The deaths, for example, of very young children, whose structures present so many varieties, even of the purest races, are extremely numerous; one reason of which with others, no doubt, may be that their structure, being within the *law of variety*, may have rendered them *nonviable*, or unequal to resist the bad effects of external influences.   In a mulatto I examined, the nerves of all the limbs were a good third less than in a person of any pure race, fair or dark. But, however this may be, the facts I have stated to you are undeniable as facts, in whatever way they may be hereafter explained.   Now, apply this to the gipsy family, some of whom had blue eyes, and you will see that, in order to explain the recurrence from time to time of fair hair and blue eyes, it was not necessary that there existed any late intermarriage or crossing, seeing that the Saxon blood might show itself a hundred years after its single introduction, and after all genealogical recollections had ceased.

The half-gipsy girl, for example, seen by me at Kirk Yetholm, when grown up might, and probably would, associate with the gipsy tribe in preference to the Saxon kindred of her mother.

In this case, though strictly gipsy in appearance,
and married to a gipsy man, there cannot be a
doubt that many of her children, grandchildren,
and great grandchildren, would show the Saxon
blood of her *mother*. On the same plan we endeavour to explain the occurrence from time to
time of Jewish features amongst other races; and
of the occurrence of other features amongst the
Jewish race.

But a totally different view of this matter has
been taken by some; and it is proper that you
hear both, or rather all, sides of the question;
a second view, and an extremely curious one, has
been suggested. It may be thus stated. As white
sheep are born from black, and white cattle from
black, and *vice versâ*, and blue-eyed and dark-eyed
persons are born under circumstances such as I
have mentioned, without the slightest suspicion of
crossing or intermarriage, may it not be that such
is simply a law of nature? and that, in order to
render such a variety a permanent one, all that is
required is, that they separate from their darker or
lighter parents, as the case may be, and live apart
—in a different quarter of the world, in fact?
Hence on this view has been explained the origin
of permanent varieties, as they are called, which
I fear is just another name for species. Thus all
sheep might spring from one pair and one species;
the black-faced horned sheep of our bleak and

barren mountains might accidentally (for the whole
is admitted to be *accidental*) produce a lamb or
two without horns; and these, by being separated
from their parents, would give rise to others, horn-
less also like themselves, and unlike their original
race.   Apply this to the gipsy; these blue-eyed
gipsies were purely accidental; according to this
view, removed from their parents and settled in
another country, their children would be comparatively fair-haired and blue-eyed like themselves,
and unlike their race, and that this accident would
constitute a blue-eyed race of gipsies; but then
these would no longer be gipsies, but Saxons or
Celts; and thus it may have happened that Saxons
came from gipsies, and gipsies from Saxons; thus
were produced the permanent varieties of mankind, kept permanent, I presume, by insulation.
That such a theory has not a single well-ascertained fact to rest on, is my most firm and solemn
belief; and it is incredible that so flimsy a hypothesis could ever have laid hold of philosophic minds.
It would, I believe, have been abandoned but for
the application of transcendental anatomy to explain the facts.   When it was pointed out that,
from the remotest historic period, animals had not
deviated in form; that neither wolf nor jackal
ever become dogs; that the wild boar never
changes into the domestic, nor *vice versâ;* that
although the species forming a genus do certainly,

when arranged as I shall presently show, exhibit difference so slight as to be barely perceptible, still they remained distinct throughout all times, the answer was that the permanent varieties only were contemplated, and not species; that permanent varieties were the product of accidental birth, and that tho present varieties in the races of man and domestic animals, though permanent, were the product of *accidental circumstances.* Transcendental anatomy was next called in to the aid of tho accidental variety theory—transcendental or philosophic anatomy—by whose aid it has been attempted to raise natural history and physiology to the rank of a science; to remove them from that prosing twaddler of detail, the professed naturalist; to elevate geological research; to connect the past with the present, and to push still further from us the region of fable and romance. This science — whose object it is to explain in a connected chain the phenomena of the living material world; to connect the history of living plants and animals with those which now lie entombed in the strata of the crust of the globe; to explain the mysterious metamorphoses which occur in the growth of animals and plants from their embryonic state to their maturity of growth and final decay; to traco a plan of creation, and to guess at that plan — these are the objects of transcendental anatomy—an appellation first given to the doctrine

by my esteemed friend and teacher the illustrious De Blainville, but a doctrine invented,
no doubt, in Southern Germany, by Oken, and
Spix, Von Martius, and others. To the South
German, to the mixed race of Slavonian and
German origin, we owe this doctrine of transcendental anatomy; to that imaginative race to

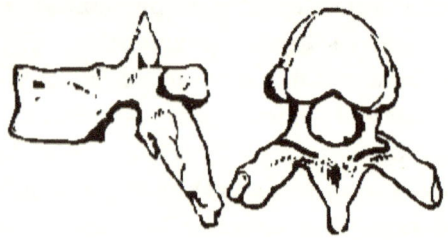

[*The human vertebra : the type of all skeletons.*]

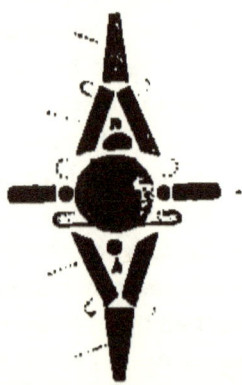

[*The ideal vertebra—itself real, however ; viewed
by Spix, Oken, and St. Hilaire, as the type of
all structures.*]

whom we owe all that is imaginative, romantic,
and transcendental in the so-called German language and German people.   To the true Saxon,
the classic German, the Swede, the Dutchman,
the thoroughbred Englishman; the Saxon, when
pure; the men of material interests; the men
abounding in common sense, and occupied with
the business of the day, what signifies to such men
the metaphysics of Kant, the reveries of Schiller
and Schlegel, the music of Beethoven; the transcendentalism of Oken aud of Spix, of Goetho
and of Humboldt?   In a vertebra the matter-of-
fact Saxon mind sees merely a vertebra; beyond
this it seldom proceeds—uninventive, unimagina-
tive.   Nor is the Celtic mind very peculiarly gifted
in this respect: the doctrines of Goetheand of Spix,
of Oken and of Geoffroy, were resisted to the last
by Cuvier and by the academy over which he held
sway.   Sir Charles Bell could never comprehend
the import of the transcendental doctrine; he stood
by the coarse utilitarianism of Paley, which with
him was the *ne plus ultra*.   Thus it was that a
theory originating unquestionably with the mixed
Slavonian and German race, inhabiting South Germany, made no progress with the would-be philosophic heads of Paris and of London.   But the æra
of Cuvier—the *siècle de Cuvier*—is gone; it embraced spiritual France and imitative England. His
narrow, empirical view of tho philosophy of animal

beings was adopted as a matter of course by the universities, who, dovetailing it with scraps from Derhan and Paley, wrought it up into a *body of doctrine*, which they trusted might serve them as long as the Aristotelian philosophy had done; save much thought, squabbling, and doubt; become orthodox and established. A witty divine furnished them with a new version of the Mosaic Record, and all parties seemed happy and satisfied. Cuvier and orthodoxy were triumphant; when all at once, in the bosom of that very scene of Cuvier's greatest triumphs, a colleague, M. Geoffroy, called in question his determinations: all Western Europe—I speak of the philosophic world—stood astonished; but being confined to the scientific world, the prudence, at all times remarkable in the English geologist, suffered it to pass unnoticed. At last a popular writer, an adept at plagiarism and at arrangement, selected from Humboldt, Geoffroy, Oken, and others, the leading doctrines of the transcendental doctrine or theory of progressive development in time and space, thus enabling the *unscientific* portion of the public to guess at the jar in the philosophic world.* Then burst out the flame of disputation and abuse—churchmen and geologists, botanists and chemists, furious in support of orthodoxy and

* " Vestiges of Creation."

Cuvier. Times are said to change, but men do not; it was the old war-cry of Aristotle and the church. In a dispute unto which even the great master of Trinity condescended to enlist his name, it must be that the audience may also feel an interest. Nor is that interest likely to cease. It is the struggle which science and scientific men have always held since the remotest times with those men in office who "in the law see justice and equity, and in the diploma see science."

BRIEF OUTLINE OF THE DOCTRINES OF TRANSCEN-DENTAL ANATOMY.

SECTION III.—All animals are formed upon one great plan; this constitutes the doctrine of the unity of organization; nor is there any reason to suppose, in so far as research has gone, that since the first formation of the globe, millions of years ago, that plan has ever been essentially altered, or any new scheme or plan of creation substituted for the first.

The extinct races of animals and plants found imbedded in the crust of the earth, in various

[*Remains of the Fossil Saurian.*]

strata, obviously of different ages, and in the
diluvial soil, seem to have appeared at certain
distant periods, more or less remote from each
other, and then to have perished—some slowly,
by apparently natural causes; others suddenly
and violently; and others in a mysterious manner,
their place being occupied by a new formation of
strata, and by a new formation, or rather by the
appearance on the surface of the earth, of animals
and plants differing specifically and generically,
as the terms go, from all which preceded them.

In these successive changes, or formations, as
they have been termed, an order appears to have
been observed. That order was, that the most
ancient strata contain the simplest forms of life;
and the more recent strata, the more complex
forms of life; as if animals and plants, simple in
construction, had first occupied the surface of the
globe, and, as they perished, others more highly
organized appeared; first came animals lowest in
the scale, aquatic chiefly; then the mollusca and
shellfish; then fishes; next birds; then quadrupeds, and, lastly, man. To this part of the theory
I do not attach much importance.

It was at first supposed by the theoretical geologists preceding Cuvier and his æra, that these
extinct animals were of the same species and
genera as those now existing. Bones of elephants
were exhibited in Germany as human bones;

fossil salamanders were mistaken for men drowned
at the deluge, &c. These miserably erroneous
notions were upset at once by a single anatomist,
by a lover of truth, a scientific man. This person
was Cuvier; he showed that the extinct fossil remains belonged to animals specifically and generically distinct from those now existing on the
surface of the globe. The scientific world bowed
to his verdict, and his views became " the law."
But he also remarked that *fossil man* had not been
found, and he concluded, or rather he left others
to do so for him, that man appeared late on the
earth, after the extinction of all the other preceding races of animals, and that his advent belonged
to the present æra, and to the now existing races
of animals. There must, in this view, have been
at least two creations, or rather there may have
been some hundred successive creations, since
the first formation of the globe. The last spelling
of the Mosaic Record (by Dr. Buckland) offered
no obstacle to this view.

But scarcely had all these difficult points been
agreed on when M. Geoffroy, availing himself of
the views of Herschel, Humboldt, Okeu, and
others, adding thereto the history of the embryo,
brought forward another bold theory to the
French Academy: that theory was based on transcendental anatomy.

When we look into the interior structure of the

grown-up animal, or man, it matters not, we perceive structures which are of no use to him or to
them individually.   These structures must have a
reference, then, to some other stage of his existence as an individual or as a race, or they must
have a reference to some great plan of creation
preceding and presiding at his formation, and so
connecting him with everything living—past, present, or to come.   Moreover, it not unfrequently
happens that man himself is born and grows up
with anomalous structures, as they are called,
such as webbed fingers and toes, the deformity
called hare-lip, &c.; or the two sides of the heart
communicate with each other, giving rise to the
formidable complaint called the blue disease; or
the arms or limbs are wanting at birth; or, finally,
he grows up with forms evidently not natural to
the well-formed, finely-proportioned, fully-deve-
loped person.   How are these anomalies to be
explained—what, in short, is their signification?

There was a period, and that almost within my
recollection, when all such phenomena were called
lusus naturæ—sports of nature—anomalies.   It
was not deemed prudent to proceed further; but
Goethe, and Spix, and Oken, and Humboldt, and
Carus, and, lastly, Geoffroy, have decided this
question. They have shown the modern anatomist
that mere details are not philosophy; that we
require *laws*, not *details*.   They have proved that

in the embryo of man and of all the higher organized animals, elementary structures indicative of
one great plan exist; that the embryo even of
man himself, whilst growing from a mere point,
as he is at first, passes through many metamorphoses, shadowed forth in the grand scale of the
animal creation, past and present; that at certain
periods he shows quadruped or even ichthyologi-
cal forms; that his fingers are, at one period of his
growth, webbed like aquatic animals; that when
he is born and grows up with them thus webbed
he merely exhibits a want of development—a persistence, in fact, of an embryonic form; and that
these embryonic forms are a counterpart of those
structures observed in some adult animal lower in
the scale, or, in other words, that anomalous
forms in adult man and animals represent merely
those forms which they pass through during their
embryonic life.   Hence the law of the arrest of
development: hence the statement of the philosophic anatomist, that whatever is irregular in
man is a regular structure in some lower animal,
and was in him a regular structure during his embryonic life.   This law, with certain modifications,
applies to everything living.   It is the basis of the
law productive of irregular form in man—the law
of deformation; productive of all those varieties
in individuals, from the slightest change to the
most striking; connects man with all creation,

past, present, and to come; and it no doubt led
Geoffroy to oppose the Cuvierian doctrine of successive creations.   A few words will here suffice
to state the outline of his great views.   We shall
afterwards return to them in a separate lecture.

The transcendental doctrine of development or
progress endeavours to explain away our existing
notions of species and even of genus.   We mistake, says Humboldt, or we may mistake a merely
historical event for a new organism.   The animals
now existing on the surface of the globe may,
after all, be the direct descendants of the animal
and vegetable fossil world; the modern crocodile
may be the direct descendant by generation of the
ancient saurians; the modern elephant of the
mammoth; the horse of the anaplotherium.   Nay,
more; what difficulty is there in imagining that
with time—to which may be added the unknown
law of progress and development, and a change
in the external media, the air, the waters, the
temperature—with time, the simple animals of the
early world (called old by mistake) may have produced by continuous generation the more complex
animals of after ages; that the fish of the early
world may have produced reptiles, then again
birds and quadrupeds; lastly, man himself?   Give
us time, said the anatomist—the geologist could
not object to this—and with time and progress in
time, and a change of external circumstances, it

will not be difficult to show that there was only one creation; that living matter is as eternal as dead matter; and that all living matter is capable of assuming every possible viable form of existence, that form varying merely in accordance with the nature of the media it then inhabits—in short, with the essential conditions of its existence.

To apply some of these theories to man himself would greatly extend the purposed limits of this lecture. I shall reserve the application, therefore, until I come to speak of the positively dark races of men—the Negro and the Tasmanian.

LECTURE IV.

OF THE COPTIC, JEWISH, AND PHŒNICIAN RACES.

1. THE COPTIC OR ANCIENT AND MODERN EGYPTIANS.

SECTION I.—Of a race I have not seen—of a people scarcely noticed by modern travellers; of a handful of men forming, so far as I can understand, the residue, the vestiges of a nation at once a race and a nation, — I naturally speak with great doubt—with hesitation—and the utmost readi-

[*The Egyptian Pyramid.*]

ness to be put right on any point whatever; for of
the Copt, whether ancient or modern, I can find
only conflicting statements. What race constitutes the present labourers of Egypt? No one
that I know of has condescended to clear up this
question. They are not Arabs, nor Negroes, nor
Jews, nor Phœnicians; the Copt forms but a
handful of the population. Like the Mongol,
they are becoming extinct; they slowly and
gradually perish; they seem to know nothing
even of their own monuments; the Copts certainly are not precisely Jews, nevertheless they
resemble them strongly. In their palmy days of
power they caricatured the Jew, representing him
with ears displaced backwards, eyes and mouth
of great length, and an indescribable mixture of
hircine and human aspect.

The modern Copt, in so far as I can learn,
resembles the ancient Egyptian, judging of these
last by the busts still preserved; but even this
fact I cannot fully make out. English travellers
are so occupied with their personal adventures,
and French with political intrigue, that there is
no getting a single new or valuable fact from
their silly books of travels. The modern Coptic
language corresponds, I think, with the ancient
Demotic. No one now thoroughly understands
the hieroglyphics, and I doubt the accuracy of all
the interpretations. The profane history of Egypt

N 2

by the Egyptians cannot, so far as I can discover,
be identified with the Jewish record; the name
and times of Shisak alone having been discovered
in an oval of an Egyptian temple. Even the
presence of the Jews in Egypt cannot be made
out by Egyptian monumental history; and the
physiognomy of the labourers of ancient Egypt,
as represented on the tombs and temples, is not
of foreigners, but evidently Coptic. Different
races of men are sketched on the walls of the
tomb opened by Belzoni, showing that the characteristic distinctions of races were as well marked
three thousand years ago as now; the Negro and
other races existed then precisely as they are at
present.

What has become of the grand Coptic race—
those builders unequalled in ancient or modern
times? We are told that foreigners and slaves
built these wonderful monuments which yet
astonish the world; I, for one, do not believe it.
The workmen employed were Egyptians. Their
disposition was to build; their innate instincts
were architectural, in this coinciding with the
Jew, the Greek, the Phœnician. Their past history is a perfect enigma to this day, nor do I
believe that a single leading fact has been well
made out. Who were the Hikshohs, the Shepherd
Kings, &c.? Did civilization travel up or down
the banks of the Nile? Did the Nile irrigate in

former times the Lybian Desert, and are the oases
proofs of such being its course ?   The sources of
the true Nile are unknown to this day.   All is
mystery, problems unsolved.   Herodotus says he
visited Egypt, but he could not have penetrated
far into the country ; and he asserts, moreover,
that the people were black, which is refuted by
every other observation, ancient and modern.

It was whilst examining the tomb, exhibited by
Belzoni in London, 1822 or 1823, in so far as I can
recollect, that I pointed out to my most esteemed
friends, Messrs. Hodgkin and Edwards, the unalterable characters of races.   Neither time nor
climate seems to have any effect on a race.

Herodotus says that the priests showed him the
mode of formation of the Delta by the slow deposit
of mud brought by the river from the interior of
Africa.   This most plausible and probable theory
is, after all, but a theory.   Three thousand years
ago the waters of the Nile seem to have been just
where they are now, and the black stone of Rosetta
was found, as its name implies, at Rosetta, on the
very borders of the Mediterranean.   If this be its
real locale it bestows an inconceivable antiquity
on Rosetta.   But Homer describes Egypt as being
in the times of the Trojan war a highly civilized
country ; what an antiquity must we then assign
to it !   The Homeric poem itself was suspected
to be Egyptian, and Cadmus brought letters into

Greece from Egypt, happily leaving the hieroglyphics where he found them.

But, in whatever way the chronological difficulties may be got over, there is a fact of curious
import connected with this pyramid-building,
mummy-making people or race. If we travel
westwards along the shores of the Mediterranean,
we discover that an offset of the race seems to
have existed in the Canary Isles, or Cape de Verds;
and the extinct Guanches closely resembled Egyptians in certain particulars. Now, cross the Atlantic, and in a nearly parallel zone of the earth, or
at least in one not far removed, we stumble all at
once upon the ruined cities of Copan and Central
America. To our astonishment, notwithstanding
the breadth of the Atlantic, vestiges of a nature
not to be doubted, of a thoroughly Egyptian character, reappear;—hieroglyphics, monolithic temples, pyramids. I confess myself wholly unequal
to the explaining any of these difficulties satisfactorily. Who erected these monuments on the
American continent? It could scarcely be the
native American Indians, as we call them; and
yet the carvings on the remains seem to portray
an American physiognomy. Still I have my doubts,
and would gladly take a view of these figures and
busts. Perhaps at some remote period the continents were not so far apart; they might have
even been united, thus forming a zone or circle of

the earth occupied by a pyramid-building people. All the literary world must no doubt remember the dispute of Byrne respecting the comparative antiquity of the round towers and the Pyramids; his mystifications, and the novelty and ingenuity of his views. No doubt he was partly in the right. The Phœnician physiognomy can easily be made out in South Ireland and in Cornwall, but these races were not Egyptians.

Thus of all races of men we, perhaps, know least about that race whose records, could we read them, would solve many of the most difficult problems of ancient history. Their relationship to the Jews cannot be questioned, but they were not precisely Jews. The uses of the Pyramids, if they had any use, have never been discovered, and the date of their erection was unknown even in the days of Herodotus. It makes one smile when they hear of Egyptian monuments being carved and set up in Egypt in the time of Hadrian; so early as the days of Augustus the Romans had commenced plundering Egypt of her antiquities; and so it has continued to the present day; from Augustus to Louis Philippe, monuments have been brought *from* Egypt, not erected there. I cannot even find that much was done during the occupation of Egypt by the Greek dynasty. Egypt had passed its grandeur, and had sunk into insignificance, when Alexander, with a handful of troops, could seize and hold it, and transmit its throne to a foreign family. The condition of Syria, of the Phœnicians, and of that section of Chaldeans called the Jews, may be judged of by this, that the historians of Alexander do not think it worth while noticing their existence. Alexander, five hundred years before our Saviour, marched through Syria and Palestine, taking possession of the country, taking possession of Judea, as if no such people existed as the Israelites.

I look on the history of Josephus as perhaps the most monstrous historic exaggeration ever penned, and I consider him as a person devoid of all truth.

To the Saxon, the go-ahead Saxon, the man who never looks back to retrace his steps,—that race to whom " to-day and to-morrow" are everything, yesterday nothing,—to the English Saxon especially, inquiries into past races can have little or no interest; they are gone, says the man of commerce—the man of to-day; what signifies their past history, what are their monuments worth to us, who care nothing for antiquarian remains? The race which looks back, resting upon its ancient deeds, reposing on its recollections, dreaming on its ancient renown—the race or the individual who does so is infallibly lost. Onwards is the word ; to look back is to invert the order of nature, to wither, and to die : to perish from the face of the earth, as the Copts have done, or are about to do.

One of the most remarkable monuments of Coptic antiquity is now in the British Museum: I mean the head of the Young Memnon, as it is

[*Bust of the young Memnon : British Museum.*]

called, although it really be the bust of Amenoph
II.: its antiquity is vast; it has survived thousands and thousands of years; of this most
remarkable bust—the highest work, perhaps, of
antique Egyptian sculpture—I shall speak in the
history of the Jewish race.

But the land of Egypt still abounds with its
ancient monuments; the race was quite peculiar,
and was, I think, African, or at least allied to the
African races. The mouth and lips all but prove
this. Nevertheless, their identity with a great
section of the present Jewish race cannot be
doubted; the young Jew of London or Amsterdam might readily sit for a likeness of the bust of
Amenoph. The resemblance, in fact, is most
extraordinary: and to me it is incomprehensible
how this had not been noticed by some one of
the thousands of sight-seers who frequent the
Museum.

Nothing is more wonderful than their reputed
knowledge of science and art; their astronomical
knowledge, their architectural. And yet, after
reaching a certain point, they stood still, retro-
graded, and finally all but disappeared.

Whence acquired they the high metaphysical
religious notions which characterized them?—the
metempsychosis, and the existence of a soul, of
a future life, and a day of judgment for the just
and the unjust? When the Jews left Egypt they

(the Jews) were profoundly ignorant of all these
doctrines, nor did Moses deem it necessary to
instruct his race in respect of them.   These doctrines, then, are not of Jewish origin, for the law
was not even written, nor the lawgiver in existence.   The barbarous and savage Turk and Arab
still lord it over Egypt; a frightful military despotism crushes down the energies of the labourer.
But who are the Fellahs, or modern Egyptian
labourers ?   What is their history ?   Let us hope
that the scientific commission headed by Lepsius
may solve some of these great questions, connecting at least the history of other races with the
monumental history of Egypt.

LECTURE V.

SAME SUBJECT CONTINUED.—VALUE OF MONUMEN-
TAL RECORDS.—THEORY OF PROGRESSIVE IM-
PROVEMENT.

THE origin of mankind, the source and origin
of life on the globe, is a problem which modern
science cannot solve. The only philosophic
attempt at a solution of this great problem was
the hypothesis of Humboldt, Herschel, Oken, and
of M. Geoffroy, commonly called Geoffroy St.
Hilaire. But against this hypothesis there lie
formidable objections, for all historical evidence
by writings, sculpture, painting, and tradition,
shows that no transmutation whatever has taken
place in the species of organic beings since the
earliest recorded time, and that, therefore, if such
transmutations had ever been effected by time, it
was required to show a lapse of ages of so vast
an extent that the hypothesis of necessity assumed
a character of wildness and vagueness clearly
removing it from the bounds of correct science;
and, secondly, that when we attempt to apply the
theory in detail, assuming as an element of the
detail that the development and progression were
forward or in advance, ameliorating and improving, then did it become evident to the unprejudiced

that the hypothesis was eminently faulty. For, without going far into such details, it were easy to show that the fish, and saurians, and mollusca, and mammals, if they were mammals, which I presume they were, of the ancient world, were at least equal to those of the present day. If the robe of the pristine carnivora corresponded to their other qualities, they must far have excelled in beauty the lions and tigers of modern times; the furs of ancient bears must have been of a quality at least equal to the existing ones—that is, presuming that the external robe or covering corresponded to their bulk. Now, there is not a shadow of reason for imagining the contrary. Again, monumental records, artistic remains, architectural designs, and utilitarian plans, prove beyond all question that the ancient races of men were at least equal, if not superior, to the modern; the Saxon and Celtic races did not invent the sciences, nor the arts, nor literature, nor the belles-lettres; they remained barbarians down to within a few hundred years ago, and when left to themselves, on the banks of the Ohio, in the far west, and in Africa, their original barbaric nature shows a strong tendency to return. If *progression* and *improvement* be an essential element in the Geoffroy theory of development, then the human race does not show it absolutely; neither the "Iliad" nor "Odyssey" were written by Saxons

or Celts, nor " The Elements of Euclid ;" nor
did the Saxons as Saxons discover the theory
of eclipses, nor calculate the periodic returns of
comets, nor build bridges over the Danube and
Euphrates, nor plan and erect the Parthenon, nor
carve the Apollo and the Venus. One thing I
admit, and that only, that the later races which
threaten to, and which I think must, become the
dominant ones, show energies, and combination
for a purpose, and mechanical applications, and
diffusive efforts, which no race before them ever
showed ; in every other quality they are evidently
inferior.

If, then, it be an essential element in the great
theory of development and progression, so cou-
rageously brought forward by M. Geoffroy at a
time when the overwhelming and overbearing
influence of Cuvier had closed all mouths, then
is it certain that such progression, in the sense
required, exists not; and here I venture to foretel
that the supporters of the hypothesis will, in their
next essay, abandon this part of the theory,
assuming simply the development of successive
eras of organic forms as a fact, disclaiming the
character of progression, excepting as to time.
The boast about the higher characters of the
present organic races * will be abandoned, and

* " Vestiges of Creation."

the law of development and progress simply
stated as it is, without a reference to successive
improvement; for *successive improvement* implies a
final purpose; a final purpose is a final cause;
to state a final cause is to guess at a purpose,
which in this case must be a purpose of the creative
power or force; but the popular supporters of
these doctrines of M. Geoffroy have declared
themselves against all such conjectures—against
all final causes as being mere effects, not causes;
they must give it up, or admit that they have
thrust themselves into the councils of the Great
First Cause.

The Mosaic cosmogony—or that, at least, which
goes by that name—cut the Gordian knot; dividing
that which it was not permitted to untie; it declares,
first, that all things were created as we now see
them—animals in pairs; man also. Further was
not revealed; why should it be? But philosophy is
not opposed to the Hebrew cosmogony—at least,
this is my opinion. The subject is mysterious,
and of vast depth. When did reasoning man
appear on the earth? If he springs from a lower
stock, what was that stock? What form had it?
How is this terrible difficulty to be got over? Is
it that the embryo is alike in all races, in point
of fact; that every embryo contains within itself
elements sufficient to assume any other form, and
to retain it, provided it be insulated and put under

circumstances calculated to bring them forth; to
exaggerate certain qualities, and give them permanency? This is, of course, a mere hypothesis
in one sense, and I think untenable. Races, however originating, have not altered within the
historic period, excepting by intermarriage: in
proof of which I have offered you the history of
the Copts, and the gipsy. Now, the Copt and
the Coptic section of the Jewish race, the Arab
probably also, are not Caucasian (if such a
phrase were of any value), but stand, as it were,
on the confines between races darker than themselves and others much fairer.

JEWISH RACE.

It was during that summer when the Dutch
and Belgians were carrying on a war after their
own fashion—marching and counter-marching,
advancing and retreating, but never fighting—
that, having a few weeks leisure from the routine
of a most laborious life, I resolved to visit per-
sonally two countries where I hoped to see two
distinct races of men, as distinct from each other
as possible, or, at least, as modern amalgama-
tions admit of; these countries were Holland and
Wales. I determined to witness for myself what
changes had been effected on the population of
these two countries by time and civilization; the
results, in as far as regards these races, shall be

submitted to you when describing the dominant
races of men; but first let me speak to you of
another race I found in Holland, favourably
placed for observation—the Jew. I had reached
London, that compound of all the earth, and I
had looked attentively at the Jewish physiognomy on the streets, as he perambulates our
pavements, and with a hoarse, unmusical voice,
proclaims to you his willingness to purchase the
cast-off clothes of others: or, assuming the air
of a person of a different stamp, he saunters
about Cornhill in quest of business; or, losing
sight of his origin for a moment, he dresses himself up as the flash man about town; but never

[*The Jew.*]

O

to be mistaken for a moment—never to be confounded with any other race. The women, too,
were not forgotten; the beauties of Holywell-
street; there they are; the lineal descendants of
those who fled from Egypt—spoiling the Egyptians—forgetting to replace what they had borrowed—but never returning to that land to which
one might suppose them attached, though it does
not really seem so—the land of promise.

But where are the Jewish farmers, Jewish
mechanics, labourers? Can he not till the earth,
or settle anywhere? Why does he dislike handi-
craft labour? Has he no ingenuity, no inventive
power, no mechanical or scientific turn of mind?
no love for war, nor for the arts of peace? And
then I began to inquire into this, and I saw, or
thought I saw, that the Jews who followed any
calling were not really Hebrews, but sprung of a
Jewish father and a Saxon or Celtic mother; that
the real Jewess admits generally of no intermarriage; that the real Jew had never altered
since the earliest recorded period; that two
hundred years at least before Christ they were
perambulating Italy and Europe precisely as
they do now, following the same occupations—
that is, no occupation at all; that the real Jew
has no ear for music as a race, no love of science
or literature; that he invents nothing, pursues no
inquiry; that the theory of "Coningsby" is not

merely a fable as applied to the real and undoubted Jew, but is absolutely refuted by all
history.

The following critique by Arpetigny seems to
me harsh and unjust :—

" Those which Poland rears form pretty nearly
two-thirds of the population of the towns.
They wear in summer a tight cassock made of a
bare and shining cloth; in winter a velvet cap
something like a thick turban, and a robe lined
with fur, fitting closely about them, with a girdle
of red wool, which serves them for a pocket, com-
pose all their dress. They allow their hair and
beard to grow long and flow free; they have an
aquiline nose, oval countenance, and pale complexion; they have long, dark eyes, full of lustre,
and which betoken cupidity; they are engaging
and polite in their manners; very emaciated, for
the most part; one would take them, at the
corners of the shops, where they station themselves generally motionless and erect, for black
cypress-trees, or pear-trees cut out like bedposts;
they throw around them I know not what reflection of Capernaum and Jericho, recalling the
impression produced by the engravings of old
copies of the Bible; they do not practise any
corporeal exercise, any fine art, making traffic
their sole occupation; to lie to secure a good
bargain, to lie to sell again at a high price, their

infamous life is spent between these two lies;
they give a preference to the calling of a courtier,
an old-clothesman, a go-between, a stock-jobber,
a broker, a publican, a banker, a tavern-keeper
—in a word, the callings where cunning of the
mind surpasses the gifts of science, the profound
knowledge of the arts, and the skill of the hands.
Against these the Jew contends by cunning alone.
They speculate openly on the luxury and drunk-
enness of others; but we owe them this justice—
that they lose nothing of their gravity, neither
under the thyrsus, nor under the caduceus.
Their hand is the same as that of the Normans,
with the palm altogether less developed, and the
fingers, as it were, square."

As I attentively surveyed the Jewish population on the streets of London, I fancied I could
perceive three different casts of features: the first,
Jewish, *par excellence*, and never to be mistaken;
a second, such as Rembrandt drew; and a third,
possibly darker, of other races intermingled. It
seems to me, indeed, that almost every race
shows, as it were, three forms of race which run
into each other, connecting them possibly with
others, so that this is not peculiar to the Jewish
race. Of the first form I need say little to you,
begging you merely to recollect that the contour
is convex; the eyes long and fine, the outer
angles running towards the temples; the brow

and nose apt to form a single convex line; the
nose comparatively narrow at the base, the eyes
consequently approaching each other; lips very
full, mouth projecting, chin small, and the whole
physiognomy, when swarthy, as it often is, has
an African look. When fine, that is in the young
person, with no exaggeration of any of the features; when the complexion is delicate, and
neither passion nor age has stamped their traits
on the face; before the energies of the chest and
the abdomen, the stomach and the reproductive
systems, have told on the features; before the over-
development of the nose and mouth has indicated
their sympathies with other organs than the brain,
and dislocated by their larger development that
admirable balancement of head and face, of brow
and nose, eyes and mouth, cheeks and chin—
constituting beauty in any face wherein it exists;
before the eye of the observer is enabled to say
at once, these features want proportion; that is,
in a word, when youth prevails, then will you
occasionally find in the Jewish face, male and
female, transcendant beauty, provided your view
be not prolonged. But why is it that you must
not prolong your view? Why is it that the female
Jewish face will not stand a long and searching
glance? The simple answer is, that then the
want of proportion becomes more apparent, and
this is enough; but there is more than this; and
I shall endeavour to explain it to you.

The living face cannot remain long unmoved; the play of the mind is at work on every feature; a passing thought kindles up the features, expands the nostrils, widens or contracts the mouth, dimples or furrows the cheeks, enlarges or diminishes the apertures of those glorious orbs through which the soul looks beamingly. Now to stand those changes, and remain beautiful, the proportions must be perfect so as to permit of change; but the Jewish woman's features do not admit of this; the smile enlarges the mouth too much, and brings the angles towards the ears; these are, perhaps, already somewhat too far back; the external angles of the eyes extend in the same direction, and the whole features assume a hircine character, which the ancient Copt, as I shall show afterwards, knew well how to caricature. If to these be added, as happens in the male face, that certain features display the internal structure, the skeleton of the face, then all beauty flies. A brow marked with furrows or prominent points of bone, or with both; high cheek-bones; a sloping and disproportioned chin; an elongated, projecting mouth, which at the angles threatens every moment to reach the temples; a large, massive, club-shaped, hooked nose, three or four times larger than suits the face — these are features which stamp the African character of the Jew, his muzzle-shaped mouth and face removing him from certain other races, and bringing out strongly with age the two grand deformative qualities—disproportion, and a display of the anatomy. Thus it is that the Jewish face never can, and never is, perfectly beautiful. I of course include not those rare exceptions which at times appear, nor those faces composed of two races which at times approach perfection. But, before I speak of this further, let me pursue my history of inquiry.

I had looked attentively at the Jews of London, but felt insecure as to my conclusions; in London we constantly meet with persons having Jewish features and Christian names; believed to be born of a Jewish father and Saxon mother, or of a Saxon father and half-Jewess, for no real Jewess will intermarry with a Saxon, or accept him as a lover, at least so I have been told; and, therefore, the Jewish blood can never alter so long as the real Jewish women, or a majority of them, are of this mind. This fact I believe to be certain; it is the same with the true gipsy, and, perhaps, with the Copt, ancient and modern; the mingling of races, however, appeared to me considerable in London. On my way to Chatham there sat opposite to me a middle-aged man, whose features reminded me strongly of a drawing by Rembrandt. His face, though swarthy, had not that characteristic look which marks the Jew of Coptic

descent; but I could not ask him if he was of
Jewish origin; so when the carriage drew up in
Chatham, and the landlord informed us of that
on which we were to dine, I objected that some
of us might be Jews. Upon this the stranger
informed me that he was a Jew, and yet had no
objection to the use of pork.

Having heard that I should find, in the Jew
quarter of Amsterdam, such an assemblage of
Jews as would give me an opportunity of perfectly appreciating the Jewish face, I was about
to embark for Holland, when, willing to embrace
every opportunity of looking at those glorious
specimens of art in the British Museum, and
especially desirous of knowing the precise form
of the ancient Coptic head, and its distinctions
from the Grecian of ancient and modern times,
I repaired to the Museum, where, again contemplating the bust of the young Memnon, new light
broke at once on my view. It seemed to me that
I had, at one time or other, and that even lately,
seen persons who might have sat to a sculptor
for a likeness of the head of the Coptic prince;
that the precise features and form, even to the
most perfect resemblance of look, were to be
found to this day unaltered in Britain; that the
Coptic blood, or at least a race analogous, remained unaltered and strongly affiliated even to
this day here in Britain; this fact, for such I felt

convinced it was, excited in my mind the deepest
reflections. An examination of the works of Ros-
selini, and also of the *grand ouvrage sur l'Egypte*,
led me almost to believe in the theory that the

[*Bust of the young Memnon: British Museum.*]

Egyptian priests and aristocracy had succeeded in crushing the national progress in art by compelling the artist to repeat only certain forms, unalterably and for ever—an attempt which has been repeated in modern times, as far as could be ventured on in a first attempt, lately here in Britain in the decorations of the House of Lords; but still I could not believe that the Coptic artist would give to the reigning prince an ideal form; he might nationalize it, but still it would be a portrait or resemblance. So soon as I began to suspect that I had seen persons in the streets of London from whose face the sculptor might have modelled the bust of the Memnon; so soon as, on re-looking and re-examining, I felt sure of the fact, I became more anxious to visit the Jew-quarter of Amsterdam, where I was told I should meet with ten thousand Israelites, male and female, walking about, or in collected groups, apart, to a certain extent, from the other race; that other race, the Saxon, strongly contrasted with the Jew: in groups assembled, kindling up deep associations with Eastern regions, with Egypt, and Jerusalem. To the result of this short visit I now earnestly beg your attention.

What I saw on landing at Rotterdam appertaining to the Saxon race I shall afterwards explain to you; it is to the Jew I wish to direct your attention. Having repaired to the quarter

of the city occupied by this race in Amsterdam, I
found the synagogue open and crowded; divine
worship was going on, the people standing in
crowds around the high altar; it was not proper
to take off the hat. Near me, almost within reach,
stood a youth about sixteen, and not far from him
others, the perfect likeness of the young Memnon.
I borrowed from him a Hebrew book he held
in his hand, that I might the better observe
his face. The whole congregation were singing,
but exceedingly noisy and unmusical, for the
Jews seem naturally to be without a musical
ear; and they have no national airs that I
can discover. The book was a Hebrew work,
beginning at the end, or what we call the end.
The women, seated in the gallery, were not
visible; but in the streets they could not be mistaken: unveiled and upright, a forward look, and
eyes fixed on you as you passed; nor did the
eyes quit their glance until you had fairly passed
them. No one turned the head, but gazed at you
until you and they passed each other. In that
fixed look nothing could be seen more than in
the statue.

    Thus I learned that originally the ancient Copt
and a large section of the Jewish people were
one and the same race, with slight differences,
however, which the Egyptian sculptor knew how
to caricature. Of the modern Copt I can learn

but little ; our British and American travellers
are so intensely occupied in describing their
culinary arrangements for crossing the Desert of
Suez, that they want time or capability to say a
word about the descendants of those who built
the Pyramids, and the Temple of Karnac; these
are trifles compared to the culinary matters; the
individual, the *personnel*. Thus what I have to
say of the Coptic and Jewish as affiliated races
must be brief. With their history I must not
touch—I mean, of course, their historic records;
but one thing, at least, is certain, that, according
to their own showing, they left Chaldea a small
family, and quitted Egypt a considerable people.
With the Egyptian, then, they had the closest
relations by intermarriage and otherwise ; we
cannot say how—for all is mystery here, and a
mystery which must not be touched. They then
mingled with the Phœnicians extensively; for
the Jebusites (who were the Jebusites?) remained
quietly in possession of their city and property,
undisturbed apparently. Now, the city of Jebus
was simply Jerusalem ; and, therefore, the very
capital of the kingdom was inhabited by and
occupied by strangers to the latest period of the
Jewish kingdom.

From the earliest recorded times the Jews had
commenced wandering over the earth, and seem
to have been trafficking in cast-off garments in

Italy before Rome itself was founded. Wanderers, then, by nature—unwarlike—they never could acquire a fixed home or abode. Literature, science, and art they possess not. It is against their nature—they never seem to have had a country, nor have they any yet. Like the Copt, they built temples, but not houses; they were, like the Copt and the Phœnician, a *building race*. The usual struggle exists amongst them as among Christians regarding the *value of tradition*; but as regards belief they present the most extraordinary spectacle the earth ever presented.

Now, nothing like so vast a difference in the matter of belief exists anywhere else, and it convinces me, with other facts, that the present Jewish race is composed of more than one: the Coptic, the Chaldee, and the Phœnician—allied races no doubt, but still distinct. With them originated monkeries They never will, of course, think with any other people. The greater number, I presume, do not believe in the existence of a soul, of a future life, or after punishments. Nothing of the sort is mentioned in the law books of Moses—these are all seemingly Egyptian ideas, derived no doubt from the East. But it is not to be forgotten that, when they resisted the power of Rome, our Saxon and Celtic forefathers were mere barbarians. When they penetrated into Britain it were impossible to say; if they came with the Phœnicians it must have been some four thousand years ago. But here they are now unaltered and unalterable. Shakspeare drew the character of the race, but he added a feature, which I believe to be impossible, namely, the elopement of a Jewish lady with a Christian—such an event I do not believe ever happened. The Christian divines translate and comment on their sacred books. Gesenius denied some important prophecies; Voltaire launched on them the whole force of his terrible satire; Buckland offers you half a dozen versions of the sacred volumes in as many weeks. Meantime the Hebrews themselves pass over all these with silent contempt—they give them not even a passing notice. Societies are got up for their conversion! Be it so. Nothing can be said against them; but in one hundred years they will not convert one hundred Jews—not even one real Jew. This is my opinion and solemn conviction. Nature alters not; remember I speak of the true, unquestioned Jew—not of the spurious half-breed, whom I notice here only for the sake of a passing remark.

About two years ago a very beautiful woman appeared as barmaid in a coffee-house on the Boulevards of Paris: all the world, as the phrase is, went to see her, so that night and day the coffee-house was crowded. She was far from

being a perfect beauty, and quite inferior to the
antique Greek; but still she possessed sufficient
beauty to attract the attention of the Celtic
capital. On looking attentively at her I felt
convinced that she was born of Jewish and Belgian or English parents.

When the Jews left Egypt they were probably
about three-and-a-half or four millions in number.
At this moment there are not on the earth more
than four millions and a half, say six millions at
the most. My opinion is that they are becoming
extinct. There are not more than 35,000 or
40,000 in Britain and Ireland. Now, they were
much more numerous in Rome two thousand years
ago. Cicero, in his *Oratio pro Flacco*, particularly
alludes to the numbers of the Jews in Rome,
to their turbulence and their restlessness. They
were supposed to have been the chief supporters
of the Julian party against Pompey, and were
accused by Flaccus of collecting the gold of the
empire and conveying it to Judea. Which, then,
was the era of the Jewish dispersion? I have
failed in ascertaining this point, which I had
once thought so simple. That they were wandering over the earth, and settled, in so far as a
Jew can settle anywhere in Rome, in the time of
Cicero, and, therefore, long before the destruction
of Jerusalem, is a fact which admits of no sort of
doubt. As I had supposed their dispersion to

be simply a historical fact, and one admitting of no dispute, I recommend the matter to theological scholars, who seem to me universally to have overlooked Cicero's observations on the race, and the important deductions which may be drawn from his remarks.

POSTSCRIPT.—JEWISH RACE.

A respect for scientific truth forbids me refuting the romances of Disraeli; it is sufficient merely to observe here that, in the long list of names of distinguished persons whom Mr. Disraeli has described as of Jewish descent, I have not met with a single Jewish trait in their countenance, in so far as I can discover; and, *therefore, they are not Jews*, nor of Jewish origin.

In my lectures some years ago in the Royal Institution, Manchester, I stated that the Jewish population in Britain was comparatively small; it now appears that it amounts to about 35,000 or 40,000. This confirms me more and more in the belief I then stated, that, but for accidental intermarriages, the race would have been all but extinct. In France, with the most unlimited liberty, they amount only to about 70,000.

My observations on the Jewish race were misunderstood, and, indeed, misrepresented by an anonymous writer in the Manchester newspapers. When I denied to the Jews any claims to literature, science, or art, which might be called their own, this writer insisted that I had denied them talents and abilities. Now, this I never contemplated. All races have produced men of ability: Confucius is said to have been a Chinese.

I took notice in these lectures of the aversion the Jews manifested everywhere to agriculture; this also was denied; but at the time, the illustrious Humboldt, I find, had made the same observation—a fact of which I was not aware and could not be, the second volume of the "Kosmos" having been translated into the English language but a few months ago. His observation is as follows:—

"They," the writings of the Old Testament, "portray the variations of the climate of Palestine, the succession of the seasons, the pastoral manners of the people, and their innate disinclination to agriculture."—Page 45, vol. ii.

One third of the Jews of the whole world are said at present to reside in Poland, amounting to about 2,150,000 Jews. It has been said, also, that in Poland the Jews have become industrious, laborious mechanics; but this is most distinctly denied by Arpentigny, and refuted by what we see takes place in Britain and in France. In addition to the authority of Arpentigny, who seems to have been an eyewitness to the really astonishing condition of the Polish Jews, or rather, I ought

P

to say, of the Jews settled in Poland, I might
quote the Russian ukase, published in 1847,
ordering the Jews to become members of muni-
cipal corporations, to follow trades, to cultivate
the ground, and to act and work like other people.
Any more remarks on these points must, I think,
be quite superfluous. Their skill in metallurgy
has not been made out satisfactorily.

On the subject of the dispersion of the Jews
and their expulsion or emigration from Judea, I
observed in my lectures that the Jews seem to
have been scattered over the then known world,
nearly as they are now, many years before the
capture and destruction of the city of Jebus by
Vespasian. I called them a *wandering race*, but
it appears that this expression is inexact, and
some of my most distinguished friends have objected to the term. My whole object being an
investigation into *the true character of the races of*
men as they now exist and have existed on the earth,
I shall ever be most ready and willing to correct
any inaccuracy of expression. If the term a *dis-*
persed race seem a more suitable one, I willingly
substitute it for that already used. But I see not
how a change in term alters the facts. That the
Jews were a *dispersed race* in Cicero's time, and
therefore dispersed some hundred years before
the taking and destruction of Jerusalem by Vespasian, is simply a fact which cannot be refuted nor

explained away; for the question always returns,
why were they a dispersed race? and why are
they now a dispersed race? No sane person
doubts their power to seize Judea if they thought
fit. One of their capitalists might absolutely buy
it from the present Turkish Government. Some
25,000*l.*, judiciously used by Lord Ponsonby, I
think, expelled the Egyptian armies and the
French party from all Syria. Now, why not use
the same means, and appeal to the all-powerful
effects of gold?

As I have been accused—in which accusation
Dr. Middleton is also included—of not clearly
comprehending the scope of Cicero's observations
respecting the Jews in his (Cicero's) times, I have
returned to " Middleton's Life of Cicero," and to
Cicero's, " Oratio pro Flacco," which on a former
occasion (at Manchester) I had quoted merely
from memory.

The passage as it stands in Valpy's edition of
Cicero, relating to the Jews, referred to by Dr.
Middleton, occurs in Cicero's defence of Flaccus
for misconduct during his prætorship of the province of Asia. He was accused by the Greeks
and Jews. Cicero disposes of the Greek wit-
nesses by showing to the judges that the Greek
race totally disregarded the sanctity of an oath;
that the whole nation, in fact, looked upon an
oath as a mere jest. In respect of the Jews,

Cicero observes,—"Sequitur auri illa invidia Judaici. Hoc nimirum est illud, quod non longe a gradibus Aureliis hæc causa dicitur; ob hoc crimen, hic locus ab sto Læli, atque illa turba quesita est. Scis quanta sit manus, quanta concordia, quantum valeat in concionibus. Submissa voce agam tantum ut Judices audiant; neque enim desunt, qui istos in me, atque in optimum quemque incitent; quos ego, quo id facilius faciant, non adjuvabo. Cum aurum, Judæorum nomine, quotannis ex Italia et ex omnibus provinciis Hierosolyma exportari solenet, Flaccus sannit edicto, ne ex Asia exportari liceret. Quis est judices qui hoc non vere tandaro possit? Exportari aurum non oportere, cum sæpe antea senatus, tum me consule gravissime judicavit. Huic autem barbaræ superstitioni resistere severitatis; multitudinem Judæorum fragrantem nonumquam in concionibus pro republica contemnera gravitatis summæ fuit. Al. Cn. Pompeius, captis Hierosolymis, victor ex illo fano nihil attigit. Imprimis hoc, ut multa alia sapienter, quod in tum suspiciosa ac maledica civitate locum sermoni, obtrectatorum non reliquit; non enim credo religionem et Judæorum et hostium impedimento, præstantissimo imperatori, sed pudorem fuisse." —p. 1510, vol. vi.

With the interpretation that Dr. Middleton has put on these remarkable passages I entirely con-

cur, although I admit that at first sight his views
may appear overstrained. I leave it to others to
decide, but in the meantime remain in the opinion
that the "quanta sit manus, quanta concordia,"
&c., have a reference mainly, if not solely, to
bodies of turbulent Jews with which Rome *at that
time abounded.*

I may now dispose of the last question—Are the
Jews a nation? This, I think, cannot be allowed
of them any more than of the present Germans,
who certainly are no nation as yet, otherwise why
this anxious search after "vaderland?" That
they are a race I admit, dispersed over the globe
since very remote times, without a country, a
home, a rallying point; but we might as well
say the Gipsies are a nation as the Jews. Such
difficulties arise from the abuse of language and
from the use of terms, which, though sanctioned
by ages, are yet merely conventional. Authors
still speak of the *German empire* as if there really
had ever existed an *empire of Germans*, which we
know was never the case. States and powers
made up of fragments of other states, of races
hating each other, as Prussia and Austria (I trust
we may not have to add Great Britain,) &c., will
now be tried to their utmost by the war of races,
which, some fifteen years ago, I foretold was sure
to happen sooner or later; but, being a new element in human affairs, the principle will be

opposed to the utmost by those who will not or
cannot understand it; and the threatening aspect
of a portion of the *Celtic race* in Ireland may render it inexpedient, impolitic, and imprudent to
discuss at this particular moment the probable
stability of an empire composed of at least two
races who cordially hate each other, even although
that monarchy may be one of *absolute perfection*
in its own estimation, and of such extent that the
sun never sets on its vast possessions.

5

LECTURE VI.

THE DARK RACES OF MEN.

INTRODUCTION.

In whatever way, by whatever means the races of men as they now are, have been formed; made to endure for centuries, preserving their specific and seemingly unalterable forms, one thing is certain; it is, the unity of the human family as a group of animal life; specific; with forms still human. That there exists no fact favourable to the theory of the conversion of any one species, or permanent variety of any animal into another, during the historic period, may or may not be true: the law, moreover, may be after all neutralized in time. The physiological law was first pronounced by Cuvier, and so far as our limited knowledge goes it would seem to be true. That no alteration or change has taken place in any animal form since the earliest historic period, is the opinion I lean to, without asserting that the theory admits of any rigorous demonstration; it was the opinion or theory which Cuvier, as I shall afterwards show, undertook to prove, with the view of refuting the geologists of *his day*, and the popular opinions of all ages, based on a false reading of the Mosaic record. And this he did most triumphantly, overthrowing them and their chronology; their diluvial and ante-diluvial periods; their one creation and all its consequences. But in so doing, Cuvier, we shall find, kept steadily in view his main object; the current English opinions of Cuvier's views are not his; his object was to disprove the all-but universal belief, that fossil remains (ossemens fossiles) belonged to animals identical in genera and species with those now existing on the earth, or at the least differing but little from them. This view, supported and maintained obstinately by priests of all denominations, he refuted. But he affirmed also that the remains of man had not yet been found amongst the ossemens fossiles. Now, his refutation, as regards animals, strictly so called, was most complete; he showed that countless species of animals had ceased to exist; that they could not have been destroyed by man, for man had no place then in creation. How they died, or why,

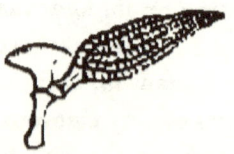

[*Fossil remains of the Saurians.*]

he offers no conjecture: that vast, speculative
void he left for the English geological-theological
school. Cautious, mechanical, precise, a lover
of fact, he resisted all attempts to induce him
to commit himself: to the history of this singular
page in human history I may hereafter devote a
distinct chapter. My object at present is simply
to point out that Cuvier did not, or would not, observe that his argument of the *permanency* of the
existing species of animals now on the globe, since
the earliest historic period (*for he went no further,*
although in England he has been made to do so;)
extends also to man himself. On the causes of
the extinction of races of animals and plants, he
offers no theory of his own, beyond the mechanical
laws of submersion and elevation of continents
and islands: on the formation of progressive
animal forms in time and space he is silent. All
this was reserved for a higher philosophy, and for
minds of a more original cast: he neither admitted nor denied the unity of man; to me the
unity of man appears evident; but if so, whence
come the dark races? and why is it that destiny
seems to have marked them for destruction?
These questions I shall not fail to discuss more
fully in distinct sections; in the meantime let me
trace rapidly the history of the so-called coloured
races of men: we, of the present time, are most interested in what is, not what is to be: creatures

of a day, the past, in one sense, affects us not; to
the future we are equally indifferent. Thus it is
with the mass. But then comes in the ever restless mind of the few; of those who inquire into
truth for truth's sake: of those who, haunted with
the desire to discover the unknown in the past,
pursue earnestly that course; of those who,
haunted with a desire to know the unknown in
the future, seek the required knowledge according to their gifts by signs and wonders, astrology,
science; and of those who, desiring perfection in
all things, compare the past, the present, and so
conjecture the future. Unquestionably had we a
sound knowledge of nature's universal law or
laws, the future might be told as easily as the
past. Did we know the law which originated the
coloured races we should be able, no doubt, to
foretel their future destiny. Whether doomed to
destruction and extermination before the savage
energy of the Saxon and Celt, the Russ and
Slavonian, or protected by the unconquerable
forest—the tropical forest; by the desert; by the
jungle and fen, the bog and marsh; by the all-
powerful tropical sun and snow-clad icy barriers
of the arctic circle; or withering and so perishing
before the as yet undiscovered laws of population,
which unseen extinguishes the hopes of races and
of nations, Mongol and Copt, American and
Saxon, yet they may stand their ground during

the present order of the material world, feebly
contending against the stronger races for a corner
of that earth, which we have been told was given
to man as an inheritance. Did we know the law
of their origin we should know the law of their
extinction; but this we do not know. All is
conjecture, uncertainty. After some 4000 years of
historic period, all we have is a chronology full of
errors and falsehood; unintelligible, incomprehensible; we find the dark races still on the earth; of
their ancient history absolutely nothing is known:
nor does it matter in what region of the globe we
first view them. They are confined to no particular
zone, but spread as it were from pole to pole;
from the arctic to the antarctic circle: if the Laps
be a dark race, then the dark races exist in Europe
as a race; Asia abounds with them; Africa has
always been considered their strong hold; and

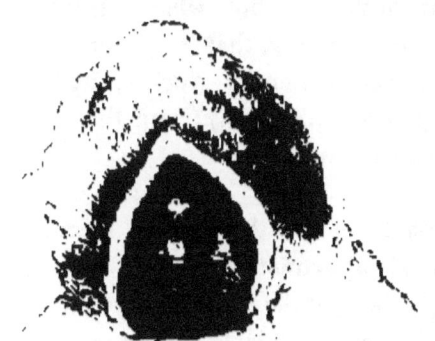

[*Esquimaux Woman.*]

unquestionably from the Mediterranean shores
to Cape l'Agulhas the thick lipped, as Copt or
Bosjeman, of all shades but the fair, prevails
throughout; but it is in America, the last discovered
by the civilized European, where we find the
strong hold of the coloured race: from the land
of fire to the ice-bound polar sea, nature had
darkened every race unmistakably; nor had the
Esquimaux or Circum-polar races escaped the
coloration.   Like their brethren in Asia, inhabiting the same zone, though far removed from
tropical heats, they also are deeply coloured; a
dark race, with the indelible osseous and other
structural characteristics of the coloured races of
men.   Hippocrates said, and modern physiologists have repeated his statement, that intense
cold darkens as well as great *heat;* from which I
long ago drew, not the inference suggested by
the great physician, but what I think a more
obvious one—namely, that Hippocrates and his
followers, from Galen to Adelon, had disunited
physiology and philosophy; and that to this day
they remain distinct.

SECTION I.—From the earliest recorded times
might has always constituted *right,* or been held to
do so. By this *right* the Slavonic race crushes down
Italy, withering and blasting the grandest section
of mankind.   By this kind of *right,* that is, *power*

or *might*, we seized on North America, dispossessing the native races, to whom America naturally belonged; we drove them back into their primitive forests, slaughtering them piteously; our descendants, the United States men, drove us out by the same *right*—that is, *might*. The same tragedy was repeated in South America; the mingled host of Celtiberian adventurers brought against the feeble Mexican, Peruvian, and Brazilian, the strength and knowledge and arms of European men; the strength of a fair or, at least, of a fairer race. The Popes of Rome sanctified the atrocities; it was the old tragedy again, the fair races of men against the dark races; the strong against the feeble; the united against

[*The savage Bosjesman;—Troglodytes; who build no house or hut; children of the desert.*]

those who knew not how to place even a sentinel; the progressists against those who stood still—who could not or would not progress. Look all over the globe, it is always the same; the dark races stand still, the fair progress. See how a company of London merchants lord it over a hundred millions of coloured men in Hindostan —I doubt the story of the hundred millions, however; the hot suns of India exalt, I have remarked, the brains of Europeans who sojourn long there; but, be it as they say, the fact is astounding. Whilst I now write, the Celtic race is preparing to seize Northern Africa by the same right as we seized Hindostan—that is, might, physical force—the only real right is physical force; whilst we, not to be behind in the grasp for more acres, annex New Zealand and all its dependencies to the British dominions, to be wrested from us by-and-by by our sons and descendants as the United States were and Canada will be, for no Saxon race can ever hold a colony long. The coolness with which this act of appropriation has been done is, I think, quite unparalleled in the history of aggressions. A slip of parchment signed officially is issued from that den of all abuses, the office of the Colonial Secretary, declaring New Zealand to be a colony of Britain, with all its dependencies, lands, fisheries, mines, inhabitants. The aborigines are to

be protected! Now, if the Crown will let them
alone, they can protect themselves; but this
would not suit the wolf who took care of the
sheep. Still, mark the organized hypocrisy of
the official opener of the letters of others: the
aborigines are not declared Britons; they are
merely to be protected!

The Indian empire, as we call it, having turned
out so profitable an investment for British capital,
although for obvious reasons it never can become
a permanent colony of England, suggested to " the
Office " the idea of founding a similar empire in
the heart of Africa. Everything seemed favourable
for the enterprise; Southern Africa had long been
ours; the southern extra-tropical part, partly
held nominally by the Portuguese—that is, as
good as not held at all—a wide desert separating
Central Africa from the Morocen, from the Celt
(in Alger) and from the present Egyptian ruler;
Central Africa, full of wealth, a productive soil,
and a feeble, black population! Nothing could
be more favourable, and I have not the smallest
doubt that the officials at the Colonial-office
already contemplated another India in Central
Africa; the wealth, the product of the labour
of many millions of Africans, in reality slaves, as
the natives of Hindostan, but held to be free by a
legal fiction, might be poured into the coffers of
the office! But, alas for land-seeking colonial

secretaries! climate interfered; exterminated the
crows of their ships, and scattered the hopes of
the patriot lord at the head of the office.

Since the earliest times, then, the dark races
have been the slaves of their fairer brethren.
Now, how is this? Mr. Gibbon solves the question in his usual dogmatic way; he speaks of the
obvious physical inferiority of the Negro; he
means, no doubt, the dark races generally, for
the remark applies to all. But, notwithstanding
the contrary opinion professed by Dr. Tiedemann
respecting the great size of some African skulls,
which he found in my own museum, sent to
me from the western coast of Africa, I feel disposed to think that there must be a physical and,
consequently, a psychological inferiority in the
dark races generally. This may not depend
altogether on deficiency in the size of the brain

[*Negro Skull.*]

en masse, nor on any partial defects; to which, however, I shall advert presently; but rather, perhaps, to specific characters in the quality of the brain itself. It may, perhaps, be right to consider first the different obvious physical qualities of the dark races, before we enter on the history of their position as regards the mass of mankind, and especially as regards those races which seem destined, if not to destroy them altogether, at least to limit their position to those regions of the earth where the fair races can neither labour

[*Caffre Race; from Burchell.*]

Q

nor live—the equatorial regions and the regions
adjoining the tropics, usually termed by romancists and travellers, and not unfairly, the
grave of Europeans.

First, as regards mere physical strength, the
dark races are generally much inferior to the
Saxon and Celt; the bracelets worn by the
Kaffirs, when placed on our own arms, prove this.
Secondly, in size of brain they seem also considerably inferior to the above races, and no doubt
also to the Sarmatian and the Slavonic. Thirdly,
the form of the skull differs from ours, and is
placed differently on the neck; the texture of
the brain is 1 think generally darker, and the
white part more strongly fibrous; but I speak
from extremely limited experience. Mr. Tiedemann, I think it is, who says that the convolu-
tions of the upper surface of the two hemispheres
of the brain are nearly symmetrical; in our brain
the reverse always happens. Lastly, the whole
shape of the skeleton differs from ours, and so
also I find do the forms of almost every muscle of
the body. The upper jaw is uniformly of extraordinary size, and this, together with a peculiarity in the setting on of the face, I find to
constitute the most striking differences. I at one
time thought that the bones of the nose were
peculiar in some races, as in the Bosjesman and
Hottentot. In these races, or race, for perhaps

they are but one, I fancied that, more frequently
at least than in others, the bones of the nose are
remarkably narrow, run together to form but one
bone, and show even an additional thin germ
mesially; perhaps mevely the anterior margin
of another bone, or an extension of the spine of
the frontal. Still the specimens are so few in
Europe, that I feel disinclined to attach much
importance to this sufficiently singular fact. I
think I have seen one of the nasal bones so short
and thin as not to reach the frontal.

In the Peruvian skull, at twelve years of age,
Von Tchudi thinks he has detected a new germ
of bone, an interparietal bone, in fact, peculiar
to the native American race; the physical differences in the structure of the Boschjiee women and
Hottentots are unmistakeable. Still be it remembered that we have no accurate account of the
structural differences of the races of *men* on
which we can depend—mere scraps of observations scarcely worthy of notice. The Negro
muscles are differently shaped from ours; the
curly, corkscrew locks of the Hottentot bear no
resemblance to the lank, black hair of the
Esquimaux. The Tasmanian and Australian
races are said to show many peculiarities in
structure.

Let it be remembered, however, that, after all,
it is to the exterior we must look for the more

remarkable characteristics of animals; it is it alone which nature loves to decorate and to vary: the interior organs of animals, not far removed from each other, vary but little. To this fact I shall advert more particularly in the lecture on transcendental anatomy; the internal structures of animals present details which we read imperfectly, connected as they are, on the one hand, with mechanical arrangements, and on the other with the primitive laws of creation.

There is one thing obvious in the history of the dark races, that they all, more or less, exhibit the outline of the interior more strongly marked than in the fair races generally. Thus the face of the adult Negro or Hottentot resembles, from

[*Bosjeman playing on the gouruh.*]

the want of flesh, a skeleton, over which has been drawn a blackened skin.

But who are the dark races of ancient and modern times? It would not be easy to answer this question. Were the Copts a dark race? Are the Jews a dark race? The Gipsies? The Chinese, &c.? Dark they are to a certain extent; so are all the Mongol tribes—the American Indian and Esquimaux—the inhabitants of nearly all Africa—of the East—of Australia. What a field of extermination lies before the Saxon Celtic and Sarmatian races! The Saxon will not mingle with any dark race, nor will he allow him to hold an acre of land in the country occupied by him; this, at least, is the law of Anglo-Saxon America. The fate, then, of the Mexicans, Peruvians, and Chilians, is in no shape doubtful. Extinction

[*Mongol; from Clark's Travels.*]

of the race—sure extinction—it is not even denied.

Already, in a few years, we have cleared Van Diemen's Land of every *human* aboriginal; Australia, of course, follows, and New Zealand next; there is no denying the fact, that the Saxon, call him by what name you will, has a perfect horror for his darker brethren. Hence the folly of the war carried on by the philanthropists of Britain against nature: of these persons some are honest, some not. I venture to recommend the honest ones—to try their strength in a practical measure. Let them demand for the natives of Hindostan, of Ceylon, or even of the Cape or New Zealand, the privileges and rights wholly and fairly of Britons; I predict a refusal on the part of the Colonial-office. The office will appoint you as many aborigines protectors as you like—that is, spies; but the extension of equal rights and privileges to all colours is quite another question.

But now, having considered the physical constitution thus briefly of some of these dark races, and shown you that we really know but little of them; that we have not data whereon to base a physical history of mankind; let me now consider the history of a few of them—of those, at least, best known to me.

Section II.—*On the Dark Races of Africa.*

What the Portuguese thought and did when they first landed at the Cape of Storms has not been recorded, in so far as I know. Records, no doubt, exist somewhere, buried in the archives of Lisbon or Coimbra. Camoens was a Lusitanian, and there may have been other minds in the Peninsula calculated by their labours, scientific or literary, to prove the race to be somewhat above the beasts of the field in their objects and pursuits. But the Portuguese who first doubled Cape l'Agulhas were in search of gold and of the Indies. Southern Africa, with its parched soil, strange-looking beasts, and still stranger men, did not suit them; they landed, but soon abandoned it, leaving the races it contained to the tender mercies of the most selfish, commercial, trading, narrow-minded, unimproving of all the Saxon race, the skippers of Rotterdam, of Amsterdam, and their descendants. These men, of whom I have spoken in my lecture on the Saxon, followed in the wake of the Portuguese; they landed at the Cape, probably in Table Bay, by the base of that romantic Taffel Berg, and though they found the country poor and generally " sonder vater," they did not altogether despise it. The Cape was on the highway to India; they found there some

long-legged, ill-shaped cattle, which the Dutch
boors maintain to this day, and sheep with wool
of a miserably poor quality; and so the Dutchman, who could neither invent nor improve,
adopted the sheep and the cattle of the Hottentot
as his own.

But what were the race or races of men and of
animals he found there? were they the same, or
did they resemble in any way, the men and animals they had left in faderland—in beloved
Holland? Not in the least; neither men nor
animals bore any resemblance to those of Europe:
the races of men they first encountered were the
Hottentots and Bosjemen, the yellow race or
races of Africa: the former word, of doubtful
origin, expresses the taller and stronger tribes—
tribes which were armed with the assagai, held
flocks of sheep and cattle, but no horses; the
term Bosjeman simply means the man of the

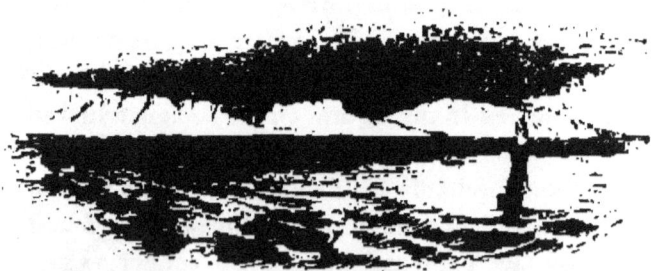

[*Table Mountain, Cape of Good Hope.   From Burchell's
Travels.*]

bush; by Bosjeman, then, we further understand
that section of the yellow race, smaller in stature
than those called Hottentots, less civilized, if such
a term could possibly be so used or misapplied;
living without flocks or herds, huts or tents; em-
ploying the bow and poisoned arrow; children
of the desert. Our present business is with the
primitive race, the aborigines, as they are called,
of Southern Africa, called by the Dutch some
three hundred years ago Hottentots and Bosjemen,—names unknown in the language of the
race, for they call themselves Autniquas, Quoiquæs,
&c. Did the Dutch, the Christian Dutch, consider
these races to be men and women? I scarcely
think so. True, they held as a theory that all
men and women came from one pair, like all cows,
and pigs, and sheep; but this was a mere theory;
in practice they held them to be a something
different. The coloured men the Dutch called boys,

[*Bosjeman, or Yellow African Race.*]

and the coloured women they called maids; in speaking of the persons composing a Commando, for example, they would say that there were on it thirty *men*, meaning Dutchmen, and fifty boys, meaning black men. *De facto,* then, the Dutch did not hold these races to be the same as their own; the fact is undeniable and incontestable. I care not for theories; the Dutch practically denied the first canon of Scripture in a body, as the United States men do now; there is no denying it. To the strange, perfectly strange, animals around them, every one differing generically and specifically from those of Europe, they gave European names: the beautiful antelope frequenting the bushy ravines of the present colony they called the bosje-bok, or bush-goat, although it be not a goat; they found also the elk or eland, although there are no elks in Africa; the very oxen and miserable sheep of the wretched Hottentot, the Saxon Dutchman adopted, cherished and maintained unaltered, until an irruption from Europe of Englishmen upset them and their soul-destroying self-opiniativeness. But we must not advert at present to these drawbacks on the Saxon character; his onward principle diffused and spread him over the colony; the go-ahead principle was at work; this, of course, led to the seizure of land, the plunder and massacre, wholesale sometimes, of the simple aborigines. Wild

principles were let loose on both sides; the gun
and bayonet became the law; and whilst I now
write, the struggle is recommencing with a dark
race (the Caffre), to terminate, of course, in their
extinction.

I have said that when the Dutch first landed
at the Cape of Good Hope they met with the race
called Hottentots—a simple, feeble race of men,
living in little groups, almost, indeed, in families,
tending their fat-tailed sheep and dreaming away
their lives. Of a dirty yellow colour, they slightly
resemble the Chinese, but are clearly of a different
blood. The face is set on like a baboon's; cranium small but good; jaws very large; feet and
hands small; eyes linear in form and of great power;

Groupe of Busjemen in the Desert.

forms generally handsome; hideous when old, and never pretty; lazier than an Irishwoman, which is saying much; and of a blood different and totally distinct from all the rest of the world. The women are not made like other women. Tiedemann says that the two hemispheres of the brain are nearly symmetrical. Though small in stature, they are taller than their cognate race, the Bosjeman; these I take to be nearly allied to the Hottentot, though different in a good many respects. They have the physical qualities of the Hottentot, but exaggerated; they are still shorter in stature. Having no measurements on which I can depend, I offer merely as a conjecture the average height of the male and female Bosjeman,—say four feet six inches for the male, and four feet for the female. Their power of sight is incredible, and this, with all other peculiarities, disappears with a single crossing of the breed.

The extent to which these singular races, if they really be distinct, extend northwards through Central Africa is altogether unknown. Dr. Andrew Smith, so well known for his travels in Southern Africa, informs me, that he saw them within the tropic, and he thinks they extend much higher; moreover, he is of opinion that they form but one race; in Harris's " Ethiopia," mention is made of a race, somewhat resembling the Bosjeman, inhabiting a wild district in Southern Abyssinia, on the equator, deeply hidden amongst woods and mountains. He did not see them, and nothing positive can be gathered from his description.

Diodorus Siculus speaks of the Troglodytes of Northern Africa, who inhabited caves and mountains, a pigmy race and of no courage ; whilst the divine Homer places, I think, in Africa, his pigmy men, against whom the cranes waged constant war.

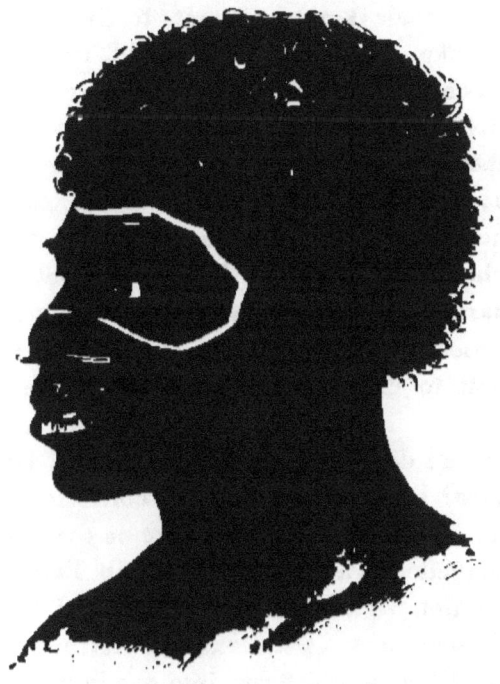

[*The Australian Race.*]

What interesting questions, geographical or ethnological, are here to solve! What a field does Africa still present! Whence came these Bosjemen and Hottentots? They differ as much from their fellow-men as the animals of Southern Africa do from those of South America. They are a dark race; but the sun has not darkened them. Without arts, without religion, and without civilization of any kind, for how many centuries had they occupied their kraals, content to live, and to perish like the beasts of the field, leaving no name behind them that such things were!

Before the go-ahead Dutchmen it was easy to see that this puny, pigmy, miserable race must retire; they did so chiefly, as it seems, towards the northward, towards the Gariepine streams and the Calihari Desert. They could not retire eastward, for this reason, that they there met the Amakosos (whom we call Caffres)—a race I was the first to describe to the scientific world of Europe.

Have we done with the Hottentots and Bosjeman race? I suppose so: they will soon form merely natural curiosities; already there is the skin of one stuffed in England; another in Paris if I mistake not. Their skeleton presents, of course, peculiarities, such as the extreme narrowness of the nasal bones, which run into one in early age not unfrequently, as we find in apes. But it is the

exterior which is the most striking; and this, no
doubt, is wonderful.   No one can believe them to
be of the same race with ourselves ; yet, unquestionably, they belong to the genus man.   They
are shrewd, and show powers of mimicry—acquire
language readily, but never can be civilized.   That
I think quite hopeless.   The Dutch endeavoured
to make soldiers of them ; and it is recorded that
they alone showed fight at the battle of Blueberg,
when all the white men ran away—I state the
story as I heard it.   We followed and imitated the
Dutch in this, as in most things, and got up a
Hottentot corps, or rather, perhaps, I ought to
say a Cape corps—for John Bull does not like
anything he finds useful called by an offensive
name.   Well, call it Cape corps, or what you will,
it is a miserable policy, unworthy the sanction of
any statesman.

In a word, they are fast disappearing from the
face of the earth ; meeting that fate a little earlier
from the Dutch which was surely awaiting them
on the part of the Caffres.   Let us now speak of
the Caffre.

When the Hottentot and Bosjeman tribes fled
before the warlike Dutch boors, they proceeded
almost due north towards the deserts, the Karoos,
the Gariepine country, and the Calihari.   The
reason for this was soon discovered: in their
retreat eastward they encountered the Caffre, a

warlike, bold, and active race of men, well armed
with the assagai, accustomed to war; though some
what feeble in their arms, yet strongly set upon
their limbs, exceedingly daring, and accustomed
to act in bodies; dark as Negroes nearly, yet not
Negroes; finer made in the limbs, and with more
energy; the head, perhaps, a little better than
the Negro, or even as good as can be found in
any dark race. These Amakosos, or Caffres as we
call them, had advanced into the province, now
called Albany, when Le Vaillant was in the colony,
in 1794 or 1795; they approached or occupied
the eastern tract of the country, the seaboard, as
it may be called. But they had neither ships nor
boats, nor any human arts; properly speaking,
they were mere savages, but at that time mild
and, to a certain extent, trustworthy; now, by
coming into contact with Europeans, they have

[*Caffre Skull.*]

become treacherous, bloody, and thoroughly
savage. Yet they have great and good points
about them, which I shall endeavour presently
to explain. First let me point out, as I did to
Europe, that there is not the slightest foundation
for imagining them to be derived in any way
from Arabian blood. This is a mere fancy. They
are circumcised, eat no fish nor fowl, nor unclean
beasts, as they are called; live much on milk,
and seem to me capable of being educated and
partly civilized. Their extent northward and
eastward is unknown, but they join at last the
Negroes of the equatorial regions: how far they
have extended into the interior is not known.
Before I speak of the true Negro, let me endeavour
to place before you a brief sketch of the race
whose contest with the British, but just, as it were,
commencing, must end by bestowing on them an
unhappy immortality.

The Caffres are closely allied to the Negro race,
and probably graduate, as it were, into them; for,
as Nature has formed many races of white men
whose physical organization and mental disposition differ widely from each other, so also has she
formed the swarthy world. It is not necessary,
neither perhaps, is it at all correct, to call a Caffre
a Negro, or a Negro a Caffre; neither are the
Caffres degenerated Bedouins, nor well-fed Hottentots, nor Saxons turned black by the sun, nor

R

Arabs, nor Carthaginians. I would as soon say they were the ten lost tribes. All those theories are on a par, and are worthy of each other, but not worthy of any notice. Their language is soft and melodious, and they seem to have an ear for simple melody. Since I first saw them in 1817 they have acquired firearms and horses; but they want discipline—the firmness of discipline. Individual acts of bravery they have often performed, but combined they can never meet successfully the European. We are now preparing to take possession of their country, and this of course leads to their enslavery and final destruction, for a people without land are most certainly mere bondmen. *Ascripti glebæ*—they would, but they cannot, quit it. The old English yeomen and the modern Dorsetshire labourer, the local tenant of Sutherlandshire and the peasantry of Ireland, are simply bondmen or slaves; there is no avoiding the phrase. The fate of the Caffre race, then, is certain, but centuries may elapse before their final destruction; in the meantime they may retire within the tropic, where in all probability the white man may not be able to follow, as a conqueror at least. There is the retreat for the Caffre—within the tropics, whence he came—to that again must he retire or perish. What travellers and others tell you about tribes of mixed breed, races of mulattoes, has no real existence; I would as soon expect to hear of a generation of mules. When the Negro is crossed with the Hottentot race, the product is a mild-tempered, industrious person; when with the white race, the result is a scoundrel. But, cross as you will, the mulatto cannot hold his ground as a mulatto : back the breed will go to one or other of the pure breeds, white or black. I have already explained all this.

And now for the Negro and Negroland—Central Africa, as yet untrodden and unknown. Look at the Negro, so well known to you, and say, need I describe him ? Is he shaped like any white person ? Is the anatomy of his frame, of his muscles, or organs like ours ? Does he walk like us, think like us, act like us ? Not in the least. What an innate hatred the Saxon has for him, and how I have laughed at the mock philanthropy of England ! But I have spoken of this already, and it is a painful topic ; and yet this despised race drove the warlike French from St. Domingo, and the issue of a struggle with them in Jamaica might be doubtful. But come it will, and then the courage of the Negro will be tried against England. Already they defeated France ; but, after all, was it not the climate ? for that any body of dark men in this world will ever fight successfully a French army of twenty thousand men I never shall believe. With one thousand white men all the blacks of St. Domingo could be defeated in a single action. This is my opinion of the dark races.

The Negro race occupies Central Africa, extending from the Kalihari to the confines of the Sahara; other races of men occupy the remainder; the Mauritanian or Moor, and the Kabyles—the race probably which the Phœnicians found there on their first settlement. But the Moor is probably not indigenous, though of vast and unknown antiquity; so, also, is the Copt. Who the Abyssinians and the Zoullahs are, it seems almost impossible to say, seeing that, from Bruce to Harris, African travellers have either started mad, or returned mad—the heat of the climate no doubt affecting their brains.

Is the Negro race confined to Central Africa? It would seem not. Report describes their presence in Madagascar, and even in Borneo, Sumatra, and in some other Eastern isles. The Australians are black, but they are not Negroes.

SECTION III.—The past history of the Negro, of the Caffre, of the Hottentot, and of the Bosjeman, is simply a blank—St. Domingo forming but an episode. Can the black races become civilized? I should say not: their future history, then, must resemble the past. The Saxon race will never tolerate them—never amalgamate—never be at peace. The hottest actual war ever carried on — the bloodiest of Napoleon's campaigns — is not equal to that now waging between our descendants in America and the dark races; it is a war of extermination — inscribed on each banner is a death's head and no surrender; one or other must fall. But here climate steps in, and says to the land-grasping Saxon, "I give you a choice of evils—cultivate Central Africa or Central America with your own hands, and you perish; employ the coloured man, your brother, as a slave, and live under the continual fear of his terrible vengeance — terrible when it comes, as come it will: unrelenting, merciless." A million of slave-holders cut off in cold blood to-morrow would call forth no tear of sympathy in Europe: "Bravo!" we should say; "the slave has risen and burst his chains—he deserves to be free."

Wild, visionary, and pitiable theories have been offered respecting the colour of the black man, as if he differed only in colour from the white races; but he differs in everything as much as in colour. He is no more a white man than an ass is a horse or a zebra: if the Israelite finds his ten tribes amongst them I shall be happy. But what has flattened the nose so much—altered the shape of the whole features, the body, the limbs? Some idle, foolish, and, I might almost say, some wicked notions, have been spread about of their being descended from Cain; such notions ought to be discountenanced : they give a colour for oppression.

Of the true Negro I need not say much; he seems to me to have qualities of a high order, and might even reach a certain point of civilization. His constitution is energetic, as proved by the extension of his race; Africa is his real country—Central Africa.   It is here that climate enables him to set the Celtic and Saxon races at defiance.   Often, often have they attempted its subjugation, but have always hitherto failed; and yet there seems to me ways to effect it, did they but adopt the wiles and the modes of Saxon traders. By ascending the Senegal cautiously and rapidly, clearing the high country, dividing its sources from those of the Niger, a thousand brave men on horseback might seize and hold Central Africa to the north of the tropic; the Celtic race, will, no doubt, attempt this some day.   On the other hand, accident has prepared the way for a speedy occupation of Africa to the south of the equator by the Saxon race, the Anglo-Saxon.

Section IV.—*Other Dark Races.*

Little is known of the dark races of Asia, even of those of Indostan.   It is a fact worthy of the deepest reflection, that neither Northern India nor Indostan Proper have altered since the time of Alexander the Great; that is, for twenty-

three or twenty-four centuries of years they have
not progressed nor changed. This I am disposed
to think decides the character of the race or
races; for no doubt there must be many races
inhabiting these widely-extended and still, I presume, populous regions. Their extreme populous-
ness I am disposed to question; their possible
improvement is questionable. I saw two of those
young persons—Brahmins I think they were, or of
that race, who were educated lately in London by
the India Company at a heavy expense, merely
by way of experiment. The result will, simply,
I think, amount to nothing. If the Company
meant to ascertain whether a few of the natives
of Indostan can be taught so much of book
learning as is usually stuffed into the head of an
undergraduate or college student, then the experiment, after all, amounts to nothing, for the same
may be done with the Negro, the Hottentot, and
the Dosjeman; it is one thing to cram a young
head with book learning, but quite another to
improve the natives of Indostan, who have stood
still in the face of European civilization so long,
unaltered and seemingly unalterable. But there
can be no harm in trying such experiments; they
form a little chit-chat for the coteries and clubs
of London. The two young men I saw, who
were natives of Indostan, were dark-coloured
persons, with heads peculiarly formed—hammer-

shaped, in fact—set on the neck differently from
the European. They wore, if I recollect right,
their native dress, showing that on their return
to India they would once more sink into the vast
gulf of non-progression.

In conclusion: researches sufficiently extensive
have not been made into the physical structure
and psychology of the dark races; even the
cranium or skeleton has not been very carefully
studied. Of the rest we know scarcely anything.
Men go to India in search of rupees, and other
stuffs of that kind. They remain as short time
as possible, and are chiefly occupied with personal
cares; the unknown is studied chiefly in the
Company's official Directory, where the anxious
inquirer learns how many require to "go out"
before his position on the list be quite satisfactory.

AMERICAN RACES.—INTRODUCTION.

The discovery of a new world by Columbus
is the most remarkable event in human history;
with the leading features of that great event all
must, no doubt, be acquainted; my object is
merely to trace the progress of races on that vast
territory, and, after a single remark on the ancient history of the American continent, I shall
resume my discourse.

When Columbus and those who followed ·him
first set foot on the islands and mainland of that

vast continent, destined to play so important a
part in the future destinies of mankind — that
land where the greatest of all experiments, to be
solved alone by time, is now progressing, namely,
the practicability of self-government, or democracy;
that land where liberty, driven from Europe, Asia,
and Africa, by whiskered dragoons and church mili-
tants, found that sure resting-place, that fulcrum
with which she may, perhaps, one day upturn the
strongholds of fanaticism and violence ; that land
which first of all brought out the true character
of the Saxon race, of the Saxon mind, in fact—in
that land Columbus and his followers, most of
whom were men of great ability—though he alone
had genius—in that land these great men found
nothing to resemble strictly the countries they
had left; nor trees, nor shrubs, nor fish, nor fowl,
nothing which lived resembled what they had
previously seen ; I had better say, nothing was
identical with the productions of the old world.
Man was there, no doubt, but he was not identical
with any other race; in his bodily and mental
qualities he differed widely from all others.
The horse was not there, nor sheep, nor cattle ;
nor the beauteous *wilde* of Africa; lions and pan-
thers, giraffe and antelope; in the virgin forests
of America stalked no elephants; the river-horse
and the terrible rhinoceros were nowhere to be
found. But other equally strange forms presented

themselves, peopling the fields, and rivers, and
forests; all differing specifically and generically,
as we express this grand and solemn fact, in
technical language; I call it a solemn fact, seeing
that it gives rise to profound reflections. Whence
came this new race of men and animals? The
answer was easy upon the old Hippocratic
theory of the effects of climate; the men were
Europeans burned to a copper colour by the sun
and wind, and other things, including the smoke
of their wigwams; and the animals were just the
same as those of the old world. Careless observers! Man had journeyed without the horse,
and sheep, and ox; he had also, I think, forgotten the cerealia; a theory was easily got up
to explain all this. Last, came men of science,
lovers of truth, enemies of romance and falsehood. Their labours proved that everything
there that lived was specifically different from
living beings on any other land; that even the
apes differed specifically from the apes of the
old world, by having an additional tooth, and by
being without that central spot or hole in the
retina of the eye, found in man and in the apes
of the old world; that the new world was an
erroneous phrase, seeing that it was a very old
world in every sense of the word; that the
copper-coloured race of America—that race which
extended throughout the length and breadth of

the land—were neither metamorphosed Welsh-
men, nor Connaught men, nor Norwegians; nor
even Polynesians; the last hypothesis, I believe,
offered the credulous for the peopling of America,
always excepting that stand-by of the thorough-
bred theorist, namely, that the copper Indians,
that is, the true Americans, were the lost tribes of
Israel, who fled there on rafts, headed, I suppose,
by Prester John.   Let us leave such sickening,
silly follies to their inventors and to those who hate

[*Native American.*]

truth—the romancists, the novelists, the tourists—
and proceed with our inquiry. Buffon concluded
that animal life was not so vigorous on the American soil as in the old world, comparing one animal with another; this simple fact, for it is one,
roused the wrath of an Anglo-Saxon, now settled
in that country, but calling himself an American;
I mean Mr. Cooper, the novelist. True to his
Saxon race, he was determined to make out, in
the face of all common sense and truth—despising
the one by his trade or calling, and being seemingly without the other—that the American soil
nourished as big animals as ever were grown in
old France or England, or the whole world;
that the buffalo was as large as our oxen, and the
turkey larger than a barn-door fowl; what a pity
he had not also added, that geese and asses of all
kinds abound, and are at least as large, as pe-
dantic, and as stupidly solemn as any the Britishers
could ever boast of. This is the Mr. Cooper who
compared, through ten drawlishly-spun pages,
the Rhino with the immortal Hudson—the everlasting Hudson—that large river which runs near
the ancient city of New York, so rich in the
association of great names and stirring events.
What solemn pedantry, what deplorable want of
taste and sense, to forget the passage of the Rhine
by Cæsar and Napoleon! These are the names
which give immortality to the Rhine, not the

amount of water it contains, nor its length nor
breadth; it is not the size of the Nile which
makes it live in the recollections of nations. Do
you not see in this miserable comparison of Mr.
Cooper the egotism of the Saxon peep out in all
its true colours? Our rivers are bigger than yours
—prettier, deeper: our horses are faster than
yours—fatter and better; our oxen are larger
than yours—sleeker and finer. You will excuse,
I trust, these critical remarks; folly and egotism
merit severe censure, whether individual or national—in fact, these terms are identical, nations
merely being aggregates of individuals. I
shall return to Mr. Cooper by-and-by, and to
his native Americans, as he calls the Anglo-Saxon
multitude who went over the Atlantic a few years
ago, and who, by settling there, as always happens with the Saxon, forgot their country, their
race, and all about it. To return : scientific inquiries have disproved all these idle romances
and errors. Let us now look at the race as we
find them.

Whilst I write this the Saxon race is at work
in America, clutching at empires. The go-ahead
principle (meaning want of all principle) is at
work; the Floridas, Texas, Oregon, California,
Mexico, all must reciprocate; the hypocrisy
called organized, but which means organic, no
doubt is at work. I blame them not; I pretend

not even to censure: man acts from his impulses,
his animal impulses, and he occasionally employs
his pure reason to mystify and conceal his motives
from others. But I have already explained all
this; let me, therefore, speak to you of the
original American races—the races found on the
American continent and its islands by Columbus,
Vespuccio, Pizarro, Cortes, and others; not forgetting our countryman, Penn, and his troop of
saints. These races still exist; in a century or
two they may have ceased to be; the American human animal is one which seemingly cannot
be domesticated — cannot be civilized. When
brought within the Saxon house and pale, he
becomes consumptive, and perishes; he is the
man of the woods, differing from all other men,
as the apes of his continent differ essentially
from those of the old world, as we term the
European, African, and Asiatic continents. But
not to the same extent, for there exists, in so far
as I know, no remarkable or specific differences
between them and us; for the apes of the new
continent have an additional tooth, distinguishing
them from the old world, and the structure of the
eye is essentially different. I allude more especially to the race known by the name of red or
copper-coloured Indians, extending, as it would
seem, from Nootka Sound and the borders of the
Arctic Circle to the rock-bound shores of the

Land of Fire, including, probably, all the West
India islands, the tribes of Brazil, and the Caribs.
At the extremities of this long and singularly-
shaped continent, it seems to me that two other
races, which may be termed polar or arctic,
exist: to the north, we are certain that the
Esquimaux differ essentially from the red Indian;* and in the south, it is probable that the
miserable dark-coloured population wandering
on the outskirts of the Land of Fire, are not
red Indians, but a race analogous to the Australian, and to the former inhabitants of Van Diemen's Land; polar or arctic races of men, dark
in colour, swarthy, peculiar; I speak particularly
of the Esquimaux: thus, in America, the races
darken as we approach the poles; the eternal
snows which ought to have whitened them, according to the theorists, from Hippocrates to
Barton Smith, have failed to bleach them. Let
me speak first of the red Indian, and next of the
two other races, that is, if the southern one be a
distinct race, which has not yet been proved.

When the European races, within the well-
authenticated historic period, discovered America,
they found, in its tropical portions, organized
kingdoms or empires, arts tolerably advanced,
and an appearance of domesticity. In the dense

* For illustrative woodcut, see page 140.

woods of South America the Indian still roamed
about, a naked savage; and in the woods of
Northern America they still found the red man
a savage, though with somewhat peculiar institutions.   They were, probably, all of one race
—the Botocudo and Patagonian; the Mexican,
Peruvian, and red Indian; the Carib and the flat-
headed Indian of the Oregon.   I say this, however, with hesitation, ready to be put right on
a point respecting which I have had so few
opportunities for observation.   But, be it as it
may, I must decline entering into any contro-
versy with those who derive them from the Welsh,
or Danes, or Mongols, or Asiatics, or Malays; or
even from the ten tribes headed by Prester John.
These are old women's fables, not worth a moment's consideration.   For after Dr. Laing has
brought his men from the Malayan peninsula to
people all America, he must also bring over in
the same boats, camels, goats, and sheep, to be
converted into llamas, alpacas, &c.   And then
the *peculiar* apes, and the two-toed sloth, and
ten thousand other American forms of life which
Dr. Laing has forgotten to allude to; and the
buffalo, which is peculiar to America.   And then
he must explain to us how it was that, if the
Malays and Mongols came there, they did not
bring with them their sheep and oxen, and horses
and pigs; for nothing of the kind was found

there by Columbus, nor by anybody else: in
short, the hypothesis is a miserable one, and
merits no attention from anybody. The Jewish
Scriptures have only suffered by such attempts
at reconciliation.

A flat or depressed forehead is the peculiar
characteristic of the American copper-coloured
race. It existed amongst the Caribs, who, I believe, are now extinct, and it is seen everywhere.
That it is produced artificially I totally disbelieve.
Persons seeing applications made to the head of
the child may fancy such to be capable of producing it, but erroneously. In certain cases it
may increase it so as to amount to positive deformity—this I will admit, but no more; the
fable about the artificial production of a flat-
headed people, is at least as old as Hippocrates,
but probably much older. He placed them on
the shores of the Euxine Sea, the America of
those days, and like all medical men, true to his
class and order, he offered a theory based on
very slight materials. But I shall discuss these
theories in a future lecture, and need not speak
further of them here. The great feature of the
red Indian, of the American race in fact, is the
flattening of the forehead, more or less, in different tribes and nations. The Caribs were remarkable for this; the Peruvians, on the other

s

hand, for irregularly formed crania, imperfect ossification, &c., as has been already shown.

When the Europeans first landed, the American was probably a race not on the ascending, but descending, series, gradually becoming extinct. They had probably passed through countless periods of existence, and were merely living on the crumbs of a past generation—the race who built and inhabited Copan. How mysterious are these ruined cities of Central America! Hieroglyphics, pyramids, mummies, columns like those of Luxor, but on a smaller scale! Egypt rediscovered as reproduced in Central America. Ye theorists, what say you now? Were these remains of former grandeur the work of the forefathers of the present race of American aborigines? or, as these have altered somewhat since the days of the Incas and of Montezuma, were they constructed by the former Mexicans and Peruvians? I should think not exactly. They must have been constructed by, or copied from others. Perhaps the continents were at one time joined where the Atlantic surge now rolls, and architects from Egypt and North Africa, from the land of the Guanches, in fact, assisted the American aborigines in raising structures whose meaning they possibly did not comprehend. Or, had Coptic and Phœnician men, the great masons of the earth, the true builders, who seem to have

taught all others, who built instinctively, as bees
construct hives, not houses, but temples — had
they ever overrun these countries, acted as in-
structors and masters, and held the soil? or, was
there a race prior to all these? or, finally, had
the American race lived its period, gone to the
full extent of their instinctive civilization, and
were rapidly declining when Cortes marched on
Mexico, and Pizarro on Peru? Did the European
find the race hastening on to a state of natural
extinction?

To these and numerous questions like these no
satisfactory answer can be given; all we know is,
but little; we scarcely have a good idea of what
this race was at the commencement of their historic period. But we do know that there are
mummies resembling the present Peruvian; that
the remains of vast buildings having an Egyptian
cast still exist; and finally, that, notwithstanding
the infusion of much European blood, the race
cannot stand its ground. Now this is the point
most worthy of our present notice.

Cast your eyes on this small spot, and see
what it portends; it is the Falkland Isles. There
a small group of Saxons have located themselves.
They could not exactly land at once on the mainland of Patagonia, and settle there; this does not
suit the organized hypocrisy which regulates the
Saxon; he settles on some out-of-the-way spot—

Aden, the Falkland Isles, Calcutta, Hong-Kong,
Borneo; something unobtrusive.   The French, a
Celtic race, try to imitate us, but they do it clumsily;
their hypocrisy is not so perfectly organized.   The
group on the Falklands are looking towards the
mainland as a counterbalance to the loss of the
United States first, and of Canada, which is sure
to follow.   But direct your attention northwards,
and see the islands we hold; precariously, however, as being within the tropics, and therefore,
wholly inimical to the Saxon constitution.   An
attempt was made on Buenos Ayres; we were
beaten shamefully — nothing scarcely equals it
in the history of defeats: the commander of that
expedition should have been hanged, and another
and another sent until we drove a plough over the
city, and blotted it from the maps.   But not so;
still the fight goes on, and we are endeavouring to seize on these fertile plains where the
European can live.   Across is Chili; northwards
Peru, and then Mexico.   Now, the fate of all
these nations must be the same; it results from
the nature of their populations, and nothing can
arrest it.   I select Mexico for the description,
but most of my remarks will apply with equal
truth, I believe, to the others, and especially to
Peru.   The original population of Mexico was
Indian—the red Indian—a half-civilized barbarian.   On this was engrafted the Spanish stock,

itself not pure, being composed of several races, but still energetic, though likewise on the wane. The product was a mulatto, or half breed, whom nature never intended should exist as a race; therefore, having ceased receiving supplies from Old Spain, mulattoes could no longer be generated from that stock; they themselves, the mulattoes, die out and out, I think, in three or four generations, unless crossed and recrossed with some pure blood, white or black; they, therefore, would have ceased to exist; the Indian blood, predominating from the first, would naturally gain the ascendant; but, as that race was seemingly dying out when Cortes seized the kingdom, there existed no elements in Mexico to perpetuate the race beyond a few centuries. Now, this is precisely what has happened: all but English statisticians and statesmen knew that the Mexican population materially decreased; and so it will be with Peru and Chili: physiological causes are at work which would have settled the rank these nations were to hold in the world, independent altogether of the Saxon sword; this being now thrown into the balance, of course decides the matter against the Indian. Had they held by Old Spain, the Mexican Indian might have continued to receive supplies of fresh energy from Europe: not good, I admit, but still superior to their own; as it is, their fall is certain, for the

Saxon will not mingle with them; the Spaniard, the Celt-Iberian, would, but not the Saxon; thus they would have surely perished, even independent of Saxon interference. The physiological laws of reproduction were against them. What are their numbers?—say five, or six, or seven millions: why, they have received more than that from Europe!—seven millions in three hundred years. They have not increased by a single soul in three hundred years. But neither nations nor individuals stand still; onward they must go, or retrograde: there is no middle course; no fixity, no finality, in that sense. I have often read, years ago, in those popular things got up to amuse the people, of the thriving state of the population of these countries; a pretty tale, dressed up for the three-halfpenny literature; a smoothly-written phrenological thing about the American republics, and the noble Mexicans, Peruvians, Chilians, &c.; white lies, dressed up with false statistics, to give them an air of truth; in the meantime no attempt at analysis — no desire to look into principles—a fine generalizing tone, smoothing over enormous errors. Mr. Canning boasted of having created the American republics; but how are they to come off? He thought, no doubt, that, being men, some few amongst them might have some common sense; but he forgot, or did not know, that he had withdrawn from them, first, fresh supplies of European blood; second, that by this he annihilated the so-called half breed, who always die out; third, that the Indian blood would finally predominate, which Indian race would never civilize, but retrograde towards that point where Cortes found them, and would also die out. These elements were not understood by Mr. Canning; if known to him, despised. In man the statesman sees a machine bound to obey the existing laws; the only power they understand to enforce the law is the bayonet. Why Mexicans or Indians (for that is really their true name) cannot unite with Saxons to form one nation, they either cannot or will not understand. But Nature's laws are stronger than bayonets—she made the Saxon and she made the Indian; but no mixed race called Mexican will she support. Already we are told that the Indian blood predominates: of course it will; but give the so-called nation another century, and then let us consider what must happen. The Castilian blood will then be all but extinct, the Indian predominating; by that time the Anglo-Saxon, true to his go-ahead principles, seizes Mexico; but no Saxon will mingle with dark blood; with him the dark races must be slaves, or cease to exist. This principle, so small in semblance, so unimportant, and so unconsequential in appearance, will yet be found

equal to the extinction of all Indian blood in
Mexico; the new canton or federated state, forming part of the union, will then be colonized by
Anglo-Saxons.   They will forget New York
and Florida, whence they came, and become
native true-born Mexicans; thus the phrase ban-
died about fixes at last on a race originally from
Scandinavia, and still quite unaltered.   But here
a difficulty awaits them: the Saxon race cannot
labour in a tropical country; they must have
slaves, or leave it; this seems the great law of
nature for the protection of the tropical races of
men; neither Celt nor Saxon can labour in a
tropical country; they may seize a country, as
we have done India, and hold it by the bayonet,
as we do that vast territory; but we cannot colonize it; it is no part of Britain in any sense, and
never will be; the white race can never till the
fields of Hindostan.

Of the remaining original races of America I
need say but little.   The southern race is but
imperfectly known to us; tho northern, or Esquimaux, have been long before the public, yet their
real history is still to write; this is my opinion.

Let me conclude this portion of my discourse
with a few remarks on the insular portion of this
continent, and on those regions in the north
which still own the sovereignty of Britain.   And,
first of these, the great Celtic family of Gaul
colonized Canada; a portion of the race settled in

it, and they carried thither, I was about to say,
their religion, manners, laws, forms of holding
property, &c.; but why not rather say at once,
that a portion of a Celtic race from France seized
on a part of Canada; that, being Celts, they carried with them the Celtic character? Is not this
enough? What else could they do? They had,
and they have yet, their seigniories and their
laws of primogeniture; their natural indolence
.and good taste; their habits of clinging to each
other and leaving the country desolate; they
huddled themselves in villages, seemingly terri-
fied to locate in the open country; they had no
self-dependence, no go-ahead notions; and so
they all but stood still, waiting the arrival of the
latest fashions from Paris. Then poured in the
Saxon upon them; seized their, territory, and
advised them to become English. With this
seemingly quite reasonable request they refused
compliance; hence the revolts—hence the attempts to re-establish Celtic authority in Canada.
This struggle can only cease when the Saxon
has become the preponderating race in Lower
Canada, which can never happen until the laws
of entail and primogeniture are abolished. These
laws perpetuate the Celtic race, and with it all the
feuds of race.* They have the same effect precisely in Ireland: Canada is merely a western
Ireland and Wales; the inextinguishable hatred

* For illustrative woodcut, see page 52.

of races is in full play; unite they never will;
one must become extinct. Now it is easy to
see which goes first to the wall; the laws of
entail, after a severe struggle, will be abolished
in both countries, and then the Saxon steps in
with his self-dependent, go-ahead principle; then
flourish commerce, manufacture, agriculture, and
every useful speculation; then will Ireland become Saxon, but not till then. So will " Le bas
Canada," as it is called, soon, under such circumstances, cease to be Celtic. In the meantime we
must not suppose that the Celtic struggle will end
here. Some ten years ago I ventured to hint
that whenever the Celtic race became sufficiently
numerous in any part of the Union, the Saxon
would be disposed to notice them. I allowed
some half century, however, to elapse before the
war of race might show itself; but in this I was
wrong, for it has already appeared in one of the
northern states, the Saxons assembling tumultu-
ously, and burning a Roman-catholic church,
with other acts of violence towards the frequenters
of that church, who of course are Celtic. We
shall see: time unfolds all events; the war of
race will some day shake the Union to its foundation. They never will mix — never commingle
and unite. Though using the same language,
they apply to some most important words totally
different meanings. The one loves war, the other
peace; the law and the constable's baton are gene-

rally sufficient for the rule of the one, and the
bayonet, on which, of course, all law ultimately
reposes, is kept out of view; but with the Celt
this, I think, can never be; he can be made to
respect the law only by means of the sword ever
drawn. It is not that he is more savage or more
brutal (the term in no shape applies to him) or
less a lover of justice than others; but his temper
is quicker, and he flies to the sword, to arms, as
his natural instinct. Against this disposition the
state must ever be on its guard. Both races talk
of republican institutions, and the Saxon may
well boast that pure democracy prevails throughout the Union; that it forms a large element in
Britain; that it is not quite extinct in Holland
and Norway, though ground to the dust in France
and throughout the rest of Europe. But the
Celt has not the most distant idea of true personal liberty. Look at him in France! See him
rebuild the bastiles he once destroyed! See
forty millions of people, warlike and courageous,
submit to become the mere tools of a miserable
dynasty.*

* This was written as the lectures were delivered, five
years ago; and prior, of course, to the late revolution. The
journalists of France inform us, no doubt, of a *republic* which
is said to exist somewhere in France; be it so: in the meantime I beg leave to hint at the following facts. Paris is in a
state of siege; walled and fortified round about; the passport
system continues in full force. A soldier of the name of
Cavaignac stands in the place of the dynasty, &c. &c.

And now of the insular part of the new world.
One great section, Hayti, has shown the white
man that he cannot colonize a tropical country;
it must revert to those races on whom nature has
bestowed a constitution adapted to labour under
a tropical sun.   Cuba and Jamaica will follow;
they will become black spots in the history of
civilization, for nothing in the history of mankind
permits us to believe in the perfect civilization of
the Negro race.   The policy of European races
would be to expel the Negro and transplant the
Coolies, Hindoos, Chinese, or other feeble races,
as labourers and workmen,—bondmen, in fact.
Why not call everything by its right name?
Over these the Saxon and Celt might lord it,
as we do in India, with a few European bayonets,
levying taxes and land-rent; holding a monopoly
of trade; furnishing them with salt at fifty times
its value; but we cannot do this with the true
Negro.

I am disposed to ascribe to the element of race
a circumstance which has occurred oftener than
once in the delivery of these lectures in various
institutions—literary, scientific, and popular. The
attention of the audience could not be so completely secured as when I spoke to them of the fair
races.   It seemed to me again a question of race.
What signify these dark races to us ?   Who cares
particularly for the Negro, or the Hottentot, or the

Kaffir ? These latter have proved a very troublesome race, and the sooner they are put out of the
way the better.   I will not say that this was expressed, but I think it was understood; it seemed
to be felt that black and coloured men differ very
much from fair men, like ourselves.   This is the
world's sympathy : they are good enough people,
but not of our kind.   Practically, all men
believe in the element of race ; it is denied only
theoretically ; thus theory and practice seldom
coincide: profession is not conduct ; fair words
do not always imply straightforward actions. Even
the daily press, so powerful an agent for the exposure of such hypocrisy, must look to those who
support it ; Negroes and Red Indians, Hottentots
and Kaffirs, neither read nor pay for daily journals.

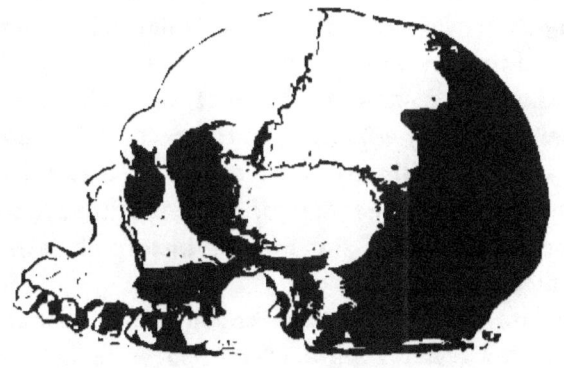

[*The Skull of the Tasmanian.*]

SECTION V.—*Physical Characteristics.*

The anatomical structure of the dark races of
men is but imperfectly known; I may venture to
say it is not known at all. The details have not
been observed and described by anatomists of
reputation: few anatomists go abroad to sojourn
in tropical countries, and opportunities for the
dissection of the dark races are comparatively
rare in the seats of learning and science in
Europe. The Hottentot Venus, who died in
Paris, was examined there, and some most distinguished men took part in the examination.
But I can find no detailed account of the structures deserving the name of a report. It is known
that the Hottentot and Bosjeman race have, in as
far as regards the female, the reproductive organs
singularly formed; but these singularities are
thought not to be peculiar to these races. I speak
of them as somewhat different to each other,
though strongly affiliated. In this respect I do not
quite agree with my most esteemed friend Dr.
Andrew Smith, the first of all authorities, however, in respect of the natural history of extra-
tropical Southern Africa.

Were the examinations conducted on a more
extended scale, I have every reason to believe
that many other differences in structure would be

found to exist. The nasal bones are narrow
and short, they usually coalesce ; the ascending
branches of the upper maxillary bones are broad,
and the breadth between the eyes correspondingly
remarkable. The power of vision is most admirable, but it is lost by a single cross with the white
race. So also are the elastic fatty cushions over
the glutei muscles and on the haunches generally,
so characteristically marked in the Hottentot
Venus. If my memory be correct, it was M. de
Blainville (my illustrious teacher, the first comparative anatomist of the present age) who pointed
out the existence of similar elastic fatty cushions
over the deltoid muscles, which he no doubt
observed in the Hottentot Venus. I did not remark them sufficiently when in South Africa, but
I do not question the fact of their occasional
presence. The truth is, that such peculiarities
are by no means universal amongst the race — at
least, so it appeared to me ; and the same remark
may be made, I think, in respect of the still more
striking peculiarities of the reproductive system.
Many other curious circumstances might here be
added, from my personal knowledge of this race,
the yellow, pigmy race of Southern Africa, but
they would not compensate for the absolute want
of scientific details, which no scientific man has
yet furnished. Neither literature nor science can
flourish in the colonies, and the disposition of the

British government is opposed to the true cultivation of science. Its utility, which is indeed often
remote, is questioned by the utilitarian practical
government of a utilitarian practical race, looking
directly and intently at immediate results and
material interests. Accordingly, no attempt that
I know of has ever been made to ascertain the
extent of the Hottentot and Bosjeman race towards the north, that is, into the interior of Africa;
a problem surely worthy a solution, for no more
singular race of men exist on the earth than the
Hottentot race.

The first Kaffir crania transmitted to Europe
were by myself, and I may claim, I believe, the
merit of having first pointed out to the learned
of Europe the true nature of this fine race. They
are not Negroes, but yet their skulls are not well
formed—they are deficient in elevation and in
breadth. They differ vastly from the Hottentot,
to whom, indeed, they bear no resemblance whatever, although it is quite possible that intermediate races between them may be found on the
Gariepine streams, or even in the Calihari Desert.
Everything is mystery here. Their limbs are of
great strength, but not their arms, and their
elongated, narrow foot, can at once be distinguished from all others. Let us hope that some
scientific man will favour mankind with a correct
history of the race before their final extinction.

When Hanno the Carthaginian led his great
colony along the shores of Africa, on the west,
they met with beings so curiously made, and
covered with hair, that the Phœnician general
was anxious to carry specimens of this race
(of men?) to Carthage.   Three were seized —
females; but they proved so troublesome to
the Carthaginians that they were forced to slay
them, and carry their stuffed skins to Carthage,
where no doubt they were looked on as great
curiosities.   Let us hope, for the honour of
humanity, that these women, so named, by
Hanno, were not women, but chimpanzees, which
still exist on that coast.

I have seen lately in England the stuffed skin
of a Hottentot woman, a great curiosity, no doubt.
Now, as the Kaffirs will in all probability soon
become extinct, it might be worth while to adopt
this method of preserving a few specimens of the

[*Chimpanzee.*]

T

race. The stuffed skin of poor Hinsa, the noblest of the Kaffir nation by birth and courage, who was killed (Lord Glenelg, if I recollect right, seemed to think murdered) on the Kei, might have figured in the British Museum, forming an exciting object of attention to the sight-seers of London. But to return.

The scientific history of the Kaffir race is still to write.

2. A very general belief has prevailed from the days of Hippocrates, and long prior, no doubt, that by artificial means the form of various parts of the human body, the general shape itself, may be permanently altered. Stating the circumstances from recollection connected with this subject, I would observe that it was Hippocrates who said that the Macrocephali inhabiting the shores of the Black Sea applied pressure to the head, altering its form considerably, and producing a deformation which continued with the life of the individual. But Hippocrates, if my memory be correct, went still further than this; he allows that the practice of thus improving the form of the head had been long discontinued in his time, but that, from being originally an accidental or artificial deformation, it had become *congenital*, no longer requiring artificial means for its production. Theories like these merit little or no attention, whether invented by Hippocrates

or by a less skilful hand. The same story has been told in modern times of the Carib of the West Indies; also of the Chenook; but I have been crania from the isles of the Southern or Pacific Ocean, if possible still more depressed even than those of the Chenook, or inhabitant of the banks of the Oregon. The natives of these countries imagine that by applying a bag of sand to the forehead of the infant at or soon after birth, and by maintaining it there with compresses, they may thereby increase to an extreme degree the flatness of the forehead natural to their race. Now, it is just possible they may do so in a slight degree, but even this is doubtful. The American race has the forehead depressed naturally; it was the same with the Caribs, a race of men nearly extinct. When we speak of the American tribes or nations being all of one race, we merely state a probability; there may have been several, though strongly affiliated races; much information is still wanting on this point.

Accident placed in my hands, a few years ago, a memoir of a distinguished French anatomist, whose name I, at this moment, cannot recollect, unless it be M. Foville. The object of the memoir was to prove that the practice, still it appears prevailing in some parts of France, of swathing the head of the infant immediately on birth, was a pernicious one, calculated to give rise to mal-

formation of the cranium, and consequently of
the brain, injurious to the health and intellects
of the sufferer. The kind of malformation observed by him consisted in a remarkable depression, extending over the vertex, in the region of
the parietal bones, sometimes more than an inch
and a half or two inches in breadth, and obviously
corresponding to the place over which the nurse
or parent had placed a tight fold of the bandage.
But it is difficult to imagine such results to flow
from such a cause, for to it M. Foville traces
many cases of idiocy and dementia. This form
of head is by no means uncommon; I have described it in my "Physiological Lectures" some
years ago; I have met with it frequently during
life, but never could observe the idiotic state of
the person as its accompaniment. This distinguished anatomist and observer must, I think, be
mistaken in his views respecting this form of the
head. It is the theory of Hippocrates, with some
additions. No deviations in form, even when
they can be produced, can ever become congenital or hereditary. Let the Chinese foot bear
witness to this fact.* For thousands of years has
this non-progressive race been endeavouring to
destroy the form of the foot in Chinese women,
without any success further than the mutilation

---

* For illustrative woodcut, see page 101.

of the individual: nor has the act of marriage
permanently altered the form of woman. *Expellas
naturam furca, tamen usque recurrat*, is the pithy
and true saying of Horace, verified from all
antiquity.

The fragments existing respecting the physical
structures are few, and in many cases not to be
depended on. Those which have been observed
are in most instances reducible to the laws of
imperfect development, as partly understood by
Harvey, and the anatomists of his day, but best
explained by the continental anatomists —
Bojanus, Oken, Spix, and others. Thus, the fold
of integument we observe in many persons, and
particularly in the young, towards the inner angle
of the eye, I have thought to be much more
frequent and much larger in the Hottentot and
Bosjeman than in the European. It has been
also described as present universally, I think, by
a careful observer, Mr. Edwards, amongst the
Esquimaux, from whose interesting account of
the race I make the following quotation:—

"I may here remark, that there is in many
individuals a peculiarity about the eye amounting, in some instances, to deformity, which I
have not noticed elsewhere. It consists in the
inner corner of the eye being entirely covered by
a duplication of the adjacent loose skin of the
eyelids and nose. This fold is lightly stretched

over the edges of the eyelids, and forms, as it
were, a third palpebra of a crescentic shape. The
aperture is in consequence rendered somewhat
pyriform, the inner curvature being very obtuse,
and in some individuals distorted by an angle,
formed where the fold crosses the border of the
lower palpebra. This singularity depends upon
the variable form of the orbit during immature
age, and is very remarkable in childhood, less
so towards adult age, and then, it would seem,
frequently disappearing altogether; for the proportion in which it exists among grown-up persons bears but a small comparison with that
observed among the young."

The deformity here described exists probably
in every human fœtus, and its continuance in
after-life is, therefore, a mere persistence of a
fœtal or embryonic form. The fold of integument does not correspond, however, is not the
analogue nor homologue of a palpebra or third
eyelid; the third eyelid exists in all animals,
being quite rudimentary, though sensibly present,
in man, whilst it attains its maximum of development in the bird.

There are appearances in the reproductive
organs in some dark races indicative of a persistence of fœtal forms to the adult or mature age.

SECTION VI.—The Chinese, Mongol, Calmuck,

and Tartar, and all or most of those tribes and
races which either inhabit the vast steppes of
Asia, extend over the Himalayan range, or
wander by the shores of the icy seas northward
from Siberia, from the north of the Obi to the
furthest land claimed in Asia by the Muscovite,
belong to the dark races of men; of these
races the Mongol was once the most powerful;
his reign was that of terror and desolation for
the rest of mankind. Twice, I think, he overran
a great portion of the then civilized world; penetrated into Europe, and then retired. What has
become of the vast races of the swarthy Mongol,
whose tented field resembled a noble city? How
were they destroyed? Why have they all but
ceased to be? A few hundred years ago they
once more threatened the liberties of mankind;
now, absorbed as a mere item in the Muscovite's
territories, they claim no separate distinction as
a power. China, which is also occupied by a
Mongolian race, must one day follow; the contest for its possession will probably lie between
the Muscovite and the Australian, for by that
name no doubt will its Anglo-Saxon inhabitants
be soon known, when, like our sons and brothers
in the Western world, they throw off our allegiance and set up for themselves. As a great
and free and a democratic nation, as no doubt
they will be, they will dispute Japan, and even

China itself, with the Muscovite. The fate of
the rest of the Mongol race is settled: Sarmatian
or Saxon, the Celestial Empire, and its sister of
Japan, must one day become. But it will not be
English: it will be Australian, and belong to the
Anglo-Saxon population of Australia. How
speedily does the Anglo-Saxon show his real
character when relieved from the pressure of the
Three Estates. In America he will not allow a
black man to be a free man; in Australia he
deems him entirely below his notice; in Tasmania he swept him, and at once, entirely from

[*Chinese Pagoda.*]

the land of his birth. No compunctious visitings about the "fell swoop" which extinguished a race.

A few years ago it was the fashion to speak of the vast population of China—300,000,000 or more; its armies, too, were described as immense; its resources ample. Now mark what happened. A Saxon nation of about twenty-two millions of population, and having a disposable force of a few thousand men at the most—never able to bring into the field, unaided by allies, a force entitled to be called an army—quarrels with this said Celestial Empire of three hundred millions, having at its disposal, as was said, an army of four or five millions of men. The result of this pretty little quarrel between the smugglers (English) and the inhabitants of the Celestial Empire is, that the former send a handful of *European* troops in ships some thousand miles across the ocean. This handful of troops, which could not have marched twenty miles inland from Boulogne without destruction, meets with no effectual resistance. It seizes the second city of their empire, and was prevented taking and plundering the capital itself merely by a bribe of six or seven millions of money—the silver we had paid them for tea.

In the meantime the army of five millions never appeared; with the greatest difficulty (as was evident, seeing that their very capital city and political existence was threatened) they scarcely mustered thirty-five thousand men; this was their largest army, and it was easily defeated by half their numbers. Surely it is time for geographical and other writers to leave off the extravagancies they have been in the habit of publishing in regard to China and Japan. In a sheet just published here in London, called "The World as it is in 1848," the authors have reduced the three hundred millions to one hundred and ninety-eight millions. How able statisticians are! They will undertake to prove you almost anything. But it may be as well to reduce their population of China by another odd hundred millions or so; for assuredly either the central provinces of China are deserts or the central government is without strength. It is impossible to come to any other conclusion but one of these. That the most ancient nation on the earth; the most populous; with a population exceeding that of Europe; reported to have been highly civilized for nearly three thousand years; productive, rich, should yet not be able to muster forty thousand men to defend its capital from the invasion of a few thousand "barbarians," as they are pleased to term us, is altogether incredible, excepting on the suppositions I have made. But now, having mentioned the term civilization as applied to China, let us consider what it may amount to amongst a Mongol race.

Long prior to the Christian era the race inhabiting China, Nepaul, and many adjoining territories, was acquainted with the magnet, the art of printing, the making of gunpowder, and with most useful domestic and mechanical arts, yet they never could turn any of these inventions to any great account. On the contrary, they remained stationary, whilst the Greek and the Roman, following the Coptic, and next the modern European, successively arose, culminated, and, with the exception of the last, terminated. In the meantime, China appears to have been completely stationary; she neither invented nor discovered; their arts must have belonged to some other race, from whom she borrowed without rightly comprehending them. Their religion is a puzzle; their morals of the lowest; of science they can have none, nor is it clear that they comprehend the meaning of the term. A love for science implies a love of truth: now truth they despise and abhor. I do not believe there is an individual Chinaman who could be made to comprehend a single fact in physical geography. So profound was their ignorance, their want of foresight and of common sense, that they could not send a single person to Europe so as to give any information about the armament which ultimately overthrew and plundered them. An English or French engineer possesses more practical knowledge than the united *savans* of their empire. Humboldt, the illustrious Humboldt, praises them, and thinks highly of them. Whilst we in Europe, he remarks, for so many centuries during the dark ages were outraging every principle of humanity and common sense, by *auto-da-fés*, and by the torturing and slaying of human beings as witches and dealers in evil arts, the Chinese were recording eclipses. These are facts, no doubt; they do not say much for the Saxons and Celts of former times; the savage nature of the elementary men of Northern Europe had not been tamed down; even yet, brutality, ferocity, frivolity, and a base and dreadful fanaticism are occasionally but too apt to surge up from time to time, in these so called European countries, telling us of the presence of those elementary hands and minds which still abound in all races; but the recording eclipses is, after all, no great effort of the mind.

Schlegel thinks them highly civilized, and instances their canals, bridges, &c.; but this is a great error—the beaver, the bee, and the wasp and ant would, in this case, be civilized; the hillock of the African termites is a more remarkable labour comparatively than the pyramids to

man; man builds, cuts canals, makes roads, instinctively, exactly like an animal; these are no
proofs of intellect or pure reason; each race
builds after its own kind; the Saxon is not disposed to build; the ancient Copts, Phœnicians,
and Greeks were, on the other hand, remarkably
so, and builders, *par excellence*.

Mere mechanical art is no proof of high intelligence. The Romans had no genius whatever,
and yet they were remarkable as builders and
for their excellence in the mechanical arts.
Historians admit that the Chinese records furnish few materials for history. It is admitted
on all hands that they are devoid of all principle,
and essentially a nation of liars. How then can
they progress? Without a military or naval force,
they resorted to tricks more worthy of children
than of grown men, in hopes of arresting the
progress of the British armament. They set up
an iron pipe on the deck of their vessels, kindling
a fire inside the tube, in hopes that the smoke
which showed itself at the top would terrify the
barbarians! They mistook the big drum of the
18th Irish Foot for an unknown and dangerous
implement of war, and kept firing at it during the
greater part of the action; they in consequence
killed nobody. Such are the Chinese.

I have, in this brief sketch, scarcely alluded to

the Australian* and Tasmanian; to the cannibal inhabitants of some portions of Oceania, if they really be cannibals (which I greatly doubt); to the Malay race; to the numerous dark tribes of Hindostan; to the Arabs, many of whom are very dark in their colour; to the natives of Madagascar; of Borneo, Sumatra, and the Eastern Isles. The reason is simple. Scarcely anything positive is known of them. The Tasmanians and Australians have never been carefully described. One thing seems to me certain, that in all the dark races the bones composing the upper jaw are much larger than in any fair race, with the exception, perhaps, of the Jew.

The reproductive organs in the Tasmanian are said to be quite peculiar in man and woman; and it has been further reported of them that the Australian woman ceases to be productive after intermarriage with one of the fair races. These would be curious facts if proved.

But the European has, in my opinion, erred in despising the Negro, who seems to me of a race of occasionally great energy. Amongst them we find the athlete as finely marked to the waist as the Farnese Hercules. Such was the head and bust of the prize-fighter Molineux, of matchless strength, could he have properly trained

* For illustrative woodcut, see page 237.

himself for the fight. Below the waist the limbs
fell off, as they do in most Negroes. He was
reported to be a Congo black. Other races on
that coast show much intelligence and energy
in commercial transactions. Most dark races
are without any ear for music, yet the Negro
seems to have some sensibilities on this point.
He is certainly at least equal to the Dutchman,
and perhaps to the very best of the Saxon race.
But the grand qualities which distinguish man
from the animal — the generalizing powers of
pure reason—the love of perfectibility—the desire
to know the unknown—and, last and greatest, the
ability to observe new phenomena and new
relations; these mental faculties are deficient, or
seem to be so, in all dark races. But, if it be
so, how can they become civilized? What hopes
for their progress? Like all other races, they
have a religion of their own: it is Fetichism.

Were they, the dark races of men, the original
inhabitants of the globe? Were they the races
which preceded ours, filling up the link in that
vast chain of life extending from the period when
first the materials of the globe were called into
form to the present day? And have these races
seen their day—passed through their determined
course and period, hastening on towards that
final exit when their remains must rank only as
the remains of beings that were, like the mam-

mals and birds of the past world, which now are
no longer to be found? Or will their stock be
replenished by the fair races, as Barton Smith
and others supposed—the Saxon being in process of time converted into the Red Indian; the
Anglo-Saxon into the Hindoo? the last descendants of the European, now flocking to Australia,
into the wretched, jet-black Tasmanian and Australian? These theories we may discuss hereafter; in the meantime, let us briefly consider an
important question—Can the fair races of man
become so acclimatized in tropical countries as
to resist the pestilential climate of such regions?
Can they become equal to labour; to till the
earth; to act as soldiers; as aborigines, in fact?
This important question will form the subject of
our next section.

COLONIZATION OF AFRICA.

SECTION VII.—*Extinction of the slave trade; future prospects of the African races. In the event of
the dark races of men being ultimately destroyed,
can the fair races cultivate or inhabit the tropical
regions of the earth? Can they occupy, as labourers
and citizens, the African and Syrian shores of the
Mediterranean?*

Long prior to the accurate researches of the
army statistician it was known to the well-informed

and educated in society, that the tropical regions
of the earth, generally speaking, were so inimical
to European life as to render it hopeless for any
European race to attempt the colonization of any
country, however valuable, however wealthy and
productive, if situated within the range of the
tract of the earth exposed to the influence of a
tropical sun. It was also known to them, not so
accurately, that other regions (as along the shores
of the Mediterranean, American, and African seas)
partook, sometimes largely, of this unhealthy
character, although not comprised within, but
adjoining, the tropical range; that tropical seas
were sufficiently healthy so long as the mariner
kept his vessel at a certain distance from the
shores; and, finally, that even in tropical countries, mountain tracts of great elevation were
healthy, and their climate compatible with European life. But, although these facts were generally known to the well-read and the educated,
it was not so with the great mass of the people,
whose ideas on this, as on most other points,
from want of a sound elementary and practical
education, are at all times miserably defective,
and not unfrequently totally erroneous: hence
originate such scenes as took place a few years
ago, when an adventurer induced a number of
persons to attempt a settlement in Poyais
(Central America), followed and preceded by

numerous other wretched occurrences, the fruits
of ignorance on the one hand, of deception on
the other.   The Texas is still advertised as a
charming, healthy country.   A very few years
ago it was attempted to cultivate Jamaica with
European or white labourers, in despite of all
previous experience!   I need say nothing of the
result, nor analyze the nonsense and falsehoods
told of the white labourers of Cuba !   It is known
to the experienced and educated that the bold
and active men engaged in voyages of discovery
have been unable, even sometimes for a few days,
to resist the deleterious effects of that perfectly
unknown and subtile agency which, like a plague,
so quickly destroys, that ships' crews, regiments,
nay, armies, have been swept off with a rapidity
equalling the plague itself.   The expedition to
the Congo, under Captain Tuckey, was one of
these; then followed that worst planned, worst
conducted of all voyages of discovery, the expedition to the Niger; the fate of the Royal African
Regiment, as it was called, on the western coast
of Africa, whilst there, gave evidence on a larger
scale; and, if more be wanted, the reader will
find in the " History of the Mortality of the
Troops in St. Domingo," and in the admirable
reports of Major Tulloch, an unanswerable proof
against the possibility of colonizing a tropical
country with European men.

Is it, then, that there exists a vast region of the earth, the richest in all respects, the most productive, which the European cannot colonize, cannot inhabit as a labourer of the earth, as a workman, as a mechanic? From which should he expel the coloured aboriginal races, he also must quit or cease to live?—which he requires to till with other hands? It would seem so; and all history proves it. This zone is the last refuge of the coloured man; like the primeval forests of these very regions, the densely wooded banks of the Amazon and the Oronoco, against which it would seem as if human efforts were of little or no avail, the swarthy Negro and kindred races, driven back, subdued, or reduced to slavery, continually recover their pristine vigour and numbers, rolling back the white invasion, forcing it into other channels, and compelling it to limit its aggressions to those quarters of the earth which Nature seems to have assigned it.

A limit, then, seems set to the aggressions of the fair races. If we are to hold India, it can only be as military masters lording it over a slave population. It is the same with Jamaica, Cuba, even Brazil, tropical Africa, Madagascar, the northern coasts of Australia, and all the islands of the Indian Ocean situated as Borneo, Sumatra, &c. An important question falls next to be discussed. Are there any regions adjoining the tropical ones—like Morocco, Algiers, Tunis, and Egypt, extra-tropical, at least in part—which may be colonized by a European race? On this question rests a circumstance of paramount importance to mankind.

When Scandinavia and Northern Germany overflowed, the Saxon race found an outlet in Central Germany and in Britain; their progress eastward was arrested by the Muscovite and the defeat of Charles XII.; southward and eastward they progressed to a certain extent against the Slavonian races, but never amalgamating. The German empire was the result of this mock union, sure to be broken in the course of time—time which strengthens races, but breaks down empires. Woe to the empire or nation composed of divers elements, of different races, and discordant principles! Let Ireland teach the incredulous.

The Saxon race or races (for this point has not yet been determined) nominally extended their power into Italy and Slavonia, sure to be forced back upon their original territory. They attempted to seize on Bohemia, and to convert it into a true Saxon territory, a "right Deutchsland," by the massacre of its Slavonian inhabitants; the contest was renewed the other day, and is sure to fall. France will interpose her power.—But to return.

Towards tho Rhino the Saxon early turned his steps, hoping to dispossess the Celt; here he failed altogether.   Britain remained: that he seized on, peopled and cultivated—the land, the richest land the sun shincs on.   Too narrow for the broad dissent which characterizes the Saxon mind, the Western world offered an outlet, more for his dissent than for his population, which required at the time no such escape.   At last, in Northern America, relieved by his own exertions from the bayonet of the furious Celt, and " fiery Hun," and brutal Muscovite—relieved, also, from the Norman government—of England, the pressure of the Three Estates—the Saxon found a place where unfettered he might display his real character—that is, the perfect democrat; the only race, perhaps, in the world, absolutely and by nature democratical.   This is the destiny of the Saxon race.

In the partition, then, of the globe, slowly effected by the hand of time, America fell to the lot of the Saxon: Asia must one day be Sarmatian.   Can Africa become Celtic?   That is now the question.   To the Celtic race naturally falls this fourth division of the globe.   Europe he cannot possess; that was tried by Napoleon— the result is known.   That the various plans adopted by the Celtic race of France for the colonization and annexation of Algeria to the

French republic are essentially vicious, there cannot bo a doubt. But with this I have nothing to do. They encountered there a bold and determined race of men—the mountaineer, the Arab; in courage and strength equalling any race on the earth. They wanted but knowledge to have again set at defiance, as they had often done before, the most powerful European armies. The journals who contrast our progress in India with that of the Celts in Africa, drawing conclusions unfavourable to them, do so in open violation of the plainest truths and facts. Their object must be to mislead, else why so systematically and habitually pervert the truth? Had India, or Australia, or Northern America, been peopled by Arabs and Mauritanians, our position in these countries might now have been widely different.

Shortly after the seizure of Algeria by France, it must have become evident that no amalgamation of the races was practicable: was not even desirable. It must have been evident that, to make Algeria French, it must be peopled and cultivated by Frenchmen, there being no slave population; no Hindoo; no Negro; no labouring class. It could not be held, then, as we do Hindostan or Jamaica. Who was to people the country? what race was to till the earth? This question is now and has been for some time

before the French Government. It is called a
question of acclimatation; for it has been supposed that in countries like Algeria, Lower
Egypt, Morocco, which are extra-tropical, the
fair races of men might with time become so
accustomed to the climate, or acclimatized, as
the phrase is, as thoroughly to occupy the territory. In Holland, for example, at Flushing
and Walcheren, and on the shores of the Scheldt,
the summer and autumnal season destroyed a
fine British army in a few months; the Bra-
banters in the meantime did not particularly
suffer. French troops stationed in these countries during the Empire suffered nearly as we
did; the natives themselves seemed to think the
country healthy enough, and were surprised at
our losses! Their immunity has been usually
ascribed to a long acclimatation; our destruction,
to the want of it.

It is not my intention to discuss here generally
this great question of acclimatation: I disbelieve
partly in its power, at least for many generations.
Let us consider merely Northern Africa, for on
the decision of this question must depend the
extension of the Celtic race into Africa: it is the
safety-valve of Europe; a successful colonization
of Algeria, or a war on the Rhine. The continental and insular Saxons, Russ, and Slavonian
(the other three great races) have their choice.

Give Northern Africa to France, to the Celtic
race: there is no avoiding the question; it is an
act of mere justice due to the race; but, as might
is right, the question will no doubt be decided by
the sword. Another affair in Morocco, and one
or two at the base of the Pyramids, will decide
the matter for a few centuries.

SECTION VIII.—*Northern Extra-tropical Africa.*

The nationalities of mankind, the results merely
of accidental and extraneous circumstances, of a
successful war under a great leader, of a geographical position, or of mere political intrigue,
have hitherto so masked the great question of
race, that to some of the most sagacious of
men its significance and overruling importance in
human affairs has appeared either entirely questionable, or, at the least, extremely problematical.
The invasion of Algeria by France, and its attempted occupation by that country as a colony
or a province, or an integral part of the empire,
was viewed in this country and throughout
Europe (I use the language of the press as inter-
preters of the feelings of the people and of the
wishes of their governments) as a wanton aggression on the part of the people called French, on
some of their peaceable neighbours, our allies,
the Dey of Algiers and Emperor of Morocco!

Their pretensions were declared extravagant and unjust. Why not remain contented with France, as we had been with England? What could they want with colonies? Was not France large enough? A few words in reply to these narrow views of would-be statesmen.

In viewing France as a nation, it was forgotten that she was peopled by a race of men, which, if not identical throughout, was more nearly so than, perhaps, any other on the globe. To the principle of nationality, that is, of political independence, she added the most glorious recollections of all times; from Brennus to Charles Martel, from Martel to Napoleon, she had never been beaten but by a world in arms. As a *nation*, then, though a nation be a mere accidental political assemblage of people—a human contrivance based on no assurance of perseverance, on no bond of nature, but on protocols and treaties, on the mockery of words called constitutions and laws of nations, made to bind the weak, to be broken by the strong—was it to be expected that France, all powerful, was to remain " cribbed up, cabined, and confined " within that territory which chance and the fate of war had assigned to her? Even as a nation! But when we take a higher view, when we remember that she represents a race the most warlike on the globe; that this race is not confined to France, but includes a portion

of Spain, of the Sardinian states, and Northern
Italy, of three-fourths of Ireland, of all Wales,
and a large portion of Scotland, of Lower Canada,
and even of a portion, perhaps, of Southern
Germany, then the *nationality* sinks into insignificance; the element of race becomes paramount; Nature takes the place of parchment;
and the Celtic race of men demand for their
inheritance a portion of the globe equal to their
energies, their numbers, their civilization, and
their courage.

But Northern Asia had been seized on by the
Sarmatian race; Southern Asia, or India, by the
Saxon-English, not, it is true, to hold as a colony,
but a mere military dependence; America, Australia, and a hundred oceanic islands were also
in the hands of the "men of commerce and of
peace;" the men of traffic, of manufacture, and
of ships; Anglo-Saxon or Holland-Saxon had
extended his race nearly over the world, losing,
it is true, his colonies nearly as fast as he acquired them, but peopling them with his race,
language, modes of thought, manner of civilization. To the Celtic race of France there remained
but Northern Africa—Africa to the north of the
equator. They had no alternative. Colonize
Africa or march to the Rhine; extend the race
into Italy or Germany, or colonize Algeria:
these were the alternatives left to France in 1830.

She adopted the latter, and on its ultimate result must depend the peace of Europe.

Let me now examine, then, with care, this great question, for such I esteem it—not whether Algeria can be made a mere colony of France, that is not the question. Can the Celtic Frenchman be acclimatized in Northern Africa, Algeria, Morocco, Tunis, Tripoli, Barca, Syrene, and Egypt, so that these countries may ultimately form an integral portion of the French empire? This is the question I mean here to discuss. Its importance will, I trust, excuse the details into which I shall be necessitated to enter.

The country of Algeria, as at first viewed by France, was deemed likely to prove an important acquisition to the empire. Its proximity to Old France; its Mediterranean coast line; its proximity to Morocco on one hand, and Tunis on the other; moreover, its extra-tropical position, seemed to combine in proving its political importance to France, and its capability of being colonized by European men of the French or Celtic race. But, after the lapse of some fifteen years or so, whilst the country of Algeria has been held by France; after being visited and reported on by scientific men of great eminence; after being ruled over by a man of abilities surpassed by few, Marshal Bugeaud, the great question remains still unsolved, or rather, I should say,

seems likely to be decided against France—
namely, is the climate of Algeria fitted or not
for the abode of the white races of men? Endeavours, no doubt, have been and will continue
to be made to show that the destructive climate
of Northern Africa depends more on accidental
circumstances than on its geographical position;
that a want of culture has rendered the climate
pestilential, destructive to the European. I for
one do not believe in this doctrine. It would be
consolatory to France to believe in its truth—
advantageous to Europe were it really true; all
this I admit. Let me examine the opposing
circumstances, for a knowledge of which I am
mainly indebted to M. Baudin. This is not
merely a medical question: it involves the abandonment of Algeria, and, as a consequence, I
think, the seizure of Italy, and a war on the
Rhine.

Abandon Algeria, says the *political* French
physician, obeying his own impulses or acting
on those which he conceives now influence his
employers; hold Algeria, and colonize it as soon
as possible, says the *social physician*, looking, no
doubt, as he thinks, towards the advancement of
his country. These terms are not mine: they
argue *two* conflicting parties, between whom *truth*
is sure to be sacrificed. To colonize Algeria by

Frenchmen, say some, is impossible; the acclima-
tization of Europeans, or, at least, of the natives
of France in Algeria, so as to withstand labour,
to become cultivators of the soil, labourers,
soldiers, and citizens, will never happen. To
effect all this perfectly, says another party, all
that is wanted is *time*.

Algeria is wholly extra-tropical; but a portion
of it is composed of plains, another part is mountainous. Of these two sections the plains are
unquestionably the most important. Prior to
the advent of the French, the climate of Algeria
was greatly extolled; but it must be admitted
that the scattered notices of travellers offered
no data from which any serviceable deductions
might be made. *The mortality* of the *civil European* population rates as follows; the figures are
taken from official documents:—

In 1842 .... 44·28 for 1000 inhabitants.
   1843 .... 44·20 do. do.
   1844 .... 44·60 do. do.
   1845 ... 45·50 do. do.
   1846 .... 44·72 do. do.

But according to M. Baudin, who probably
more nearly approaches the truth, the statement
ought to stand thus:—

In France, the mortality per 1000 is 23·6
In Algeria, the mortality per 1000 is 62·5

This mortality approaches the desperate condition of our ill-fated squadron on the western coast of Africa.

On the other hand, the Jewish *race* in Algeria show different results. Mortality as *races:*—

1844.

Jews............... 21·6 for 1000 inhabitants.
Mahometans . 32·4   do.   do.
Europeans .... 42·9   do.   do.

1845.

Jews............... 36·1 for 1000 inhabitants.
Mahometans . 40·8   do.   do.
Europeans .... 45·5   do.   do.

From 1839 to 1847 the average mortality of the Jewish race was 27·3 for every 1000 of the population of their race.

The mortality of European children born in Algeria, taking the period from birth to fifteen, is *four* times greater than in England.

The European population, then, of Algeria, *decreases* annually by seventeen per thousand. Let the statistician, then, add this seventeen to 4·9, the annual increase per 1000 in France, and he may then have some idea of the present sacrifice of human life in that prosperous colony; or, as stated by M. Daudin, whilst Ireland doubles her population in fifty years, precisely in the same period of time would the European population be swept from Algeria, but for the influx of emigrants.

The open country is more unhealthy than the towns, being the reverse of what happens in Europe. In 1843, thirty-eight Trappistes (monks, we presume, of the order of La Trappe) established themselves at Staoueli: eight died in the course of the year; and of 150 soldiers assigned as labourers to them, as a commutation of punishment (deserters, we presume), thirty-seven died; the remainder were attacked with the most serious disorders.

Marshal Bugeaud, whose views respecting the military colonization of Algeria formed the subject of much discussion in France, and even in England, when called on to defend the measures adopted by him, easily did so, by merely describing the deplorable condition of the civil population of the territory. Families were continually being reduced to hopeless destitution by the death of the father and of the sons equal to labour; women became prematurely old; orphans abounded everywhere, demanding the immediate interference of a Christian government! Such is M. Bugeaud's *official* statements, which none have ventured to gainsay. On these grounds he recommends the establishment, rather, of military colonies; and herein, no doubt, he was right. But a man of his energy and originality became,

of course, troublesome to the rotten dynasty of
Orleans, and he, I think, resigned, or was recalled
from the government of Algeria: a prince of the
dynasty, with a host of courtiers, was thought a
safer government for the colony.   Let us hope
that we have seen the end, at least, of this enor-
mity, as regards Algiers.   But France has much
to do before Algeria can become a portion of
the French empire, inhabited by able, healthy
Frenchmen: Will this ever happen?   Would it
not have been better to have imported a Negro
population as labourers?   In India we have the
Coolies and the labouring servile population of
Hindostan.   In Jamaica the Negroes.   In the
southern states of America our Saxon descendants employ the Negro; it is the same in Brazil,
Cuba, and all tropical countries.   In Morocco
and Peru it was precisely the same: the coloured
population alone could labour; the European was
unequal to it.

Dr. Lesneur, a military surgeon in the French
service, reports (10th of April, 1847) that, after
having raised expensive barracks and other military works at Foudouk, it was discovered that
man (Frenchmen) could not live there.   It was
the same at the camp of El Arich.   In 1844
every possible effort had been made to improve
the place; all that labour and genius could do
was done, without the smallest benefit.   In the

month of August two-thirds of the garrison were
in hospital.   Of twenty-five births there was not
a child alive six months thereafter.   The civilians
were in the most deplorable condition, and to
preserve a garrison there it seemed most advisable
not *to attempt acclimatation*, but to replace the
troops rapidly by others, so as to prevent the
deleterious influence of the climate taking full
effect.   So much for the acclimatation of French
troops at El Arich.

"At Mered, as at Mahelma," says Marshal
Bugeaud, " I was constrained to associate the
military colonists in pairs, in consequence of the
severity of the climate."

Dr. Boudin has no faith whatever in the theory
of acclimatation ; I was all my life, also, sceptical
on this point ; but Holland furnishes some curious
facts in favour of the theory of acclimatation, to
which I may afterwards return.

Neglecting less important details, the following
table will tend, perhaps, to clear away the delusion in respect of those charming countries, those
Mediterranean shores, around which centered the
civilization of the ancient world :—

ALGERIA.

Military.—1837.   100 deaths per 1000.
                1841.   108   „   „
                1840.   140   „   „

X

Civil.—1842.   44.28 deaths per 1000.

   1843.   44.20 „ „

   1844.   44.60 „ „

   1845.   44.50 „ „

   1846.   44.72 „ „

Although, for many reasons, I cannot venture to consider this important question decided, namely, the probability of the colonization of Algeria by Frenchmen (its abandonment is quite another question), I may yet venture to remark that, although England has not colonized India, and never can (she never even proposed so mad a scheme), she thinks not of abandoning it.

It may here be worth while considering for an instant if Algeria ever really was cultivated by European hands,—by the white races of men now or formerly existing in Europe. M. Boudin believes that it never in this sense was a colony of any European race. The Carthaginians may be said to have been in possession of Algeria as colonists and agriculturists, but still this is doubtful; not that they did not hold possession of the country, but that they were the *bonâ fide* cultivators of its soil. Even as soldiers they never seemed to me to have been numerous. The Carthaginian armies were recruited in Gaul, that is, in France. The victories of the Thrasmene Lake, of Cannæ, and a hundred others over the Romans were decided chiefly by the Celtic men of ancient

France. When driven back to Carthage, Hannibal could not induce the warlike French to
follow him into Africa; and then the Carthaginians were easily defeated at Zama, on their own
territory, when left to their own resources.

But admitting that the Carthaginians did exist
in Africa as cultivators of the soil, which is
extremely doubtful, wo must not forget the
difference of race. The ancient Carthaginians,
of whom we know so little positively, were an
Asiatic people—Phœnician, no doubt—allied to
tho Jews. Now the Jews stand their ground very
well in Algeria; in their race the births exceed
the deaths. *But they do not labour.*

General Cavaignac, whose name stands so prominently before the world at the present moment,
brought this question some years ago before his
Government:—

" Avant tout, il faudroit savoir jusqu'à quel
point l'Europeau peut se naturalizer en Algerie.
Jusque ici l'expérience est douteuse."—(General
Cavaignac, " De la Régence d'Alger," p. 152.)
" Above all, it is essential to know to what extent
the European can become naturalized in Algeria.
Hitherto experience is doubtful."

These important words, by a man of such
ability, should have roused France at once to a
sense of her position in respect of extra-tropical
Africa. Then was the time to have engaged the

Negro labourer; then was the time to have sent a
powerful armed force, accompanied by a large
trading community, up the Senegal, across the
mountain ridge, and seized on the valley of the
Niger and Central Africa; then was the time to
have invited the Saxon labourers from Northern
and Central Germany to have joined with them
in this great enterprise—the Saxon farmer, agriculturist, trader, manufacturer, each of whom
respectively is worth a hundred French Celts.
But France did not do this: she was cruelly
oppressed by a filthy dynasty, seeking merely
place and patronage for their flunky partisans.
The result is known. But the question still remains—Can extra-tropical Northern Africa be
colonized by the Celt; can he establish here an
African republic of Frenchmen?

There exist no historic proofs that Northern
Africa was ever colonized by European hands,
as agriculturists. This is M. Boudin's strong
expression, and I perfectly agree with him. The
researches of Messrs. Dureau, De Lamalle, and
Enfantin, seem equally to prove that the Roman
dominion over the cities of Northern Africa
amounted merely to a military occupation, much
as the French rule in Corsica; or, in other words,
that these cities were to Rome what those of
Corsica are at present to France; that is, cities
and a country inhabited by a race of men called

French citizens, but who, in fact, are not of the French or Celtic race. Verily, the history of the races of men must be rewritten from the beginning. Nothing is correctly known of the Corsican race; still less of the Sardinian; the remains, no doubt, of primitive races once inhabiting the shores and islands of a series of lakes now comprised in the Mediterranean Sea; primitive races, like the Basques, of whom so little is known, who yet may, in remote ages, have played a conspicuous figure on the globe, before Sahara was a desert, or the Atlantic a sea.

Thus it would appear that the Corsicans are called Frenchmen by law, as we call the Celtic Welsh, Irish, and Highland Scotch, Britons; citizens of Britain; and sometimes, which is most amusing, Englishmen! The same legal fiction extends to India, and to Caffraria, and to New Zealand. The Hindoos, then, are Englishmen, as the Corsicans are Frenchmen, and the Mauritanian inhabitants of Northern Africa were called Roman citizens! Human contrivances, to mystify, to job, to rob, to plunder. It is a portion of the organized hypocrisy which marks the statesman wherever he exists. France has never colonized Corsica, which remains in the hands of its primitive inhabitants; England has never colonized Ireland, three-fourths of which remains in the hands of its original Celtic inhabitants.

The manufactory of Roman citizens was an extremely profitable business for Rome; it became a trade, and a thriving one too. England has done a good deal of business in this way; it has a decided influence over the revenue. It is mentioned by Plutarch, * that the three hundred Roman citizens mentioned by Cato in Utica were *merchants*.

I have been greatly surprised to observe a statement by Messrs. Foley and Martin, in the *Gazette Médicale*. They ascribe to *pride* the dislike of the European to labour in a tropical country. Statements like these merit not the slightest notice; they are opposed to the most direct observation and experience. Admirable as is the climate of extra-tropical Southern Africa, I have some doubts as to the competency for severe field labour by the European, even there. I allude more particularly to the country extending from the Great Kei to the tropic. The country to the west and north of Natal is not healthy, and the banks of the rivers in and about Delagoa Bay are sickly places for Europeans. It appears to be the same in Northern Africa.

In England the mortality of children from birth to fifteen, is twenty-six per 1000. In Algeria it stands thus :—

* Quoted by M. Bondin.

In 1841 .... 63 deaths to 1000
    1842 .... 45 ,, ,,
    1843 .... 79 ,, ,,
    1844 .... 75 ,, ,,
    1845 .... 78 ,, ,,
    1846 .... 97 ,, ,,

For every twenty-two births there is one still-born, or dead birth.

France entertained, and perhaps still entertains, hopes that her armies in Algeria might in time become acclimatized; in these hopes the nation is almost sure to be disappointed. It is still a mere hypothesis, and the existing facts are all against it. Suggestions have been made to send thither the inhabitants of the South of France, which seems a reasonable enough proposal; but there still remains the question of race, which has its influence not merely in one climate but in all.

In 1843 the Prussian Government directed statistics to be made in respect of the numbers and condition of Posen, forming at this moment a portion of the Prussian territory, and no doubt considered in this country as a place inhabited by the loyal subjects of his Majesty the King of Prussia. But how stands the case? Posen is occupied by at least three races, who have not, nor ever will mingle with each other. These races are—

The Slavonian,
The German,
The Jew.

Now, the tables of disease for the three races
give the following results :—

For 1000 Slaves   ....   29 sick.
     1000 Germans   18   „
     1000 Jews   11   „

These are the leading facts, then, as to the
colonization of extra-tropical Northern Africa by
a European race of men, the Celtic race. Great
difficulties lie in the way, and none of them has
as yet been overcome. England, more fortunate
than France, holds India, lording it over a feeble
race; France encountered in Africa a deadly
climate and a brave and energetic race; *Arabes
indompti*—the unconquered Arab. Her proper
plan is to penetrate as fast as possible to the
mountainous districts of the country; her armies
should avoid labour. But an agricultural class is
wanted for Algeria; we shall see presently how
this may be remedied.

I incline, then, to the opinion that the dark
races may for many ages hold the tropical
regions; that many countries now in the military
occupation of the fair races may and will revert
to the dark; that it would be a better policy, perhaps, to teach them artificial wants and the habits
and usages of civilization. Commerce alone, I

think, can reach Central Africa; the Negro must
be taught the value of his labour. When this
happens, the slave-trade will of necessity cease.
Of other admirable regions adjoining the tropical
ones to the north and south I have my doubts,—
doubts as to the possibility of acclimatation by
the Saxon and Celtic races. We have seen that
Algeria, so wide of the tropic, is about to prove a
failure as a colony; the Arab race will become
extinct or retire to the desert and to Central
Africa; no *coloured* population is there to succeed
them. The French would do well, perhaps, to
encourage the immigration of Coolies or Negroes
as we do to the West Indies. The trade (a modified slave-trade) is free to all. Call them *appren-*
tices as we do; there is much in a name: or by
sending a force up the Senegal sufficient to
protect French commerce, the mountain range
dividing the sources of the Senegal from those of
the Niger, and shutting out the western territories
from Central Africa, the valley of the Niger and
the rich basin communicating, perhaps, by a port-
age of no great distance with the waters of the
White Nile, may thus be reached. A chain of
forts extending from the mouth of the Senegal to
the sources of the White Nile would put France,
and with her the Celtic race, in possession of a
country as rich as India; secure for her ultimately
the military possession of Algeria, Morocco, and

Tunis; enable the race to extend themselves, their language, their commerce, and civilization over a considerable portion of the globe; offer an escape, or safety-valve, as it is called, to Europe, by the employment of her restless, idle, warlike population; relieve Europe from a portion of the five hundred and forty thousand armed men who must be employed some way or other; extinguish the slave-trade, and secure for a season the peace of the world.

I here conclude this brief and hasty and imperfect sketch of the dark races. No one seems much to care for them. Their ultimate expulsion from all lands which the fair races can colonize seems almost certain. Within the tropic, climate comes to the rescue of those whom Nature made, and whom the white man strives to destroy; each race of white men after their own fashion: the Celt, by the sword; the Saxon, by conventions, treaties, parchment, law. The result is ever the same—the robbing the coloured races of their lands and liberty. Thirty years ago a military *rhazia*, composed of English soldiers, Dutch boors, and native Hottentots, devastated the beautiful territory of the Amakoso Kaffirs. We reached the banks of the Kei, and the country of the noble Hinsa, where wandered the " wilde" of Nature's creation. All must disappear shortly before the rude civilization of the Saxon boor—antelope and hippopotamus, giraffe and Kaffir.

I shall conclude with a single remark on the position of the copper-coloured race or races of Northern America, and on the *progress* the question of race has made since the delivery of my first course of lectures on the races of men.

When, some ten or fifteen years ago, I maintained publicly that neither the Saxon nor any other fair race transplanted into the American continent would during a historic period or era exhibit any important modifications in physical structure or psychological character, as a result of climatic influences or governmental—that is, conventional human arrangements (for all governments in church and state are merely accidental circumstances and human contrivances usually arranged for particular purposes)—my opinions were met by such observations as the following. I was told, for example, that the men of the United States already differed from their Anglo-Saxon, German-Saxon, and Celtic (for the Celtic race abounds in America) forefathers and brethren, physically and morally. My opinion then and now was that these assertions are devoid of all foundation, and are based on a surface view of society. This opinion I developed more fully in a course of lectures delivered before the Philosophical Society of Newcastle about five years

ago, in which I endeavoured to show that the
races had not altered by being transplanted to
another (the American) soil; that the Celtic race
had carried with it all its characteristics unaltered
and unalterable; that historians, journalists, and
mankind generally mistook the slight modifications impressed on form and character for permanent alterations in the organic forms of humanity,
fancying they saw in the civilized Celt or Saxon
a being totally different from the uncivilized one.
This is the delusion I have always combated;
and, although at first the doctrine met with almost
universal opposition, it makes its way with most
unexpected rapidity; judging, at least, from some
articles which have appeared lately in the daily
press.

In the brief reports of my lectures, at various
philosophic institutions, it will be found that the
amalgamation of races, in America or elsewhere,
had been distinctly denied by me for a period of
more than thirty years; and in my first course of
lectures, carrying the doctrine to the American
shores, I ventured to point out that, after many
ages, the Saxon, Celtic, Sarmatian or Russ, and
aboriginal or copper-coloured Indian, would
remain, and be found to be quite distinct; that
these *races*, transplanted to the New World, would
endeavour to carry out their destinies as they had
done, and were now engaged with, in the Old

World; and that *nationalities*, however strong, could never in the long run overcome the tendencies of race. An article which appeared lately in a leading London newspaper, on the future destinies of the races in America, is, as nearly as may be, a reprint of my views and ideas on all these great questions; but the editor has not shown his usual candour; for the reprint does not acknowledge the source whence the information was derived; and there is in the reprint the usual mystification of the compiler.

In my next lecture I proceed briefly to examine the history of the dominant races of men: the Celtic, (the Saxon has been already described:) the Slavonian, and the Sarmatian.

LECTURE VII.

HISTORY OF THE CELTIC RACE.

THE Lowlands of Scotland not offering me the opportunity of observing the Caledonian Celt on his native soil, I visited, in 1814, the mountainous tract of Caledonia proper, the Grampians and their valleys. It was here I first saw the true Celt: time nor circumstances have altered him from the remotest period. Here I first studied that character which I now know to be common to all the Celtic race, wherever found, give him what name you will — Frenchman, Irishman, Scottish Highlander, Welshman; under every circumstance he is precisely the same, unaltered and unalterable. Civilization but modifies, education effects little; his religious formula is the result of his race; his morals, actions, feelings, greatnesses, and littlenesses, flow distinctly and surely from his physical structure; that structure which seems not to have altered since the commencement of recorded time. Why should it alter? But this great and oft-debated question I have discussed when considering the history of the Coptic, Jewish, and Gipsy races. The fact is sufficient for us here, that climate, nor time, affect man, physically—morally. Let the history of the Gauls speak for itself.

From the remotest period of historical narrative —usually called history—the abode of the Celtic race was Gaul on this side the Alps—the present country called France. This was the country which Cæsar subdued and formed into a Roman province. But long prior to his time, the Celtic race had overflowed its barriers, crossing the Alps, peopling the north of Italy, and making permanent settlements there— the Gallia Cisalpina of Roman writers. They had sacked Rome; they had burst into Greece, and plundered the temple of Delphi. War and plunder, bloodshed and violence, in which the race delights, was their object. From Brennus to Napoleon, the war-cry of the Celtic race was, "To the Alps—to the Rhine!" This game, which still engages their whole attention, has now been played for nearly four thousand years. I do not blame them: I pretend not to censure any race: I merely state facts, either quite obvious or borne out by history. War is the game for which the Celt is made. Herein is the forte of his physical and moral character: in stature and weight, as a race, inferior to the Saxon; limbs muscular and vigorous; torso and arms seldom attaining any very large development—hence the extreme rarity of athletæ amongst the race; hands, broad; fingers, squared

at the points; step, elastic and springy; in muscular energy and rapidity of action, surpassing
all other European races. *Cæteris paribus*—that
is, weight for weight, age for age, stature for
stature — the strongest of men.   His natural
weapon is the sword, which he ought never to
have abandoned for any other.   Jealous on the
point of honour, his self-respect is extreme;
admitting of no practical jokes; an admirer of
beauty of colour, and beauty of form, and therefore a liberal patron of the fine arts.   Inventive,
imaginative, he leads the fashions all over the civilized world.   Most new inventions and discoveries
in the arts may be traced to him; they are then
appropriated by the Saxon race, who apply them
to useful purposes.   His taste is excellent, though
in no way equal to the Italian, and inferior, in
some respects, to the Slavonian and peninsular
races.   The musical ear of the race is tolerably good; in literature and science, they follow
method and order, and go up uniformly to a principle; in the ordinary affairs of life, they despise
order, economy, cleanliness; of to-morrow they
take no thought; regular labour—unremitting,
steady, uniform, productive labour—they hold in
absolute horror and contempt.   Irascible, warm-
hearted, full of deep sympathies, dreamers on the
past, uncertain, treacherous, gallant and brave.
They are not more courageous than other races,

but they are more warlike. Notwithstanding their
grievous defeat at Mont St. Jean, they are still the
dominant race of the earth. On two great occasions they have saved Europe and the Saxon race
from overwhelming destruction and worse than negro slavery ; twice have they stemmed the tide of
savage Asiatic despotism as it pressed on Europe,
threatening the final destruction of freedom :
Attila they defeated ; Charles Martel forced the
Crescent to retire for ever from the West ; the
time seems approaching when the Celtic race may
once more be called on to bring to the decision of
the sword the oft-renewed contest, the oft-debated
question; shall brute-force, represented by the
East, by Moscow, succeed in extinguishing in
Europe the political influence of the Celtic and
Saxon races? and will that influence blot out from
the map of the world all hopes of the future civilization of mankind ? A leading journal, whose
object seems of late to be the misrepresenting all
that is good in human motives and actions, speaks
of " the combination of Eastern against Western
Europe." Why mystify the question? By the
selfish conduct of the German population, the
apathy and timidity of the original Scandinavian
nations, the brutal, treacherous, and cowardly
Houses of Brandenburgh and Hapsburgh have been
allowed to butcher the noblest blood of ancient
Germany ; the Slavonian race has been outraged

Y

and insulted in Posen, Poland, and Bohemia, by
the selfish, commercial, grasping Saxon ; and, as
a consequence, the entire race has been thrown
into the hands of the Sarmatian or Muscovite.
Why mystify questions so plain as these, foreseen
and foretold years ago? But to return to the
Celtic race.

A despiser of the peaceful arts, of labour, of
order, and of the law, it is fortunate for mankind
that the Celtic race is, like the Saxon, broken up
into fragments. The great and leading family of
the race is in consolidated, united, all-powerful
France. The Gallic Celt is, if we may so say, the
leading clan. Next, in point of numbers, is the
Hibernian Celt; then the Cymbric, or Welsh;
and lastly, the Caledonian. In the New World
there are the Canadians, the Habitans—Celtic to
the core, as when they first left France. In the
free states of Northern America the Hibernian and
Scoto-Celt abound. Their numbers I do not know,
but their increase for a time is certain. Change of
government, change of climate, has not altered
them. Children of the mist, even in the clear
and broad sunshine of day, they dream of the
past: nature's antiquaries. As looking on the
darkening future, which they cannot, try not, to
scan, by the banks of the noble Shannon, or
listening to the wild roar of the ocean surf as
it breaks on the Gizna Briggs, washing the

Morochmore; or listlessly wandering by the dark
and stormy coast of Dornoch, gaunt famine behind
them, no hopes of to-morrow, cast loose from the
miserable patch he held from his ancestry, the
dreamy Celt, the seer of second sight, still clinging to the past, exclaims, at his parting moment
from the horrid land of his birth, " We'll maybe
return to Lochaber no more."

And why should you return, miserable and
wretched man, to the dark and filthy hovel you
never sought to purify? to the scanty patch of
ground on which you vegetated? Is this civilization? Was it for this that man was created?
Chroniclers of events blame your religion :* it is
your race. Why cling to the patch of ground
with such pertinacity? I will tell you : you have
no self-confidence, no innate courage, to meet the
forest or the desert; without a leader, you feel
that you are lost. It is not the land you value as
land, for you are the worst of agriculturists; but
on this spot you think you may rest and have
refuge. Now look at the self-confident Saxon:
the man of unbounded self-esteem; an enormous
boaster, but in a way different from your race.
Does he fear to quit the land of his birth? Not
in the least; he cares for it not one straw.
Landing in America, he becomes a real American

* Macaulay.

y 2

—a Kentuckian, a Virginian, a furious democrat.
In Oceanica he becomes a native Tasmanian,
Australian; in Southern Africa he calls himself an
Africaner.   Holland and England are nothing
to him; he has forgot for ever the land of his
forefathers, and, for a consideration, will fight to
the death with his own brethren. He has shaken off
the pressure of the Three Estates, the Church
and State incubus, and feels himself a free man.
Then comes out his real nature—his go-ahead
principles.   See how he plunges into the forest;
boldly ventures on the prairie; fears *no labour*—
that is the point; loves that which you most abhor
—profitable labour.   What is to him a patch of
ground?   All the earth he is prepared to cultivate, and to sell to the highest bidder, so that it
suits his purpose.   You cling together in towns
and hamlets; he, on the contrary, will not build
a house within sight of his neighbour's, if he can
avoid doing so.   With him all is order, wealth,
comfort; with you reign disorder, riot, destruction,
waste.   How tender are the feelings of the Celtic
woman—how soft and gentle is her nature!   Her
tears flow at every tale of distress: her children
are in rags.

On a subject so vast I must be extremely brief.
The Celtic race presents the two extremes of what
is called civilized man; in Paris we find the one;
in Ireland, at Skibbereen and Derrynane, the other.

Civilized man cannot sink lower than at Derrynane, but civilized man may, perhaps, proceed higher even than in Paris. But of this I am not quite sure. Beer-drinking, smoky London, with its vaults and gin-shops, its Vauxhalls and Cremornes, its single gay street, and splash of a short season, cannot be compared with Paris. As a race, the Celt has no literature, nor any printed books in his original language. Celtic Wales, Ireland, and Scotland, are profoundly ignorant. There never was any Celtic literature, nor science, nor arts: these the modern French Celt has borrowed from the Roman and Greek.

Of French literature I need say little; it is of the highest order, and, to a certain extent, peculiar to, or rather deeply influenced by, the race. Of their literature I may mention especially the epopée, which, though not peculiar to them, characterizes the race. The "Maid of Orleans," by Voltaire, "Hudibras," by Butler, "Don Quixote," by Cervantes, describe the characters of their respective races. The first, refined, witty, alarmingly sacrilegious and licentious, is a type of the mind of the race, when set free from the trammels and usages of common life. The second, by Butler, no less depicts the Saxon. Coarse, brutal, filthy, but pithy; practical, utilitarian, abounding with common sense, and with that pleasant and comfortable feeling which measures the worth of all things,

from a bishop's office to a bale of cotton, by its
value in money :

> " For what's the worth of anything,
> But as much money as 'twill bring."

Paris is the centre of the fashionable, the
civilized world ; always in advance, in literature, science, and the fine arts. Their Academy has no equal anywhere, and never had.
Even in ship building they transcend all other
races; but they cannot man them ; they are
no sailors.   In taste they can never sink to
the low level of the Saxon race, whom it is almost
impossible to maintain at even a respectable
standard.   Hence the efforts in Britain and elsewhere to educate, to found literary and philosophic societies, Mechanics' Institutes, Athenæums,
Polytechnic Institutions. All these will gradually
sink and disappear, to be replaced by others, in
their time again to give place to others; for in
their very constitution such institutions display
in its highest perfection the besetting evil tendency of the Saxon mind: division, disunion,
jobs.   No dozen men can agree to form a liberal
institution.   In London, forty distinct societies
do not supply the place of one Academy.   There
is no Polytechnic School in any Saxon kingdom ;
in Britain it would not be tolerated for a day.
Court, gentry, clergy of all denominations, would
combine to suppress it.   It is otherwise in Celtic

countries, where centralization and high education
are not so much dreaded; yet even there the Polytechnic School has frequently proved a source of
great anxiety to the government.

All over the world the Celtic race is, properly
speaking, Catholic, even when not Roman; for
France is thoroughly Roman Catholic; so is Ireland and Canada; in Wales and in Caledonia
they still hold their ground. The reformed Celts
have never joined the churches "as by law established." It is the Saxon who accepts of his
religion from the lawyers; the Celt will not.
Accordingly, the Welsh and Caledonian Celt
are strictly evangelical. All this display of true
faith seems not to be inconsistent, or at least is
not incompatible, with a laxity of morals which
would astonish the world, if fairly described.

The Celtic race has had in its hands more than
any other its own destinies. Chance placed at
their head the greatest of men that ever appeared
on earth. Him they sold and betrayed. Still their
power is terrible, and quite an overmatch for
any other single race. Nothing could prevent them
again marching to Moscow and Petersburgh,
were the contest to be merely between the two
races. By such a contest mankind would be
greatly benefited. Even as it is, France can no
longer be assailed by any foreign force. Paris is
fortified, and were the territory again polluted

by a foreign foe, the true republican flag would
be once more hoisted, sure to be pushed
forward to Berlin and Vienna, Moscow and
Petersburgh. The horrible degradation of the
Celtic population of Ireland may perhaps be best
judged of by this one fact: that they are not
aware of the existence of forty millions of *the
same race* within two days' sail of their shores!
Ignorance is a dreadful thing.

It is amongst Celtic nations that terrible con-
vulsions of necessity arise in respect of the property in land, arising from the erroneous nature
of the Celtic mind in respect of true liberty, freedom, equality; on all these points their ideas
are innately and inherently vicious.

No Saxon man admits, in his own mind, the
right of any individual on earth, be he who he
may, to appropriate to himself and to his family,
whether to the eldest or any other son, any portion of the earth's surface to the exclusion *in
perpetuo* of the rest of mankind; but, sensible that
the earth must be cultivated by some one, which
cultivation never can give any further right in
the soil than the value imparted to it by the
labour of the *ad vitam* occupant; treating it, in
fact, as any other goods or chattels, he makes it
liable for the debts of the occupant, and further
ordains that at his death it shall be sold to the
highest bidder, for the behoof of widow, children,

and creditors, if any; the ultimate object being
to restore the land to the community at large.
If it be otherwise in many parts of England, it is
because the government is not Saxon but Norman; that is, the government of a dynasty and
aristocracy antagonistic of the race. Were the
evil attaining any great magnitude it would revolutionize England. But to revolutionize is Celtic;
to reform, Saxon; and so, probably, with time,
feudality and primogeniture, the two greatest curses
that ever fell on man, may, at last, peaceably be
driven from this semi-Saxon country. Still, I have
some doubts of this. It is the last stronghold of
the Norman dynasty and their defenders; and
the question may yet, even in England, be
decided by the sword. It was introduced, no
doubt, into England chiefly by the Norman conquest, the greatest calamity that ever befel
England—perhaps, the human race.

Now, contrast these Saxon ideas with the
Celtic. From time immemorial the land belonged
to the chief; the clan was entitled to live on it,
it is true, but it did not in any shape belong to
them. By degrees, nearly all the soil of France
came into the possession of the crown and court,
the clergy, the high aristocracy. A nation without land, became, of course, a nation of slaves.
Then burst forth that mighty revolution which
shook the world, whose effects must endure for

ever. Court, clergy, and gentry, were swept into
the ocean. But did the Celt thereby put the land
question on a right footing? Not in the least.
He created merely another class of landed proprietors ; an immense body of men of matchless
ignorance and indolence, mostly sunk in hopeless
poverty. He abolished the law of primogeniture,
it is true, but he had not the soul to rise up to
the principle of abstract justice. Restore the
land to the community ! Put it up for sale to the
highest bidder! Divide the amount raised amongst
your heirs ! You have no more right to appropriate this piece of land to your family, to the
exclusion of the rest of the nation, than had the
ancient noblesse of France ! But you have no
individual self-reliance, and so you divide and
sub-divide, in the Irish cotter style, the bit patch
of land left you by your forefathers, until your
condition be scarcely superior to the hog who
shares it with you : to sell the land; to divide
the proceeds amongst the family ; to accept of
your share, and plunge boldly into the great
game of life, is a step you dare not take. It is
not that you are deficient in courage : no braver
race exists on the earth ; but you have no industry,
no self-esteem, no confidence in your individual
exertions.

ON THE PARIAH RACES OF FRANCE.

Scarcely any nation, certainly no great nation, can boast of such unity of race as France. She is, in fact, all but wholly Celtic: hence her strength and her weakness; her dangerous character in war; her helplessness in peace.

Yet even France has her outcasts—not to speak of Jews and Gipsies—outcast tribes of unknown races, scattered here and there throughout her vast territory.

In a work lately published, abounding with details, there is a full account of these races or remains of races, for they are now but vestiges: yet despite tho centralizing power of Louis XIV., the irresistible edicts of Napoleon in their favour, and the spread, to a certain extent, of liberal notions, lurking prejudices still exist against even these vestiges, which time itself may fail to efface.*

Physiologists and historians, statesmen and philanthropists, ecclesiastics of all denominations, generalizers of every shade, delight in speaking of the various European races of men as forming one great family. Like other great families, these races cannot be made to agree with each other. The closer, in fact, the pretended relationship may be, all the more are they disposed to quarrel

* Histoire des Races Mundites de la France et de l'Espagne. Par Francisque Michel. Paris: 1847.

and fight; to add to the confusion in this happy
family, they speak totally different languages,
which never approximate, but rather diverge;
they happen also to differ in religion, customs,
laws, manners, literature, art, science.   Nor is this
difference confined to the moral—it extends also
to their physical structure ; for countless centuries
has the bold, erect, bulky, fair-haired, blue-eyed
Scandinavian occupied the identical regions giving
shelter and place to the dark, black-haired,
diminutive Finn, the Lapp—the smallest of men
—the Esthonian, the Livonian, the Slavonian, the
yellow-bearded Muscovite; yet all these races
remain to the full as distinct as they were long
prior to the appearance of Cæsar on the Rhine.
To these self-obvious, but not the less curious facts,
the author, tho title of whose work we have quoted
above, adds others no less singular, no less worthy
of inquiry.   He shows that nationality, a thing
conventional no doubt in itself, but of great importance in human affairs—nationality, so doated
on by most men, so easily understood, the war-cry
of crafty politicians, dynasties, and serfs—Michel
shows that even nationality, though wielded by
the most gigantic grasp the world ever witnessed, failed to extinguish in compact, national
France, the hatred, the antipathies, the dislike of
race to race.   There is, there can be, nothing
more wonderful in human history than this dislike

of race to race: always known and admitted to
exist, it has only of late assumed a threatening
shape. Analyze the late revolutions of Europe,
and you will find that in the first of the great
struggles which must successively arise before the
final emancipation of Europe from the tyrannic
dynasties which now oppress, crush, and destroy
the fairest portion of mankind, the question of
race saved the dynasties for a time; the old war-
cry of nationality was raised by the two contending powers, sure to terminate in favour of the
dynasty.

In this war of race against race, France stands
pre-eminent; whilst shouting "Egalité, Fraternité!" he violently extruded from his land a few
hard-working English labourers: this was his
first act, his first practical demonstration of his
notions of egalité and fraternité: his common
sense, his sense of common justice to men, his
education, his religion, all, all are arrayed in vain
against the innate dislike of race to race.

It appears that, for at least ten centuries, there
have lived in various parts of France and Spain,
a few families, called by a variety of names, but
most generally Cagots, detested and despised by
the surrounding population. To ascertain the origin
of this name—the race of people to whom it has
been applied—if to one or to several—and the
reasons of their exclusion from the pale of society,

whether by reason of physical or moral leprosy—
forms the subject of M. Michel's inquiries. It has
become one of considerable difficulty, for, in course
of time, documents become scarce and rare; rare
as to the Cagots of the south of France, and to the
Caqueux of Brittany; still rarer as to the Cagots
or Colliberti, of Annis and of Bas-Poitou. The
notices are confined, indeed, to two valuable but
very short passages in Pierre de Maillezais—that
is, until the time of M. Dufon. Maillezais'
notice dates as far back as the eleventh century.
He says that the Cagots of Maillezais were the
remains of a body of Scythians, who entered
France with the king of the Alani.

As usual, there are twenty other opinions concerning these Colliberti.

To what race of men was the term *Collibert*
applied?—this is precisely the question. Plautus
uses the term, meaning by it an enfranchised
slave set at liberty with another. But in Celtic,
col means 'to serve,' and *ber* means 'man:' so, in
Celtic, Collibertus might mean a slave. So much
for the derivations of words.

At this period the natives of France were the
most abject of slaves, bought and sold precisely
as cattle. The same was the case in Merry
England.

And thus, although it be not improbable that
the Colliberti now spoken of may be after all but

the refugees who fled with Charlemagne from
Spain after the affair of Roncesvalles, still nothing
of all this has been proved. They live still
amongst the waters in barges; they are fishermen,
and keep aloof, and are still somewhat distinct
from the adjoining population.

The antiquarian speaks more confidently of the
Chretins of Majorca. They were simply Jews;
and, although they professed Catholicism, their
scuffles with the Inquisition were annual. Their
history, whilst in the hands of the Inquisition,
makes the blood run cold, and shows clearly that
certain races possess demoniacal feelings, which
they will always exhibit when they can.

By a decree of Charles III., in 1782, they were
emancipated; but the tyranny of the mob prevailed in shutting them out of all offices and
honours, even so late as the close of the century.
It was an Irish affair: English justice to Ireland.

Of the origin of the Cagots, or Vaqueros, of the
Asturias, nothing is known for certain. They are
shepherds, inhabiting the slopes of the mountains
of the Asturias. By the Asturians they are
despised; the Vaqueros repay this with defiance
and hatred. Intermarriages, therefore, seldom
occur, and hence the Vaqueros are thrown on
their own population. Rome profits by this, and
dispensations are frequent. A portion of the

village church is still railed off to separate them
from the Asturians—the orthodox and legal faithful!

The Marons of Auvergne are a repudiated
caste — pariahs. Our great dramatist says,
" What's in a name?" But a name is everything.
" Give a dog——" we need not add the rest;
Marons they are called—come from where it will:
the negroes at Jamaica, who revolted to secure
their liberty, were called Maroons; so were the
rayahs of Auvergne.

The Moors are said to have escaped from Spain
during the terrible time of Philip III.: but if this
were so, nothing can be so easy as to determine
the point; for if the Marons of Auvergne are of
the Moorish race, the blood will show itself for
ever; it is curious to see the historian, the anti-
quary, the statesman, beat about the bush in a
matter of this kind.

The Spanish monarch—not imbecile, but wholly
wrong—resolved that Spain should be of one race.
The excuse set forth was that she should be of one
religion, but the real question was that they
should be of one race: this was the whole affair.
Hence came the expulsion of the Moors—their
escape into France during the reign of Henri
Quatre, and then to Africa. France behaved
nobly; but it was Henry alone.

But for the clergy of France, the southern

regions of that country would have possessed at
this moment a vast Moorish population, superior
in all respects to the lazy, worthless Celt; an
active, energetic, industrious body of artizans.
But the clergy would not listen to it; and so the
noble and gallant king was compelled to send the
refugees from Spain across to Tunis, and to Africa
generally.

Yet many must have remained—even some of
those whom Charles Martel defeated. There cannot be a doubt but that Moorish blood must
abound in Southern France. Hence the term
Marons applied, in all probability, to small
colonies of these Sarrazins. If still existing, they
will show the Moorish blood in their countenances,
their forms, their organization, their mental disposition. These never alter. Modified they may
be by time and circumstances, but they alter
not.

The imperfect inquiries, leading to scarcely
any solid result, on the preceding races, are
followed in the work I allude to, by others
equally unsuccessful, into the history of the Or-
seliens of the duchy of Bouillon; the Harel-
ponnais and Lyzelards; the inhabitants of Cour-
tisois and of Ricey; the Cacons of Paray; the
Jews of Gevaudan; the Saracen colony on the
banks of the Saone; a small people on the banks
of the Loire; the Thierachics; and the Celots of

Poictou,—all more or less hated and despised by
their Christian neighbour, the Catholic Celt.
Superior to the Celt in most points, (a cause, certainly, for the Celtic dislike,) they yet form a class
apart—even yet, so relentless is the implacable
hatred of the brutal mass, when stimulated, as in
most of the cases above, by a fanatical clergy, the
accursed instruments of debasing tyranny. In a
word, of all these peculiar castes, their origin,
their history, scarcely anything is known for
certain.

It is generally admitted that the songs and
poems of a country are calculated to throw light
on all inquiries into race; accordingly this has
not been neglected by M. Michel. He collates
and translates (for the *patois* of these songs of the
canaille require this) the popular songs and
poems in Bearnais, Gascon, Basque, Breton, composed by and against the Cagots. But whether
from a want of original material, or that such
never existed, the collection is scanty and unpro-
ductive of any results. France generally seems
early to have lost its Celtic language, Celtic
music, Celtic dress. All this seems to have happened long prior to Cæsar's time. Her music she
has never replaced; for it can scarcely be said
that at this moment she has a good national air,
song, or poem—a circumstance at once curious
and inexplicable.

LECTURE VIII.

WHO ARE THE GERMANS?

THIS question I put to myself many years ago, and I have since put it to many others, Germans as well as countrymen. It is not a question of mere curiosity; nor vast as is its political import and influence over the future destinies of Europe and of mankind, does this include all: even these, great as they are, yield in some measure to another bearing on European civilization. Whence comes the element of mind which created the so-called German literature; German science; German art; German metaphysics, and modes of thought? None of these are Scandinavian or Saxon; no one can imagine them to be of Saxon or Scandinavian growth: I should as soon expect to hear of a Dutch poet; a Swedish opera: a Platonist addressing the practical men of England and of Holland, and securing their attention to his address.

Five years ago, when I first delivered these lectures, I again put the question to the public, Who are the Germans? and, Where is Germany? By many of my audience the question was wholly misunderstood; by others it was thought para-

z 2

doxical; some thought it a pity to stir such questions.   But soon the question could not be
blinked; could not be concealed.   Within a
couple of years of the time I first placed the
question before the public, there suddenly arose
a cry of millions in central Europe; a cry of
liberty; liberty to the German race!   Now who
is this race?   Are they Scandinavians? that is,
Saxons.   Are they composed of two races com-
mingled—namely, Slavonian and Saxon? or are
they a third race, not yet described; not yet
understood; not even yet named?   One thing is
certain; for fully a hundred years have some forty
millions of people been in quest of a spot which
they might call Germany; a central spot; a unity
of race; a common flag; a political union; but
above all have they sought the solution of this
question—Who are the Germans, and where is
Germany?   And these forty millions have utterly
failed in making this out, unless we accept their
last solution, by means of a national song: that
"all are Germans who speak the German tongue,
and that Germany, Fatherland, is wherever the
German tongue is spoken:" and now I ask of
those who thought my views paradoxical, to answer the question in a straightforward way;
politically, geographically, ethnographically.

Before entering on a description of the two
great eastern races of Europe, the Slavonian and

Sarmatian, it seems right that at least an attempt
should be made to analyze the word *German:* to
ascertain to what race it of right belongs; and
whether or not we are to include in the same
category the thick-headed, pipe-clayed, and drilled
automatons of " Mon maitre le Roi de Prush ;"
the bold and free Holsteiner and Saxon; the
grasping accumulative Hollander; the versatile
and puerile Austrian; the manly Norwegian; the
Swede, inferior to none of his race; who, at
Lutzen, stood between the continental Saxon and
destruction, who saved Europe from the abhorred
despotism of Austria, heading the Slavonian race;
these are indeed the progenitors, not of all
Englishmen, but of *the men of England who are
of Saxon blood.* It was unquestionably a great
error in Dr. Arnold to confound under the common name of Teutonic, races so diverse as those
of whom I am now about to speak; no minds are
more distinct than the Saxon and the Celtic; the
Slavonian and the Sarmatian: they cannot be
classed together under the name of Teuton.
Does the German of South and Middle Germany,
the German properly so called, belong to any of
these races? are they a mixed race? or are they
a distinct race not yet described?

Mind is everything: the history of man is the
history of his mind. What is the quality of
mind which most distinguishes one race from

another; ono individual from another; man from
woman; the dark from the fair portion of mankind? It is the power of generalization; of abstract thought; of rising from detail to general
laws. There is a small knob of bone growing
upon the inner side of the arm-bone of man, in
most persons scarcely apparent. All the Saxon
nations on earth could not, in twenty centuries,
have explained the nature, the meaning of this
nodule of bone; perhaps might never even have
observed its presence. But from a race of men
in Central and Southern Germany, as the countries on the Upper Rhine and Danube are sometimes called, this, and a thousand other phenomena, inexplicable by the men of material
interests; the matter-of-fact men; the men of
detail; the Saxon men; these met with a full
and complete elucidation. They, the men of
South Germany, discovered, in fact, the transcendental theory of organic bodies—the greatest
discovery which has ever been made; not even
excepting that law of gravitation—that theory of
fluxions, a discovery shared with Newton by the
German, Leibnitz.

As early, then, as 1820-21, I became convinced
that the element of mind to which the German
owes his vast reputation as the most philosophical
of all men; the most abstract in reasoning; the
most metaphysical; the most original; and, in a

word, the most transcendental; the element of
mind which produced Kant, and Goethe, and Gall,
Leibnitz and Oken, Carus and Spix, and a thousand others whom I could easily name, is not,
cannot bo Saxon—cannot be Scandinavian. The
antique and primitive races who inhabited the
marshy forests of ancient Germany, the Lettes,
Esthonians, &c., are, it is said, still to bo found
by the shores of the Baltic, and extensively scattered through Prussia; but from such races nothing is to be expected. I have been assured by
observers, on whom I could depend, that whilst
travelling through a portion of the Black Forest,
there are still to be met with villages, whose
population exceed in coarseness and ugliness all
that can bo imagined; with enormous hands and
feet, and an expression indicative of the lowest
intellectual qualities. To these primitive people,
who, no doubt, occupied all the so-called German
territory before tho advent of the Northern Scandinavian and the Southern and Eastern Slavonian, who plundered them of their lands, driving
them before them into desert and woody marshes,
and who still exist in the peasantry of some
portions of Flanders, no one, I imagine, will conjecture that modern Germany owes any of its
genius, any of its intelligence. But the Northern
German or Scandinavian is not inventive; has no
genius for the abstract ; no love for metaphysical

speculation; cares not one straw for the transcendental; is the sceptic of nature's own making
—a reasoning man, who tests all things, even
his religious faith, by his reason: to such a
person, and to such a race, who will pretend to
trace the diablerie of Germany? the craniology
of Gall? the homœopathy, the hydropathy of
the same country? It is not, then, to the classic
German of Livy and of Tacitus, that we can trace
this element of mind? the fair-haired, large-
bodied, blue-eyed classic German, is now exactly
what he was two thousand years ago; he is the
Saxon or North German, and occupies nearly
the same ground he did when, crossing the Rhine,
he was routed by Cæsar, who chased the Saxon
Boor with his Vaans and Parde Vaans back again
across the Rhine: there they are to this day, no
doubt, unaltered and unalterable. But Central
Germany furnishes another race; a darker, and a
differently shaped race. Whence come they?
To them, and to the pure Slavonians, belong
German literature, science, and art. Two hypotheses offer an explanation—the first, perhaps,
the true one.

1st. Intercalated between the true Northern
German or Saxon and the Slavonian race of the
Danube, intermingling deeply in Prussia with
the Pruss, the Sarmatian and the Slavonian, and
especially the Saxon, a seemingly distinct race

extends itself towards Flanders, mingling with the
Flamand; to the South and East it encountered
very early the Slavonian, who seized Bohemia, the
Grand Duchy of Posen, and Poland, advanced into
Finland, driving back, on one hand, the Sarmatian,
on the other, the Saxon. This race called themselves Germans, and came in time to be mistaken
for the classic German of Livy and Tacitus. That
the greater part of this German race, so called,
are not Saxon, may easily be shown from their
physical and moral nature. They assisted the
Houses of Hapsburgh and Brandenburgh in all
their efforts to crush the liberties of the true
German: they are Catholic, which no Saxon, no
true German, ever is; they opposed Gustavus
and his bold Swedes; they fought under Walles-
tein; Austrians is their proper name, not Germans. The literary world cannot, I think, but
soon be disabused as to the true nature of the
Middle and South German; that is, if he be a
pure and original race, which I long doubted,
giving a preference to the next hypothesis.

2nd. As the modern German bears no resemblance in mind or body to the pure Saxon
German of Northern Europe, differing in features,
in feelings, in thoughts, and actions, it has been
surmised that such differences may be explained
on the hypothesis of his being a mixed race;
composed partly of Saxons, partly of Slavonians,

in as it might be nearly equal proportions; at the
sources of the Danube and adjoining countries, the
Elbe included, or on the banks of the Rhine and
its tributary streams from the east and north, the
two races met: the result was the modern German,
unlike either, but most unlike the Saxon. I have
just been favoured with a third hypothesis by a
distinguished German scholar, himself a good
specimen of this contested race. The modern
Germans, always meaning the Germans of Middle
and South Germany, are, according to his view,
a mixed race, composed of Celts and Saxons.

Now, of all the hypotheses offered, this is the
least tenable, for the race I speak of have none
of the qualities of their supposed parentage. If
we must view them as a mixed race, it is clearly
to the Slavonian and Saxon we must look; or to
the Slavonian, mingled with an unknown and
undescribed race. But against such theories,
admitting the strong admixture of Slavonian
blood with the Austrians, and all the so-called
South Germans, great physiological laws are
opposed. No mixed races can, or ever did,
exist for any length of time. The race seems to
me an original race; the people whom the
Romans called Goths; who overthrew the Roman
empire; who lived in Austria, and in the Danubian provinces, before Rome was founded, and
who live there still; who have for four or five

centuries been endeavouring to persuade the
world that they are of Saxon origin; Scandinavians, in fact; who dislike their Slavonian
affiliations; who stand, and always have stood,
on middle ground between two races, of greater
energies and larger numbers: the race to whom
I shall feel disposed to think Germany owes all its
intellectual superiority over the rest of mankind.

But, be this as it may, the architecture called
Gothic belongs to them; to them and to the
Slavonians belong the waltz and the polka, and,
perhaps, the Mazourka; the music of Bohemia,
soft and enchanting: they produced the Mozarts
and Beethovens, and many others. They divide
with the Slavonians the taste and genius of
Germany. No native Pruss has ever been found
fit for anything. They were described by Voltaire. But when the prince of critics lived—the
founder of philosophic history — the modern
German race had scarcely shown themselves.
The brutalizing wars of the Imperialists and
Pruss seem to have crushed the intellects of both
races, Slavonian and South German. The philosophic mind shrank from contact with Spandau
and Schoenbrunn, Potsdam and Ulm. Over Italy
the leaden sceptre of Hapsburgh, the lineal and
literal descendant of the Danubian Goth, waved
ominously for man. Thus were crushed for centuries the most gifted of mankind. Then came

the career of the mighty Napoleon, who first struck down these abhorred dynasties, showing their intrinsic weakness and rottenness. That they ever recovered was simply due to England. Next came the war of race, which must continue whilst race exists, and war confined to no particular region, but extended over the earth. It has been sometimes called a war for conscience' sake—a religious war; at other times it blushes not to own its commercial character and origin; and at times the cross has been raised, and the extermination of the heathen loudly demanded. But after all, the basis is difference in race, that key-stone to all human actions and human destinies.

It seems to me, that in claiming for the German so many works of merit, the illustrious Quetelet has not drawn a clear distinction,—I had almost said, has failed to observe, that Scandinavian or true German, that is, the classic German of antiquity, has no pretensions whatever to the literature he has assigned to the people he calls German; that the whole of it is either South German or Slavonian. The same error runs through most modern writers, such as Morrell. The Scandinavian German who rallied around Gustavus at Lutzen, is a noble race; a protestant; Nature's democrat: the only free race in the world, as proved by the greatest colony ever founded—

the United States of America; but he is not philosophic nor is he transcendental. There is the less
occasion then for ascribing to them qualities they
never possessed. That much of these high qualities of mind, the appanage of the Middle and
South German, is derived from their contact, and
possibly, admixture, with the Slavonian, I am
willing to concede; at one time I felt inclined to
ascribe it wholly to the Slavonian, and did so in
several courses of lectures. But a matured reflection compels me to leave the question still open.

Defeated in their last great effort, extending
from Baden to Vienna, the fate of the German
people or race I now speak of is uncertain.
In their last struggle, the best Scandinavian
blood stood aloof; no Gustavus appeared to lead
them to victory; no such person, perhaps, ever
belonged to their race. They sing songs when
they should fight; these pretended Germans are
not Saxons. Saxons, no doubt, abound amongst
them, but the mass is not of that race. To the hypothesis, that the modern German is a hybrid between the Celt and Saxon, I reply, first, that there
are no hybrid races; and, secondly, the accidental
mixture of Celt and Saxon produces, for a time,
a body of people of uncertain character, inde-
finable; they are occasionally to be met with on
the eastern coasts of Scotland and of Ireland, and
they may be found, no doubt, in great abundance

in the great manufacturing towns of England,
Scotland, and Ireland.   They die out of course,
or return to the pure races; but this I will say,
that in no instance have I ever observed them to
bear any resemblance to the modern Middle and
South German.

LECTURE IX.

THE SLAVONIAN RACE.

HISTORIANS, the chroniclers of occurrences and
events, of the ups and downs, the rise and fall of the
political unions called nations, have not failed to
record and to present to mankind as " philosophy
teaching by examples," how the kingdom of Poland
was once a kingdom of some consideration ; how
the monarchy was elective ; how there was also
a kingdom of Bohemia, forming a part of the
German (!) empire ; how, somehow or other, the
German empire quarrelled with those Bohemians,
and although both people were thoroughly Christian, orthodox, and up to the mark ; Bohemia
forming also a part and parcel of the great and
united empire of Germany, the said German emperor not only quarrelled with these Germans (!)
born in Bohemia, but filled the country with human
cut-throats, utterly to exterminate these Bohemians ; how they failed, notwithstanding, in doing
so, Bohemia being still in the hands of these same
Bohemians ; how the said German empire changed
its name, acquiring that of Austrian; at first Gothic,
then holy Roman, then German, then Austrian: but

they have not told you that the whole of this was
a fraud, and an imposture; they have omitted or
misunderstood the essential facts of the history.
They have not told you that the true Germans
always rejected the head of this empire, refusing
to acknowledge him or it as their head; that the
political union was a jumble of heterogeneous
materials, ready to fall to pieces before an invading force; and that like every fraud on sense and
nature, the artificial and unnatural power would
cease to be. Accordingly, the Austrian empire
fell before a mere handful of men, who would no
longer submit to be the most wretched of all slaves;
the emperor fled from his palace; the sagacious and
far-seeing Metternich had no advice to give, no aid
to offer. He was the first to run: he, who for thirty
years had enjoyed the plunder of a most rich and
fertile territory, inhabited by more than thirty millions of industrious and most intelligent people;
he, when the hour of danger came, had not a friend
to strike a blow in his defence. Recovering from
their panic they were next overthrown by a handful of Hungarians: all but beaten out of Italy, and
finally rescued by the gold and bayonets of another
race; to endure, or be endured, for a short time
longer, and then to cease for ever.

I have for many years been observing with much
interest, and not without some admiration, the
skill with which the British press contrives to

elude the question, which, during the last two
years, has shook the world. When I predicted
some years ago the certain downfal of the Houses
of Hapsburgh and Brandenburgh, and the approaching conflict between dynasties and races,
I was told that the kingdom of Prussia was a
strong and united kingdom—consolidated: that
all distinction of race had long disappeared : that
it was the same with Austria: that these drum-
head governments were the very best in the world;
the people educated and happy; models, in short,
for the British people. But this profound ignorance of the actual state of Europe would now
seem to have been confined to Britain, and perhaps to France: the Slavonian and German
questions were perfectly well understood and
acted on by the various dynasties; especially
was it essential for the Houses of Hapsburgh
and Brandenburgh, to prevent the agitation of
these two questions—to break up these two, or,
rather as they may now be viewed, three races,
the Saxon or Northern German, the Southern
German, and the Slavonian : it served the views
of a fourth race—above all, the Sarmatian—a race
grasping at the possession of the ancient world.
In Britain, to suit the taste of the public, the
press, from the *Quarterly* to the ephemeral
daily journal, affected to wonder, how two or
three different races could not live peaceably

A A

under the same government; they forgot Ireland
and Canada—but it did not matter; and they
reversed, in as far as regarded the Continental
nations, that term which they are fond of claiming
for themselves—namely, that a government is
intended to serve the people, and not the people
the government.

Whilst looking at the map of Europe, some
twelve or fifteen years ago, and recalling, in as
far as I could, the narrative of a few centuries;
the causes assigned for triple and quadruple alliances, and their probable real causes—the osten-
sible reasons for wars and partitions of states,
the thought occurred to me, May not the question
of race explain some of these, to me otherwise
inexplicable, historical events? I said to myself,
who are the Slavonians, the Tzeks, the Huns?
What race occupies South Germany?   What
occasioned the thirty years' war in Bohemia?
What led Gustavus Adolphus into the centre of
Europe to head one portion of Germans against
the other?   It was in the course of this inquiry,
that I ascertained that a race of men, whose
history is still to write, of whom we know neither
their physical structure nor mental qualities, extends from the mouth of the Danube, occupying
both banks, but chiefly the southern, to the confines of Austria; that from thence, proceeding
northwards and eastwards, the same race, occa-

sionally modified by unknown causes, occupy the
whole of Bohemia, Poland, the wide plains of
Cracovia, the grand Duchy of Posen, a portion
of Lithuania, and of the southern shores of the
Baltic—and lastly, extending still further to the
north, they stretch into Scandinavia, peopling
Finland with a race whose origin, no doubt,
must be looked for in southern and eastern
Europe; a Danubian race—in western Europe
as in Prussia, mingling, but not uniting with the
Saxons and Southern German; in northern
Europe with the Sarmatian; in Hungary with
the Huns; in Turkey with the Greek and Tartar;
mingling, but never uniting; distinct from all
these races before history began—distinct now.
There are some who stickle for the fusion of races,
placing them in a Utopian theory of progress:
let them try the question by the Slavonian race.
The Tzelks occupied, beyond all question, the
same countries they do now, long before Rome
was founded—they are there now: assuming the
modern South German to be the Goths of Roman
writers, the Slavonians joined them in the overthrow of the Roman power: with some of the
Scandinavian tribes they formed the great mass
of barbarians who overthrew the Roman Empire;
they gave rise to the dark ages, and it is not the
fault of the House of Hapsburgh that these happy
ages, the paradise of churchmen and barons, were

not made permanent. " I want good men, not
great men," was the reply of Ferdinand to Scarpa,
when the gifted Italian had shown this imbecile
Goth how the reign of the Goths in Italy had
destroyed the intellectual character of the Italian
Peninsula, reducing all to miserable mediocrity
or coarse brutality.   The sticklers for the amalgamation of races had better try the question in
Posen, or Finland, or Prussia, or Austria; in
what number of centuries do they look for such
an event? The position of the Slavonian has
been known for fifteen centuries, and may be
guessed at for fifteen more, yet we have no visible
signs of amalgamation, nor any explanation of the
fact, unless by the falsifying of historic facts.

Little seems to me to be known of this noble
race, the most intellectual, probably, of all. They
are said to be remarkably deficient in elegance of
form; external beauty does not belong to them,
according to some; they are short in stature, with
dark hair and complexion—cheerful in disposition
and fond of pleasure.   Superior to the Saxon and
Celtic races in their taste for music, architecture,
and the fine arts, generally—above all gifted with
high feelings, leading them to view Nature's laws
abstractedly, and to see in her operations principles imperceptible to others. The element of
mind which leads to transcendentalism is distinctly
Slavonian—at least, so it seems to me. Call it

also German if you will, it is not Saxon—not
Scandinavian. The rationalism of Strauss belongs
to no Scandinavian; Oken was not a Saxon; nor
Spix; nor Von Martius: Bathyani and Kossuth are
not Germans: De Haen was a court physician in
Vienna about a century ago; he wrote on magic!
the author of the Philosophy of History, published
but lately, sees evil agencies everywhere at work;
the Diablerie of Faust is evidently of Slavonian
origin, or at least South German, whose relation to
the Slavonian is close and intimate—affiliated races
not yet understood. In the desire to get at first
principles, they overlook *manifestations;* these with
their external forms, whether organic or not, are of
but little moment: it is the essence, the principle,
they aim at. With them originated the transcendental philosophy, claimed in part I believe, by
the *South German.* I pretend not to dispute this
claim, having no data to guide my opinion. In
my younger days I was taught, as most have
been, no doubt, that the Caucasian family was
one—the Caucasian *nations*, of one race, of one
mind therefore; this, I think, is a fair deduction
from the premises. Now try this simple statement by an appeal to fact; explain the transcendental theory of organic life, the metaphysics of
Fichte, Schelling, Hagel, to a Saxon audience;
English, Dutch, North German, Swede—show them
the nodule of bone I spoke of to you, found on the

arm bone of man, and ask them the meaning, the
signification of it—ask them the signification of
the limbs—the meaning, that is the reason, why
two small additional bones are found occasionally
attached to the upper part of the breast bone; the
signification of two small folds of membrane traversing loosely the knee joint in man, and be
assured that the mechanical race who will have a
mechanical reason for all things, an intelligible
utility, that is a utility intelligible to them—be
assured that the race will reply, as has been done
for them from Derham to Paley, from Paley to
Charles Bell, "all these structures have a reference to animal mechanics —their mechanical
utility is obvious, and for that were they created."
Confounding the pure high-minded spiritual doctrine of the Slavonian with their Celtic modifications: mistaking their parentage, and fancying
them French, a cry is raised that the doctrines
are material(!) and sceptical, being French; but
this great question, the results on philosophy
by the introduction of the Slavonian element of
mind into civilized Europe, I must not discuss
here, although appropriate, until I shall have com-
pleted this brief sketch of the Slavonian race,
together with a still briefer one of the Sarmatian.

The future destiny of the Slavonian race is, if
possible, more problematical than any other. Like

the continental Saxon, they want a leader. About eighty millions in number, they groan under the despotisms of three dynasties or families—Haps-burgh, Brandenburgh, and the Muscovite. Part belong to the Mahomedan of Turkey, with whom it would seem that honour and humanity, and common sense, driven from civilized (!) Europe, are about to make their last stand. They want a leader. It would seem that the Ban Jellachich is their hereditary chief, but he let the golden opportunity slip through his fingers—betrayed, no doubt, by the court of Vienna. Still the Slavo-nians demand a political unity—the South Ger man does the same; the North German or Scandinavian despises them both, but he also would fain be free. For union he cares nothing: it is liberty the Saxon aims at, that liberty which originally belonged to him, and to him only. They desire to shake off dynasties, which, of all races, they most abhor—to establish republics—united states, peopled not by slaves, but by free men. Liberty of conscience and of action—equality before the law—the reign of the law instead of the reign of a dynasty. The North German or Scandinavian race, then, may some day be free as they once were, but still it is doubtful. The Pruss, so admirably described by Voltaire, extinguished freedom but lately in Saxony and on the Rhine; the war of 1815

blotted the republic of Holland from the map of
Europe; the best blood of the race, that is, the
Swede and the Dane, and Norwegian, is over-
awed by Russia; the Western Saxons of Prussia,
and the smaller states of the Rhine, could not
resist for a day the combined attack of Sarmatian
and Slavonian, led on by their respective dynasties.
England, half Saxon, wholly commercial England,
fancies she has a direct interest in the perpetuation of these iron dynasties of Europe. But, of
the Slavonian race, it would be difficult to conjecture the future.   Not so, I think, of the people
called German, that is, South German, Austrian,
&c.; surrounded by those purer races, their chance
of independence is small; they may, assisted by the
Slavonian, have founded the Gothic empire—this
I pretend not to question—but neither they nor
the Goths, whom Jornandes traced from, instead
of to Scandinavia, ever were Saxons.   Thus, I
reply to Arnold and to Prichard; to the amalgamation theorists; to the progressists, the edu-
cationalists of all denominations. I ask them to
look again at Central Europe, its state in 1815,
its condition now. The Slavonian wants a leader;
so does the South German; so does the true
Saxon or North German. They are quite sensible that at present, though broken into fragments,
the day may come when nature must again assert

her rights in despite of treaties and protocols, partitions and adjustments. The balance of power
in Europe must ultimately rest, not with families,
but with races: the question of European civilization must repose on the same basis.

362

LECTURE X.

OF THE SARMATIAN RACE.

THE Muscovite power, which at this moment
threatens the destruction of human liberty in
Europe and in Asia, is, as it were, of yesterday.
To the dominant race of this political dynasty,
for it rules numerous other races, to be described
hereafter, I have ventured to give the name of
Sarmatian, instead of Russ or Muscovite; by this
I mean not to trace their history to the ancient
Sarmates, but merely to designate thereby a race of
men clearly distinct from all others, in physical
structure and moral character. Whether they
are, or are not, the lineal descendants of those

[*Modern Greek and Russian Profiles contrasted with
each other.*]

who, crossing the Euxine, attempted to seize
on Byzantium during the decline of the Eastern
Empire, I leave to others to determine. One
thing is certain, I think, the element of mind
peculiar to them did not show itself in Europe
until very lately. Christianity they modelled like
the other races, to suit their physical and moral
nature; the Greek formula of religion was that
they adopted: as the Celt and Slavonian adhered
to Romanism, and the Saxon nations, so soon as
they dared do so, threw off the yoke of Romanism
with its hideous mummeries, reducing their religion to a formula sanctioned by their reason; a
protesting utilitarian race, averse to extremes, and
fond of common sense; so the plastic robe was
easily moulded into these three great forms, or
adaptations, suited to the moral and physical
structure of the European races.

We know nothing of the origin of the Sarma-
tians, nor of any other race. Aided by the course
of events, and the gradual extinction of the Mongol, (a race evidently becoming decayed, and
ultimately, perhaps, extinct,) they hold the great
Steppes of Asia—a large portion of Europe. The
Mongol held them in cruel slavery for nearly two
hundred and fifty years, traces of which may
still be seen in their institutions; they have now
enslaved the Mongol; China and Thibet are at
their mercy when they choose to subjugate them;

a single rail-road will do it; and with that rail,
our power in Indostan ceases.

The struggle between the Muscovite and Saxon
was soon over; it was decided at Pultowa; the
contest with the Pruss may be said to have ended
also in his favour, the dynasty of Brandenburgh
being merely a tenant-at-will of the Muscovite.
If you desire to see his power over the Northern
Saxons or Scandinavians, attempt a constitutional
monarchy or republic in Sweden or Denmark, and
watch the result; he now aims at the Slavonian
—this is his best game—it leads to the gates of
Constantinople, and the possession of Greece.

Before Dr. Edward Clarke, of Cambridge, published his travels through some parts of Russia,
the real character of the Muscovite seems to have
been wholly misunderstood.   He is the true

[*Calmuck Woman.*]

Xanthous race, the dark skinned, yellow bearded
man : the *homo duri frontis ;* hollowed out face,
square shaped orbits, projecting brow and chin;
apathetic; torso without shape; tall, yet not
robust; strong, yet without energy. They are
described by Dr. Clarke as a nation without
principle ; liars all. But Clarke had a heated
imagination and a diseased brain, of which he
died, and so great allowances must be made for
him, and all his ideas must be viewed as over-
wrought; his colouring too high, his perception
of the frail side of the Sarmatian morbidly acute.

Retzius says, that the crania of the Russ and
Slavonian races are shorter than those of the
Saxon and Celtic: but this most distinguished
observer made but a few measurements. One
thing seems certain, they are admirable linguists,
profound dissemblers, and, as a consequence, good
statesmen and politicians. They have a language
peculiarly their own, a music also superior to
Celt or Saxon; without inventive genius they
are yet admirable imitators ; that is, living auto-
matic machines ; in progress of time they will
probably have an architecture and fine arts of
their own : for the present, they no doubt borrow these things from others. Stubborn, without
bravery, their quality as " food for powder" was
tested at Borodino; but they ran away from Napoleon and a handful of young conscripts at Lutzen

and Batzen—their emperor and staff being the
first to run.   But for the gold of the Ural and
Georgey, the Hungarians would have given Europe
a good account of Paschievitch and his savages.

Of the literature and science of a race to whom
free thought is denied, what can be said?   If
neither exists, it surely is not their fault.   Their
government has even attempted to falsify history,
imitating the Stuarts in this respect.   No fair race,
perhaps, were ever sunk so low in the scale of
humanity, and the morals often correspond to this
physical degradation.   Asia is their field into
which they should be driven.   The Turks are a
highly civilized race compared with the Russ—in
morals they cannot be compared.   A Turk's word
is sacred as his oath; of the value of that of
the Sarmatian and modern Greek I need not say

[*Russian Soldier, in the time of Paul: from
Clarke's Travels.*]

one word.   They are Christians it is true, and he
is Mahommedan, follower of a false light ; what a
pity it is that even Christianity, the everlasting
truth, cannot alter humanity—cannot alter race.

It was remarked to me by Dr. Roussell of Finland, that the Russ being the latest race to appear,
bade fair to become, in his turn, the dominant race:
that most races have had their day, and that the
tide was now with the Sarmatian.   What will the
progressists say to this ? More than four thousand
years ago, men were born of a race who carved
the Venus and the Apollo, wrote the Homeric
ballad—built the Parthenon.   Demosthenes dis-

[Venus.]

coursed in Athens; Thucydides, Euclid, Aristotle,
were persons who lived a very long time ago.
The people who listened to them understood them
perfectly; they were not, therefore, prodigies.   If
the Russ be the last development, human course
cannot be forward, but retrograde; it is a progress
backwards, tending towards some unknown goal.
Why not? we know nothing of Nature's plan;
the Russ may be her BEAU IDEAL—her highest

[*Apollo; the Greek Profile contrasted with the other
extreme of the fair races—the Russ.*]

and last development. The world, for countless
thousands of years, was inhabited only by fishes;
could they have spoken, and left us records, we
should have found, no doubt, that they considered
themselves as the most perfect of all Nature's
works, and the beings for whom the seas, at least,
if not the dry land, had been made. Then came
bears and hyænas, called antediluvian without the
shadow of proof—and they, no doubt, could they
have reasoned, would clearly have demonstrated,
not only their right to the earth, but that the
globe was made for them, and all that it contained, whether they made use of it or not.
Then came man, and he finds everything made
for his use—serpents, crocodiles, and hyænas
—very useful things in their way, and, beyond
all question, made exclusively and solely for
his profit and advantage : without serpents in
certain countries, mice would be troublesome;
and crocodiles and hyænas occasionally save
man the trouble and expense of funerals. The
Russ, after all, may be the highest developed as
he is the last. If obedience to "the powers that
be," truly form the greatest quality of the human
mind, then does the Russ stand as high as the
Saxon is low. I leave the question to the statesman and theologian.

LECTURE XI.

I WAS, I think, the first, or amongst the first, to
point out to the reading world the antagonism of
the present Norman government of England to
her presumed Saxon population. From " the
element of race," advocated by me as a leading
feature—*the leading feature* in human thoughts and
actions, the deduction was direct. No right-think-
ing person could avoid coming to the conclusion,
that, in the present dynasty and aristocracy of
Britain, the descendants of William and his Norman robbers had a perfect representative. What
the sword enabled him to do, the sham constitution
of England qualifies the present dynasty to attempt.
England is perfectly feudal: the results are not
quite so apparent, it is true, in a Saxon country, in
consequence of the energy of the race ; but in
Celtic Ireland, Scotland, and Wales, "the system"
has produced its full results. I was amongst the
first to point out that the land of Ireland, and of
Caledonian Scotland, was in the hands of the
hereditary descendants of the Norman ; and that

broad England itself was daily following in the
same steps: patronage, and corrupt influence,
and enormous wealth, effecting now what brute
violence and its armed followers accomplished in
former times.

I was in Sheffield when an agitation was attempted to be got up in favour of " financial reform." Some most esteemed friends advocated
this *unprincipled* (I do not use the word in the
common acceptation,) — *unprincipled* measure,
hoping great things from it. The opinions I gave
them were the same then as now; the same as I
held when the ludicrous Reform Bill came in
under " our Sailor King;" you " are entirely in
the hands of a Norman government—united,
wealthy, all-powerful; your Church is rampant,
Norman, and bloated with wealth—corrupt beyond imagination; your population priest-ridden.
*The land of England is not in your hands. Go at
the land in preference to every other measure.*"

And now it appears that these great and vital
truths, based on the simple fact—namely, the existence of a feudal Norman government, in semi-
Saxon England, antagonistic to the majority of
its inhabitants—is beginning to be understood by
all ranks; the expressions then used spread, and
are coming into daily use.

M. Guizot has written a work on the Causes
of the Success of the English Revolution; he

must mean " the failure :" for never was a failure
more complete. Church and State remain as they
were ; nay, they are worse than prior to 1088.
The military force at the disposal of the government for the crushing down and intimidating the
freemen of England is more effective, more insulated from the people, than in the most despotic
European state.   The wealth, patronage, and
power of the country, are concentrated in the
dynasty and its supporters.

In the so-called colonies, matters are still
worse : the sham is greater : the officials more in-
solent ; occasionally imbecile, at others insane.
The Smiths, the Wards, the Torringtons, the
O'Ferrals, carry out the views of the Norman
government of England in distant lands.

Had a statesman of Rome been told that a
small nation would one day arise on the confines
of Europe, secured by its insular position from
the rude grasp of continental tyrannies ; that
this nation, after founding the greatest colony
(North-American Union) the world ever saw,
should, through the folly and tyranny of its government, antagonistic of its race, aided by the
brutal ignorance and intolerable selfishness of its
own people, lose that colony for ever ; be driven
from it with ignominy, leaving in the minds of a
growing population of millions and millions a
rancorous and eternal hatred for the parent king-

dom; an abhorrence of her, and her rotten institutions; that statesman would have declared at
once, that no country could survive the shock of
such an event. Yet England has stood it.

All men love liberty, in one sense or another;
but all do not attach to the term the same ideas.
Each race interprets the expression differently. Four times, I think, within the memory of
man, has the Celtic race of men in France
achieved their absolute freedom — their entire
liberty to form whatever government they might
choose. Four times they have betrayed the hopes
of mankind. No trust can any longer be put in
them. Look at the Celtic man in Canada, Wales,
Scotland, United States, Paris—it is always the
same : he does not know the meaning of rational
liberty. Look at Paris, after a revolution the
most complete, the most successful, the most
daring the world ever beheld : the dynasties of
Europe, from St. James's to Moscow, struck
dumb; aware of their extreme danger, but afraid
to move; the very " *Times*" itself shrinking into
nothing with alarm and fear. Now visit Paris!
A fortified camp, espionage, police, gens-d'armes,
passports, all in full force : the reign of Napoleon
was a farce to this terrible mockery.

A rumour prevails at this moment that it is
intended to abate one of these alarming nuisances,
by abolishing the passport system. It may be so,

but I for one do not believe it. Come when it
will, it will take the whole race as much by surprise as it will do me. Even then, let it be
remembered, that it is not the act of the Celtic
French themselves, but of *a foreigner*. A Celtic
man, even the most furious democrat, cannot be
made to understand how the system of passports
is incompatible with human liberty.

Each race has its own ideas of liberty. There
is but *one race* whose ideas on this point are sound;
that race is the Saxon. He is the only real democrat on the earth, who combines obedience to the
law with liberty. But the law must be made by
himself, and not forced on him by another; hence
the successive revolutions in England to overturn
the Norman law and the Norman government;
hence the struggle now approaching, which will
not be the last.

If we now inquire into the history of the Anglo-
Saxon colonies, keeping in view the element of
race, we shall find that on quitting his native soil
the Saxon loses all respect for it. He is totally
devoid of the weakness called patriotism. His
adopted land becomes his fatherland. With the
first opportunity he shakes off the despotism of
England and sets up for himself: hence, in time,
England must lose all her colonies. It is a
singular event in history that she has not lost
Ireland; but that is no colony as yet: it is a

conquered country, where the Norman is in full
force, where he rules with the sword, and into
which Saxon laws were never introduced. The
occupant race is Celtic. Under a bold military
leader they might have driven out the Norman
ruler and recovered their freedom, for the English
are quite aware that Ireland is not a colony, but
merely a country held by force of arms, like
India; a country inhabited by another race.
They are aware, too, that, in point of fact, it is
merely a fief of the reigning dynasty and a few
of the *noblesse*; they would not, *for them*, support
a long and *unprofitable* war; so that Celtic Ireland
might have recovered her *nationality* by a single
well-fought action. But she could not have recovered *her liberty :* Rome was there, and O'Con-
nell, and a thousand influential haters of true
liberty. Allowing, which was probable enough,
that, carrying out the destinies of their race, after
driving the Norman oppressor from their soil,
young Ireland had risen, and, imitating their
brethren in France, they had pushed at the point
of the bayonet from out the soil of Ireland the
abhorred demagogue and his fiend-like church,
still, as a Celtic race, they must either have fallen
into the hands of a military leader, or relapsed
into a state of barbarism similar to the Caledonian
Celt prior to 1745.

All races of men equal to a social condition,

which in courtesy we may call civilization, will,
I think, obey *the law*, if made *by themselves*; law
and government are identical and nearly syno-
nymous terms. If in accordance with *their race*,
the law is obeyed cheerfully; the ruffian populace,
who do not constitute the people in any country,
but a turbulent section, were mercilessly shot
down on the streets by the mayor of New York,
and a handful of *citizens*, armed merely for the
occasion; it was an ominous event for the Norman and other dynasties of Europe, showing them
what the Saxon becomes when *the law* is of his own
making: a Saxon republic: unconquerable Holland, as a republic, might, with the aid of England,
have defied Europe, but for Napoleon; as a kingdom! even the Belgians beat her on her own
frontier.

If there be one feature more remarkable than
another in the history of the existing dynasties of
Europe, it is their general imbecility; the Norman
government of England is no exception to this.
Let us look at its policy with regard to her
colonies.

That Saxon men will on leaving England become furious democrats, I admit; nothing will
ever satisfy them but self-government. Adopting,
moreover, the land of selection for their own, *the
English* become Canadians, Americans, &c., as
the case may be; the Dutch assume the name of

Africaniers ; the English, Australians : always
Saxon, they view *nationality* as a thing of no
moment, unless it refer to the community of
which at the moment they happen to form a part.
Hence no government can long hold a *Saxon*
colony, do what it will, because their insolence
and demands will always rise with their numbers
and wealth.

But this great lesson, taught the Norman
government of England by the American revolution, was lost on the dynasty ; and they pursue,
true to their nature, the same course with respect
to the few *real colonies* England yet has : Canada,
tho Cape, Australia, Tasmania ; the rest scarcely
merit notice, as yet : India is merely a conquered
territory. The *system* followed out leads almost
uniformly to the employment of officials, *whose
rise in life were impossible*, under any other circumstances, but in tho atmosphere of a court. Owing
everything to *patronage, they despise every other
human qualification*. All places of trust and profit
thus, in time, become filled with *placemen ;* of the
character of theso persons I need not here speak.
The results show themselves most strongly abroad:
Malta, Corfu, Now Zealand, Tasmania, Canada,
the Cape. A mere handful of Saxons, disunited
on most points, scattered, unarmed, poor, have
beaten our flunky official, with six regiments at
his back, to the wall. It is a lesson not merely

for England, but for the world: a subject of amusement and ridicule to those who know the country, its resources in able hands, and the ease with which an able man could have set the Boor at defiance. I have examined this question in a note, to which I beg leave to refer the reader.

The really momentous question for England, as a *nation*, is the presence of three sections of the Celtic race still on her soil: the Caledonian, or Gael; the Cymbri, or Welsh; and the Irish, or Erse; and how to dispose of them. The Caledonian Celt touches the end of his career: they are reduced to about one hundred and fifty thousand; the Welsh Celts are not troublesome, but might easily become so; the Irish Celt is the most to be dreaded.

It was natural for an amiable man, of a vigorous understanding, great energy and courage (I allude to Mr. John Bright), to ascribe Irish misery to the misrule of her race; and to trace this misrule not to the English people, but to the imbecile, treacherous, and disastrous government of her Norman dynasty and Norman nobility: of a corporate body of foreigners, who would still fain look on England as *theirs by right of conquest*, and on the soil of Ireland as a mere hunting-ground for the recreation and profit of the mighty barons. But Mr. Bright is, in the main, in error. The Norman government of England has, it is true, done its best and its worst in Ireland. If you wish to see what such a dynasty can do, go to Ireland; still, the source of all evil lies in *the race*, the Celtic race of Ireland. There is no getting over *historical facts*. Look at Wales, look at Caledonia; it is ever the same. The race must be forced from the soil; by fair means, if possible; still they must leave. England's safety requires it. I speak not of the justice of the cause; nations must ever act as Machiavelli advised: look to yourself. The Orange club of Ireland is a Saxon confederation for the clearing the land of all papists and jacobites; this means Celts. If left to themselves, they would clear them out, as Cromwell proposed, by the sword; it would not require six weeks to accomplish the work. But the Encumbered Estates Relief Bill will do it better.

Then will come, a hundred years hence, a more momentous question for England: a *Saxon population* in Ireland will assuredly forget that they ever came from England; at all events, they will bo *born* in *Ireland*, and their property is there, and that will be enough for them. Then will come the struggle of self; the Saxon against Saxon. A Saxon colony in Ireland! But long before that, the tri-colour flag may wave over the United States of Great Britain and Ireland. This is the march of the Saxon onwards to democracy; self-government, self-rule: with him, self is everything.

LECTURE XII.

SOME REMARKS ON JEWISH CHRONOLOGY.

SECTION I.—In drawing up this brief sketch of the history of these three remarkable races of men, the Copt, Jew, and Gipsies, my attention has been forcibly attracted to two points; first, to the absence of sound historical data in respect of all three; secondly, to the extraordinary proofs they offer of the incorrectness of that view which would assign to an ideal family of men, called Caucasian, not merely those elements of mind which belong to other races, and which no one of these three seem ever to have possessed, but by a still grosser error, would ascribe to this ideal Caucasian race mental qualifications and physical structure excelling all others; superior to all; not to be surpassed.   From these abstractions of Blumenbach, Prichard, and the English school, although they scarcely merit the name, have flowed other serious mistakes and incongruities, depriving the view of all title to the term philosophic ; the singular spectacle of a wandering race living in the midst of civilization, of conventionalism, of restraint, yet refusing for centuries to recognise

these adjuncts to humanity, preferring the life of
the beasts of the field, has never been fairly met.
Yet this, the Gipsy, is called a Caucasian race,
and by some thought to be beautiful and of
the highest order. Another *dispersed race*, for
it would seem I must not call them *wanderers*,
remain dispersed for some thousand years: till
not, fabricate nothing, create nothing, live in a
seeming vision of the past, a host without a leader.
Adopting in part the civilization of the surrounding races, they yet themselves have neither literature, science, nor art; nor wish to create them,
nor power to invent them, nor ability to perform.
Yet here is another of the said Caucasian family
of Prichard; the oldest, as is said—the best—
beaten by the rough energy of the rude Scandinavian.   Loftiest of the Caucasian family! show
me your doings, your labours.   In energy and industry you are inferior to the Negro; in muscular
frame, mechanical skill, and accumulative power,
overmatched by the Saxon; in taste and elegance,
in war and peace, the Celt leaves you immeasurably behind; last and greatest, the Slavonian
and South German, or Goth, transcend you in
that very philosophy called transcendental, considered by many as the great peculiarity of your
race.   Yet Blumenbach, Prichard, and their followers, call you Caucasian!

A third race, also called Caucasian, erect

monuments of surpassing grandeur; attain seemingly the highest civilization at a period when the
Scandinavian, Celtic, and Slavonian lay grovel-
ling, and but little raised above the beasts of the
field. Yet where are they now, these companions
of Sesostris? Your Coptic civilization has passed
away seemingly with the race; and so has the
Arabic or Saracenic also with the races. A
ruffianly mixed population of blacks and browns
occupy your fields, to become extinct in time, as
all mixed races must. But are your Copts of
antiquity extinct? Here is a question for the
physiologist; and if so, how came it to pass?
Do races of men become extinct, like the beasts
of the field?

To this question I shall soon turn; but before
discussing it, let me direct your attention to the
present position and past history of the Jew.

SECTION I. *The Jewish and Coptic Chronology.*

The chronicle of the events which have happened to races, nations, and remarkable individuals, has been, with few exceptions, so imperfectly
written as to render human chronology nearly
worthless. It solves no great questions in a complete manner. The monumental records themselves of Egypt, the most valuable and probably
the most ancient, explain but little; each
successive discovery adding ænigma to ænigma,

doubt to doubt, merely. I have always, therefore, avoided, without, however, overlooking or despising, discussions on chronological questions, generally speaking, and excepting in a very few instances, I attach no importance to them: human history, whether recorded or monumental, I esteem but a drop in the ocean of time and of events. The greatest of all questions, in one sense, is no doubt a chronological one. Its adjustment would form a new æra in human history. Give us the precise date of the building of the Great Pyramid—the name of the dynasty of the period—the relation of the Egyptians of that period to the surrounding nations. Show us the exact condition of the Esquimaux, or yellow races of Africa, 3000 years ago. Nay, inform us rigorously of the nature of the race inhabiting South Britain when Cæsar landed. Give us any fixed starting point in history. But there is no such point; all is surmise and conjecture, contradiction and ænigma. No one could have felt this more than the celebrated historian Niebuhr. It was incomprehensible to him how " the Germans," as he called the middle and South Germans of his day, were dark-complexioned men, with dark hair and eyes; whilst in the time of Marius, of Livy, and of Tacitus, *the Germans* were a fair-haired, blue-eyed race. Niebuhr neglected the element of race, and hence his difficulty. The present or modern South German does not belong to the race described in classic Roman history; they are *not Scandinavians or true Germans, and never were a fair race.*

Long prior to the appearance in an English dress of the immortal historian's works, I had arrived, after much anxious thought, at the conclusion that Jewish chronology was worthless; that Coptic written history could not be trusted; and that Coptic monumental history — the most valuable, I admit, existing — with its inexhaustible but mysterious hieroglyphics, had added hitherto no substantial, no decisive fact to human history, saving one, that civilization, and arts, and mankind generally, were of a much more ancient date than was generally supposed.

These opinions I have always expressed cautiously before public audiences, knowing the deep prejudices existing throughout Europe generally on all these questions, and the determination of the mass, not merely of theologians, but of the world generally, to assign a historic character to the Mosaic record, and to take for a chronological history of mankind that history, which, if complete and understood, would no doubt have explained all things, but which, as it now stands, is no more a history than it is a work of science.

My present remarks will be very brief. Literary men and theologians dispute for victory : I

aim merely at truth. To me it is a matter of the
most perfect indifference whether the Jews ever
were in the land we call Egypt, or not. The
Rev. Mr. Beke, who, I believe, is an orthodox
divine, says that they never lived in the land we
call Egypt, but in the now wild and desolate
region between the River of Egypt (which I need
not say is not the Nile) and Syria. Be it so; I
leave this matter entirely to theologians. Let me
return to the history of the Jew and the Copt,
adhering strictly to what has a reference to the
element of race.

Niebuhr observes, in a note to the first edition
of his great work, that the chronology of the Jews
of the Mosaic record is beneath all notice, and
merits merely contempt. These too strong expres
sions theologians have generally and prudently
overlooked, contenting themselves, I think, with
expunging the exceptionable passages from subsequent editions. Dr. Arnold, whose works are a
mere copy of Niebuhr's, takes no notice, I think,
of these and similar passages. Bishop Usher's
views on chronology have been stereotyped in
England by clergy and laity. In Catholic
countries there is no occasion to reconcile any
contradictions, however monstrous: the Church
is infallible. To minds so constituted, a difference
amounting to a trifling 1600 years or so is nothing. To such minds, truth in history is of no

c c

value; science they detest; all scientific men
they place in one category.

I may hereafter discuss the influence which discoveries in physical science have exercised over
chronology. My present object is with the verifi-
cation of certain events connected with Jewish and
Coptic history, keeping ever in view the question
of race.

It is and always has been the practice of every
race and nation, whose intellectual faculties were
sufficiently elevated, to connect their history with
the origin of all time, and, under one denomina-
tion or another, to identify themselves with the
great creative Power. This practice seems not to
have been confined to the fair races *exclusively*;
for the Chinese, Mongolians by race, Japanese,
Hindoo, Copt, are all more or less dark-coloured
races, have, notwithstanding this, traced their
origin to the gods, and their priests made " common cause" with the Creator of all things. This
practice prevailed to such an extent, becoming
so deep-rooted in human minds, that to this
day stealing from a building called a church is
termed sacrilege, as if any one building made by
human hands could be more sacred than any
other; and millions of educated and superior
men still think it necessary that some mummery
be repeated over a portion of the earth's surface
before that earth can be fit to receive those frail

and rotten remains, which mythology and philosophy alike inform us, sprung originally from it.

Whilst the human mind remains in this degraded condition, truth is not wanted. Millions
and millions of brave men, Romans, believed that
a priest did divide a whetstone with a razor.
The same race (Italian) have superstitions still
more numerous, offensive, and degrading to humanity. They believe in the liquefaction of the
blood of St. Januarius, and in the efficacy of " the
red tunic." We hear kind-hearted men speak of
the progress of mankind! What progress do
they mean?

The Jews are said to be descended from one
family, one man: I speak of the so-called historic
period. This expression is really devoid of any
meaning; for his descendants returned on all and
every occasion to Chaldea, if he was really a
Chaldean, for wives from other families of the race.
Lot, not a remarkably over-scrupulous or tight-laced
man, was his kinsman—I think his brother. His
heir-male of entail lived in Damascus. Nineteen
hundred years, then, before our æra, there was a
town, a city at Damascus; the Syrian plains were
fully occupied—so also, no doubt, was Lebanon.
Thus mingling with a section of the Chaldean or
Babylonish race, the Jews progressed in numbers
and wealth: the Abrahamidæ were a section of a
wandering race who had already wandered into

Syria before the appearance of Abraham in that
country—wanderers over the earth from their earliest records to the present day; a scattered race
by the nature of their instincts.

The race whence the Abrahamidæ sprung was
left somewhere in Chaldea: travellers ought to
find them there to this day. They are the *origin*
of the race of Israel—the *original stock;* the purest
blood must be there, and also the most numerous
tribe; for the offset which wandered into Egypt
was a branch, sure to perish but for fusion with
other races. This accordingly happened; and in
Egypt the race assumed that Coptic physiognomy
and form, unalterably stamped on the family,
now visible everywhere, under all climates, under
all circumstances. As the modern Jew, then, is
chiefly Egyptian, a question arises as to the real
character of the primitive race, their physiognomy,
and form, and mental disposition. This, I think,
must be sought for in Chaldea, from whence we
are told they came. It is a subject worthy the
inquiry of a Lepsius or a Humboldt.

The race, now remodelled, leave Egypt with a
view to the extermination of the Syrian inhabitants of the country, the utter extermination of
the race or races of Palestine, and the substitution
of themselves for all others. Their utter failure
was complete; but still not more so than that of
all other races under similar circumstances. That

they should fail in the extermination of another
race ; that, after the lapse of many centuries, they
should find themselves in their first position,
scattered over the earth, few in number, without
a rallying point, has nothing in it wonderful.
Equally so is their distinctness from all other
races : I have shown the fusion of race, or amalgamation of races, to be a theory refuted by all
history.

In briefly reviewing these two great facts, let
me supply the physical evidence deduced from
the theory of race to which I venture to lay
claim. 1st, By his *nature*, the Jew, or Chaldee,
is a wanderer over the earth; like the Gipsy,
whom he greatly resembles, he has no settled
home; the restoration of Palestine to the Jew
would not in the least degree render the Jew
less a wanderer. From Chaldea he wandered
into Egypt; from Egypt again to Palestine.
Famine could not have been the sole cause of
this ; a pastoral people, as they are stated to have
been at the time, could suffer nothing by a scarcity
of *grain*. If all the wheat in South Africa were
destroyed for seven years, the people would
suffer not in the least, so long as pasture remained sufficient for their flocks and herds. The
inhabitants of South America live on animal food,
caring nothing for grain. 2nd, Originally Chaldee,
they acquired the Coptic cast of features in

Egypt; this was quite natural. In Persia they
got Persian blood; in other countries they received from time to time accessions of foreign
blood; hence their numbers, which would otherwise dwindle away to a mere handful, are partly
maintained. But the leading part of the Jewish
physiognomy naturally remains. That physiognomy was probably Chaldee; it differed somewhat from the Copt, who caricatured it on his
monuments. 3rd, Phœnician or Syrian blood
mingled largely with the original race; even their
capital, Jerusalem, remained in the hands of the
Jebusites. David's conquest was merely nominal,
or at least a compromise with the original inhabitants of the city of Jebus.

That they should have failed in exterminating
the Syrian race or races, and taking their place,
is simply what has happened to all other races.
The Turkish empire withers and declines, as I
have shown elsewhere, from the same causes: its
population is becoming extinct; the country will
return into the possession of its original inhabitants, whoever they were. Ireland, Caledonia,
are even yet in the hands of the Celtic race—
hence their terrible condition. Charlemagne
and his bold Franks have ceased to live—France
is Celtic to the core. It is the same all over the
world. Why should the Jews form an exception
to nature's great law? South England is far from

being Saxon; neither Holland nor Flanders show
much Spanish blood; the South German has
made little or no progress against the Slavonian
and Hunnish races; and a mere accident prevented
these two races from again crushing the German,
as they had done before.   Their want of union
saved the dynasty of Hapsburgh.

I find it difficult to obtain from the literary
man, theological or otherwise, a clear statement
as to his views on another point of Jewish history;
some maintaining the doctrine, 1st, That, under
all climates the Jew continues the same; or 2ndly,
That he differs under every climate, but remains
steady to his race.   Both opinions cannot be true;
nevertheless they are alternately maintained by
the same class of writers.   The relation of the
Arab to the Jew is not merely doubtful, but it does
not exist: I speak of them as races.

In the successive devastations of Syria by
various conquering people, from the Persian to
the Turk, the Jews were not the only race who
suffered; all must have suffered equally.   But
these races, being aboriginal, recovered their
population: the Jew, a foreigner, did not.

The story of the Jew, as told by himself, is a
plain and simple story enough: in the hands of
the writers of other races it becomes a rhapsody.
That of the Copt is really wonderful; their monumental history surpasses all on earth besides

The Jew has no monumental history. He never had any literature, science, or art: he has none yet. "Their completeness and wonderfully preserved individuality"[*] has nothing in it in the slightest degree curious. All other races are in precisely the same position; and, in this respect, also, the Gipsy is superior to them.

It is admitted that the Jews have no rural population at present in Judea: it seems to me that they never had a rural population anywhere. In all Syria they are supposed to amount to 30,000.

But I admit it to be singular enough that they should still maintain their handful of a population on the earth; explicable only on the ground of the race receiving occasionally supplies of fresh blood from other sources. A recent traveller[†] informs us that the Jews do not multiply "in the capital of their race;" the writer should have said, "in the city of Jebus," which was not their native city, but one which they had long occupied in common with the aboriginal inhabitants. This correction of an otherwise important passage is essential to truth and science. "Jew children," it is added, "seldom attain to puberty; and the mortality is altogether so great that the constant reinforcements from Europe scarcely

* The Cross and the Crescent, 187.
† Warburton.

maintain the average population."[*]   I submit
these curious facts without comment to the scientific reader.

When I first delivered these lectures, orally,
to the public, the investigations of Bunsen and
Lepsius had not appeared. Nor yet have I had
an opportunity of perusing their works. But,
from various scattered notices, I believe that
nothing has been made out to invalidate my first
impressions in regard to Coptic history. The
opinion I had formed was unfavourable to the
accuracy of Herodotus; and this view is now, I
believe, admitted to be the correct one. It was
from the Coptic monumental history that Cuvier
drew the result, that no animal had sensibly
altered its character; that no ancient species had
been metamorphosed; no new species had arisen
since the historic period—that period being as yet
undetermined, but marked by records respecting
which there could be no mistake. The illustrious
anatomist forgot to mention *man*—forgot to include
him in the list of unchanged and seemingly unchangeable species of animals: I add him now;
requesting my reader to remember that the term
"historic period" denotes a mere speck in the
ocean of time. The persistence of species can be
admitted now as extending merely through limited

[*] Warburton, p. 196.

periods of time ; the discoveries of De Blainville
seem likely to settle this great question.   There
has been, there can only be, " one creation ;" all
successive forms must proceed from others preceding them.   Life on the globe is but one, not
many.   Forms vary agreeably to the eternal laws
of development regulating these forms.   They
appear in succession, but they are still one.   To
living forms there can be no limit, saving " the
essential conditions of their existence."

Coptic chronology is still to write; the hieroglyphics have taught little or nothing—the expla-
nations hitherto offered are extremely doubtful.

CONCLUDING LECTURE.

WHEN the world was yet, as it were, in its
infancy, a race of men appeared in the stream
of human history, with intellects and frames
so glorious, that no parallel to them was ever
found in history. That race was the ancient
Greek. The precise period of their appearance
on the earth is, of course, not known; I say of
course; for if there be one fact better made out
in all history than another, it is this—that human
chronology, as it now stands, is all but worthless.
Of Homer and Troy we know nothing; the precise date when the noblest of all statues were
carved is equally a mystery. One thing is certain—the statues remain; the ruins of the Parthenon may yet be found; the Homeric ballad, the
grandest of all human works, is still extant; and
Plato and Socrates, Iskander and Aristotle,

Euclid and Herodotus, are names as familiar to
the men now living as household words.

Wonderful and most mysterious race! divinest
chapter in human history! unparalleled, unequalled, whence came ye? Whither have ye
gone, fading away into the mists of the past?
What is Parthian, or Mongolian, or Roman, or
Germanic glory, compared with yours? And
even now, whilst I write, reducing to some sort of
order the thoughts and reflections of many years,
a trafficking, commercial, strong-armed, buy-and-

[*The Parthenon.*]

sell race beset your Piræus; a coarse, barbarous, vulgar crew, point their artillery at Athens. It is a *money question* seemingly—a commercial *question* really; the savage Russ claims you for his brethren on the score of the gross and idolatrous worship which disgraces you as men, and renders you contemptible in the eyes of the rest of the world; the "grande nation," whose claims to the term "great" repose mainly on the merit of having plundered the Romans of those monuments they stole from you, affect to sympathize with you. But you are not the descendants of the ancient Greek; and this is the point I mean first to moot.

It is a fact, in as far as so ancient a historic recollection may be esteemed a fact, that the northern nations as they are called, the Scandinavian, the Celtic, Germanic (South German or Goth), Slavonian, and Sarmatian, existed not merely as they now are, physically and morally, from the most ancient times; but that they were ever formidable and troublesome to the Peninsulas of Italy and Greece before the real historic period. Unequal to originate within themselves any form of civilization; deficient in originality or genius; strong-armed, common-sense barbarians, many of them, they knew that in the south were sunny climes, and rich wines, and wealth. In the time of Marius, some 2,200 years ago, they plundered Italy and Greece; but they had been there as

victors a thousand years before that; masses of barbarians, a moving nation, a swarm in search of a
new habitat. Devastating Greece and Italy and
Asia Minor, they still founded no new states, but
mingling with the existing population of a land,
and a clime, and a centre of life which was not their
focus of origin, and in which, therefore, they could
not continue to exist, they merged in the original
population, finally to disappear as a race; leaving
vestiges of their being, of their qualities, good
and bad—thus modifying for centuries the destinies of these lands. In the meantime, cut off
from the parent line, these northern aborigines
fail to continue their own race. Confronted with
a more numerous one, the aboriginal inhabitants
of Italy, Greece, and Asia Minor, they naturally
yield and disappear; their blood is merged in a
wider stream; it mingles, and is lost. The purest
stock, left in Northern Europe and Asia, remains
barbarous as it was; unequal to the invention of
any literature, science, or art, beyond the common
household wants, the exigencies of war, the inflic-
tions of climate, the northern hives remain as they
were—wonderful spectacles of barbarism, to which
Kentucky, Canada, Florida, would soon return,
were they cut off for two or three generations
from the rest of mankind; to which England
itself would return; to which the greater part of
Ireland has returned, and from which, to this day,

the Sarmatian or Russ has never emerged. Look
at the condition of the Saxon boor as he herds
his flocks on the vast plains of Southern Africa;
read the history of those Englishmen, who have
re-peopled Tasmania and Australia; of the Celt-
Iberian and Lusitanian, hunting as guanches the
pampas of South America. A professing Christian is not necessarily a civilized man. Civilization and Christianity are identical, it is true; but
then it must be real, and not sham Christianity—
the actual, not the shadow.

And thus did the northern hives, as they are
called, pour masses of men and women from their
woods towards the south, without, however, really
founding any new states. Even in Cæsar's time,
Gallia Cisalpina had lost its sympathies with
Gallia Transalpina. Separated from each other
by the great central chain of the Alps, the Celtic
colony which had seized on Northern Italy had
already lost a portion, and a great one too, of its
Celtic character. That race, the Celtic, if I mistake
not, is now nearly extinct in Northern Italy, the
population having, no doubt, returned to that race
which preceded the Gallic invasion: that invasion also, be it remembered, is much beyond all
human history. As it was with Italy, so it was
with Greece, using the term in its widest sense,
and therefore including a great part of Asia
Minor. Three, or more likely four thousand years

ago, the Celtic and Scandinavian, and Gothic
or Germanic blood, perhaps even the Slavonian,
was mingled deeply with the aboriginal inhabitants of Greece and Macedonia; the peninsula
and its isles; with their colonies everywhere;
with the original race, which I shall venture to
call Pelasgic; they mingled, not by thousands,
but by hundreds of thousands. Hence arose a
new race of men, destined to cease at a given
period; a race which could not stand their
ground against Nature's laws; a *mixed race*, an
anomaly on earth; a thing repudiated by the
organic laws of man and animals; a race of men,
if it merits the name, whose possible existence
depended on an annual influx into Greece of
Scandinavian and Celtic hordes; that is, of an order
of things which never yet happened to mankind.

This, then, is the theory I offer. There never
existed *a race* of men and women formed like the
Apollo, the Venus, the Dian, the Hercules, the
Niobe, the Bacchus; but there existed a combination of circumstances in the Peninsulas of Italy
(Southern), Greece and her Isles, and Asia Minor,
which gave rise to the production of numerous
persons, of whom some equalled, still more approached these glorious figures I speak of.
Matchless and perfectly beautiful, they had only
to be seen to be immediately understood; genius
—lofty genius abounded everywhere. The robust

energy, the vivacity and vigour of the Scandinavian and Celtic races, came to be mingled with
an Oriental race or races, of which we know
nothing, but of whose sublimity of mind the
Cyclopean walls leave unmistakable indications.
Oriental minds, allied to Copt and Chaldee;
monuments analogous, but not identical, with
Egyptian Thebes and Asiatic Nimroud and
Babylon; with men who lived beyond the Babylonish and Coptic period. The Italian Peninsula
no doubt was once also theirs, as well as Greece,
and, it may be, the Lusitanian. These fine and

[*Bust of the Venus.*]

D D

classic regions, the northern, that is, Saxon,
Celtic, and Gothic barbarians, have constantly
invaded, hoping to make them their own; they
have as constantly failed; for no race can permanently locate itself in a continent in which it
had not been placed by Nature.   And now, the
populations of Italy, Greece, and Asia Minor,
having returned pretty nearly to their aboriginal
condition in respect of race, are as they were
before, timid, cowardly, unwarlike; serfs by nature;
slaves of the horrible and brutal superstitions of
the Roman Catholic and Greek Churches. An idiot,
vulgar Goth reigns in Greece: the imbecile House
of Hapsburgh lords it in Italy; the savage Turkoman scourges Asia Minor. From the people themselves all traces of the men who form the glory of
this world have disappeared, leaving behind them,
in their nearly aboriginal condition, that population
on which the Scandinavian and Celtic and Gothic
blood being once engrafted, originated all that
was great and glorious; but now, left to itself,
exhibits to the world a spectacle most lamentable
and deplorable.

In the circumstances of which I have spoken,
the union of different races, and its result on the
physical structure and moral qualities of the
descendants or progeny, originated the classic
days and age of Greece.   To the Scandinavian
blood the aboriginal Pelasgic hordes, whether

European or Asiatic, Greek or Italian, owed the
occasional beauty of their complexion; that matchless hue which Homer compares to the colour of
" the elephantine bone, fresh from the hands of
the turner." The Maid of Athens had blue eyes,
a divine and matchless colour, bestowing on
woman's looks an expression above all earthly
passions; fair and flowing locks, full bosomed,
fleshy, and large-limbed, seem to have been
the character of Grecian women : look at the
Niobe, the Venus of Gnidos, and a hundred
others. All these show Scandinavian blood, for
no such persons are to be found anywhere else.
It was Sir Charles Bell, I think, who said that the
grand facial line or angle of the antique Greek
cannot now be found! Never, I think, was so
great an error of observation committed, for the
streets of London abound with persons having
this identical facial angle; and it is in England
and in other countries inhabited by the Saxon or
Scandinavian race that women resembling the
Niobe, and men the Hercules and Mars, are
chiefly to be found. I shall speak shortly of the
differences unquestionably existing between the
ancient Greek or classic head and the modern
Scandinavian ; the Niobe and the Saxon matron.
These differences reside chiefly in the *form* and
position of the eyes, for in the antique head the
eyes are deeply set; but they are not confined to

these organs, as we shall afterwards find. To the
Scandinavian, then, Greece owed her grandeur
of forms, especially in woman ; her disunions,
obstinacy of character, common sense, mechanical genius, large-limbed men, athletæ, matchless
perseverance.   To the admixture of Celtic blood
may be traced her warlike disposition, energy,
vivacity, wit ; and to Slavonian and Gothic we
must trace, I think, the transcendental qualities
of her philosophy and morals ; the substratum
was an Oriental mind, not Coptic, least of all
Jewish ; but these latter elements now prevail, I
believe.   The grand classic face has all but disappeared, and in its place comes out a people
with a rounded profile ; the nose large and
running into the cheeks, like the Jew ; the chin
receding ; the eyebrows arched.   Anti-classic in
all things, how Greece has fallen !   Yet this was
the country which produced the men who fought

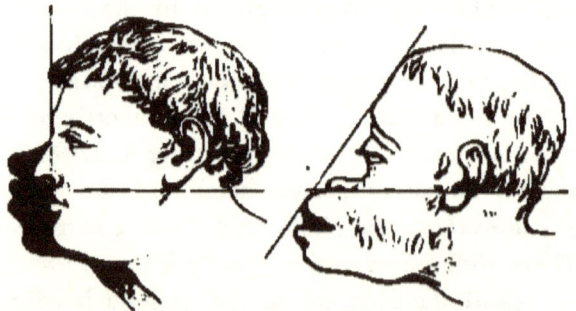

[*Profile of Negro, European, and Oran Outan.*]

at Marathon and conquered on the banks of the
Granicus; Pyrrhus belonged to them and Peri-
cles; Aristotle and Plato; Socrates, Demosthenes; Iskander, equal to Napoleon; Archimedes,
Euclid, Thucydides, Herodotus, Homer, Pindar,
Anacreon, Phidias, and they who carved the
immortal and transcendant Venus and Niobe!
Where shall we commence, or where end? If
many brave and good men lived before Aga-
memnon and Achilles, when did classic Greece
commence? Homer was not, could not be the
first: before Homer there were others. Homer
could not invent a civilization which did not
exist; Shakespeare described Nature as he saw
her. He invented nothing. Great minds see
truth, and truth only; they have no fancies;
legends and miracles are out of their sphere; St.
George and the Dragon; mountains skipping like
lambs; Bel and the Dragon; the eleven thousand
virgins drowned at Cologne; armies of martyrs
fighting in the clouds; St. Jago charging the
Paynim on a white horse; these inventions belong
to other minds and other races. They exist still,
but under other names; a volcanic fire kindled
in Snowdon; the subsidence of the centre of
Britain would reduce the English mind to the
imbecility of the tenth or twelfth centuries. No
greater error was ever committed than that of
supposing that *the mass* of men change or pro-

gress: *Le peuple n'est rien*, was the expressive
but satirical expression of Voltaire. No greater
truth was ever uttered. How was it, then, with
the Grecian people in the classic days I speak
of? Just as now; they were nobody; they
merited no particular notice, further than that
they produced men, such as have never been
seen since. A higher taste also than is common
they must have had; yet philosophy in Athens
was of course confined to the schools, and the
council or senate of Athens, the working, state-
corporation of Athens, gave it as their opinion
that Aristophanes, the poet and comic writer, was
wrong in taking so much notice in one of his
comedies of *an unknown person like Socrates*. But
they, the people, knew enough of him as the
representative of philosophy and of truth to
dislike him mortally; their animal instincts told
them that he and they were of different natures.
Truth and science, which is, or ought to be
truth, are ever disliked by the mass.

In Galen's time, if I mistake not, gladiatorial
scenes were of almost daily occurrence. Hundreds
and thousands of human beings were butchered
in cold blood in presence of Roman audiences;
of a people abandoned in vice below imagination;
but Galen dared not allow it to be known that
he had examined for the purposes of science
some human bones, which he did by stealth,

and secretly. This is man. But to return to Greece.

Against her schools of philosophy and science Greece ever waged war. Yet art and science stood their ground. The civilization of mankind is based on what it received from Greece; whilst in respect of the fine arts, more especially the modelling and drawing the human figure, which forms the only basis of all art, it is not possible to imagine what might now have been the actual state of the fine arts but for the discovery of those wonderful remains, the antique marbles. These revealed to the world wonders at least as great as the telescopes of Galileo; they revealed the beautiful, the perfect, the matchless, the highest and noblest physical manifestation of nature; consequently, the only being corresponding to the highest gift of the mind; in these, then, the moral or metaphysical world, the world of mind, found at last that which it must ever aim at—" the perfect."

How they rose and fell, as a nation, belongs to the chroniclers of events. I have traced their progress as a race; a race which is gone, which cannot re-appear; climate aided them. They never, properly speaking, formed *a distinct race of men*, and hence could not stand their ground, any more than the Romans. The physiological laws of the species were against them. But I pretend not to trace their history. Some curious

points of resemblance between the women of
classic Greece and the thorough-bred Saxon
women of England, or Holland, or Sweden,
might here be pointed out; but this I must leave,
for the present, at least, to some "Historian of
Manners,"* not forgetful of the element of race,
like Guizot and the Thiers school. There are
curious points of resemblance, independent of the
Amazons; bacchanals and festivals, not altogether
unlike scenes at Wapping and Portsmouth Point
in the glorious old times, the good old times of
George the Third. A hint, I presume, is enough.
It was Hippocrates who said that the Greek
women could drink deeper than the men; and
that they were somewhat liberal of their charms
all history, I think, maintains. The whole reminds
me much of Holland and of the Saxon generally;
beautiful women who sold their favours for money
were much esteemed in Athens; the same class
meets with all respect in most Saxon countries.
In republican Holland they were not merely
tolerated, they were protected, the state deriving
an income from them.

But we now return to consider the Greek mind
solely under one point of view—its relation to
art. It is to this relation I mean now to direct your
attention, for it is in this that we purpose tracing

* Histoire des Mœurs.

the germs of all that is great, because all that is
human in the human mind. All nature's works,
we have seen, are wonderful; but it is man alone
who can reason about them; understand them, at
least to a certain extent; view them in relation
to himself, and himself in relation to them: man
is the problem to solve; his presence here, his
origin, his purpose or end. I do not mean that
the Greeks were the first to moot these great
questions; neither did they, perhaps, solve them;
but their arts showed that amongst them existed
minds which understood and comprehended the
universal, the transcendental, which can alone be
truth.

THEORY OF "THE BEAUTIFUL," AS DEVELOPED IN
THE ANTIQUE STATUES OF GREECE.

As I stood by the banks of the Koonap, gazing
eastward over the grassy plains which lay between
me and the Indian Ocean, alone, unattended, a
stranger in the land on which I stood—an alien by
my race to all that was around me—I sought in vain
to connect myself with that landscape, *by theory*, yet
I felt myself identified with it; I said to myself, this
park-like scenery, resembling beautiful England,
but still more beautiful; grander, more vast, more
romantic, more perfect; that transparent and deep
blue sky—glorious light and shade; deep gloomy

ravines of the Anatolo and Winter Bergen; bulbous flowers of all hues and fragrance; delicate mimosa and fantastic aloe; these are not European—these belong not to the land of my birth—to the continent from which I sprung, yet the *wilde* (for man had done nothing here since man was on the earth) was beautiful, tender, melancholy, romantic. Why then, if the landscape before me be *beautiful* and *perfect*, do I gaze at these Anatolo mountains, scanning with a strong glass each ravine and bushy dell? Is not the scenery exquisite? What more can be desired? Why look beyond it? I will tell you.

Man alone is beautiful; the human *form* alone satisfies the *human mind*. Other objects have their attractions—we admire them and are pleased, but they do not solve the problem of "the beautiful," which must be sought for in man alone.

Whilst meditating on these abstract yet pleasing topics for thought, I naturally asked myself the source of pleasure derived in the contemplation of the landscape before me. The term *picturesque* rose on my memory, and all but startled me from my reverie—deep-felt reverie, absorbing my whole soul with thoughts and meditations for which language had no expression. The word *picturesque* all but banished from my mind the solemn scene before me; it recalled to me the nonsense I had read about the fine arts: it placed before me the artificial man,—the Cit, the Cockney, the model man, " trying the pittoresque,"—" coming the picturesque" near London or Amsterdam; the artificial man—the would-be civilized man—cribbed, trammelled, and confined; the thing in harness—the state flunkey; the biped in harness; the clock-regulated animal; the creature with a soul composed of associations of ideas.[*]

But before I consider why even then so young I rejected the flimsy theories of the civilized hack, be he churchman[†] or layman,[‡] orthodox,[§] or sceptic,[‖] all tending as they do in one direction, let me first submit to you a brief analysis of " the beautiful;" the To Kalon of the Greeks; " the sought-after" of all high minds, of every age and race.

The human *form* alone is beautiful; *woman* presents the perfection of that *form*, and, therefore, alone constitutes " the perfect." It is not youth, nor intellect, nor moral worth, nor associations of any sort, which constitute the beautiful and the perfect; nor is life required, nor complexion, nor motion; it is *form* alone which is the essential.

Let us consider this proposition carefully; it has been since I first announced it much contested, and will continue to be so, no doubt. It strikes at innumerable prejudices, feelings, pas-

---

[*] Alison, Jeffrey. [†] Alison. [‡] Jeffrey.
[§] Paley. [‖] Voltaire.

sions—above all, it limits and defines the term beauty, that happy field for interminable dispute since Socrates to the present day. From a race, the Saxon, to whom utility is as a deity; who admire in general, as a race, only what is useful, I naturally expect every opposition. It will not be easy to persuade a race of utilitarians that anything can be beautiful but in the ratio of its fitness, its utility; then, why may not a wheelbarrow lay claim to the title of beautiful? or a pigsty? or a pair of Jack-boots? and as the large, firm, hard, spatular-fingered hand must clearly be the most useful, so a preference ought to be given to it over the slender, taper-fingered, jointless looking hand of the Venus.

But what say men of taste? What say those who love *form* for the sake of the form itself? Do you select a person devoid of a musical ear to sit in judgment over Mozart's thrilling notes? Would you give a preference in the matter of

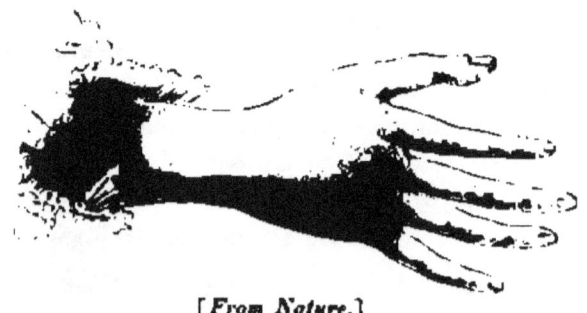

[*From Nature.*]

colours to those who think any one colour as
good as another? who paint landscapes all blue
or all green, or all red or brick-dust colour, as the
case may be? Why then take the opinion in respect of *form* of those to whom all forms are nearly
indifferent? But perhaps I debate a matter which
will be conceded me even by a utilitarian race;
grant that all forms are not of equal beauty; that
some are confessedly beautiful, others not; that
when divested of prejudices of education, and of
prejudices of ignorance, all the world admits certain forms to be at the least much more beautiful
than others; let us consider then,—1st. What
are these incontestably beautiful forms? 2nd.
Why are they beautiful? in other words, What
is your theory of high art—of the beautiful—of
the perfect?

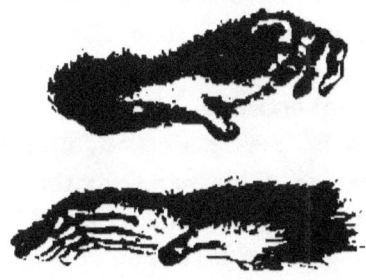

[*Oran Outan.*]

Place before you an antique statue of Venus—
the youngest daughter of Niobe—the Venus of

Gnidos; look carefully at the proportions and forms—if you have the least doubt, compare them with the living, or with modern sculptures; do this repeatedly, and I think you will be inclined to arrive at the following conclusions :—1st. That the figure before you is perfect, transcending all other material objects; that its forms and proportions are perfect, since the slightest alteration of them by the substitution of others, deranges the effect and destroys the beauty of the part—that the figure satisfies *the eye for form*, and by so doing the highest and deepest of all human feelings; for on form depends the living world in as far as we are concerned. The material world itself—the stellar universe itself—all is *form*; without it, Nature can have no existence *to us*. This is the first link, the first sympathetic cord which ties man to the material world or to material manifestations—to none else whilst mortal can he be linked. What exists not materially is to him as non-existing. Finally, through this human form he sees perfection, thus satisfying the deep craving of his mind for the perfect; it is, moreover, in the ancient Greek, and in no other race, that he sees the perfection of form, and this links him to eternity.

2nd. If you now examine this figure still more carefully, you will discover a mysterious and wonderful secret, hitherto, I think, unobserved; or if observed, not fully appreciated. A living

being is composed of an interior and an exterior:
the latter alone is visible, and intended to be so;
the former, Nature carefully conceals when she
aims at the perfect and the beautiful. In the
exterior, beauty resides—that alone she decorates—all within is frightful and appalling to
human sense—never beautiful, but the reverse;
always horrible. In proportion as any figure,
whether human or bestial, displays through the
exterior, that unseemly interior, which has no
form that sense comprehends, or desires, so in the
same proportion is that figure beautiful or the
opposite. Why are the forms of age displeasing?
Why of extreme youth? Why do we place under
the same category those whom disease or penury
have withered and deformed? It is this—it is
not age, nor extreme youth (new-born children;)
nor disease, nor poverty, which bring out the feeling I now speak of—it is the exposure of *the
interior;* that dreaded interior, sure emblem of
dissolution and death. It is the feeling of dissolution, of annihilation, which instantly seizes
unconsciously on the mind of the spectator: an
unknown dread of a something which must happen
to him, although he were never told it—a dread
of dissolution, that most dreaded of all events.
Thus, already do we see what Nature has done
for the beautiful figure, it being her highest material manifestation in the existing order of things.
She has fitted it to satisfy the craving for perfec-

tion and for form, thus calling forth two of the
grandest and deepest sympathies of our nature:
she has concealed beyond all possibility of detec-
tion or even suspicion, the emblems of mortality*
—that is, *the interior,* thus carrying the mind
furthest away from the most dreaded of all events,
dissolution: nay, more—by this concealment of
the interior, and those beautiful and perfect forms,
she has called forth in the human mind that other
grand feeling of the soul—the contemplation of
eternal ever-reviving, ever-returning youth—the
youth of the universe; the bright gleam of hope;
of a to-morrow and a future; of a nature that will
never die.

The object of art is to call forth the grand sen-
timents, feelings, and passions of the soul—the
tender, the pathetic.   When it fails in this, it is
no art.   The works of ingenious industry, of
luxury, must not be confounded with the fine arts.
All the diamonds in the Tower are not worthy a
moment's gaze, when compared with the hand or
foot of a beautiful woman.   I speak not of the
head or of the torso—nature's masterpiece.

But this is not a work on art, nor intended to
be so ; and I shall therefore bring these remarks
to a conclusion.

The beauty of children is proverbial—of their

* See drawing of Human Skull, p. 427.

hands and feet especially — yet they are deficient
in proportions and forms; the torso is shapeless;
and the statuary should know this, and avoid as
much as possible carving the nude child. What,
then, is it we admire so much in children; and
why is their company so sought after in preference to the aged; the young ever courted,

[*The Infantile Form, loved not for its form, but as
an emblem of youth.*]

E E

ever admired? Is it their ingenuity, their com-
plaisance, their simplicity, their innocent curiosity, even their listlessness, their complaints, their
tears? All these add, no doubt, to the deep
attraction man feels for them, but they do not explain it. To him they present those *emblems of
youth* which call forth in his mind the hopes that
nature will never die; that all things will not
wither and decay, but be for ever young, for
ever at least restored to youth—eternal youth.
Nature never dies; she always was, and for ever
will be. Compare the bright green leaf of May
to the yellow scar of autumn; the lambkin to the
aged ewe; the coming summer to the past; the
child to withered, hoary, stricken age; one category, one principle, one theory, embraces all. It
is not merely youth, then, as Winckelman supposed, which is beautiful. Youth never attains
the perfect and the beautiful, whilst disease, or
penury, or vice, can transform the child into an
object of pity or disgust, by taking away the characteristic emblems of his youthful condition.
Age, time, years, are nothing; they have no existence; what to us looks young is young; what
looks aged, is aged.

And now this were the appropriate place to
trace the history of the Fine Arts, properly so
called, which no doubt emanated from Greece;
to show how all races—I mean all civilizable

races—have their fine arts peculiar to themselves;
to trace the source of pleasure we derive from the
fine arts, and their utility to a nation; but this I
must not think of here. In speaking of the various
races, I have already glanced at these topics; and
in my notes appended to these lectures, I may
again return to this subject in a more practical
manner; but the introduction of the disquisition
into a theory of the beautiful was forced upon me
here by the necessity of connecting the history
of race with the perfect; to trace to it the laws of
formation, leading to the perfect; and from it the
laws of deformation, leading to the imperfect; or,
in other words, to explain the origin of race, or
at least to connect the history of race with the
great laws regulating the living organic world—
the laws of unity of organization, another expression for the law of variety, or of imperfect formation; and, finally, with the law of perfect formation—that is, of specialization—towards which
nature aims and tends; which is, in fact, her
ultimatum. We have seen what the law of specialization has done for the human form—it has
produced the Venus, a real, not an ideal form.
The correct mind rejects everything which is
ideal, or what never had an existence. The
monstrous creations of the disordered Hindoo,
Chinese, and Saxon minds; these are ideal, fic-
titious, false; the Venus is real. Let us now

attend to the universal law of nature, the law of
unity of the organization ; that universal principle
—identity of life, identity of structure, identity of
result for all living things, at their origin, in space
and in time. For all individuals are connected,
as we shall find, with space and time ; specializations have only their day; they form a part, no
doubt, of nature's great plan ; they are, in fact,
the result. It is the laws of development we are
now to trace—the history of the gradual and successive development of living beings—of progress
also, as it may be, although I doubt the theory of
progress as now offered. It smacks of utilitarianism—of the Paley school—of final causes, which
are no causes, but effects. It is presumptuous and
anti-philosophic, and, as applied to the great mass
of the organic world, positively untrue. All that
can be said in its favour is, that man appeared last
on the surface of this world. But even this has
not been proved. He may have come first. Let
us attend first to the facts, and next to the arguments.

We have seen that the exterior alone was decorated by nature ; in it resides chiefly her specializations ; species, distinct races and kinds, for-
bidding all error or mistake, all confusion. But
rightly to understand this exterior, we must also
examine the interior, seeking for truth with the
torch of science.

What does that interior reveal to the scientific inquirer, to him whose temper leads to the search after the unknown, in the present, in the past, in the future? it reveals to him that man and all the organic world is linked to the past, seemingly without break or interruption; that the organic world, of which he forms a part, has obeyed for ever two great laws (like the inorganic), the law of specialization, or of perfect formation; the law of unity, or of imperfect formation: Formation and Deformation. Between these two laws is balanced the living world since the earth was, since, as a sphere of various dimensions, it has rolled through space.

This great fact is proved, then, 1st, from an examination of animal bodies—of animal bodies, as they now exist, and compared with each other; 2nd, from an examination of the embryo, or young of man or of any of the higher animals. This inspection tells us, that, from the moment of conception or of independence, that living point, that embryo, passes through a succession of *forms*, shadowing forth the organic world as it now exists, from the highest to the lowest; shadowing forth the organic world as it has existed from the dawn of creation to the present day— this is proved by geology; and shadowing forth the organic world, or worlds, no doubt, which are yet to come. For there was but one creation—

there could not be two, or three, or twenty, as
Cuvier has it, or rather his followers, for he himself never maintained such opinions. Unity of
idea, unity of result—life once created, once called
into play, could never cease: it appeared, no
doubt, with the globe itself—contemporaneous,
coeval. Its primitive form, that is, the form it
first assumes, is conjectured to be a cell—a
sphere or globe—minute, microscopic. This at
least seems probable; but it must always be remembered that *we* merely see the *material* manifestation of *life*, and not life itself; not the living
particle, the living essence, which must also be
material.

It has been finely remarked by Humboldt, that
when we look at the stars through the telescope,
we discover a past and a present, and we conjecture a future; and when we look into the structure
of the globe, the solid strata of its surface, the
fossil world which lies imbedded reveals to us also
a distinct past and a probable future. So we
have seen it with the embryo of man; it also reveals a past; the present is before us; a probable
future may be surmised. What is the result of
these three observations, seemingly distinct? It
is, that *unity* pervades all living things—the past,
the present, and the future—unity of structure,
unity of life, unity of purpose. What that purpose is we know *not*. Some will have it that it is

progress. Progress towards what? The idea has
been thrown out by a utilitarian mind,* an unconscious disciple of Paley ; a nibbler at philosophy,
who scarcely understood the thing.   Ho wished
to give *a reason* for everything : a Saxon, no
doubt, and so he thrusts himself unwittingly into
the councils of the Great First Cause.   And so it
ever is with the half-educated; the utterly ignorant,
the *canaille,* flee at once in all arguments to a
first cause.   They know no other, and can understand no other.   With them all is mystery, a *lusus
naturæ,* a visitation of Providence, a direct interference; with them the Deity is ever present; he
has no power to bestow secondary laws on matter;
with them attraction has no real meaning; every
animal required a distinct creation.   A material
Jove still thunders.

   That all animals are formed on one great plan,
that a unity of *plan* at least exists, is supposed to
have been first announced by Newton.   This is
not the place to inquire into a historic point like
this; such also, no doubt, was the view of Leibnitz, and of many others before their time.   But
unity of plan scarcely implies unity of structure,
as M. Geoffroy (St. Hilaire) seems to have
thought.   That unity of structure also existed,
was most probable ; but what was the structure ?

* Vestiges of Creation.

Independent of all other considerations, it had
been made evident, even to the "mere formulist,"
"the external character" man, that in the animal
kingdom two distinct forms of structure prevailed,
or, in other words, that life clothed itself with two
great forms, seemingly distinct, and widely apart
from each other; and fossil remains of previously
existing worlds proved that these two forms had
existed from the remotest of periods.   The names
of vertebrate and invertebrate had been given by
the philosophic Lamark to these two kingdoms of
nature, as they were called; animals with, and
animals without a vertebral column (back-bone).
But waving, for an instant, the question, after all
but a secondary one, though much dwelt on by
Cuvier, that in reality two distinct forms of life
exist, let us consider, first, what is meant by
Unity of Structure in any class of animals.

By dissection, the dead are analyzed or reduced to certain assemblages of organs, holding
relations, often mechanical, to each other.   They
all perform certain functions, some of which have
been imperfectly guessed at; made out in a coarse
way: organs of locomotion exist—bones, liga-
ments, joints, muscles, or flesh; organs of sensa-
tion, and thought, and will; the brain and spinal
marrow; the nerves; organs of digestion and
assimilation, the stomach and digestive tube, and
their appendages; lastly, organs of breathing,

essential to life; the lungs, by which we draw from the air the breath of life. Blood-vessels acted on by a heart carry the blood through the frame. Out of this vital fluid the body is constructed, repaired, formed. Now if we select any one of these organs, or sets of organs, we shall find that, in one shape or another, it extends through the whole range of vertebrate animals, most probably through the entire range of animal life, but under a shape or form no longer recognisable by our senses. A few instances will suffice to explain this to my audience. There is no occasion for any minute or technical exposition of facts, which are, as it were, on the surface. Let us first turn our attention to the skeleton. Not that this assemblage of levers proves better than any other set of organs the unity of structure, the unity of organization sought to be superadded by the German (and Slavonian) philosophy, to the unity of plan laid down by Newton; I do not even think so well; but it presents materials easier to be handled, easier to be inspected, obtained, and understood.

The basis of the skeleton before you, whether mere animal or man, is a series of bones jointed or articulated with each other. In common language it is called the back bone. You see how violently inaccurate such a term is, when

applied to a series of bones perfectly distinct
from each other, possessing most of them a distinct mobility.   These bones we call *vertebræ;*
here is one of them.   When studied by the surgeon or medical man, it is viewed by him merely
as a portion of the skeleton ; to the philosophic
anatomist it becomes the type of all vertebrate
animals, of the entire skeleton, limbs and head
included ; of the organic world, vertebrate and
invertebrate.   Carried further, it possesses the
form of the primitive cell ; of the sphere ; of the
universe.

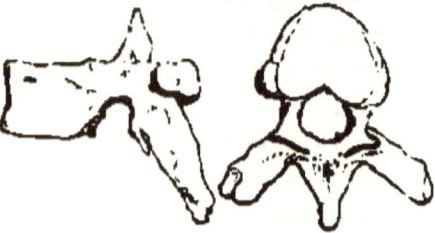

[*The human vertebra.*]

Now look at this bone in man—it appears
simple, but it is not so.   Originally, that is, in
the young, composed of many distinct portions,
which afterwards unite with each other, but which
remaining distinct in many animals, as in fishes,
proves to us, that throughout the whole range of
animals so formed, the vertebræ do not really
differ so much from each other as might at first

appear: that, in fact, the elements forming them seem the same almost numerically, giving rise to the well grounded belief, that, in the embryo, the elements of the skeleton may be, after all, the same in every animal. From man to the whale, all is alike; one theory explains all; one idea or plan pervades all.

Let us trace this chain of bones upwards and downwards; see how downwards (coccygeal vertebræ) certain elements cease to be developed, or do not grow: still the plan is the same; identical; analogous, as regards the individual, that is, repeated; homologous or identical, as regards one animal compared with another. Look to this section of the skeleton, called the head; the bones seem widely different from the vertebræ; but it is not so. They are merely vertebræ, repeated, upon a larger scale as may be required: a chain of vertebræ form, then, the head or cranium.

[*Cranium.*]

These great truths we owe exclusively to the illustrious South German and Slavonian schools of
transcendental anatomy; to Oken and Spix, Au-
tenrieth, Frank, Goethe, and a host of others.
Resisted to the last by Cuvier, they were looked
on with strong feelings of alarm in England; to
this day rejected by most, a garbled view is now
admitted by some, merely to save appearances,
and to make it appear that a something is known
of these doctrines on this side the channel. A
school of *low transcendentalists* has arisen (I use
their own phrase), who think that a portion of
Goethe's and Oken's views may be admitted without causing scandal, or risking their positions with
orthodoxy and Oxford. Others, and they are by
far the most numerous, stand out for the good old
Galenic nonsense, that every animal has its own
plan, and every part was formed for itself. That
ribs are ribs, and nothing else; that the hyoid
bones of man were made expressly for him, and
that they are neither the homologues nor the ana-
logues of the branchial arches of fishes. When
my brother discovered that the knee-joint of the
ornithorynchus and echidna was divided into two
distinct cavities, by a completing of the alar liga-
ments, I asked Sir Charles Bell what purpose it
might serve? Merely to strengthen, was the reply
of my esteemed friend; an orthodox answer, quite
safe, and entirely mechanical.

But to return.

A vertebra must have a type; that is, a plan, sufficiently comprehensive to include all forms of vertebræ. Now where is this to be found? Is it an ideal type not yet discovered? Or is it to be found in any extinct or living animal? I apprehend that it may or it may not have been found, but this in no way interferes with the principle that there must be a type laid down by nature; eternal; equal to all manifestations of form, extinct or living, or to come.

But the discovery of such a type could only be made were the anatomy of all animals that ever lived known to us; perhaps not even then; for the future must be wrapt up in the past; and what seems to us now a mere speck of bone, a nucleus, a point unimportant, nay, scarcely discernible, may, in a future order of things, become an all-important element. As thus:—

If birds did not exist, we could scarcely conceive the high organization to which the third eyelid, in man a mere rudiment, attains in them. Not wanted in man, tho organ sinks to its rudimentary and scarcely perceptible condition. Of essential service in birds, it suddenly acquires its seemingly highest development. Yet the organ was always present, rudimentary in one, developed in the other. Let us take another instance.

The adult, or grown-up man, has, as you all

no doubt know, three bones to each toe, with the
exception of the first; these three bones are connected to each other, and to the metatarsal bone,
their supporters, by three joints.   In the feet of
birds you meet with four or five bones in certain
of the toes; and it might seem to you that the
feet of birds were formed on a different numerical
plan, at least; but it is not so: for in man, as in
birds, each digital bone is formed of two elements,
or distinct bones, at first, that is, in the young of
each: as the bird grows up, they remain distinct
—in man, on the contrary, they unite—that is all.
The arrangement is not only analogous, but
homologous or identical, in the strictest sense of
the terms.

Again, remember that a thousand similar instances might be given: I merely select a few of
the easiest understood.

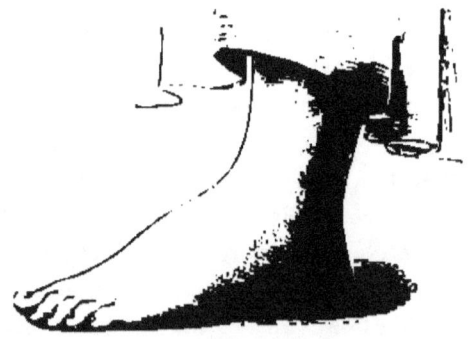

[*The European foot.*]

In man there is a little cartilage, scarcely perceptible, connected to one of those bones occupying the nostrils, called turbinated bones. It may or it may not in him serve any purpose; that is a matter of pure indifference. It is a rudimentary and a useless organ seemingly. Now, mark the extension and development of this cartilage or organ in the horse—still more in the whale. In the horse, where it most admirably serves to shut off the great cavities of the nostrils from the vestibular cavities in front—thus protecting them from foreign bodies: in the whale, acquiring their presumed highest development, these living cartilages, now grown to the size of bolsters, return after breathing into the vast nostrils of the whale from which they had been momentarily withdrawn, filling them up, sealing them hermetically against the pressure of a thousand fathoms deep of water, which they sustain with ease, when, plunging into the vast abyss of the ocean, the giant of nature seeks to avoid his enemies.

Let us now briefly review the progress we have made in this the highest of all analyses: deepest of all theories: most important to man. Man, we have seen, stands not alone, he is one of many; a part and parcel of the organic world, from all eternity. That organic world is the product of secondary causes. During his growth he undergoes

numerous metamorphoses, too numerous even for
the human imagination. These have a relation to
the organic world. They embrace the entire range
of organic life, from the beginning to the end of time.
Nature can have no double systems; no amend-
ments or second thoughts; no exceptional laws.
Eternal and unchanging, the orbs move in their
spheres precisely as they did millions of years ago.
Proceeding, as it were, from an invisible point endowed with life, he passes rapidly, at first, through
many forms, all resembling, more or less, either
different races of men from his own, or animals
lower in the scale of being; or beings which do
not now exist, though they probably *once* did, or
may at some future time. When his development
is imperfect, it represents then some form, resembling the inferior races of men, or animals still
lower in the scale of being. Moreover, what is
irregular in him is the regular structure in some
other class of animals. Take for example the
webbed hand or foot occasionally found in man,
constant in certain animals,—as in the Otter and
Beaver; constant also in the human fœtus, that
is, the child before birth. Take for example the
cuticular fold at the inner angle of the eye, so
common with the Esquimaux and Bosjeman or
Hottentot, (the corresponding yellow races of the
northern and southern hemispheres,) so rare in
the European, but existing in every fœtus of every

race. Nor let it be forgotten that forms exist in the human fœtus which have nothing human in them in the strictest sense of the term; that the fœtus of the Negro does not, as has been stated, resemble the fœtus of the European, but that the latter resembles the former, all the more resembling the nearer they are to the embryonic condition. Unity of structure, unity of organization, unity of life, at the commencement of time, whether measured by the organic world or by the duration of individual life. Lastly:—

Whence then arise those varied forms of man and beasts, plants, and living things, which now clothe the earth, giving to it the sole interest we possess in its existence; without which it were, in our conceptions, a barren waste, an immeasurable wilderness, a world without an object—what sympathies could we have with it, though its strata were gold and silver, alternating with rubies and emeralds? What signifies to us the stellar universe? The earth we inhabit is the field for the immediate inquiry of man. That inquiry, stifled for thousands of years, reopens from time to time; checked by fraud and force, it cannot be put down. A chapter on its history ought to form my concluding lecture.

Section I.

WHAT a pitiful thing is human history! Up to
the period of my own existence it was a current
matter of belief with all nations, all creeds, the
learned and the unlearned, that the earth, as it now
exists, was some 5641 years or so old; some felt
disposed, though with great caution, to venture,
in a humble and beseeching way, to add 1600
to these 5641, making a good round total of 7200
years since man and plants, birds and beasts, appeared on the earth; since the orb commenced
its wild path through space. By this it was hoped
to " reconcile" all things sacred and profane; to
give a concordance to the writings of a race, to
whom truth in chronology was a farce;* a race
without science, literature, or art; a race who
never originated a single discovery calculated
to benefit mankind—to advance civilization, to
humanize the animal part of the human kind.
One discovery upset this quiet dream; one man
taking up the views of others, and *carrying
them out to their legitimate length,* upset all existing
ideas as to the history of the earth and its
organic inhabitants. That man was George
Cuvier; his biography is well worth writing, that
is, his true biography; what has been done in

---

* Prideaux's Concordance.

this way is below criticism—I mean to glance
at it here merely in a scientific point of view,
with a reference to the aid and to the resistance
he offered to the progress of science; the solid
aid he gave in disabusing the mind of a system of
the grossest delusion and falsehood which had
prevailed for at least four thousand years; the resistance he offered to the spread of those doctrines
which, not appertaining to him, nor to his era,
not French, not Celtic, nor Saxon, but Slavonian
and South German, he dreamed as calculated
to terminate his own era before his own extinction;
the opposition, in fact, he offered to the extension
into the schools of France of the doctrines of transcendental anatomy. Of the English schools I
speak not—they took no part in the struggle at
first; to these followers of Paley, nearly to a man,
the philosophy of nature, as expounded by the
laws of transcendentalism, could have no meaning.
Within these two or three years, a few persons,
for the credit of the country, have ventured to
attempt the formation of a school of low transcendentalists, (I use their own phrase,) nibbling,
but with great and becoming caution, at the transcendental doctrines. The school, if it can be
so called, is beneath all notice in the history of
science.

SECTION II.—*Discovery of the real antiquity of*

the earth and of the organic kingdom—era of Cuvier.
The publication of the " Ossemens Fossiles" by
M. George Cuvier forms an era in the history of the
human mind. It set aside for ever all existing
chronologies of the organic and inorganic world,
its duration and formation. It revealed in a way
not to be called in question any more, the astounding fact, that for millions of years the earth had
been inhabited by plants and animals of races
now (*seemingly*) extinct. He declared them to be
extinct, and so in one sense they are. He showed,
what others had indeed done before his day, but
neither so fully nor so clearly as he did, that
the existing continents had been under water, not
for forty days, but for ten times forty thousand
years. That they had risen and been immersed
repeatedly; life, in the meantime, varying with
each elevation and submersion; that the now living
forms do not resemble the ancient forms: that
they could not be their direct descendants; that a
new Fauna and a new Flora had appeared and re-
appeared repeatedly on the earth's surface. There
ended the dreams of all previous scientific (!) men,
geologists, historians, theologians. And had
the remains of *man* been found coeval with some
of these fossil remains, the human mind would
have been set free at once, and by one mighty
effort from a chronological incubus which still
oppresses it. Scientific men all over the world

saw this; the pseudo-scientific, whose chief
habitat is England, availed themselves to the
full of the curious anomaly: man, they observed,
came last, late, but yesterday; Cuvier supported
this view himself, in an elaborate preliminary discourse, in which he wandered far from the matter
in hand. He showed that human fossil bones
could nowhere be found; that the most ancient
of human labours dated but a few years back;
that the Pyramids themselves were but of yesterday, compared with the antiquity of the Anaplo-
therian and Plethiosaurian remains; that the *homo
dilixvii testis* of Schultzer was merely a fossil sala-
mander; that the bones of the *giants* preserved
in Germany belonged to the fossil mammoth.
What a mass of hideous ignorance has not anatomy removed from the human mind; anatomy
and a *geology based* upon it; twin brothers, which
cannot and ought not to be disunited.

Reflecting on the wonderful step in advance of
preceding ages, our wonder ceases that Rome and
Oxford should have felt alarmed; but the flood
could not be arrested, and each took its own way
to meet it. The former, truculent to the last,
never ceased its hostility. Ever-watchful, it instructed the greatest of all Irish impostors, and
that is saying much, to offer an uncompromising
resistance to the establishment of colleges in that
happy and enlightened country, in which colleges

or schools *Anatomy* and *Geology* should be taught by any one *not appointed by the Roman See!* By the hierarchy drawing its inspirations from the Catholic unity of Rome! *This* failed, no doubt, but they will try again. The object of the Romish Church was to teach falsehoods instead of truths; to suppress the facts of anatomy and geology; to explain away, to expound, to twist and contort; to jesuitize all human knowledge.

Of the tactics " of the Great Dissent"* I mean to say little here. Finding the stream too strong to be resisted, they threw themselves into it with the utmost energy and vehemence; stereotyped Cuvier's imperfect researches; made them orthodox, and, as is their wont, prohibited all further inquiry. Cuvier was to be to them in the place of Aristotle, and to endure for as many centuries.

In the meantime, the stream of science could not be arrested. A bold attempt was made to stereotype Paley's coarse, mechanical views upon the schools of philosophy;† it also must fail; *final causes* are not causes, but *effects;* all philosophers ‡ admit this. Let us return to Cuvier and to his œra.

Prior to the publication of the " Ossemens Fossiles," the instinctive desire for accurate anatomical

* English Church. † Bridgewater Treatises. ‡ Fontana.

knowledge had led Cuvier to undertake the most
extended researches into the anatomy of the actual
existing order of living animals. His beautiful
work on this subject is classical, and cannot be
excelled. Such researches he mistook for philosophical anatomy; these comparative examinations
of the special anatomy of various natural families
and species of animals he mistook for comparative
anatomy; the results, for comparative physiology.
His subsequent inquiries into the fossil remains
of previous worlds should have taught him otherwise. But he had established a reputation, an
æra, and that was enough. Accordingly, he
watched, evidently with gloomy apprehensions,
all attempts to alter or extend his views. He had
proved, as he thought satisfactorily, the existing,
living races of animals to be totally, and specifically, and generically, distinct from their predecessors; his views warranted the doctrine of
successive generations of plants and animals,
although I am not sure that he ever said so; but
if he did not, it was said for him, in England and
in France. He had proved, moreover, as he
thought, that the existing order of animal life had
not changed since its appearance on the earth;
that neither plants nor animals had changed their
forms, at least since the building of Carnac and
the Pyramids; but he avoided speaking of man.
Cautious to an extreme, he failed to remark that

the same observation applied strictly to man himself; that he, also, had not changed during the
lapse of time alluded to. Thus he was using a
double-edged weapon without being, perhaps,
aware of it.

I first saw Cuvier and his illustrious opponent,
Geoffroy, in 1821; Oken was in Paris, and many
others. It was easy for me, intimate with both,
in almost daily conference with Geoffroy—aware
of the views of my illustrious friend, De Blainville, the first of all living anatomists—it was easy
for me, so situated, to foresee a coming storm. " It
is to be regretted," said Cuvier to me, " that our
friend Geoffroy is not an anatomist." Now, that
was no doubt strictly true : he was no anatomist,
in any sense, but he was an observer of nature,
of lofty transcendental views; a man of genius
and original powers of thought, beyond the logical
mind of the celebrated author of the " Ossemens
Fossiles." The result was briefly this. Strongly
impressed with the ideas of the unity of the
organization, unity of structure, unity of plan in
nature's works, a portion of the great transcendentalism taught him and Europe, by the
master minds of Slavonia and South Germany,
he made an effort to introduce them into France,
and even into the bosom of that Academy where
Cuvier reigned triumphant. A failure was the
certain result. Cuvier easily withstood the attack,

and returned it with great advantage; ridiculed, as they deserved, the illogical views of my esteemed friend in respect of analogous and homologous structures, and succeeded, for a time, in suppressing the transcendental doctrines in France. So early as 1821, I had pointed out to my most esteemed friend Geoffroy, that he must not play fast and loose with analogy and homology; that organs were not convertible, as he thought; that the branchial cartilages could not be converted into ribs, nor ribs into branchial cartilages; that nature had laid down certain types or plans which it was our business to investigate and, if possible, to discover, but not to determine *à priori*. I could easily see that my illustrious friends were both partly in the wrong; Cuvier most. The event has proved it. Let us consider how this was brought about.

The immortal discoveries of the South German and Slavonian Schools in respect of Embryology, the doctrine of the skeleton, of unity of the organization, and of a universal type or plan, had by this time, in despite of Cuvier and his school, made a progress scarcely to be resisted. It is true that Geoffroy's loose views, based on analogies and homologies alternately, could not be sustained; no more could the formula of Meckel and the North German school be admitted as true theories; they had discovered the source of

all human aberrations of form to consist in an
arrest of development; this I showed could not
be true of all; not, for example, of that most
remarkable perhaps of all deviations in human
structure, which I had the good fortune to discover—the structure of the arm of the tiger found
in man. I had shown, moreover, with others,
although few took the same views, that lungs
and gills were not convertible into each other
in the vertebrata; that every vertebrate animal
seemed to possess both, whilst in the embryonic
state, and that this extended to man himself; that
the same doctrine applied to the generative system ; and that Meckel's views and formula were
wholly untenable. Still, this did not affect, in
the main, the soundness of the transcendental
theories; it merely showed that false applications
had been made of them. As early as 1827, I
proposed a modification of the views, substituting
the doctrine of type for the then existing theories.
But, foreseeing the differences certain to arise
between my illustrious friends, and sure of being
referred to as witness of Geoffroy's earliest researches ; satisfied that in the coming struggle
there was one anatomist at least*—one, too, of the
highest reputation, who could, as a right-hand
friend, have preserved M. Geoffroy from all

* M. Serres.

serious anatomical errors, I ceased all correspondence with these illustrious men for many
years. But I have promised the result as regards
this dispute ; it may be stated in a few words.

In his place in the Academy of Sciences, M.
Geoffroy, at last made the following bold proposition; long had he meditated it, but had not
the moral courage to do so; he foresaw that it
must disunite him with Cuvier, and, in some measure, with the Academy. The proposition may be
thus summed up:—" The existing animals and
plants—the Fauna and Flora of the present world
—are connected with the past by direct descent;
generation following generation uninterruptedly.
There never was but one creation. Time, the
laws of development, changes in the external and
circumambient atmosphere of the globe, in the
frame of the globe itself, effected all the rest.
In the structure of one animal all the forms are
included; the embryo proves this; so also do the
phenomena which fossil anatomy has already unfolded. There is then, after all, but one living
principle, one animal, one eternal law. Forms of
animal life, forms of vegetable life are, to a
certain extent, unimportant. Matter assumes, no
doubt, certain definite forms; naturally, nothing
exists by chance, all is in harmony with the
great First Cause—the end or object no man can
foresee, no man can foretel. Meantime, let us

investigate truth; the opposite course has led to
tragedies of an appalling nature."

Thus did Geoffroy, foremost in France, but last
in Germany,* bring forward and advocate the
views of the illustrious Oken and Göethe, Leibnitz, and a host of others; applying the doctrines
of transcendental anatomy to the past and present
and to the future. Much requires to be done to
give to these doctrines all the accuracy of a
finished inquiry; the whole subject is but yet in
its infancy.

" There is but *one animal*," said Geoffroy, " not
many," and to this vast and philosophic view, the
mind of Cuvier himself, towards the close of life,
gradually approached. It is, no doubt, the correct one. Applied to man, the doctrine amounts
to this,—Mankind is of one family, one origin.
In every embryo is the type of all the races of men;
the circumstances determining these various races
of men, as they now, and have existed, are as yet
unknown; but they exist, no doubt, and must be
physical; regulated by secondary laws, changing,
slowly or suddenly, the existing order of things.
The idea of new creations, or of any creation
saving that of living matter, is wholly inadmis-
sible.   The world is composed of matter, not
of mind. The circumstances giving rise, then,

---

* See note on the views of Spix and Von Martius—the
human skeleton.

to the specializations of animal and vegetable forms, giving them a permanency of some thousand years, are as yet unknown to us, and may for ever remain so; but that is no reason why they should not be inquired into. Some speculations into this, the most important of all human inquiries, will be found in the notes appended to this lecture.

In conclusion: the permanent varieties of men, permanent at least seemingly during the historic period, originate in laws elucidated in part by embryology, by the laws of unity of the organization, in a word, by the great laws of transcendental anatomy. Variety is deformity; deviation from one grand type towards which Nature, by her laws of specialization, constantly aims: those laws which, once established, terminated the reign of chaos. To every living thing they give a specific character, enduring at least for a time; man also has his specific character to endure for a time. Certain forms, certain deviations, in obedience to the great and universal law of unity, are not viable in the existing order of things; but they may become so. If the deformity, that is, a return more or less to unity, be too great, too antagonistic of her specific laws, the individual, whether man or mere animal or plant, ceases to be, and thus the extension of variety of forms, which we call " deformations," ceases.

The perfect type of man was discovered by the ancient sculptors of Greece: it cannot be surpassed; all attempts to improve on it have failed. Towards this, nature constantly tends. Certain races seem to be approaching the condition of non-viable races; it would seem as if their course was run: they hold the same position to mankind as the individual or family in whom the laws of unity, superseding in part the laws of specialization, have given rise to deformations, monstrosities, incompatible with reproduction, or with individual life. These races may then probably disappear, and this may be the fate of man himself under every form, his intellectual nature notwithstanding. For millions and millions of years the world rolled through space without him; his absence was not felt; he hopes his presence to be now eterne: Creature of yesterday! Such would have been the language of the ancient saurians, could they have spoken —" Look at our might, our strength; look at the glorious world around; the vast and beauteous forms which everywhere decorate the earth. This can never come to a close." But it did, and that frequently too: from the past, judge of the future.

APPENDIX.

In the history of the Jewish, Coptic, and Gipsy races, the great question of the extinction of race has been considered. These races, placed by theorists with the so-called Caucasian race, and at the head of the Caucasian family, I consider as belonging to the dark races of men. They are African and Asiatic, not European. The purest of the Jewish race is a dark tawny, yellow-coloured person, with jet-black hair and eyes seemingly coloured: there is no mistaking the race when pure:* it is Egyptian—that is, African. The same remarks apply to the gipsy, who is of Asiatic origin. A series of incorrect observations, commencing with Blumenbach, but not terminating with Prichard, led to errors which no doubt will hold their ground for centuries. For this reason I have, in a preceding lecture, reviewed the history of these three races, the Copt, the

* See Engraving, p. 193.

Gipsy, and the Jew, and in so doing, briefly
examined the question of the extinction of race, as
applicable to all. Of the destiny of the dark races
it is not my intention to say much. Originating
from the same stock with their fellow men of all
colours; formed into distinct groups by the laws
of development, obeying geological æras; these
groups or natural families preserve, as in the case
of all other animals, their specific forms and mental
qualities, for at least a term of years which history
does not yet enable us to determine, but of sufficient duration to convey to the limited mind of
man the idea of eternal. Thus it was that Cuvier,
assuming the brief span of man's written history,
and of man's pictorial history, as shown on the
monuments of Egypt, to be the beginning and
end of man's history, leaped to the conclusion
that animals (he avoided speaking of man *on this
point,*) had not altered their forms in *the slightest
degree* since the historic period commenced; as if
that historic period were anything but a day in
the history of the globe, and of life. Thus it was
that his followers, denying the slightest change
to any other animal for thousands of years, though
exposed in every possible way to climatic influences, claimed for man the privilege of everlasting change, though protected from these
influences by his inventive genius, mental faculties, and powers of combination; of changes in

form and exterior, so great that in any other
animal they would of necessity form groups which
science could not permit to be confounded with
each other.[*]

And now, inquiry shows us, that these groups
of the darker races of men I have just spoken of,
touch, by diverging rings, all other races; showing
the deep affiliations depending on the unity of
human life—of all life: of the great laws of unity
of organization, suspended merely for a time by
those specific laws which give to life its forms and
order in space and time. By the Central American[†]
they seemed to have touched the ancient Euxine
race described by Hippocrates; by the Hottentot
and Bosjeman they touch the Mongol and Tartar;
by the Nubian and Abyssinian they approached
the Copt and Jew; and through them, Asiatic,
Greek, Syrian, Armenians. Furthest removed by
nature from the Saxon race, the antipathy between
these races is greater than between any other: in
each other they perceive their direct antagonists.
The wild and savage South African; the Tasmanian, the uncultivated Negro, merely feel the
instinct; the semi-civilized Chinaman, Malay,
Negro, Afghan, both feel and understand the
results. The mandarin sees, in the contest with
a Saxon race, the extinction of his own; he acts

[*] See Engraving, p. 224.
[†] See Drawing of Cherokee, p. 246.

accordingly.   Could he be taught; could he read
and understand the rise and progress of the Anglo-
Saxon in America, then war to the knife would be
the first and last words of a Chinaman, a Kaffre,
a Red Indian, a New Zealander.   But they cannot
be taught: history has no examples for them.
Animals of to-day, they look not for a to-morrow;
the present is theirs.   Destined by the nature of
their race to run, like all other animals, a certain
limited course of existence, it matters little how
their extinction is brought about.   Starting from
a stronger stock at first; fresh and energetic, like
the young oak, their forms of civilization, peculiar,
of course, to themselves, preceded that of their
fairer brethren.   This is at least my present opinion, from historic data, I admit, of doubtful authority.   In their progress, each group showed its own
tendencies towards the civilized, or rather towards
the human condition; towards a show, at least, of
humanity, and the decencies and order of human
existence.   The Central Asiatic race, the Mongol,
the Tartar, when pure, revelled in tents and arms;
plunder and the pomp of war was their whole
aim.   The other group, the Chinaman, proceeded
somewhat further; his tendencies were domestic
and trading: his taste for pagodas and lanterns is
characteristic; his notions of beauty of form peculiar; in all things peculiar; in architecture,
literature, fine (?) arts, peculiar; and having car-

ried out his destiny, attained the maximum of his
civilization, and being unequal to the full adoption
of any other, he progresses not, standing on the
verge of that destruction awaiting him, when
Saxon and Sarmatian will contend with each
other for the plunder of Nangasaki and Pekin,
with high hopes, no doubt, of supplanting the
Asiatic race, or at the least, of converting China
and Japan into another Hindostan. This I doubt;
not the attempt, but the result. But to this, also,
I have already devoted a few remarks.

On the American continent, the central group
of the aboriginal coloured races was running their
narrow course when the Celtiberian and Lusitanian races burst in upon them; upsetting their
idols and temples; their pyramids and obelisks;
as the semi-barbarous Saxon and Celt and Goth
burst on Rome; with the same results; the substitution of one form of civilization for another;
of one race for another; none to hold their ground,
but all to dwindle into a mere shadow. Look at
modern Rome and modern Mexico; Jerusalem as
it is, and as it was; Babylon as it is, and as it was;
Karnac; Egyptian Thebes with its hundred gates;
immortal.

The Southern Asiatic also had his day; his rise
and fall. In ancient times he built structures
in Hindostan, which his pitiful descendants look
at with awe and wonder, but attempt neither to

repair nor renew. In Central Africa the true black or negro race seems to have attained his ultimatum centuries ago. He has his own form of civilization, but, unfortunately, it includes neither literature, art, nor science. Yet he is industrious, good tempered, energetic, accumulative, a lover of order and of finery; a fatalist and a worshipper of Fetisches. The stronger-headed men of his race dispense with their respect for the Fetisch as Aristides and Cæsar did with the heathen gods of Rome, leaving all such frivolities to the " rascal multitude." * Yet from that mass they spring, and to it they return. When the race attempts the civilization of another, Celtic or Saxon, for example, the whole affair becomes a ludicrous farce, and even grave men laugh at it. The after-piece is being played in St. Domingo, where they have elected a black emperor! In Liberia they will elect a sham president. It can come to nothing in either case. Each race must act for itself, and work out its own destiny; display its own tendencies; be the maker of its own fortunes, be they good or evil. A foreign civilization they cannot adopt; borrow they may, and cunningly adapt, calling it national, native; but the imposture, like all impostures, becomes manifest in time, whether practised by the negro or the Saxon.

* The appellation usually applied to "the million" by my great ancestor, John Knox.

They elect a president in Hayti; in recollection of
Napoleon; he declares himself emperor; standing
in the same relation to that name which the oran-
outan does to the Apollo. He even sets an example
to the President of the backward republic of Celtic-
Gaul; See, he says, how forward *we are*. He founds
a dynasty; black Thiers and swarthy Guizots
cluster around to establish the dynasty and maintain the " juste milieu;" they spout philosophy,
and praise the virtues of the reigning dynasty;
the majesty of the law; the divine rights of kings
and emperors; the sacred rights of property
and privilege, however acquired. The whole is
a farce when acted in Hayti; a melo-drame with
tragic episodes when Gaul is the stage; and so it
is ever with the most skilful and able of impostors, that is, of imitators; sooner or later the trick
comes out. A noble mind builds St. Paul's! a
copy, it is true, and an imitation of a greater; but
a noble imitation, satisfying all minds. The thing
is vaunted as national! native! straightway, as if
to unmask the imposture, a certain building appears in Trafalgar-square; a hideous bronze or
two show themselves about Hyde-park; natives,
no doubt; quite original. But I forget that my
present chapter is on the dark races, or rather
the darker groups of the dark or coloured
races. I have already spoken of their affiliated
races, the Gipsy, Copt, and Jew; and of that

race which far excelled all others,—the ancient Greek.

I have sometimes thought, that even the yellow race of Africa, the degraded Hottentot and Bosjeman, the Quaquoes and the Antniquas, must have had their æra; their attempt at civilization and its failure; instead of being a recent oppressed race, they are perhaps a most ancient and fallen race; fallen, never to rise again, not merely by having come into contact with more powerful races, but simply as a result of the history of development and progress. In ancient times the race seems to have extended throughout all Africa; I have alluded to this in my history of the Troglodytes of Homer; the desert or dry places of the earth seem always to have been their dwelling-place. Where placed near stronger races, they would imitate their civilization in as far as their physical organization admitted; just as the Hottentot of the Cape does, or would do if left to himself. The towns he would build would not be strictly European towns, but clusters of mud closets, raised on each other, should necessity, that is, a want of room or a common danger, compel them to live huddled together in groups. They would occupy, in a half civilized condition, some insulated hill or rock, driving their flocks and herds to the plains during the day-time, and retiring to their fastnesses on the approach of

night or of an enemy, thus leading a dreamy,
dreary, life, " flat, stale, and unprofitable." The
history of a day is the history of their lives. Such
were the Namaquas when first visited and described by Kolben and Le Vaillant, bating the
fastnesses and densely populated hill town, to
which no necessity had ever given rise. Gradually diminishing and fading away, prior even to
the advent of the Saxon-Boor in Southern Africa,
they seem to have never attained any higher condition of civilization there; but could we suppose
for an instant, that the peculiar and almost indescribable race of men whom Mr. St. John found
in the Oases of Northern Africa, and especially in
that of Jupiter Ammon, are the descendants of
the Troglodytes of Homer, then we have a solution
of the question as regards the yellow race or races
of Africa. In Northern Africa they had attained
their highest element of civilization possibly even
before Egyptian Thebes was built; or wandering
over the deserts, they imitated, in their own
fashion, the doings of stronger races; built their
hovels on a hill, and for self-defence lived together. But they had run their course before
Carthage appeared; then came the Roman, dispossessing, as to power, Juba and Masanissa;
then the Saracen and the Moor; they too, sink
before the climate and the returning dark races;
returning to the land from which they were often

expelled; themselves gradually fading away, to
be replaced by the *wilde* and the desert, perhaps
the ocean.   The Arab and the Turkoman supplanted the Copt in Egypt; but will they hold
their ground? observing travellers seem to think
that they cannot; the Coptic face is still to be
seen on the banks of the Nile; the Negro gives
ground; the desert also progresses; and thus may
the motley population of Egypt perish, failing
to represent its ancient inhabitants.

If there be a dark race destined to contend
with the fair races of men for a portion of the
earth, given to man as an inheritance, it is the
Negro.   The tropical regions of the earth seem
peculiarly to belong to him; his energy is considerable: aided by a tropical sun, he repels the
white invader.   From St. Domingo he drove out
the Celt; from Jamaica he will expel the Saxon;
and the expulsion of the Lusitanian from Brazil,
by the Negro, is merely an affair of time.

Section II.— *The Antagonism of Man to Nature's Works.*

The citizen—the man of to-day—the formulist
—the being whose mind has been clept and
fashioned from its earliest dawn, as his garments;
forced to adopt the " spirit of his times," taught
to talk largely of the rapid progress of man—of

his civilization, meaning the form which society
has assumed in the warren-looking row of dwell-
ings, in No. 4, or 6, of which he is for a brief
space located; to this trammelled and harnessed
animal, " the wilde" is a mere plaything, an unintelligible freak of creation. Having no occasion
for thought, it occupies no part of his attention;
and should so idle a question arise in his mind
as " the object of its creation," his remaining
special and specific instincts which the artificial
existence he chooses to call " civilization" has
failed quite to extinguish, teach him that to it
his nature is antagonistic. Thus be he savage
or boor, citizen or man, coloured or fair, war to
the knife is the cry with Nature's Fauna and
Nature's Flora; destroy and live, spare and
perish, is tho stern law of man's destiny. Whence
this antagonism? and why? To the profound
philosophers of the Bridgewater school, to the
sturdy Utilitarian, the dogmatic Jew, to the man
of happy self-conceit, who in all things sees two
sides of a question, of which the one of his adoption must be the best, who thinks that two and
two make four, or five, or one, according as the
matter is viewed; who sees in the enormous destruction and seeming waste of life—of early
infant life—innocent, pale-faced, sweet and beauteous youth, struck at by stern, remorseless, piti-
less death, " a wise dispensation of Providence

for the multiplying of pleasure:"* to him, or to them, for they are a school, I leave the jesuitical task of discovering in physical and moral suffering a benefit and a pleasure, and proceed, disclaiming all knowledge of " the why" and " the wherefore," pretending not to an initiation into the mysterious ways of the Creative Power—its intentions, its plans, its views, its theory—but merely to inquire into the reality of the fact and its consequences.

That animal and vegetable life is produced in an abundance exceeding all belief; that a half, at least, of everything born, perishes from unknown causes when young; that another section or division afterwards perish, being destined as food for others; that man himself, an animal mortal and frail like others, is included to the full in this stern category; that there would even seem for him a worse fate than for the others, is simply a fact undeniable, explain it as you may. Mental and bodily diseases of all hues, harassing pestilence and famine ; wars of opinion! war to the knife! promising utter destruction and final extermination to those who prefer the evidence of sense to the erring reason of man, stupidly maintaining that bread is not flesh, and that wine cannot be turned into blood until

* Buckland, Bridgewater Treatise.

digested and assimilated. Man's fate, then, is severer than that of the lower animals; they have no aristocracy, no priests, no kings; they are spared this triple curse; nor can a dark and fearful future be depicted on their brains, in terms so strong as to make them believe that millions of invisible beings walk the lower regions of the atmosphere, wholly occupied in leading him to destruction.*

Whatever, then, be the cause, life is produced on the globe in extravagant and unintelligible abundance—life clothed in forms, some simple, others more complex. To this life, as produced by nature, clothed with the forms necessitated by development in time, or by time (for this has not yet been fully resolved) man, also a part of Nature's plan, else he could not be present, is the perpetual antagonist. Against the floral and faunal *wilde* he carries on perpetual war; if civilized, even the natural herbage does not escape him; for it he substitutes an artificial crop. His domestic animals, as he calls them, seem never to have been really wild. They are not, nor ever were, found in a natural state; it is the same with vegetable productions; his destiny is, multiply sheep and oxen, and wheat and cabbages, until the earth be filled therewith; to extrude and destroy, if he can, all that is wonderful

* Modern Theology.

and beautiful on the globe as it came from Nature's
hands.   In dealing with this astounding, yet certain truth, let us be cautious how we apply the
word man.   Are all the races of men antagonistic
of Nature's work?   Probably they are, but differ
in this antagonistic power immeasurably from
each other; nor is it improbable that, with certain races, the amount of antagonism would in
no conceivable period of time have reached
the point of extermination.   But for the rifle,
the American bison might for thousands of
years have maintained his ground against the
feebly armed Indian; the grizzly bear might
have become in time the assailant; the wolf
have forced the copper-coloured Indian to fortify
his camp against a midnight attack; and the
jaguar and alligator and boa reigned masters
of the wooded banks of the Maranon and Ori-
noco.   I know not of any means possessed by
the Circumpolar races for the extermination of
the seal and walrus, the polar bear, the whale;
no powers of combination, no powers of invention equal to the task.   For how many ages to
come might not the ponderous elephant and un-
wieldy hippopotamus have grazed by the banks
of the remote Kei, or harmlessly gambolled in
the Keis Kamma or Gariepine streams?   For how
many centuries yet to come, but for the interposition of the Saxon and the rifle, might not the

stately giraffe, with the gazelle eye, have adorned
the southern edge of the Calihari, by your
beauteous reaches, clear and crystal Gariep?
Who shall say? The wild man was obviously
unequal to their destruction; even the baboon he
dared not attack in troops; the buffalo and the
rhinoceros he could scarcely encounter under any
circumstances; and, in despite of Bosjeman and
Hottentot, and Kaffir, the lion stalked at mid-day
on the open plains. This have I seen whilst
wandering in South Africa, traversing slowly the
Bosjeman land, or wistfully gazing over that
beauteous field, looking from the Koonap eastward, then calm and peaceful, now marked by
scenes of pillage, plunder, and relentless massacre.
On this field the naked savage met the disciplined
savage, the semi-barbarian met nature's man.

In my early days, and whilst still a youth,
a friend placed in my hands five enchanting
volumes, full of nature and of truth, " The
Adventures of Le Vaillant." Ten years afterwards I stood on the spot where, crossing the
Groote Visch Rivière, he ascended the slope
leading to the undulating Table-land, through
which the Koonap and the Chumic, the Keis
Kamma, and many other streams make their
way, directly or indirectly, to join the Indian
Ocean. Wandering alone on the afternoon of a
bright sunshiny day, such a day as can be seen

only in Southern Africa, and ascending the long
and gentle slope, thus reaching the level of the
grassy plains stretching eastward towards the
Koonap, the neutral ground lay before me.   To
the north and east might be traced the wooded
range of the Kaha and Anattola mountain range,
part and parcel of the lofty Winterbergen; and
as I stood musing on the scene before me, the
past and the future rose on my imagination like
a dream.   What was the living scene before me?
Nature in all her wondrous beauty and variety;
the dark-eyed antelope, of nearly all varieties,
covered the plain; in the distance, stalked slowly
the majestic ostrich; over head soared, silent and
sad, the vulture; bustards of all sizes; harmless,
peaceful, grain and insect-loving animals; the
zebra and the quagga; the acacia, the strelitzia,
the evergreens, the pasture and the bush, planted
by nature; the field which plough or spade had
never turned up, on which the cerealia had never
been grown.   And what is this scene to me, I
said?   Beautiful though it be, where is man?   It
seemed, in my sight, a vast stage, decorated, picturesque, lovely, but the actors were wanting; it
was a panorama, a picture—a living picture, yet
desert and without that life to which man ever
looks.   But now the glass discovers on the wooded
slopes of the Chumie mountains the curling smoke,
telling of the presence of man.   Now who is the

man who watches that fire? It is the savage Bosjeman, or still fiercer Kaffir; the race looked for
by Le Vaillant many years before, from the same
spot on which I now stood. Nature, then, had
stood its ground in that lapse of time; she had
remained seemingly unaltered for countless ages
up to the moment I then noted her; Why should
not this continue? I will tell you: a new element
had appeared, the Dutch-Saxon and the Anglo-
Saxon were now hanging on the skirts of the old
African world. A new element of mind had appeared about to create a new South African æra:
the Saxon or Celtic element, bringing with it the
semi-civilized notions of Europe—the power of
combination, fire-arms, discipline, laws. Before
this new element, antagonistic of nature, her
works are doomed to destruction, in as far as man
can destroy. The wild acacia he wastes as fire-
wood; the Chumie forests he utterly destroys,
converting the timbers thereof into rafters for
barracks and other hovels, for men to congregate
in like pigs. Over nature's pastures, over the
iris, bulbous plants of surpassing beauty, over the
strelitzia, and a thousand other wild flowers, he
passes the ruthless plough. The antelope is
exterminated or disappears; the zebra, the gnoo,
the ostrich, the bustard, escape from the land, or
are shot down; the mighty onslaught of an antagonistic element, seemingly too strong for nature,

defeats even the rhinoceros, the elephant, the lion,
so that their skins are become rare, so rare as
to be prized for European museums. Last comes
man himself—the coloured man—the man placed
there by nature; he also must of necessity give
way; his destiny apparently is sealed, and extinction in presence of a stronger race seems
inevitable. The yellow race, the feebler, will
naturally yield first; then the Kaffir—he also
must yield to the Saxon Boor, on whose side is
right, that is, might; for, humanly speaking, might
is the sole right. Retiring northwards towards
the Calihari, and perhaps crossing it, he and the
wilde with him may gain Central Africa, and so
escape for a time the destruction threatening
them. But is this destruction certain? In
front of the Saxon Boor stands the desert;
that he cannot conquer. As he advances
northward and eastward, he encounters the
tropical line, within which generally he cannot live. Thus, after all, his dominion may be
limited to Southern extra-tropical Africa; nor
is it quite certain that he may always stand his
ground in that healthiest of all countries. He
has not yet *laboured* there as a cultivator; he has
not yet been left to his own resources. But this
question I have already discussed — I mean the
destruction of one race by another, and the substitution of one race by another. Man's gift is to

destroy, not to create; he cannot even produce
and maintain a new and permanent variety of a
barn-door fowl, of a pheasant, of a sheep or horse.
This, then, is the antagonism of man, of certain
races of men, to nature's works — of those races,
at least, in whose minds civilization forms a
natural element — natural or acquired; of men
educable and progressive, at least to a certain
point. With other races it seems different. That
the Saxon and Celtic races may maintain their
ground in Southern Africa is possible, but not
proved. The history of man, as I have already
shown, is against the theory, which indeed is
mainly maintained by the arrogance and self-suf-
ficiency of the race. But this great question I
have already discussed : let me therefore conclude
by rapidly surveying the opposing obstacles to the
identification of the Saxon and Celtic races with
the soil of Southern Africa.

There is first the Kalihari or Southern Sahara;
the Karroo, not yet cultivated; the labour question
he has not yet met; to the northward, the tropic
he dare not enter as a cultivator; the dark and
more numerous races he must there encounter.
To these the Saxon bears an eternal, deep-rooted
hatred; but not so other races — the Celt, for
example, and the Celtiberian. As he proceeds
towards Central and Eastern Africa, he will encounter the Arab and the Moor: by these he has

H H

hitherto been kept in check. But it is the tropic
which must protect the dark races ultimately
against the antagonism of the fair. With the
wilde it is otherwise. There man may destroy—
this is, indeed, his aim—progressing onwards, as
he thinks, when the earth shall support only oxen
and sheep, and cabbages and man,* and Saxons,
of course; adopting the theory that the Saxon
race is the highest development. Pleasant theory!
So would have reasoned the saurians, could they
have reasoned—the sivatherium and the dinotherium! Contemplating their gigantic, and, it may
be, splendid forms, with the great and sublime
around him : tortoises that might sustain an elephant on their backs ; bears the size of horses ;
tigers and oxen of gigantic stature, and robes at
least as beautiful as those of the present day ;
was it not natural for the man of that day, as no
doubt there was such a man, to have said to himself, "This is the last development, the highest
effort of nature! She can produce nothing more
sublime than the world now before me!" But now
the aim of the Saxon man is the extermination of
the dark races of men—the aborigines—the men
of the desert and of the forest. I have shown you
the obstacles to his progress—the forest, the
growing desert, the overwhelming sands of the

---

* Mulder, the chemist.

sea-shore; the terrible results of earthquakes and
of volcanoes; the subsidence of land under the
ocean; the advance of the bog and the heath.
These affect all races, more or less; so does
climate—more powerful than all—the present
climate of the earth as it is known to us. Extend
the phrase climate to times past, and to times to
come; ask yourselves what climatic changes destroyed the mammoth, the aneplotherium, the
dinotherium, the sivatherium? the fishes of the
ancient world? the saurians? Man destroyed
them not; yet their race is run. Why dies out,
almost before our eyes, the apteryx? The Irish
elk, the gigantic fossil ox, the dodo, have not
long ceased to exist. The destroying angel
walks abroad unseen, striking even at the races
of men. But nature dies not; ever young; ever
returning; ever reviving; she is eternal. The
form is immaterial; the essence is the same; first
and last.

NOTES.

Note 1.

NATIONALITY *versus* RACE.

In despite of the lesson taught the Saxon race by the United States of America, a lesson without a parallel in the world, the Norman government of England persists in the same colonial policy which caused her the loss of America. Whilst I now write there is a scheme to found a *British colony*, with true *British* feelings, in New Zealand. It is to be called New Canterbury. Nothing can teach certain men. The promoters fancy that they can alter human nature; the Saxon nature: that *British feelings* or *nationality* is to prevail over the eternal qualities of race. So little do they seem to know of human nature, that they fancy it possible to extend British nationality to the descendants of a race, coming from England no doubt, but born and brought up in New Zealand. They actually deny to the Saxon his greatest quality, self-esteem, self-dependence. Scarcely will *these* New Zealanders have seen the fourth or fifth generation, before they will set Britain, with all its mock institutions, at defiance. They are Saxon men; that is, democrats, by their nature; and they will throw off the Norman rule the instant they can. They did this in the United States; the Cape will follow next; then Australia. Looking at the present condition of Britain, it were grievous to think otherwise.

NOTE 2.

About fifteen years ago, the Prussian system of education, as it was called, came into notice in England. Interested greatly in everything pertaining to the education
of man, I carefully weighed its probable results on any
people who unhappily might adopt it. The conclusions I
then formed, and of which I made no secret, were, 1st,
that the Prussian system was not intended to educate, but
to destroy the human mind. 2nd, that as nothing good
could come from the House of Brandenburg and its drum-
head government, it ought to be at once refused admittance into Britain. At that time I could get none to agree
with me on these points: to-day, however, I find that
even in the House of Commons, where truth penetrates
latest, the execrable scheme has been exposed. This really
infamous plan to destroy by misdirected State education
the mind of the rising generation, was not confined to
Prussia; it extended all over Austria.

NOTE 3.

I have introduced into the text a woodcut of the head
of one of those races supposed to have cannibal propen-
sities: but I have always doubted the fact of cannibalism
having ever existed. A patient inquiry into the history of
the American race satisfied me that the cannibalism of the
New World was the pure invention of the Catholic missionaries: the cannibalism of the East may, I think, be
traced to a similar source. I never met with any one who
had been present at such a banquet. In Africa no such
practice exists. The whole affair is, I think, a romance,
but it has served its purpose with those who think that
the end vindicates the means.

NOTE 4.

No mixed race can stand their ground for any long
period of years. The Danish (Scandinavian or Saxon)
blood, which must have existed in sufficient abundance in

South England during and subsequent to Canute's time, has given way before the Flemish races, which preceded the Saxon, and now prevails everywhere. All traces of the Scandinavian and Celtic seem to have left Greece. The mingled Italian races, the product of so many others, seem fast reverting to a primitive race, which occupied Italy before Rome was founded. A mixed race may then be produced, but it cannot be supported by its own resources, but by continual draughts from the two pure races which originally gave origin to it.

The character of such a race may be judged of by what ancient historians say of the Sybarites, even before the time of Pyrrhus, and by the accounts which some modern travellers give us of the present Neapolitans and South Italians, including the Sicilian. For the sake of humanity I should hope that these accounts are exaggerated; it has been said, that after thirty years of age all the characters of the vilest passions appear strongly on the South Italian countenance, in an unmistakable way. There must still be a good deal of Pelasgic blood in Campania and Sicily.

Note 5.

No existing race is equal to the colonization of the whole earth. They cannot even extend themselves from one continent to another. Already the Anglo-Saxon rears with difficulty his offspring in Australia: it is the same in most parts of America. But for the supplies they receive from Europe the race would perish, even in these most healthy climates. We have the authority of Mr. Warburton for a fact I long suspected, but could not fully ascertain. Jewish children cannot live in Jerusalem; and the whole race would die out in a few years in the promised land, but for the influx of stranger Jews from other countries. A great section of the Jewish race was probably Chaldean; for on the Nimrod monuments the Jewish cast of features is quite discernible. Another great section was Coptic. A Syrian section must have existed or grown up by intermarriage. No Jew lived in

Jerusalem until after David's time, and even then the original inhabitants, the Jebusites (Syrians), continued peaceably to occupy the city. It is probable, then, that in time the race may return to the original Chaldean ; but in England the Coptic features show remarkably in some families.

NOTE 6.

The *Saxon race*, as a race, is the tallest in the world, but, *cæteris paribus*, they are not the strongest. The Celt is stronger, and so, probably, is the Arab : the Congo black, Molyneux, was much stronger than any Englishman of his day. But in this climate, tall men frequently die early, of pulmonary consumption ; and hence the greater mortality of the Foot-guards, and the difficulty of maintaining the standard of recruitment. They enter the service, moreover, too young. When sent to fine climates, as the Cape and Australia, such persons live readily ; they escape consumption. The descendants also of the Saxon race seem to become a taller race in these latter countries; but this arises merely from the circumstance that the tall children, who would die in Europe, survive at the Cape, and in Australia.

The Saxon despises soldiering, so that his armies generally are heavy, cumbrous, and expensive. He is trained or disciplined with great difficulty. The *pure English peasantry* make wretched soldiers : they have neither the shape nor the qualities fitting them for war. The proper field for action of the Saxon is the ocean.

The Saxon, then, is not warlike, and he hates unprofitable wars ; but he is as brave as any man, and his strength and obstinacy make him a formidable enemy. As the Saxon by becoming a soldier loses the esteem of his fellow Saxons, so the status of the English soldier in society can never be raised ; the meanest *independent* labourer despises him ; he has sold his independence, the natural birthright of the Saxon. The Celtic race, destitute of all self-esteem, does not understand this : the Celt makes the best of soldiers : at sea he is all but worthless.

Note 7.

Homer must have seen a Scandinavian woman, else he could not so have described Penelope. The complexion he assigns to her exists in no other race.

Climate alters not complexion permanently; individual alterations never become hereditary. My esteemed friend, Dr. Andrew Smith, informs me, that, curious to know the truth on this point, he attentively looked at a family descended from forefathers who came to South Africa with the first settlers. Three hundred years, then, had elapsed since their first arrival. Their descendants at this moment are as fair as the fairest of Europeans.

The Dutch at the Cape (Saxons) have a perfect horror for the coloured races; it extends to the Mulatto, whom they absolutely despise. The placing a coloured man in an important official situation in South Africa, has caused to Britain the loss of some millions, and laid the basis for the ultimate separation of that colony from Britain.

Note 8.

Nationalities are always odious. Of all *nations* the English, in consequence of their nationalities, are the most disliked by the rest of mankind. They owe this in a great measure to the large admixture of Saxon blood which prevails throughout England. The Saxon portion of the United States men carry these bad qualities to the utmost extent; the press must, of necessity, support the nationalities, however odious and disgusting they may be. A most amusing paragraph in an American newspaper was shown to me lately, written, I think, at a place called Buffalo—a beautiful name for a city. The writer, like modern Saxons, tries his hand at statistics. "Sixty years ago, there were only six millions of Saxons in America; now there are twenty-six. In another century they will be sixty millions; and they will spread over the earth until the globe be theirs!" Admirable statistician! Effective writer of common-place! How coolly and softly you dis-

pose of the other races of men! But perhaps I do wrong
in noticing such nonsense.

NOTE 9.

Many are disposed to think that England is becoming
everyday more and more Saxon; I am not of this opinion
since residing in the South of England, where the population is mostly Flemish. Dynastic influence—Church and
State—and an executive backed wholly by a strong military force, never were more rampant in Britain then at
the present moment.

NOTE 10.

Since this work has gone to the press, I have been informed by a military friend, an excellent observer, that
the Saxon-Dutch at the Cape have seldom numerous families. I entertained myself at one time the opposite opinion,
but I feel now convinced of the correctness of my friend's
remarks. This explains the slow increase of population in
Southern Africa, and is another confirmation of the great
physiological law I have been the first to propose—namely,
that no race, be they who they may, can appropriate to
themselves any other continent than the one to which they
are indigenous. The ultimate extension, then, of the Saxon,
or of any other race, to other continents than their own, is
a dream or vision, opposed to all previous history. What
Providence may do for that, or for any other race, I do not
pretend to know. Under Providence we were driven
shamefully out of Affghanistan; and at Buenos Ayres, and
at Rosetta; dispossessed of the United States; Walcheren
tells a sad tale; and always under Providence the amount
of juvenile delinquency and crime exceeds in England probably all that at present exists on the globe. I leave the
matter in the hands of the theologian, who, whether he be
Lutheran or Catholic, Greek or Mahometan, will, no
doubt, reconcile all contradictions. I pretend to nothing,
but, simply inquire.

The Huns are interlopers from Asia; their fate seems

certain. It is the same with the Turcoman. The Jew never could make good his ground in Syria, nor the true Arab in Africa. The Celts of England, Ireland, and Scotland, are just where they were a thousand years before Cæsar landed. So are the Normans or Flemings of South England before William landed: so are the Saxons of Eastern England and Scotland. Spain seems returning to a single primitive race, existing there long before the Phœnicians landed in the Peninsula. Italy seems to be undergoing the same process.

Note 11.

It was, I think, in the spring of 1821, that I met the celebrated French traveller, Le Vaillant, in Paris. He was no traveller, nor was he a scientific man in any sense of the term. But he was a good naturalist, a collector of specimens, and a simple, honest, public-minded man. His description of South Africa was most accurate, so far as he went; but he forgot to say that the country was in the hands of the Dutch Boors. To have said so would have destroyed all the delightful romance of his inimitable work. Barrow hints that the Abbe Phillipon wrote Le Vaillant's works; now this is absolutely impossible. Retouched they may have been in Paris I admit, but that is all. Every word bears the impress of the mind of the man I met in Paris. Not one word of what Barrow said against Le Vaillant is strictly correct. No two men differed more widely than Barrow and Le Vaillant: the latter, a simple-minded naturalist, a lover of truth, a good observer, with some genius or originality; the former, destitute of all powers of original observation; a hard, cast-metal, cold-blooded, hack official, a model clerk of a model board; the mouth-piece of a Bureaux, the English Admiralty, in which it would be difficult to say whether incapacity or dishonesty most prevail.

Note 12.

Humboldt remarks in his "Kosmos," that the ancient mind (Greek and Roman) differed from the modern or that

now existing, in nothing more remarkably than in the view
each took of external nature; the landscape; the forest; the
ocean; the solemn grandeur of mountain gronps, touching
by their granitic pinnacles the clonds themselves. Of all
these the ancient mind took little or no notice; the modern
dwells on them even to nausea. This is not the place to
explain the cause of so wide a difference: this work already
exceeds greatly the extent which I promised my publisher.
I may therefore merely observe, that in contemplating the
external world and its material manifestations, man and
his instinctive and intellectual results; his physical structure and his mind are really the only objects in this world
which tonch the human feelings deeply. All else is desert:
all else is surface: there exists no corresponding sympathies
but with *one*, primitive and elementary; it is the aspect of
the earth in a state of natnre (South Africa), or in a state
resembling nature (South England), which speaks directly
to the soul, reminding us of our condition as man, our real
relation to the globe as opposed to conventionalities of
civilization. But a glance at the Parthenon, at the Venus,
at the smooth brow and sparkling eye of beauteous
woman, when just entering womanhood; a few moments
passed in presence of the frescos of Angelo and of Raffaelle,
or of the ruins of Karnac, will, I feel assured, convince
any correct mind, that these are the objects calculated to
bring out our noblest sympathies; to elevate the mind,
and to raise ns immeasurably above the rest of the animal
creation. With these, that is, with man and his works,
the elevated sympathize; not with the unseen powers of
nature; not with the secondary laws, as they are called,
which destroy and reconstruct planets. With these we
have no sympathies, and cannot have; their manifestations have forms, but not our forms; to us they must ever
appear as abstractions, though real.

Note 13.

There are persons who must for ever, and on all occasions, thrust themselves into the counsels of the Creative

Power; guessing at its plans and schemes—the grand scheme of nature.

They are generally persons who, not having received a regular education in science, employ the same terms sometimes literally, sometimes metaphorically. Some fossil remains of a former organic world, they call " Foot-prints of the Creator," as if the creative Power had feet and hands. With them all is miracle; all is final cause, though profoundly ignorant of what that cause (which is an effect, and not a cause) may prove to be. The universal system of nature must have been formed by fixed, unalterable, eternal laws; it is still regulated by them. The globe we inhabit, and all that it contains, forms no exception to this: in it rather we find the proofs that such laws have always existed. Nor does the creation and maintenance of the organic or living world form any exception to this statement; the organic and inorganic worlds have coexisted, no doubt, from all eternity. Perhaps they form but one. But be this as it may, of one thing we are sure—the antiquity of the organic world is immeasurable. The Hindoo theory, then, on this point is more minute in its details, if not more philosophic than the Hebrew. The latter has the advantage in simplicity and grandeur, the former in scientific truths.

The creation of the organic world by fixed laws. was the discovery of the South German and Slavonian schools; it is due mainly to Oken, Humboldt, Spix, and Von Martius, with some others. St. Hilaire was also explicit enough many years ago. "There is but one animal, not many," was the remarkable expression of Geoffroy; it contains the whole question. What was, now is, under other forms; but the essence is still the same. So long as this great truth was announced in merely scientific language, the schools of Britain took no notice of it; when clothed by a plagiarist in plain language, it burst on the English utilitarians like a thunderbolt.

In some minor points the theory of Oken differs from Geoffroy's; but they are not of great importance. That nothing was created as it is, is the common theory of both;

all is development from a microscopic point. But Geoffroy endeavouring to become intelligible in France, where the development theory was never well understood, added the further statement, that one genus or species of animal might produce another; "that the present saurians are the direct descendants of the ancient or extinct saurians." He went further; he said that, *in time*, by the force of external circumstances, an animal of a totally different group of life, might assume a new form: his views were based on the unity of life. The difference, if any exist, and this I doubt, simply amounts to this: 1. From the first, the germs of life differed specifically from each other; or, 2nd. At first, they were precisely the same, the subsequent specializations being the result of external circumstances. In either case, nothing was ever formed or created as it is.

Out of elemental bodies all living forms arise. Their course and existence are fixed and determined. In time they are developed, having special forms which endure for a time. The law of this progression has not been discovered; but man plays a part in it. What that part is cannot even be guessed at, in consequence of the failure of civilization to better man's condition on the globe.

Those who look for intermediate forms of life being produced, as it were, under our own eye, or rather during the present geological period, err, I think,—1st. In their estimation of the antiquity of the globe; 2nd. In their estimate of the characteristic differences marking all external circumstances during successive geological periods. The developing powers are not the same. The salmo estuarius (estuary trout) differs specifically from the fresh-water trout, and from the sea trout; but this specialization was not caused by his living in brackish waters. He forms part and parcel of the existing order of things formed at the last geological æra. The dark, circumpolar races of men were not darkened by the snows of the Arctic circle: they belong to an anterior geological period. Some writers have confounded the theory of development with the theory of progress. They are quite distinct.

Note 14.

The origin of man is a myth, which each race interprets in its own way, formulæs after the fashion of its own intellectual bearing; retouches as it makes progress in arts, literature, and science; that is, in civilization.

I mean not here to discuss these myths. The Jewish myth seems to have been a purely material one; philosophic, and sublimely simple, it offers no details. The Coptic and Hindoo was spiritual and lofty, but debased by shocking obscenities; the minds of the races were not equal to the perception of the perfect and the beautiful. The Scandinavian myth was coarse and brutal; material in its essence: the hideous representations of the Deity in India, China, Mongolia, and Polynesia, indicate the sad character of the minds of these races.

The precise geological period when man appeared on the earth, has not been determined; nor what race appeared first; nor under what form. But it is evident, that man has survived several geological æras. On those points all is at present conjecture; but as man merely forms a portion of the material world, he must of necessity be subject to all the physiological and physical laws affecting life on the globe. His pretensions to place himself above nature's laws, assume a variety of shapes: sometimes he affects mystery; at other times he is grandly mechanical. Now, all is to be done through the workshop; in a little while, the ultimatum (what is the ultimatum aimed at?) is to be gained through religion: and thus man frets his hour upon the stage of life, fancying himself something whilst he is absolutely nothing. For him worlds were made millions of years ago, and yet according to his own account he appeared, as it were, but yesterday. Let us leave human chronology to the chronicler of events; it turned the brain of Newton.

THE END.

LONDON:
PRINTED BY SAVILL AND EDWARDS, 4, CHANDOS STREET,
COVENT GARDEN.

AN INQUIRY

LAWS OF HUMAN HYBRIDITÉ.

--- --- ---

CHAPTER I.

PART I.

THERE is scarcely a physiological inquiry which presents greater difficulties than the one I now attempt. Hitherto it has been mixed up with animal hybridité in general. What was held to be true of one species of animal was presumed to be applicable to others; hence many errors, for every species has its own laws and peculiarities, and the very terms species and specific imply this. All analogies are doubtful, and the greater number wholly fallacious. In this respect modern inquirers have not advanced beyond the strictly logical reasoning of the time of the historian Livy, or rather of the Consul Manlius, who lived some hundred years before the celebrated Roman historian. The arguments used by the consul to persuade his army that the Gauls settled in Asia were not to be held in the same esteem as warriors as their ancestors who overthrew the Roman army at the Allia and sacked Rome, are based on the effects of climate on living beings. "Climate," he says, "has done its work. The Gauls settled in Asia as an exotic race, and, like all exotics, have degenerated." Had the consul been educated at Oxford or Cambridge, he could not more logically and skilfully have handled the question of climatology and its effects on plants and animals, and, by inference, on man himself. "It

I I

is not unknown to me that, of all the nations inhabiting
Asia, the Gauls have the highest reputation as soldiers.
A fierce nation, overrunning the face of the earth with its
arms, has fixed its abode in the midst of a race of men
the gentlest in the world. These tall persons, their long
red hair,* their vast shields, and swords of enormous length;
their songs, also, when they are advancing to action, their
yells and dances, and the horrid clashing of their armour
while they brandish their shields in a peculiar manner, practised in their original country; all these are circumstances
calculated to strike terror. But let Greeks and Phrygians
and Carians, who are unaccustomed to, and unacquainted
with, these things, be frightened by such; the Romans,
long acquainted with Gallic tumults, have learnt the
emptiness of their parade. Once, indeed, in an early
period, they defeated our ancestors on the Allia. Ever
since that time, for now two hundred years, the Romans
drive them before them in dismay, and kill them like
cattle; there have, indeed, been more triumphs celebrated
over the Gauls than over almost all the rest of the world.

" It is now well known by experience, that if you sustain
their first onset, which they make with fiery eagerness and
blind fury, their limbs are unnerved with sweat and
fatigue; their arms flag; and though you should not
employ a weapon on them, the sun, dust, and thirst sink
their enervated bodies and their no less enervated minds.

" We have tried them, not only with our legions against
theirs, but in single combat, man to man. Titus Manlius
and Marcus Valerius have demonstrated how far Roman
valour surpasses Gallic fury. Marcus Manlius, singly,
thrust back the Gauls who were mounting the Capitol in a
body. Our forefathers had to deal with genuine native
Gauls; but they are now degenerate, a mongrel race, and,
in reality, what they are named, Gallogræcians. Just as
is the case with vegetables; the seeds not being so effica-
cious for preserving their original constitution, as the properties of the soil and climate in which they may be reared,
when changed, are towards altering it.

* They could not have been Gauls, but Teutons or Scandinavians.

"The Macedonians who settled at Alexandria in Egypt, or in Seleucia or Babylonia, or in any other of their colonies scattered over the world, have sunk into Syrians, Parthians, or Egyptians. Marseilles, by being situated in the midst of Gauls, has contracted somewhat of the disposition of its adjoining neighbours. What trace do the Tarentines retain of the hardy, rugged discipline of Sparta? Everything that grows in its own natural soil attains the greater perfection; whatever is planted in a foreign land, by a gradual change in its nature, degenerates into a similitude to that which affords it nurture. You will, therefore, fight with men of the like description as those whom you have already vanquished and cut to pieces; those Phrygians, encumbered with Gallic armour, in the battle with Antiochus. I fear that they will not oppose us sufficiently so that we may acquire honour from our victory. King Attilus often routed them and put them to flight. Brutes retain for a time, when taken, their natural ferocity; but after being long fed by the hands of men, they grow tame.

"Think ye, then, that nature does not act in the same manner in softening the savage natures of men? Do you believe these to be of the same kind that their forefathers and fathers were? Driven from home by want of land, they marched along the craggy coast of Illyricum; then fought their way, against the fiercest nations, through the whole length of Pæonia and Thrace, and took possession of these countries. After being hardened, yet soured, by so great hardships, they gained admittance here; a territory capable of glutting them with an abundance of everything desirable. By the very great fertility of the soil, the very great mildness of the climate, and the gentle dispositions of the neighbouring nations, all that barbarous fierceness which they brought with them has been quite mollified.

"As for you, who are sons of Mars, believe me, you ought from the very beginning to guard against and shun, above all things, the enticing delights of Asia; so great is the power of those foreign pleasures in extinguishing the vigour of the mind, so strong the contagion from the relaxed discipline and manners of the people about you.

i i 2

One thing has happened fortunately, that though they will not bring against you a degree of strength equal to what they formerly possessed, yet they still retain a character among the Greeks equal to what they had at their first coming; consequently you will acquire, by subduing them, as high renown among the allies for military prowess as if they had kept up to their ancient standard of courage."*

It has been generally taken for granted that all mankind are of one *species*, thus assuming as a fact the very matter in question. The parties who commence the inquiry after this fashion are the same who ascribe the obvious varieties in mankind to climate or to the accidental mixture of races or varieties accidentally produced; and, finally, they are the same persons who deny the influence of race over the destinies of nations, and compel by fraud and violence the assent of nations to a chronology of mankind notoriously in contradiction with unquestioned and unquestionable historic evidence. Their chief support they find in modern logic, borrowed from the sophists of Athens, whose aim is not truth, but the fulfilment of "the logical necessities of the case."

" A hybrid is a living being, the product of a mixture of two species more or less remote."† When such an individual is produced from the admixture of two species lower in the scale than man, the being is called a mule; but as this word is more generally applied to the product of a cross between the horse and ass, I shall use the term hybrid as more appropriate and liable to no equivoque. To assert that these human hybrids are unprolific like the mule, without further inquiry, would be to commit the error I have just criticised—namely, the assuming as a fact, proved and demonstrated, that men are of different species; whereas, like the antagonistic theory, the opinion rests on mere conjecture. Is it necessary, in order to arrive at the truth, to go back to the origin of things—of life and species on the globe? Buffon thought so, and

---

* Tit Livii, Histor. Roman.
† So defined by an author, M. Paul Broca, who has given to this great question more attention than any other inquirer of modern times.

after him Goethe, Lamarck, Oken, and Geoffroy (St. Hilaire). I feel disposed to doubt this, for the following reasons. It is a question deeply mingled up with the theological opinions of many races and nations, as is that of the antiquity of life on the globe. In my younger days the belief that life appeared first on the globe a few thousand years ago was all but universal, and now such a theory is scouted by all scientific men. Let us wait, then, but a short time, and in all probability the fact may become demonstrable that man's antiquity on the globe (for this is the real question) is coeval with life itself. I wait patiently; the facts are sure to come. If life on the globe originated in the development of germs, conversion of inert into living matter, or in the existing from all eternity, there can be no necessity for inquiring into its origin. To the fact that man forms a part of the animal creation, as proved by his organic structure, may now be added that other fact, no less certain, that in the development of his organs from the embryo to the adult and aged, there exist proofs of a consanguinity with all that lives, demonstrable by anatomy, supported also by the structure of the adult existing generation of animals, and, as far as can be discovered, from the osseous remains of the species and genera now extinct—a discovery we owe to De Blainville. Thus the field of inquiry becomes narrowed; mysticism and miraculous interpositions are set aside; the unseen principle—that is, the transcendental—becomes known to man by its visible interpretations or realities. Let us adhere to these. If, by the mixture of two different races or species, a third new to history can be produced, then the question of the origin of new species may be considered as definitely settled. But the facts must be drawn from observations made directly on man, none other being applicable to the case.

The distinguished ethnologist * to whose remarkable work I have already alluded, is disposed to think that distinct species, not necessarily nearly allied to each other (*espèces voisines*), may be crossed and mingled so as to produce durable results; that is, I presume, mules or

* M. Paul Broca.

hybrids, which being self-supporting, constitute, in fact, *new species*. The solution of this question is deeply intermingled with human history.

I. That species have not altered since the earliest historic times was the opinion of Buffon, and was adopted by the immortal Cuvier. It was also that of Voltaire. To this opinion, which admitted of demonstration, and was, in fact, true, Cuvier added the hypothesis, that species had never altered, and never did alter, or assume any other but their original forms. This was hypothesis first. The second was forced upon him, and he never very clearly assented to it; it amounted to this, that the extinct or fossil animals had no *consanguinité* with the existing; that they perished *en totalité*, giving room for another creation; that these distinct acts of creation formed epochs in the history of life on the globe; and that, consequently, each new creation argued a new interposition of a First Cause. Such interpositions exclude at once all science and all philosophy. These opinions still hold their ground, and are not confined to any particular school. Cuvier never altogether assented to them. But he was an anatomist, and although by his race a German, he despised the Teutonic philosophy; in his opinion such men as Goethe, Oken, and Geoffroy were mere dreamers, and I have heard him say so at least fifty times. He saw instinctively in these theories an indirect attack on his great work, "Sur les Ossemens Fossiles," on which his vast reputation wholly rested. The outer world, composed of men whose minds are unfitted by education to weigh any scientific questions of this kind, adopted the hypotheses of Cuvier; to doubt them was to cease to be orthodox, and to be put to the ban by all the governments and governmental institutions of Europe. With infinite tact Cuvier avoided all these difficult and dangerous questions; in short, man formed no part of his animal kingdom. To the question of the unity of the human race as one species, he gave little or no attention. To derive all the varieties of men from a primordial pair is a pure hypothesis, but not more so than the theory which derives them from several primitive pairs.

Of the two hypotheses, the latter is the more improbable. In fact, neither rests on any scientific inquiry ; they are mere assertions unsupported by any proof.

In the course of the inquiry it became necessary to define species. Naturalists have generally admitted that animals of the same species are fertile, reproducing their kind for ever; whilst, on the contrary, if an animal be the product of two distinct species, the hybrid, more or less, was sure to perish or to become extinct, unless its continuance were insured by the infusion of new blood drawn from a pure race; in other words, that the products of such a mixture are not fertile. In this way species are unalterable and eternal, or, at least, permanent. Those who hold this hypothesis reject all opinions, such as those of Aristotle, and of those who fancy they can see in climate the efficient cause of the origin of species. They deny by inference the animal series, all existing relations between the past and the present, the present and the future. They deny by inference the doctrine of a chain of creation ; the mystery of mysteries, the extinction of the fossil animals, and the appearance of new species on the earth, they solve by an appeal to a First Cause.[*]

II. I have promised to confine my attention mainly, if not solely, to human hybridité. Is it true that all the races of mankind intermingle freely with each other, giving rise to a fertile progeny? Look over the world as it now exists, and say where such a hybrid race exists ; for to prove that all races mingle freely with each other, it must be shown, not only that this is so, but that there results a self-supporting progeny, characterized by all its newly acquired moral and physical properties, without recourse being had to either of the primitive races. Now this has never happened either in respect of dogs or men—the two genera which have been chiefly appealed to in this inquiry. But I wish it to be understood that I refer only to the historic period. When Goethe, many years ago, and long before any of these discussions commenced as to the *origin of species*, remarked, that in a Sicilian valley

* Cuvier, Broon, &c.

he saw a herd or drove of most beautiful cattle all resembling each other, gentle, quiet, and wholly unlike the
wild of the bovine family, he said to himself, "this is not
a new species of ox, and yet in one sense it is; it is a
breed formed out of the primitive, savage, suspicious,
timid, and ferocious bos, by a domestication of a million
of years." This bold conjecture or hypothesis of Goethe,
made many years ago, is the source of all the modern
philosophies as to the origin of species with which
the public has been amused and startled during the last
thirty years.* It is an ingenious hypothesis, and has great
claims on our attention as a new philosophic reading of
the phenomena of life, but—it is not science. Let us return to man, the aim and object of all useful inquiry.

I have already proved, many years ago—and was, I
believe, the first to do so—that from the earliest historic
times, mankind were already divided into a certain number
of races, perfectly distinct; and I called on those who
maintained that the distinctness in the races of men was
the product of climate, to say in *what time* such a change
could be effected. To those who, like Goethe, conjectured
man to have been on the earth a million of years ago, I
said, "your hypothesis is a probable one—the most probable—and that in time, and by the influence of external
causes, new species appeared, the direct descendants of
the old, but new to the world." This view did not originate with M. Geoffroy (St. Hilaire), but he was the first
to announce it in France. The Academy rejected it at
once; it touched a reputation (that of Cuvier) of which
France and the Academy were justly proud. It was
loudly objected to in England by all geologists and
zoologists, most of whom are still alive, but who now
adopt it to the full, or are prepared to do so. One of the
great objections to the view was, that paleontology did not
reveal to us the intermediate forms of life between the
past and the present. It was reserved for De Blainville
to prove that it did. Transcendental anatomy, also,

* Oken, Geoffroy, " Vestiges of Creation,' Darwin on the " Origin of
Species," &c. &c.

supported this view, based on paleontology, embryology, and the history of zoological individual development. If in the young of a species of a genus embracing many species, we find all the external characters of all the species included in that genus, then to comprehend when certain species disappear from the earth and others previously unknown take their place, we have only to note in the history of the natural family in question the regular progress of all that lives to decay and dissolution, and the as constant renovation, under other forms of life, on the globe. In other words, as the embryo of every individual of any species belonging to the natural family contains within itself the characters of the adults of all the species, it is then but a question of time and circumstances which species is to die out, and which to take its place.

But this theory of Goethe's requires, if it is to be applied to man, a time almost infinite, or at least indefinite. The theologian holds that two or three hundred years are sufficient to give rise, under the influence of climate, to all the varieties of man. His view is untenable, and his chronology is flatly contradicted by evidence of an unanswerable character. All this I pointed out in my first lecture on the Races of Men. M. Broca has taken the trouble to go over the ground again, and even condescended to correct the theologian in his translation of certain passages of the Hebrew writings, showing that he (the theologian) has no grounds whatever from that book for his theory as to the origin of the Negro race. M. Broca's clear refutation will not put a stop to the infamous hypothesis which has been engrafted on the Book of Genesis by modern divines.[*]

Our first knowledge of species and of genus, or natural family, is not derived from science, and, indeed, has nothing to do with it. In a knowledge of species the savage is often much more expert than the highly civilized and learned man. But when men are called on to *prove* that

* To understand the full import of this atrocious calumny on the Negro and Coloured races generally, see Livingstone's "Travels in South Africa."

certain animals which more or less resemble each other externally and internally, are yet perfectly distinct species, they very naturally appeal to the method by experiment, basing the inquiry on facts derived from daily observations. These facts show, then, that many animals closely allied to each other never naturally seek each other's company, so as to give rise to hybrids—that is cross-breeds. Secondly; by experimental science they learn that these animals may, however, be made to produce hybrids or cross-breeds, which, when left to themselves, they never do; and that of the cross-breeds so produced, some are fertile for several generations, others not at all. Zoologists, availing themselves of these facts, brought out by experimental science, base a doctrine thereon which seems to me scarcely scientific; it is this:—If the hybrid produced be prolific and self-supporting, the parents *must* be of the same species, however different they may seem in their external and internal characters; if the hybrid be not fertile, then the parents, how greatly soever they may have resembled each other, were of different species. I am not indisposed to admit this view, although to me it seems not founded on a scientific basis. But if facts are in its favour—that is, if there are certain hybrids produced by species hitherto held to be distinct, which hybrids prove fertile without any limit—then I am still disposed to think, in opposition to M. Broca, that the species, after all, were not distinct. Let it be borne in mind that the doctrine leads directly to an explanation of the origin of species, for such a hybrid would be a new form of animal life not heretofore on the earth. For whether its parents were of different species or of the same, the observation opens up a field of inquiry touching the very essence of the origin of the varied forms of life. If we admit the unbounded fertility of a hybrid, the product of two individuals hitherto recognised by all men as of distinct species, we destroy the last test of species which man possesses; the others—that is, a difference in anatomical structure and in external characters, in the *morale* and the *physique* of the species—sink into insignificance so soon as

it becomes known and proved that these species, seemingly
so distinct, are yet the same. But, I repeat, such is not
my opinion. With time the hybrid breed will gradually
lose its peculiar moral and physical nature, compounded
of those of its primitive parents, some of the offspring reverting to one species, others to the other. Ancient
monuments do not seem to show that such hybrids ever
existed. But this is no reason why they should not appear.
Be it understood that I speak of self-supporting hybrids,
requiring the infusion of no fresh blood from the parent
races or species. But if, on the other hand, the hybrid be
self-supporting, have we a right to conclude from this that
the original parents were of the same species? With
the utmost respect for the matured opinions of so distinguished an ethnologist as M. Broca, I think we have ;
but I quite agree with him that here, as in most zoological
questions, experimental science alone, and not any *à priori*
reasoning, can decide, until at last, the hybrid qualities
entirely disappear, and the product reverts to one or other
of the primitive races. Time must be allowed for this
great depravation of species. By the cross of a white man
with a mulatto woman of no very deep die, dark blood has
been observed to hold its ground in the descendants for a
hundred and fifty years, although all the subsequent intermarriages were with one race—the fair.

PART II.

THIS great ethnological and physiological question early
attracted my attention. It was brought forward in my
work on "The Races of Men," but I had already examined the theory of human hybridization in many public
lectures, long prior to the publication of that work. Whilst
collecting materials for these lectures, it was impossible
for me to overlook numerous important facts, or at least
phenomena and reflections, open to all who have the courage
to embark in the inquiry. Like most ethnological ques-

tions, it intercalated with, or involved, several others not
less important, and to these I shall allude in the course of
the present chapter.

At the period of my commencing the inquiry, certain
physiological ideas prevailed almost universally. To get
at the source of certain of these ideas, we must go up to
the instinctive thoughts of unscientific men. It is the
most natural thing in the world for scientific men to
imagine that mankind owes to them all exact knowledge
as to the nature of things, but no idea is more erroneous.
The learned mathematician imagines that he invented
mathematics, simply because by his reasoning powers he
demonstrates their truth; but the most untutored of men
understand their practical application quite as well as he
does, whilst all the great mathematical principles of natural
philosophy were perfectly well understood before science
appeared. In assigning to reason its full influence over
man's progress on the earth, let us not forget the universality of another mental power—instinct, which, combined
with simple observation and the experimental test resorted
to by the savage as well as by the followers of Bacon,
seldom misleads. Let us apply this to zoology.

The idea included in the word "species" is as clear,
precise, and positive in the mind of the merest savage as
in that of the most highly educated zoologist. It has
nothing to do with science, and was not the invention of
scientific men. The specifically distinct characters which
constitute species are as well known, and have ever been
so, to the merest savage as to the most highly educated of
men. On conversing with the wild Bosjiemen and savage
Caffres of Eastern Africa, I have sometimes fancied that,
in respect of a knowledge of the specific characters of
animals and plants, they excelled the civilized man. That
these characters were what we call external in a great
measure may be admitted; but the teeth and feet do not
come under this head altogether, and to these the savage
and the uneducated carefully attend. Generally, also, these
simple-minded men are free from the prejudices which
beset civilized man, and which he acquires by means of

that other form of ignorance called erudition. Their ideas
of species being thus clear and precise, as derived, partly
from instinct, which so seldom errs, partly from daily
observation, lead almost directly and unconsciously to this
conclusion—namely, that as all these species are thus
distinct from each other, avoid each other, and never
intermingle, they must be, and are, wholly distinct from
each other, and have ever been so; for were it otherwise,
the field of observation, the zoological and vegetable world,
must long since have presented thousands and thousands
of living beings, impossible to name, impossible to comprehend. To this natural conclusion, the savage, the uneducated of all countries, of all races, and of all times, arrive.
He learns from the aged around him that it was precisely
so in their younger days and in those of their forefathers,
and instinctively he arrives at the same results attained by
the elaborate researches of the immortal Cuvier, the dis-
coverer of the fossil world and the inventor of true descrip-
tive comparative anatomy (a discovery not inferior to the
first, and leading directly to it)—namely, that the various
species of animals, man included, have never varied, are
immutable, unchangeable, if not eternal; that as they are
now, so were they when man first commenced to engrave
on stone or record on parchment what he saw in the
external world. The law of living beings was obviously
that every living being should bring forth after *its* own
kind, and this law, based on daily observation through
countless centuries, assumed the form of a truth, to doubt
which implies an aberration of intellect amounting to a
condition of mind closely approximating that of the sceptic
who calls in question the truth of a geometrical problem.
This law or laws (for there are more than one) handled by
the scientific zoologist, assume an imposing form, although
in reality they are not based on science nor on any inquiry.
Species became, in the hands of the illustrious—and, I think,
we may say immortal—Buffon, the eternal moulds of nature,
unalterable, unchangeable. A demonstration of the unalterable character of species was attempted with great
success by one whose claim to the title of immortal cannot

be questioned, and thus the immutability of species and
the eternity of species assumed at last the form of a
scientific dogma.   Let us return to the simple observation
of the savage—the uneducated.

It was known that, although species remained thus
distinct, it occasionally happened that two species intermingled (as the horse and ass), and that the result was a
being partaking of the character of both parents, yet
distinct from both. How did it happen, then, that mules
had not spread over the earth, thus giving rise to a *new
species* of horse ? The answer was obvious and at hand ;
mules are sterile or unprolific, proving, as Buffon would
have remarked, that Nature had resolved to preserve her
primitive moulds from all change, whether that lead to
improvement or to degradation. Experimental science now
steps forward and shows various degrees in this infecundity
or sterility of hybrids, some proving unfruitful at the first
generation, as the mule properly so called ; others only
after two or more generations ; lastly, the experiments of
M. Roux, as detailed in the admirable memoir of M.
Broca, tending to show that two distinct species may produce a mule breed, a new species, fruitful to the end of
time ; thus originating a *new species*, unknown heretofore
to man ; unknown in the past ; appertaining, therefore, to
the future, and, to a certain extent, giving to the philosophical romance of Aristotle a distinctly scientific character. For he first launched the theory or hypothesis,
as it really was, that the variety and extraordinary characters of "the wilde" of Africa was owing to the for-
tuitous crossings of species as they met in vast numbers
by the margins of lakes or the pools of partly dried-up
rivers, in that land which still merits the name bestowed
on it by Rome's great lyric poet, " the parched nurse of
lions."●

It is easy to see in what direction the scientific must of
necessity follow these questions. Sharing with the savage,
from whom the idea springs, the theory that two distinct
species cannot produce a fruitful mule, they assigned this

" Arida nutrix leonum."—Hor.

fact as a *proof* of what ought to have been proved experimentally. "If the product was fertile, the parents were held to be of the same species; if unfertile, they were of different species." This is precisely the theory or opinion of the savage and of the uneducated; it partakes of the nature of an instinctive feeling, supported by the past history of the animal creation. Recent experiments, however, have shown that the mule produced by the hare and rabbit is productive or fruitful, if not for centuries, at least for several years. Time alone can try this question of the self-supporting character of the *leporides*, the hybrid product of the hare and rabbit; in the meantime I remain of the opinion that the hare and rabbit are distinct species and have been so for countless ages, and that the *leporides* will in time return to one or other of the species from which they sprang. If we admit the fecundity of the hybrid *leporides*, we have a key, no doubt, to the origin of new species, and their appearance from time to time on the earth. Extend the theory a little, and it will explain the disappearance of species which once existed merely by assigning to them a limited vital force. Lastly, to admit the theory to its full extent is to do away, in a philosophic sense, with the idea of species, and to substitute for exact science the philosophic romance of Goethe, of De Mallet, and of Lamarck, so often reproduced since their time, and more especially by Oken and Spix, Geoffroy (St. Hilaire), by the author of the "Vestiges of Creation," and by Mr. Darwin; a theory which may be thus expressed:—All may spring from all; every form of life is possible; the ideas of species and genera are fast leaving men's minds, being merely conventional terms invented by man to express distinctions in living beings, which, by their long continuance, he fancies to be eternal, a word of which he is very fond, and greatly pleased to apply to himself and to his works. Thus, to the theory of the influence of climate in so altering species as to cause them to assume the form of new species (a theory wholly unsupported by facts), and to the influence of domesticity (a principle which could only be applied to a few species, such as the

ox, sheep, goat, dog, horse, ass, camel, elephant, lama, and
of a few domestic fowls, and which over most of these has
never exercised any influence whatever,* and in which the
varieties so produced require for their maintenance the
constant attention of the breeder) came now to be added a
third hypothesis, the principle, namely, of crossing of
species, giving origin to a fertile, self-supporting hybrid.

In part third of this chapter, I shall examine more
fully this question as it regards the lower animals ; a few
remarks, therefore, may suffice here. 1st. As regards
climate ; a European species transferred to another climate
either stands its ground or becomes extinct. If crossed
with species of the same natural family peculiar to their
adopted country, they produce a hybrid *breed*, which
maintains its ground only so long as the crossing continues.
Left to itself, it speedily resolves itself into its primitive
races. 2nd. As regards domesticity, its influence on some
species is sufficiently remarkable, although even this may
be fairly questioned. On others it exercises no influence
whatever. The ass, lama, elephant, camel, and several
others, seem to me to come within this category. Goethe
thought the Sicilian ox to be the gift to man of domestication through a million of years. This is not science.

How stands this question as regards man ? Certain of
the various races of men seem to form distinct species ;
they differ from each other by their external characters
and internal anatomy quite as much as most of the species
held to be distinct by zoologists ; what applies to them
may fairly enough be applied to man. In my former
works, I endeavoured to add to the zoological characters
others drawn from the *morale* of the races, showing that in
this, as well as in the *physique*, the differences were unmistakeable, and that in reality they were specific. But it
was objected to my view, that as all the races of men breed
freely with each other, and that the product (which in this
case we can scarcely call a hybrid) was in all cases uniformly fruitful, it was evident that all must be of one
species, since in no instance was the true hybrid product

* Ass, elephant, camel, buffalo, lama, &c.

of two species known to be so. To this my reply was, that
the statement as to the fruitfulness of the human hybrid
rested on no sure data; that history disproved the assertion by showing that the human hybrid in time became
extinct; further, that the hybrid was a degradation of
humanity and was rejected by nature. In support of this
latter view, I instanced Mexico, Peru, and the Central
States of America, foretelling results which none attempt
now to deny; to this I added the history of the hybrid
population of South Western Africa, of Portuguese India,
&c.; lastly, the history of race as exhibited during twenty
centuries in Northern Africa. A distinguished physiologist
and anatomist,* who shares with me the opinion that the
races of men constitute distinct species, yet doubts the
theory of the absolute sterility of the human hybrid, and
does not think such a fact at all necessary to prove the
theory that men are of distinct species. Fertility or non-
fertility of a hybrid, he thinks, in no way proves or disproves the idea of distinctness in species. For my own part,
I still cling to the theory, almost instinctive, and common,
I believe, to nearly all men, that the non-fertility of a
hybrid proves beyond cavil that the parents were of distinct species; whilst the converse shows, at least, that if
they are not of absolutely the same species, they partake
of a nature so affiliated, so nearly related to each other,
that the fecundity of the hybrid need not be wondered at.
It is quite possible, then, that the human hybrid—the product of two strongly affiliated races—may be fertile and
self-supporting; but I do not find this view to be supported
by history. The hybrid produced between the male
European and the female Australian seems to be altogether sterile from the first. Hybrids between other races
seem to be *less sterile*, if I may so say, but I think it only
a question of time. Proofs of hybridism may remain for
centuries, but history and common observation show that
they become extinct at last. But should it be proved, as
it is not yet, that individuals descended from parents heretofore held to be distinct species, not only by the vulgar,

* M. Broca.

X X

but by the scientific, may give rise to a hybrid race partaking of the characteristics of both parents, yet distinct from each—self-supporting and enduring, then I confess that the term *specifically distinct* cannot well be applied to the parents. For on what shall we ground the proofs of distinction of species, but on the sterility of the hybrid? Buffon was the first, perhaps, to give to the theory a scientific formula, and to eliminate from the absolute fact itself the various objections which might be raised against it on the ground that certain species produce, by intermingling, hybrid products which continue fertile and self-supporting for a time. Now this fact I do not dispute, and never did; the natural *consanguinité* which connects members of the same genus or natural family sufficiently explains the fact; to what extent this may proceed can only be determined by experimental science, in the prosecution of which in this direction let us never forget that we attempt a task which nature has declined for the last six or seven thousand years at least.

The obvious physical degradation of the European races long settled in the United States, I do not ascribe to the intermingling of the European races on that continent, but to the influence of climate, which sooner or later disposes of all exotics; neither do I think that the amalgamation of all the races of men on the earth would lead to the extermination of mankind,[*] for each race would separate, and after the lapse of centuries revert to its original type.[†] The tribe of Griquas, on the Orange River, has been often cited as proof of the existence of a self-supporting hybrid race. Now the Griquas whom I have seen seemed to me a bastard Hottentot race, in no way self-supporting, but constantly maintained by primitive races in contact with the tribe. Hasty observations have greatly injured ethnology, as they have done science in general. The Griquas return rapidly to the African blood. M. Broca has taken the trouble to refute Dr. Prichard

and his adherents in respect of the existence of certain
Eastern self-supporting hybrid races. I never had the
smallest belief in such theories, which, indeed, I knew to
rest on no scientific inquiry. But the distinguished French
ethnologist thinks that it was not necessary to go to Polynesia or to the desert banks of the Orange River in order
to find a self-supporting hybrid race. He bids us look
nearer home, and we shall find the race we inquire for in
modern France and in other European countries. In other
terms, if I rightly comprehend the meaning of the distinguished author, he bids us apply the test of experimental
science rigorously; by this test he has made it extremely
probable that, as in many species of animals experiment
has proved that the hybrid of remote species is unfruitful,
whilst the offspring of naturally affiliated may prove fruitful and self-supporting to all time, so it may be with the
races of men : the hybrid of a Papuan Negro or Boajiemen
with a European race may be unfruitful ; the hybrid of a
Teuton or Celt with a Scandinavian or Italian, a Sclave or
Goth, may lead to the establishment of a self-supporting
hybrid race permanent and enduring.

The *consanguinité* between different species of the same
natural family is proved by the resemblance of the young of
all the species to each other ; the young, in fact, are *generic*
animals for a time, and only become *specific* as they grow
up. I have demonstrated these facts* respecting the *consanguinité* and its obvious effects on the young of all the
species of a natural family, and shall return to the question
in a future chapter.

The two great nations raised by accident to be at the
present moment arbiters of all human affairs, are supposed
by those who support this view to be composed each of a
hybrid race, distinct, self-supporting, and possessed of
mixed moral and physical characters, distinct from those of
the primitive race from which they spring. To me, on
the contrary, it appears that modern Gaul, after having
been overthrown by several races, has in the course of
centuries depurated itself from all exotic elements. Teu-

* See " Trans. Lin. Society" and *Lancet* for 1837.

tonic blood no longer exists there, but that Gaulish race
which the immortal Dictator described in terms as true
then as now. He admits that "the Belgians, Aquitains,
and Celts differ from each other in their language, customs,
and laws; but they are all Gauls, and have all a Gaulish
look." The "Commentaries" seem to me to have been
written long after the conquest of Gaul, and not hurriedly,
but from notes taken at the time of the occurrence of the
events. He does not mention the Cimbri, known to him
probably by the name of Belgians. The immortal Dictator
speaks of "the levity of the Gauls, who are very changeable
in their counsels and fond of novelties;" and, if I rightly
remember, speaks of their "religion as of a gloomy and
ferocious character."[*] Cæsar takes no notice of Cisalpine
Gaul, nor of the distinct race of the Basques. The Cisalpine Gauls have become extinct, and the character of the
natives of Savoy is anything but Gaulish. The Dictator
describes the Gauls as being extremely superstitious; the
Germans, on the contrary, "acknowledge no gods but
those that are objects of sight." The distinction remains
to this day. There exists no hybrid race in Holland, the
people being either Scandinavian or German; whilst the
Kymri, a Gaulish race, have remained distinct from the
Celt to the present day.

Of Britain the Dictator's description is equally clear.
The people he met on the shores were Belgians, and in
their nature are so now. "The inland parts of Britain are
inhabited by those whom fame reports to be the natives
of the soil." Of these he says nothing. They were probably the Kymrai, a Gaulish race, dispersed and broken
up before his time. With this Belgian and Kymraig races
the race or races we call Saxons largely intermingled.
These so-called Saxons were in reality the Jutes, Angles,
and old Saxons from North Germany, composed mostly
of Germans or Teutons. The true Scandinavian, or Dane,
appeared afterwards. Now these races, to which may be
added the Norman, gave rise to no new or hybrid race,
but the mixed population amongst whom all these elements

[*] I quote from memory; the observation may belong to Tacitus.

and several others—such as the Phenician and Celt, Iberian or Spanish—are distinctly recognisable.

This extremely plausible and even probable theory is therefore not supported by history. In the chapter on the Past, Present, and probable Future of Africa, I shall endeavour to show that the attempts made on a large scale in that continent to produce a hybrid race, have entirely failed; for the present, I shall confine myself to a few observations which no doubt have often occurred to others.

1st. How is it that no trace of the Visigoths is to be found in Spain? Were the two races (the Teutonic and Celtiberian) so distinct as to render the formation of a hybrid race impossible? The Arab was expelled from Spain, but not the Goth.

2nd. The Gauls who invaded Asia Minor are said to have been a fair-haired race, and therefore were not pure Celts, but a mixed race, as the Kymri of Wales have dark hair. It is probable that with the Gaulish force there proceeded into Asia many Teuton or Germanic tribes; but be this as it may, it is generally admitted that all traces of these Europeans have disappeared from Asia Minor.

3rd. Gallica Cisalpina—that is, Northern Italy—was in Cæsar's time and long after, a Gaulish territory, entirely occupied by the Gauls. They built Milan. What has become of these Gauls, call them by whatever name you will? Did the conquerors at Magenta and Solferino find any sympathy in the native population? Did the victors at Marengo find in the aborigines the descendants of their Gaulish progenitors, even the remotest trace that the ground on which they stood had once been as essentially Gaul in respect of its population as the banks of the Loire and the Seine?

4th. In Cæsar's time there were in Gaul three distinct populations—the Celt, the Belgæ, and the Aquitanians. The immortal Dictator does not say that they were of one race, but he ascribes to all "a Gaulish aspect." How full of truth are these observations! From the observations of others I learn that these three populations, with "a Gaulish look," are there now. He makes no mention of the Kymri, the people we now find in Wales, Ireland, and Caledonia; they are to be found generally mingled with the Celts. Both races migrate in great numbers to the United States of America, but they mingle not with the Anglo-Saxon nor with the Teuton; true to their nature, they await the advent of a leader—a sultan whom they will be sure to follow.

5th. The Teutonic Franks conquered France, and gave a name to the country; but this Teuton blood has altogether disappeared. I can find no Roman colonies anywhere. An ingenious writer in the pay of Russia,[*] and evidently a Sclavonian, endeavours to show that the present population of France is formed out of three distinct elements:—1st, Celtic; 2nd, Roman; 3rd, Teuton. I have no faith in such a theory, which, moreover, is at variance with all the well-ascertained facts bearing on the question. Climate, no doubt, exercises a mysterious influence over the continuance of non-indigenous races, as has been all but proved in the case of the Mamlooks in Egypt. They have become extinct, and the same fate awaits the Turcoman. Where, in the meantime, are the hybrid races which ought to be found in that country?

The physical, and possibly the moral, degradation of the Italian race, or races, constantly followed the successive irruptions of other races into the Peninsula. In England and the Lowlands of Scotland we have two races—the Teuton and Scandinavian combined, and the Belgian. They are not much mingled yet, and certainly there exists no hybrid race properly so called. The *morale* of these two races is quite distinct, and requires but a social or political question to bring it prominently out. The three races in Prussia (German, Pruss and Sclave) have never been intermingled, and to this day are held together by the sword. As regards remotely affiliated races, M. Broca allows my view to be correct—namely, that by their admixture hybrids are produced which are not fruitful or self-supporting. There exists, then, scarcely any real difference between M. Broca's views and mine. He thinks that some

* *Times*, Jan. 1861.

strongly affiliated races produce fertile hybrids, and I confess that I lean strongly to his opinion, but feel bound to await the proofs. Other races, he frankly admits with me, produce hybrids which are not fertile. If this be so, we have the best proof required to constitute these races into distinct species. Buffon himself, were he alive, would accept the theory. Cuvier excluded man from the history of zoology.

The races of men differ from each other, and have done so from the earliest historic period, as proved—

1st. By their external characters, which have never altered during the last six thousand years.

2nd. By anatomical differences in structure.

3rd. By the infertility of the hybrid product, originating in the intermingling of two races.

4th. By historic evidence, which shows that no distinct hybrid race can be shown to exist anywhere. Thus the infertility of the hybrid probably extends to most, if not to all, the races of man. These distinctions in race cannot be traced to the influence of climate, nor to any physical causes known at present to exist. This immutability of species during the so-called historic period was proved in respect of the lower animals by Cuvier. Buffon was also of the same opinion; but it does not disprove, as Cuvier thought it did, the descent by direct generation of the present living world from the past. Paleontology daily brings to light the absent links connecting the past with the present, whilst in embryology we have the proofs that the forms of many species are included in each and all. The realization or specification of these forms does not require the interposition of a new creative impulse—that is, of a First Cause—as Mr. Broun thinks, but merely an alteration of the physical circumstances in which the young may be placed. Though of distinct species, all the races of men belong to the same natural family, the embryo of each species containing within itself the rudiments of all the others. The human family stands profoundly apart from all others, implying that in the great chain of beings constituting nature's plan, some natural family filling up the link has disappeared.

Future palæontological inquiry may solve the difficulty, which however I do not look on in the light of a difficulty. When human fossil remains shall have been discovered, their general resemblance to the osseous remains of the races of men now on the earth will not furnish adequate proof that they were of the same race; for distinctions in race or species are mainly connected with the exterior, which has naturally perished in the course of ages. Cuvier himself admitted that in the anatomy of the Equidæ we do not find the distinctive characters of species which must be sought for in the exterior. So it is with man; the skeleton differs, no doubt, in the various races as in the Equidæ, but not so strongly as to furnish at once a sure characteristic. A glance at the exterior removes all doubts.

In 1821-22, I pointed out to Dr. Edwards, at that time on a visit to London, that the drawings in the Egyptian Tomb, arranged for exhibition by Belzoni, represented several races of men precisely as we find them now. This distinction in race, then, has existed for at least 4300 years; but according to Lepsius and Bunsen, who have investigated carefully Egyptian history, for a much longer period. By leaving man out of his zoological view, the immortal Cuvier avoided discussing these troublesome questions. Climate seems, then, contrary to the opinions of Hippocrates, to be unequal to the transmutation of one race into another, or to the formation of a new race; but it has always appeared to me that intrusive or heterochtonous races perished, or became extinct in time in the land of their adoption. The presence of an indigenous race may contribute, no doubt, to this result, but it is not the sole cause. The Mongol, who at one time extended so far into Europe, has all but disappeared; the Turcoman follows, and the same remark is applicable to the Arab. Flushed with success, and fed by the annual importation of half-a-million of Europeans into Northern America, the men of the United States, as is the custom of that race to which they mainly belong, talk loudly of becoming in a short time masters of the earth! Already symptoms of decay appear in the race, who, deprived for a short time of their European supplies, would soon become extinct, following the fate of the Spanish and Portuguese races on the same continent. To the history of the Hispano-hybrid races of Mexico, Guatemala, Chili, Peru, &c., I beg again to refer the reader. They are a disgrace to human nature. I foretold their career nearly a quarter of a century ago, the cause which led to it, and their certain destruction.

To Buffon we owe the idea of "centres of creation." As regards the zoological world, these centres remain even now distinct. The centres were not always continents, although as regards man and most animals and plants, the observation was undoubtedly correct.

The distinguished ethnologist[*] to whose unanswerable memoir I have so frequently referred in the course of this chapter, admits that even were it proved that there exist races of men whose progeny when intermingled is not *sterile*, the doctrine that men are of the same species receives from this no support. With this question I commenced my ethnological inquiries at least forty years ago; the sterility of certain hybrids, the product of the intermingling of two distinct races of men, seemed to me even then to admit of no doubt. M. Broca, and many others who strongly opposed my views at first, now admit the correctness, or at least the great probability, of the theory. In this case we have the proof which Buffon required as to the distinctness of species, and are at liberty to apply it to the natural family of mankind. On the other hand, M. Broca thinks that this test of species is not the only one, and that it is not conclusive, since there are distinct species (as the hare and rabbit) whose hybrid product is perfectly fruitful and self-supporting. I confess I have my doubts, and instinctively, as it were, adhere to the opinions of Buffon, that sterility of the hybrid is the only certain character of distinctness of species in which all men will agree. Nevertheless, I quite agree with this distinguished observer that

* M. Broca.

the hybrids of certain species, both of animals and man, are more fruitful than others—that is, for a time ; and that absolute sterility does not invariably happen. As in all that regards life, such questions cannot be decided by any *à priori* reasoning, but by direct experiment. Men speak of the historical unity of the races of men, as they did in my younger days of the creation of the zoological and geological world some four thousand years ago ; this latter theological hypothesis has been unanswerably refuted, and the other must speedily follow. In the meantime, political, religious, and social questions have arisen and mingled with the scientific, but they are wholly foreign to science. Truth is not their object. To these questions I shall return in the sections of this work which treat of the future of the races now located on the African and American soils. In the same sections suitable occasions may be found for discussing the question as to the superiority of one race to another, a problem already attempted as regards literature by the illustrious Quetelet;* but literature is only one item—the most important one, no doubt, in civilization. In the sections to which I refer, all the elements of civilization will be kept in view. In Europe, between the more or less fair races it is merely a question of national interest, and, instead of causing or aggravating natural antipathies, might be turned to good account by inciting the various races and nations to strive for superiority, not by the invention of steel-plated ships of war and Armstrong guns, but by the advancement of true civilization—literature, science, and art. In America it is otherwise,—there an intrusive European race condemns to the most horrid bondage the feeble Negro, who he is told by the Book he worships is his *brother.*†

The mingled races of Europe are not hybrids; the Basque remains distinct from the population of old Gaul, and the Sclaves retain everywhere the peculiarities of their race.

* "Sur l'Homme." Translated by R. Knox. Chambers.
† I have read with horror the ravings of Mr. John Bachman, a slave-holding parson. The expression "whited sepulchre" must have been invented for the class to which he belongs. They are very numerous in England.

The " flat-nosed Frank " is not to be found in any numbers
in France, although M. Arago mistook them for the progenitors of the present French. "The old Pruss" is still
distinct from the Scandinavians, Sclavonians, and Teutons,
who groan under his abhorred rule. Molder of Bonn is
the worthy descendant of Freytag of Frankfort, immor-
talized by Voltaire ; and since Jena and Fleurus, Aus-
terlitz and Jemmappes failed to cure the race of its self-
conceit, we must look upon the disease as hopeless. But
they are not German, nor ever were, neither is there any
hybrid race in Prussia. The original Moorish or Kabyle
blood is said to prevail in the island of Sardinia, whilst
Gallia Cisalpina contains no Celtic blood. Of all countries
Italy is the one which ought to have proved, by its population, the substitution of a hybrid for a pure race. Nothing
of the kind exists.

The sterility of hybrids is the check which nature employs for the preservation of her primitive forms of life.
There is a *consanguinité*, no doubt, in all that lives ; for
life, being a property inherent in matter, must at its
origin have been one, but this *consanguinité* does not extend to or exclude specialities. It goes no further than their
genera, and most commonly not so far. Hence the study
of generic differences is in the main an abstraction,
not bearing on the practical world but on the philosophic. In these men obtain occasionally a hurried
glimpse of nature's scheme of development. The young of
all animals display generic forms at first ; these gradually
give way as the specific forms are being developed.

CHAPTER II.

ON SOME ANCIENT FORMS OF CIVILIZATION.

PART I.

The term civilization is a conventional term, admitting of no precise definition. If we limit it to the invention of those social arts essential to the existence of a nation or race, under the circumstances in which, for the time, it happens to be placed, then the definition must include all mankind, all being equal to such inventions. There are conditions of humanity, nevertheless, so low as scarcely to merit the name of civilized, whilst there are others so lofty as to embrace to a certain extent all that man is capable of in science, literature, and art; these combined constitute civilization in its highest form.

It must always interest man to know how ancient races stood in respect of civilization—the ultimate and highest aim of humanity. An inquiry extending through many years, has convinced me that much may be learned on this subject by a careful examination of the remains of art still subsisting, added to what has been written by the races or nations themselves. Of these ancient races, some, as the Chinese, Japanese, and Mongol, generally have perpetuated to the present day the form of civilization invented by themselves and peculiar to their race. The Hindoo may also be included in this class. Others, as the Kopts and Assyrians, have left us only the remains of art and some linguistic or literary records, which hitherto have been very imperfectly deciphered; whilst others, as the ancient Aztecs and Peruvians, have only left artistic records, which we must endeavour to read and comprehead without the aid of written documents. One thing seems to me certain; all these races invented their own forms of civilization, borrowing little or nothing from others. To make this clear, I shall preface my inquiry into the remains of those races by discussing, as briefly as I can, the nature of art, its origin and progress, and the influence which race exercises, not only over all human inventions, but over the view each race takes of nature. This sketch of the origin of the arts, and the influence of race over their development, will be extremely brief, as it is my intention to reconsider the whole subject at greater length in a subsequent memoir.

The arrival in France and England of the Assyrian marbles, discovered by Messrs. Botta, Layard, Rawlinson, and others, strengthened me in the opinion I had already formed of the real origin of art, and its intimate relation to race. Like the Coptic remains, they offer to mankind a view of the social history and physical aspect of a race which, though not extinct, has long ceased to exist as a nation; of a nation whose history was interwoven with the annals of another race in whom the Christian world takes a deep and enduring interest. No one could fail to regard them with as deep a feeling as it is possible to bestow on the past. The story of Nineveh and Babylon, taught us in our earliest years, is impressed in a thousand ways on the memory, and we are instructed by every educational device to accept the story as related to us by an Oriental race, the Jewish, to whom philosophy and science, the art of criticism, and a desire to discover the truth, were absolutely unknown. And now artistic records of this Assyrian and Babylonish race reach Europe, to be read by each according to his prejudices. If they fail to give us confirmation of any existing history, if they are found to be equally at variance with the chronology of Herodotus and of Josephus, one thing at least is certain, they represent the physical aspect of a nation which does not now exist as a nation, but traceable as a race still wandering by the banks of the Tigris and of the Euphrates; and they further prove that, when the race figured as a nation, they were equal to the formation of a civilization peculiarly their own. As a nation they ran their course, leaving monuments attesting their power, their physical character, the nature of their religious belief or folly, their social condition, and the view they took of the external world. The meaning of the phrase "the external world," I shall first endeavour to explain.

ORIGIN OF ART.

The external world, or globe, we inhabit, may be looked on as composed of two classes of objects ; one great class, *invented* by man—the social arts, as they are called; of a second great class of objects, formed, created, or developed by nature.* The objects made and invented by man constitute a large portion of human civilization, and, indeed, without them civilization does not exist. As wealth and the civilization mainly occupied with the invention of the social arts advance, the nation and race recede further and further from nature, according to the disposition of the race; for nature's objects they substitute the artificial, their own inventions ; and this may go on, as in China, until nature be all but put out of court. A race strongly disposed to admire their own inventions are generally despisers of nature and of truth, which resides only in those objects which nature forms. Thus, in estimating the character of a race, we have only to discover from what point of view they contemplate the material or external world; what value they attach to their own inventions, and what to nature's creations. The arts which man invents,† and which so many races, and individuals of all races, admire and esteem beautiful, are constructed on principles addressed to certain faculties and instincts of the human mind which man values highly. They are addressed to his love for parade and magnificence, order, symmetry, grandeur, nicety of workmanship, difficulty of execution. When the objects thus invented and carried to perfection

---

* I exclude from this view the mineral crystallised masses, of whose origin we know nothing. The organic is never crystallized.

† I exclude the fine arts from those of man's inventions.

are presented to him, he calls them beautiful, esteeming them highly as the perfection of human handiwork. But he never imagines that there can be any truth in them excepting the mechanical, and he does not look for truth, knowing that utility is their aim; as regards all such inventions there is no standard of taste, each generation despising the inventions of the past, and more especially of the labours of the immediately preceding age. The reason why each generation when in its prime and vigour despises the inventions, thoughts, ideas, actions of the immediately preceding generation more than any more ancient one, is this: the generation about to depart is before them in a senile, feeble, decaying, and decrepit form, and the thoughts of the young and vigorous naturally class together the declining race and their inventions. In the presence of the aged and enfeebled everything connected with them, mentally or physically, seems redolent of antiquity—dress, thoughts, inventions. It is not so with the generations which have passed away, of whom we are more likely to remember whatever was vigorous, youthful, and great. But in contemplating nature's creations, and the imitations of such objects by the *true artist*, whether in marble or on canvas, the highly organized mind sees in the object the truth of nature, and demands in the imitation by the artist the presence of beauty and of truth. He is sensible that man cannot alter, cannot improve, although he may disfigure, nature's creations. A garden, to be perfect in man's eyes, must be laid down on mathematical principles; now these are peculiarly of human invention. The grass must be smoothly cut, the shrubs kept in order, trees disposed symmetrically and in rows; there must be no wild flowers seen anywhere, and, least of all, any appearance of sloth or neglect. The object aimed at here, is to show how perfectly man has carried through, regardless of time, labour, and expense, the object held in view. How different is the natural landscape. Both are admired, the garden and the landscape; but let us never forget that the one is invented, as it were, by man, the other created by nature; that the one addresses itself to qualities which are strictly human;

the other strikes at our deepest sympathies—our sympathies with what lives, with that wherein resides the mysterious principle of life. With the one class there is a deep *consanguinité* which language in vain endeavours to express; in this class, that is, in nature's creations, we find the absolutely beautiful—that is, woman's form; to this must be added our profound ignorance as to why or wherefore these objects were so created, while all that man makes and fashions can be traced at once by human reason to the baser qualities of human nature, to utility and necessity which rule the world.

I exclude from these considerations true, or fine art, as it is usually called, as not being a human invention. It originates in no necessity, aims not at utility; it is strictly an imitative art, by which man expresses his capability of perceiving in nature the absolutely true, the perfect, and the beautiful; in other words, the view man takes of the external world. To represent nature's creations in marble or canvas is, perhaps, the highest gift which has been bestowed on man; and in proportion as man can execute and nations admire such works, so it will be found that the race or nation so gifted excels all others in those intellectual endowments which form the greatest ornament of humanity.

Food, clothing, and a dwelling form the object of all the social arts; necessity is their parent, utility their object. The existing generation* in possession of the earth despises the labours of past generations, more especially of its immediate predecessor. It is gone and passed, never to be revived. Not so living nature; for ever renovated, the youth of life is being constantly placed before us; with nothing else are we entirely pleased or satisfied. In all the objects of nature we admire, we demand the presence of the emblems of youth and the absence of those of decrepitude, decay, and dissolution. Together with their inventions the aged pass away. In the eyes of the existing generation all the inventions of the generation passing away seem antiquated—furniture, dress, equipages, gardens, mansions,

* Men and women between 20 and 45.

instruments of war, ships, roads, ideas—all share the same fate. In common language they are said to be out of fashion, but this does not express the feeling which lies at the bottom of all this. They belong to a generation no longer in possession of the earth. Another, a younger and a stronger, fierce in its youth and strength, feels the necessity of thinking and acting for itself, and refuses to accept the past as its rule of conduct. Thus it is, and ever must be, with all the inventions of man. They originate chiefly in human necessities, and pass away with the circumstances that created them. Each succeeding generation is aware of this, and looks only to its own era. Without this contempt for the past, human progress would cease ; and as works of social art must of necessity address themselves to the wants, views, and feelings of " the race in possession of the earth," so must they ever represent the existing order of things. Quite otherwise is it with nature's works, and with the imitations made of them by the true artist. They are never old ; never old fashioned ; never represent an order of things with which man has lost all *sympathy ;* they belong to all ages.

The Assyrian marbles, to which it is my intention presently to request the attention of the reader, are pictures in stone, representing the ideas of the artists, and, to a certain extent, of the race to whom they belonged. By applying to them the principles just laid down, we may arrive at an approximation of their place in history and in art. In the Coptic, Indian, Chinese, Mexican, and Peruvian remains, we have, I think, materials for such an inquiry into the history of those races. Certain Oriental races still exist as nations, others merely as races; in either case it is interesting to inquire into their past history, even although we should fail to discover the causes of their rise and fall. They stand in strong contrast with the Greek and with the western European nations. The true and the beautiful in nature they could not perceive. They viewed man simply from a social and domestic point of view, which they mistook for the highest civilization ; and by thus thrusting out nature from their view of the

external world, the otherwise highly gifted races of men
from the Euphrates and Nile to the borders of the Yellow
Sea and the still more distant isles of Japan, have excluded
from their history as nations and races those grand elements of *truth* first discovered and only rightly understood
by the antique Greek.   To reduce any nation or race to
the condition of ancient Egypt, Assyria, and Babylon, or of
modern China, they have only to blot from their recollections all remembrance of Greece and her productions, and
raising a great altar to "utility," sacrifice on it, as an offering
to the goddess they worship, the eternal works of nature.

As it might be said of the Assyrian, ancient Coptic,
Chinese, and Indian, that they never came in contact with
Greece nor with the European races or Western world,
and were thus deprived of those advantageous opportunities afforded by the imitation of the works, labours, and
ideas of other races more highly gifted by nature, I shall,
before entering on the consideration of the antique races
I have just alluded to, briefly sketch the history of the
rise and fall of the Arab race.   In their history, authentic
beyond doubt, we have the history of an Oriental race who
not only came into contact with the western races of Greece
and Rome, but did their best to imitate and follow them in
their progress towards a higher civilization.   The result
was a total failure, proving that no race can successfully
adopt a civilization foreign to its nature, or, in other terms,
that each race must invent for itself and adopt the view of
the external world bestowed on it by its instinctive nature.

I am anxious that the principles I am about to apply in
the appreciation of ancient forms of civilization be clearly
understood.   A knowledge of many useful arts is essential
to the existence of man, nor is it easy to imagine the possible existence of any race, or even tribe, totally ignorant
of the useful arts.   On the other hand, to perceive the
absolute truth and to represent *this* in marble or on
canvas, to place before the eyes of men correct imitations
of what nature has created, is the highest of gifts.   In proportion as the individual or race gives a preference to the
objects invented by mankind over nature's creations, so

will the taste of that individual or race be low, unintel-
lectual, and remote from truth ; his sympathies with the
living world have been thrust into the background by the
mathematical and logical inventions of human nature ; he
traces all to *utility*, the goddess he worships, and boldly
proclaims that Nature herself in her inventions had
utility in view. Without being aware of it, he worships
human reason, and denies that anything exists beyond it.
By carefully noting the artistic efforts of a race, we may
arrive at a tolerably clear idea of the view that race took
of the external world; now in that view are included the
character and nature of the civilization of the race.

When so highly gifted a race as the Arab failed in
adapting their nature to a civilization foreign to their race,
we need express no surprise on finding that other less-
gifted races should also fail.

THE ARAB RACE.

In the time of Augustus, the Arabs were unconquered ;
they are so now. The mighty conquerors reported to have
ruled Egypt and Persia never subdued the Arab. Nineveh
and Babylon rose and fell, leaving the Arab race free in
their deserts. Alexander, the all-powerful, shunned Arabia,
and so did Jengis Khan and Tamerlane ; Rome civilized
and ruled many races and nations, but ventured not to
carry her arms into the land of the Arab. The great king
they held in contempt. What progress the race had made
in the meantime must be gathered from the writings of the
age of Mahomet. A part of the race settled in towns had
invented many useful arts; their religious faith could
scarcely be called folly, as it was of the purest. But disunited and at war, tribe against tribe, their united strength
for good or for evil had never been tested ; in other words,
they formed a race, but not a nation. Thus their capabilities for the higher forms of civilization had not been
ascertained, and could not be guessed at, the opportunity
for progress not having occurred. At last, one great man
appeared—Mahomet. He polluted their otherwise simple
faith by the usual trick of impostors, that is, by claiming

a divine mission and the powers of inspiration. Thus an impostor obtruded himself upon the Arab race, and the imposture was readily perpetuated, like every other, by the mixture of fraud and violence usually called education and the law. Thus prepared, the Arab race arose in their might; they had found a leader and they overran the world. The history of the race brings out the questions of the future of intrusive races into continents of which they are not the aboriginals; the influence exercised over the invading race by coming in contact with those of a higher or a lower civilization; the value of the hypothesis which speaks of the ancients as our *precursors*, as if an intelligent race required, in the discovery of the arts of social life, any precursors, any stimulus but that of necessity and opportunity; lastly, the causes of the rise and fall of every race. The object of the inquiry might almost be summed up in a single phrase :—What was the view which the Arab race took of the external world? By the results we shall know if the Oriental mind was equal to the perception of *the truth*, or whether they substituted for moral and physical truths, an artificial, conventional, unreal world of their own invention. The results will show themselves in the character of the literature, science, and art of the race.

When the Arab race at last found a leader worthy of the name, they rapidly conquered the civilized world. Within a few years, they overran and settled in, as colonists and conquerors, Syria, Africa, Sicily, Asia Minor, Persia, India, Spain. A mere accident prevented the conquest of France, Germany, and Britain. But although confronting many forms of civilization, and inventing themselves many arts, their Oriental character never changed. They ventured even on the cultivation of science and philosophy, the only cure hitherto discovered for fanaticism and folly; but even this bold attempt did not succeed in deeply modifying the Oriental mind. A stern and pure republican, like Thomas Jefferson, might be disposed to ascribe this unchangeable character of the race to their religion (the Koran), " which forbids the admission of science and philosophy among the people;" but this may be said of all religious codes.

Had the victorious career of the Arab not been arrested

by Charles Martel, the Koran might now have been taught at Oxford and Cambridge as "the Book" which must supersede all others. As it was, the Arab race finally succeeded in establishing themselves in Spain, amongst a race which may be called European, although mingled with others of undoubted African and Syriac origin. Let us now observe the result. In possession of wealth, of peace, and power, the opportunity had arrived for the full development of the genius of the race, whatever that might be. Accordingly, we find them introduce into Spain an architecture of a grand and noble character peculiar to the Saracenic race, and which by a mistake easily explicable has been called Gothic; all the arts of peace flourished; luxury prevailed everywhere; but the arts were Oriental, and so was the character of the luxury they had adopted; what they could not invent they borrowed from the race amongst whom they dwelt, adapting all they borrowed to their own nature. And now came the attempt to test the Oriental mind as to the progress of which it was capable in respect of literature, science, and art—that is, fine art, for by these three the genius of every race must ultimately be tested, its progress defined and settled, its relation to the eternal truths of nature be finally set at rest.

Now, history informs us that, despite the Koran, the Arabs of Spain attempted the acquisition of science, and turning their attention to literature, created a form of literature peculiar to themselves. With the works of Greece and Rome before them, they were not benefited by them; they could not alter the nature of their race. The city, palace, and gardens of Zebra, the Alhambra, and numerous other noble edifices, attested the splendid imagination of the Orientalist; but with him it was for ever decoration—pearls, gold, and precious stones. All they admired was merely of human invention, the labour of skilful mechanics; a single Greek statue was of more value than all the barbaric pomp of Saracenic Spain. But this great truth the race could not see, could not comprehend. In their eyes nothing was of value but human inventions. As wealth increased, they added the pursuits of profane science to the study of the Koran. The works of the Grecian masters were translated into Arabic; colleges were founded and amply endowed; an Arabian literature appeared, which continued for nearly five hundred years, until extinguished by the great irruption of the Mongols. This literature, though confronted with the Greek and Roman, and in some measure based on them, was distinctly Oriental; experimental science did not exist, and as the study of anatomy was unknown, the philosophy of the living creation was equally so. Greek and Roman history they declined to read, or could not comprehend; their knowledge of man prior to their own age was a tissue of fables; and however we may hesitate in criticising the literary labours of a race we perhaps do not well understand, their deviation from truth is so palpable as to furnish materials sufficient for their condemnation.

Conclusion.—Placed under the most favourable circumstances with one exception—the existence of the Koran— the Arab race made no progress, never in reality improved. The existence of the Koran may have been the cause of this,* but I doubt it. There were others, amongst which the most powerful was race.

1. They never suspected that their caliph was a tyrant and their prophet an impostor. This was effected by the education of the youth, and so perpetuated. The instinct of superstition took alarm even at the introduction of the abstract sciences.

2. Their colleges taught no truths; their writers and lecturers were engaged in theological discussions, polemics, mystics, scholastics, and morals.

3. Their works of art were got up to please and gratify the minds of a race wholly incapable of admiring the beautiful and the true. Fine art did not exist, and what was mistaken for it were the works of the architect, the gardener, the mechanic—the labours, in fact, of ingenious artificers.† What the race admired were the inventions and

* The works of Calvin extinguished science and literature in Scotland for more than 200 years.

† Decorative art is based simply, as I have proved long ago, on the mechanical principles of natural philosophy, or mathematics. Squares, arches, triangles, straight and curved lines constitute its elements; its aim is to gratify our love of order, symmetry, proportions, &c.

handiwork of skilled workmen in apparel, gardens, armour, palaces, decorations, marble columns, pearls, and gold. Each generation, as was natural, setting aside the inventions of its predecessor, substituted for them others more costly, more highly finished. In their palaces they raised trees of gold and silver, birds made of the same metal sat on the boughs warbling their natural harmony by the aid of machinery. In a word, true to their race in their view of "the world to be admired," no place was left for beauty or truth.

Thus the Arab race rose and fell, nothing remaining of them worthy of notice but their architecture, which we call Gothic. Vestiges of the race may still, it is said, be found in Sicily, but this is doubtful. They muster strong in Northern Africa. Though mingling freely with many other races, nowhere have they given origin to a hybrid race, which could not indeed exist beyond a few generations. They have all but returned to their original limits, the peninsula of Arabia, from which they started to conquer the world.

What question does the history of the Arab bring to an issue?

1. Brought into contact with many races, they adopted the inventions of none; they accepted of fables for truths; science and philosophy they arrested by a perpetual reference to a First Cause. The Koran was the tomb of truth in science, literature, and art.

2. Though brought into contact as conquerors with many races, they gave origin to no hybrid race. The civilization of Greece and Rome affected them not.

3. They never altered their view of the external world: full of inventive mathematical genius and a lofty imagination, cultivators of the purest faith, they could under no circumstances perceive the beauty and the truth inherent in nature's works, substituting for them the inventions of man.

4. They attempted settlements or colonies on three continents, and failed. Nature gave them desert Arabia as their home, and there only do they thrive.

PART II.

As the principles I have laid down in this section apply to all the races of men, I shall be as brief as possible in respect of the ancient Assyrian form of civilization. They were an Oriental race, devoid of all love of nature or of truth.

The Father of History, Herodotus, says that the Assyrians, who built Nineveh, and perhaps Babylon, were formerly a leading power in Asia. They formed the eastern riverine population of the Tigris and Euphrates. To Messrs. Botta, Layard, Rawlinson, and Loftus we owe the discovery and transference to Europe of the marbles called Assyrian, now in the Louvre and in the British Museum.

Many of these marbles are covered with a writing which cannot now be read. This at least is my opinion, in which however I differ from many learned men and distinguished scholars. The architecture of the race or races to whom these monuments belonged has not been discovered. These marbles are pictures in stone of the Assyrian race, and give us an idea of the view they took of the external world; their ideas of domestic and fine art; their religious folly; their mode of warfare, &c.; above all, the physical character of the race; in this they resemble the Coptic. The marbles were discovered and dug up at Mossul, a modern town, presumed, on tolerably good authority, to be the site of ancient Nineveh. We have, it is true, no historical evidence for this; Nineveh had disappeared before the times of Herodotus and Xenophon. Five hundred years before Herodotus—that is, about 960, B.C.—the Assyrians were a leading power in Asia, and he says that their capital was Nineveh; but Diodorus points to a much higher antiquity, and this would carry us back to a civilization as ancient as that of China, Indostan, or Egypt.

The arrow-headed characters forming the written characters of the nation and race are not peculiar to the race; they are found in Persia and in Babylon. The hieroglyphics of Egypt were confined to the valley of the Nile.

The marbles represent a peculiar race differing from all others, but most resembling, if not identical, with the present Armenian. Modern travellers are not agreed as to the race which may be considered as directly descended from the ancient Assyrians. By some the Yzidis* are supposed to be the race in question; others give a preference to the Nestorians and Chaldees; but I have always understood that these terms do not characterize races, but merely religious differences in tribes.

The war scenes represented on these marbles are combats with men of the same race, who lived in towns on the banks of rivers. To this there are two exceptions. Mounted on horses and camels, certain persons escape from the battle-field. They may have been Arabians. Defiling from a captured town is a string of prisoners of a dark race—not Negroes, but dark men; probably some of the degraded races who then, as now, lived by the shores of the Persian Gulf. In all other instances the marbles represent but one race; the Jew is not there, nor the Copt, nor any European or Mongol race.

On the black obelisk (supposed by some to represent prisoners and spoils taken in Syria and Egypt), the elephants are of the Indian species, and the camels are Bactrian. The translation of the inscription must then be incorrect. In as far, then, as we may infer from these marbles, the Assyrians, like the Copts, made no distant conquests. The ancient Copts seem to have been wholly unacquainted with the elephant and with the camel. History offers no satisfactory reply to such extraordinary facts. If the artists represented facts, it is useless to attempt connecting these marbles with the history of Judea,

* Ainsworth.

or with any events mentioned in authentic history. They represent battles, such as Homer has described them. The forces employed on both sides were infantry and war-chariots; cavalry was not in use. The religious folly of the Assyrians was also peculiar to the race; not borrowed from any other race, nor shared in common with any other people. Of Bramah or Dudha, Jupiter and Juno, Isis and Osiris, these people knew nothing. Their worship seems to have been Zoroastrian; but be this as it may, they stood alone, borrowing no great features of their civilization from any other race. We must not measure their power by the value or extent of their artistic remains. Be their antiquity greater or less—whether they were a nation and a power when the Pharaohs ruled Egypt, and built the Pyramids; when Bramah and Guadama lived, and China invented all the domestic arts, does not in the least signify; neither the Persian nor the Assyrian borrowed from these races.

The marbles we now consider instruct us as to the mode of warfare of the race; they lived in walled towns, and so did their enemies, who were of the same race; with the exception mentioned, if the artist who carved the marbles adhered to the truth. That race is now represented by the modern Armenian. They knew nothing of the elephant, Asiatic or African, and as an arm of war they never encountered them. Of cavalry they made no use. In these respects they resembled the ancient Copts.*

The artistic products of a race—I mean the labours of the true artist (not the skilled workman or artificer, so often mistaken for an artist)—ought, to a certain extent, to instruct us as to the view of the external world taken by the race or nation to whom he belongs. Generally the artist must of necessity be influenced by the race for whom he works, even although by force of genius he may rise above and despise them. In so far as he is competent to

* The Asiatic elephant is carved on the black marble obelisk now in the Museum, but it is not harnessed; it is being led along with some captives. The Bactrian camel is carved on the same obelisk. It represents, therefore, some razzia in the direction of Bactria and India, and not, as Sir H. Rawlinson thinks, towards Egypt and Syria.

observe the truth in the external world, and is permitted
and encouraged to express it in his works, to *imitate* the
objects of the external world with truth and fidelity, and
last and greatest, to place on canvas or represent in
marble man, his thoughts, actions, and the grand expressions of the inmost workings of human sentiment and
passion, and those sublime forms which nature (the great
artist) at times displays for the admiration of mankind;
so will art in his hands reach perfection, and the approv-
ing race be placed highest in the scale of humanity. The
aim of all artists is, or ought to be, to reach the heart.
Homer, Horace, Burns, Shakespeare, and Pindar, by a few
words; the skilled mechanic aims at a baser principle, but
strictly human;[*] he cares not for the heart but the reason,
conscious that he addresses principles equally potent in
human affairs; he asks us to turn from nature's landscape
to the Italian garden; from the oak and cedar to his
neatly trimmed alcove ; from the Medicean Venus to the
court lady of the reign of Louis Quatorze, or of any other
court, where the milliner and the modiste have succeeded
in withdrawing your attention from nature's grand outlines to the costly silks and velvets, the trimmings of
gold and silver, the pearl necklace, and coronet studded
with diamonds of unknown value. It answers for a time,
and the artificer's labours are declared to be beautiful—by
the present generation. By and by a new race appears,
and the finished works of the artificers of the past age are
pronounced to be antiquated, wretched, intolerable, and
out of date. But why out of date? Is the virgin forest
ever out of date? the Medicean Venus, or the Apollo?
The paintings of Angelo, Raphael, Leonardo, Rubens,
Teniers; the descriptions of Homer, Shakespeare, Horace,
and Burns? Never! They are the works of men who
saw the beautiful and the true in nature, and represented
it as it is. They worked for all generations.

Fine art, like a lofty literature, is the test of the cha-

* Mechanical, mathematical, numerical principles instinctively inherent in human nature, and common to all the races of men, and
requiring neither science nor taste to develope or invent.

racter of every race. They reveal to us the view the race
or nation takes of the external world, its regard for truth,
in literature, philosophy, and science. Without this
innate feeling there never can be any lofty civilization;
for the race which substitutes utility for truth and beauty,
which worships only the useful, can never be made to
comprehend the truth. They create a world of their own,
and admire and worship it; and as they work only for the
present generation, that which follows holds them in contempt. The goddess such races worship is utility.

If we try the Assyrian marbles by this scale, we shall
discover in them all the defects of the Oriental mind. The
colossal human-headed and winged bulls imply a vivid
and powerful fancy on the part of the artists; but fancy is
not imagination, any more than romance is history. The
inscriptions on these figures have never been explained
satisfactorily; one thing we must not forget; the most
ancient bricks of Babylon are uniformly marked with
similar inscriptions in arrow-headed letters or characters.
All this is mysterious, and implies some very ancient form
of civilization of which we know nothing. Homer himself points to the era of Troy and its destruction as
belonging to an age—

> Whereof the faint report alone
> Has reached our ears, remote and ill-informed.[*]

In Homer's time, whatever that be, the Grecian mythology had assumed a perfect character. Let us fix the era
at 900 years B.C. But it had not penetrated into Assyria,
the proof of which we have in these marbles. On the
other hand, the primitive Parsees were fire worshippers.
Thus the religious folly of the Assyrian was not borrowed
from Persia; whilst, as regards the character of true or
imitative art, no two races were ever more opposed than
the Greek and the Assyrian. According to the conjectures of the celebrated travellers, Messrs. Layard and
Rawlinson, the winged human-headed lions with human-
shaped ears, and the winged bulls with ears of the brute

---

[*] Nos vere famam solum audimus;
Necque quicquam scimus.—*Clarke's Translation.*

skilfully diminished so as not to offend the eye, and now
in the Museum, formed part of the decorations of a
temple of the god of war, and were erected by Ashurakbul
or Sardanapalus, about the year 721, B.C.; that is, about
250 years before Herodotus visited Babylon, at which
time Nineveh had ceased to be. This is not trustworthy
chronology, neither is it history.

The features of the human heads of these colossal figures
represent the race; it was the same with the Copt and the
Greek, Brahmin, Chinese, and modern Italian; to their
idols they gave the head and features of their race. To
the human-headed colossal bulls the Assyrian artists gave
the ears of the brute, but smaller and proportioned to the
human physiognomy; to the man-headed lion he gave the
human ears, with earrings and pendants, as was the
fashion of the race. These figures, invented by the race,
spoke to its feelings, instincts, and prejudices; they were
emblems of ideas long departed. We know not so much
of them as we do of the Hindoo and Chinese idols, the
literature of these races being still extant. Herodotus
says that the Greeks borrowed their mythology from the
Copts, but the "Iliad" and "Odyssey," and the Egyptian
monuments still more forcibly, refute this idea. The so-
called Dagon, or Fish God, represented on the Assyrian
marbles, is merely a human figure with the skin of a fish
drawn over it. The Assyrian sculptures represent one
race; and the artist being an Oriental, and unequal to the
perception of beauty and of truth, represents all figures
and every age, male and female, king and priest, lord and
servant, on the same model, from which he never varies.
This model is the adult male figure of the then existing
Assyrian, and of the modern Armenian, coarse, abounding
in impossible attitudes, and with such a display of the
interior, or of the naked anatomy, as to banish from the
whole group the slightest pretensions to beauty and truth.
The limbs are coarse, muscular, and large, with the intermuscular lines or partitions deeply chiselled, as we now
see them in the Modern Assyrian and Turcoman generally.
There is not a correctly formed hand or foot to be seen,

nor woman's form anywhere; even the beauty of youth
and childhood, which with the beauty of form and proportion constitutes the absolutely beautiful—the το καλον
of the Greeks—they could not perceive, though it must
have been constantly before them.

We learn from these slabs that the zoology of these
regions was similar to that described by Xenophon (B.C.
401). They hunted the lion and wild ox, the antelope and
wild ass or horse, and the ostrich, perhaps no longer to be
found in Mesopotamia. Of camels and elephants there
were none; the Asiatic elephant was unknown to the
Persians in the time of Xenophon, and was not seen by
any European until the time of Alexander (B.C. 331).
In the representation of some of these animals, the
Assyrian artist, escaping from the fetters imposed on
him by his race, displays much tact and genius; the truth
is finely told, and shows us that, but for the race and the
nation, the artist was, perhaps, not unequal to look nature
in the face. The truth with which they have represented
the chase of the lion, the wild ass, and the pursuing
dogs is unquestionable. The ostrich is not to be found
on these slabs, nor the buffalo, but the deer, the antelope,
and the ibex. Thus, in what regarded merely animal life,
the Assyrian artist was equal to the perception of truth;
but in attempting to portray man, he encountered the
prejudices of Oriental civilization, which forced him into
the most common of all errors, the mistaking for truth and
beauty the artificial, the fashionable, the conventional, the
national, the studied, fanciful, and extravagant; in a word,
the theatrical—the figures he found on the world's stage
in Nineveh and in Babylon. Thus beauty and truth escaped
them, as it has done so many other races and artists—all
indeed but the antique Greek, and a few inspired artists—
to be found probably amongst most races. Fine forms
they did not comprehend; the beauty of youth was unintelligible to them; its emblems exercised no influence
over their minds, and they were equally indifferent to the
emblems of decay and dissolution. Thus skeleton and

muscular forms appear on the surface, forms which
nature never intended should be seen, and which in the
beautiful figure she does her best to conceal.* The same
result happened here, with nature before them, as we have
seen occur in the history of Arab civilization. The grand
models of Greece and Rome were before the Arabs, but
they could not benefit by them. Nature was before the
Assyrian artist, but he could not, or was not permitted, to
imitate what he saw. Yet even then, the true theory of
high art was perfectly known to the Greeks, as may be
gathered from the works of Homer.†

* A theory has been offered by M. Bonomi to explain away some of
these deep errors of the Assyrian artist, but it is not satisfactory. He
suggests that the deep intermuscular grooves were chiselled inten-
tionally by the Assyrian artist to bring out more forcibly the outline of
the figures placed in the gloomy darkened chambers of the palace of
Nineveh. To this plausible and ingenious theory numerous objections
might be made. Even admitting the theory to be partly true, it does
not explain the total contempt for fine forms.

† The theory of the highest art of which man is capable—sculpture,
was perfectly known to Homer, who is thought to have written the
"Iliad" about 200 years before the period assigned to these sculptures.
He unfolds the whole theory of painting in his description of the shield
of Achilles. The essence of the beautiful and the true is wrapt up
in his narrative of the means by which Venus decorates Penelope when
about to meet Ulysses, and the converse when it is her intention that
Ulysses should remain not only unknown, but be mistaken for an
object of pity and contempt. To effect this, Minerva

    " Touched him with a wand,
    At once o'er all his agile limbs she parched
    The polished skin ; she withered to the roots
    His hoary locks, and clothed him with the hide
    Deformed of wrinkled age ; she charged with rheum
    His eyes, before so vivid, and a cloak
    And kertch she gave him, tattered both and foul,
    And smutched with smoke ; then casting over all
    A huge old hairless deer-skin, with a staff
    She filled his shrivelled hand, and gave him last
    A wallet patched all over, and that
    With twisted buckle, dangled at his side."

Neither poet nor artist has ever placed before human sight in so
matchless a way the emblems of decay and dissolution ; it extends to
the dress and equipment ; nothing is omitted, and it is easy to see that
in Homer alone could we find such a picture.

If in our western and European world there be many educated and
superior-minded men who cannot be made to comprehend this theory
and its results, it may be consolatory to them to know, that Cicero
himself, educated in Athens, never could comprehend it. The Europeans

Thus, excepting as regards composition, the artists of the race had no other artistic qualities. They knew not the value of emblems, and how deeply they influence the human mind. That the feet and hands of the race were generally skeleton-formed in the adult, as in the modern North American Indian, Caffre, &c., may be true, but this does not prove that no model of beauty could be found in the Assyrian race. The Copt *committed* the same error.

Conclusion.—Fine art was as low with the ancient Assyrians as with the Chinese, the Indian, and the Copt; their extended conquests were mere fables, as with the Egyptians. The Babylonians and Chaldæans were probably of the same race as the Assyrians, or at least strongly affiliated. No Jews are represented on these sculptures, nor any other race but a few prisoners, seemingly of a dark race, defiling from a walled town with other prisoners of the Assyrian race. The Arabian was then in the field, just as he is now.

Over the desert plains of Mesopotamia the Emperor Julian led an army, many centuries after Xenophon had described them. Another race, the Persian, held then the supreme power of Asia, but the leading features of the Orientals had not changed. Ancient Babylon and Nineveh had long ceased to be, and Julian marched on Ctesiphon, finding on all sides the characters and circumstances of the ancient Assyrians.

Of their architecture I can say nothing: the Orientals excelled in this art all other races, perhaps even the Greek. But architecture is merely a domestic or useful art, it is

are the descendants of the strong-armed barbarians, who never, in so far as I know, invented anything. Settled down at last into nationalities, they have acquired, some of them, a language and a literature which, though not of the highest order, is yet equal to the expression of human thoughts and actions. Mechanical science they have greatly advanced, and the principles of commerce seem to be better understood than they were even a century ago; out of the remains of Coptic, Indian, Mongol, Assyrian, Greek, and Saracenic architecture and fine art, they endeavour to identify something with the national feelings, and call the edility thus produced national architecture and national art! But it is impossible to overlook the fact, that a nation merely as a nation can never originate a form of art or literature: this natural gift belongs to a race, whether formed into a political power or not.

not a fine art; it therefore furnishes no proof in favour of
the artistic abilities of any race. Races low in true art aim
at effect, in literature vulgarly called clap-trap. Neither
the Copt nor the Assyrian could have ever made any progress in high art, the character of the races being opposed
to such progress. Thus it is that in the domestic arts,
man continually changes and sometimes improves; of
these he is the solo inventor. They spring from his
wants, necessities, circumstances, and the progress or
change is caused by the advent of another generation on
the stage of life. As regards imitative or high art, the
object of the Coptic and Assyrian artist was effect—not
truth.

The remains of art, proving the existence of very ancient
forms of civilization, instruct us as to some curious facts
in the history of mankind. Had not the Coptic monuments survived the havoc of time and the destroying
hands of other races, no man could have been persuaded
that such a race as the Coptic ever existed. The same
may be said of the ancient Aztecs, without giving credit to
more than a half of what the gifted Prescott has written
concerning them. No fact of any value can be gathered
from the Jewish records respecting the condition of ancient
Egypt or Syria; whilst but for the remains of art, the world
would call in question, and has repeatedly done so, the
marvellous history of ancient Greece.

These fragments of ancient history deeply affect the
human race, for man is interested solely in what concerns
man. The fossil remains of other animals disinterred from
the ancient strata of the globe, and first interpreted by the
immortal Cuvier, took men by surprise, inasmuch as they
overthrew all existing cosmogonies and chronologies; but
as man was not included in these discoveries, the surprise
gradually subsided and ceased to interest. Not so with
what regards man. Disinter a fragment of human bone
from an ancient stratum of the globe, discover in such a
stratum an object of human industry, and you startle the
Christian world. As we have no proofs that the Assyrian
marbles are of very remote antiquity, I need not here

discuss the all-important question of the antiquity of man
on the globe.

Conclusion.—At the period, whatever it might be, when
these marbles were sculptured, civilization had culminated
to its highest point in Assyria; the race had wrought out
its destiny, nor would the invention of a thousand objects
of domestic art have altered the character of the race or
influenced its view of the external world. The same had
occurred in Egypt, Hindostan, and in China, in Mexico
and Peru. There the Indo-American race carried out to
the utmost the peculiar form of their civilization. When
swept off by the Spanish conquests, the race relapsed to
its primitive barbarism, unequal to adopt the civilization
of another race.

It was the same with the Babylonians and Assyrians,
Copts and Syrians. Though brought face to face with the
Greek and Italian races, they could not adapt themselves
to the new forms of civilization offered them; that is, they
could not look on the external world otherwise than the
instincts of their race prompted them to do. Then arrived
in these fine countries other barbarous races—the Arab,
the Mongol, the Turcoman, and all civilization fell at once,
to re-appear under another form created by the conquering
races.

The great error of modern times is to undervalue the
character of ancient forms of civilization, a sure corrective
of which will be found in comparing the progress of Alexander and Cæsar with modern European heroes and kings,
and in a careful study of the letters of Cicero. Of these
ancient races the Chinese still survive as a nation; and in
Hindostan we have the direct descendants of many races.
Copts strongly resembling their ancestral drawings still
wander by the banks of the Nile. The modern Armenian
retains all the Assyrian features. The Jew is not to be
found upon any Coptic or Assyrian monuments; and the
conquests of the ancient Egyptians must unquestionably
be mere fables. They were ignorant of the use of cavalry
and of the elephant as an instrument of war, though
limitrophic with Elephantina, the country of elephants.

The Arab at all times defied all these races. Of their literature we know nothing ; but if it resembled their pictorial and sculptural arts, it must have been inflated, false, theatrical—in a word, Oriental. They originated their own social arts, borrowing from none. Their fine arts display the view they took of the external world ; in this view the beautiful and the true held no place.

CHAPTER III.

AFRICA,

ITS PAST, PRESENT, AND PROBABLE FUTURE.

CHANCE, which regulates the fate of all that lives—chance, which the divine Homer called fate—led me a good many years ago to Southern Africa, a portion of that enigmatic continent so well designated by the Roman poet as the " parched nurse of lions," and as a land which ever offers something new to the traveller. Of this vast continent the Greeks and Romans knew but little; its interior is still, to a great extent, unknown to the European world. A climate the most deadly excludes the white man from its tropical portions; no great navigable rivers give access to its central regions, whilst vast deserts all but insulate the northern extra-tropical from the tropical sections of the continent. Thus, although abounding in gold, in animal and vegetable life profusely lavished on it by all-bounteous nature, and further, although the cradle of a race of men who, from an inferiority of intellect or natural feebleness of character, have suffered, and still suffer, at the hands of European races all the cruelties and horrors of transportation into hopeless bondage, the continent of Africa has hitherto escaped, to a great extent, the desolating conquests which have everywhere characterized the progress over the earth of the European races of later times. Before attempting an explanation of this sufficiently curious fact in the history of Africa, I shall make a few remarks in illustration of the main object of this lecture,* which is intended briefly to introduce to the notice of my audience the great question of modern times, the moral and physical characteristics of the various races of men now occupying the earth, with a reference more especially to

* The substance of this chapter was delivered as a lecture about three years ago in the Philosophical Institution of London.

those aboriginal and intrusive races soon to meet on the
African continent. The contest between those who openly
maintain might to be right, who quit their native homes in
order to appropriate to themselves, on various pretexts,
the land of others, has already commenced on the African
coast. The nations representing the Saxon, and Scandinavian, and Celtic races, precipitate themselves into Africa.
Their object is plunder, conquest, annexation, if possible ;
these are the ends they seek in the invasion of the African
continent. They invade from the north and from the
south, from the east and from the west. Political and
other circumstances rendering the exportation of the Negro
from his aboriginal soil no longer practicable, or at least
attended with unpleasant political complications, they
follow him to the cradle of his origin, the land of his birth,
trusting to repeat on that land the sad tragedies which
followed the invasion of America by the Saxon and Iberian
races ; of India by the Saxon and Gaul. Man, some maintain, is progressive, but history does not support this view.
In what is he progressive? Is it in practical Christianity ?
Is it in the humanizing arts of civilization ? Look at India,
Africa, Mexico, and Australia ; think of the history of
North and South America. Does the progress consist in
the simple fact of a greater accumulation of what may be
called the social arts? Then proceed with me to Northern Africa, and let us see what we have on that soil,
encumbered with the vestiges of five successive forms of
ruined civilization, to compensate for the past ; what exists
to mark the progress of humanity, Pagan, Christian, or
Saracen. I am no stickler for the superiority of the
ancient forms of civilization—of which, by the bye, we after
all know but little ; I am not an admirer of the institutions
of heathen Rome, any more than the most distinguished
orator of the day ;* but I love truth. Now, I do not find
in the history of the conquests of the ancient Greeks and
Romans that peculiar savagery, ferocity, hypocrisy, and
licentiousness which mark the progress of modern Christian races and nations over the earth. The bulk of the
African continent has hitherto escaped, to a great extent,

* Mr. J. Bright.

the grand humanizing and civilizing progress of the Anglo
and Dutch Saxon and Celtiberian races in America and
India, which are being now repeated in Southern Africa,
and which, unhappily, instead of elevating, as the Romans
did, the rude aborigines, depress and enslave, hopelessly
and seemingly for ever, the native races. This is the
first question I mean to consider. The second, naturally
flowing from the first, will be, "the probable future
of Africa," which may, I think, be conjectured from the
past. The elements for the solution of this problem, the
future of Africa, are, the character of its aborigines and of
the European races who now anxiously desire to intrude
themselves into that vast and comparatively unknown
land.

If the races of men here in Europe are so distinct from
each other, why, you may perhaps say, go to Africa in
order to explain their characters and differences? If the
Gaul, the Scandinavian, and the German, or true Frank,
whom M. Kossuth mistakes for mere nations, confounding
the German with the Scandinavian (although he must
know that the true German never, properly speaking,
formed a distinct nation), be so absolutely distinct, why go
to Africa to establish the importance of this *natural history character?* My answer is this:—The story of the
conflict between the intrusive and the aboriginal races on
the American continent belongs to history ; the events are
past and gone ; they no longer interest humanity. It is
the same with India. Clive and Pizarro, Cortes and Albuquerque, have long passed away to render their last account ;
even the atrocities of Rosas are already forgotten. Africa,
on the other hand, is now present; here the conflict is
about to be resumed—nay, has already commenced; the
enormities which Bourmont and Pelissier practised in
Northern Africa, Pretorius and his Dutch Boers have
already rivalled in the South. It is Clive and Pizarro,
Cortes and Albuquerque again, without the pomp and circumstance which shed a horrid and unearthly glare around
the progress of these strong-headed savage filibusters.
The struggle now carried on by the Celtic race of France

in Northern Africa is with petty sheiks and wild chiefs of two barbarous races. In the south, the intrusive Saxon fights with Caffre kings at least as savage as the Bedouins and Tibboo of the north; in tropical Africa, the feeble Lusitanian race maintains a contest with the still feebler Negro, which it enslaves, brutalizes, and sells as he would the beasts of the field. Now, the aim of all the fair races is the same,—namely, plunder and conquest; and, although the Lusitanian race rapidly becomes extinct in these regions, as must ever happen to Europeans in tropical countries when not fed by a continual immigration from their native land, still, by means of the mulatto, they for a time may stand their ground against a race so inferior in intellect as the Negro. But the Mulatto will also in time disappear, and all will return to the gloomy shades of the aboriginal stock, and thus extinction under both forms threatens the Lusitanian race in Africa.

Now it is this circumstance, the actuality of the contest, which renders the African continent so interesting: it is its present relation to the races and nations of men, and especially to the European brigands of the present day, which has induced me to select it as the chief topic of my discourse. There is a question I have often deeply meditated, but to which I shall merely allude here: why, for example, the rapacious, intrusive, and unprincipled European races of comparatively modern times avoided Africa to a great extent, selecting the Asiatic and American continents and their islands as the grand fields for their filibustering expeditions: why, for example, the Scandinavian and Saxon Hollander and English (the Anglo and Dutch Saxons as they are called) preferred America as their field for plunder and violence to Africa; why the Lusitanian, Celtiberian, and Celtic races also sought those continents in preference to Africa, though so much nearer their own shores; and how it was that even the ancient Roman, Greek, and Persian, in their filibustering career over the earth, confined their exploits in Africa to a comparatively narrow territory embracing not a tenth of Africa's great continent. The solution of this question might be found, I think, in the character of the African soil and its population. With a view to the elucidation of this question. I shall make a few brief remarks on the early history of Northern Africa. The earliest race which can be discovered in Africa north of the Sahara, is the Libyan, Kabyle, or Berber. They seem to have occupied the entire tract of country from the borders of Egypt to the Atlantic, and from the Mediterranean to the southern border of the Sahara, or the land of the Negro. On some linguistic grounds the race has been traced to the East (India), but this has not been proved.* We may view them, then, as primitives or aborigines until other facts refute this view. The Negro race never penetrated into Northern Africa, and it is asserted that even now the true Negro cannot extend his race in Northern Africa. The first intrusive race who entered this region of Africa was the Phœnician, to whose history I have alluded in the chapter on the Assyrian Marbles. One circumstance only I may mention here. The Phœnicians who emigrated to Africa are said to have been a motley crew made up of men of various races.† If this were proved, it would of itself explain the extinction of the Phœnician race in North Africa; for the motley or hybrid race was sure to die out in time, if not fed by some pure race. The Berbers or Kabyles now occupy the country under the name of Moors, having survived the Phœnician intrusion ; and, secondly, the Greek.

The first Greek intrusion took place 651 years B.C. It was on a small scale. The fugitives came from Thera and founded Cyrene. But Cyrene after all was never more than a Greek oasis in the midst of a desert. Alexander first thought of Egypt which he took from the Persian, also an intrusive race into Egypt ; but his destiny led him to Asia, and thus the Phœnicians escaped. Subsequently an adventurer of the name of Agathocles invaded Northern Africa with an army of Greeks, but failed ; and thus the Greeks as an intrusive race make no figure in the history of Northern Africa.

Another race, usually held to be Asiatic, but of whom

* Sallustii Hist.   † Ferrier.

many seem to me to be descended from the Copt, also penetrated into Northern Africa. These were the Jews. Long
prior to the destruction of their nationality by the taking of
Jerusalem, the race had wandered into every country of the
then known world. At one time they abounded in Cyrene;
they now flee from Morocco as they formerly did from Spain,
taking refuge in Algiers. M. Duprat thinks that the Jews
cannot be traced into Spain earlier than the destruction of
their nationality by Titus. It may be so; but I have shown
in my work on the "Races of Men" that they were extremely
numerous in Rome in the time of Cicero; that they were
numerous, wealthy, and, consequently, influential—a fact
which historians seem to have overlooked. They fled
from Spain in the reign of Ferdinand and Isabella to the
number of 300,000, most of whom sought refuge in Mauri-
tania. The remains of the race, reduced to 26,000
people, now flee before the Moors to seek a refuge in
Algiers.

The next intrusive race was the Romans, who civilized
all Northern Africa; but their race as a race made no progress, and we now know that they have been long extinct.
In 429 the Vandals appeared, amounting probably to more
than half a million of people; they also have been long
extinct. The destruction of their power in Africa was
effected by Belisarius and his motley crew of Byzantines;
but their occupation of the country was merely a military
one, so that we must look to their successors, the Arabs,
for the intrusive race which most deeply affected the
character of the population of Northern Africa. There
are some grounds for supposing that colonies of Arabs had
settled in Northern Africa long prior to the rise of the
Mahometan power; but they were in no strength, and
could not influence the population. It was quite otherwise
with their invasion in 632, which led to the complete
conquest of Northern Africa, and to the establishment of
the Arab race upon its soil; some centuries afterwards
they were followed by the Osmaulis or Turks, who now
give place to the Celtic race of France. None of these
intrusive races have displaced the primitive Berber; they

have been more or less mingled with them, but such mingling never ends in the production of a hybrid race.

Conclusion.—As respects Northern Africa, when the Celtic race of France took possession of Algeria, they first met the remains of the Turk or Turco-man, and the Turco-Arab or Coulouglis, a hybrid population sure to terminate in extinction. These people occupied the towns. They next encountered the Arab of the plains, the descendants of those who first overran Northern Africa, and founded the Mahometan sovereignties. These the French mistook for a united people, although in reality they form but a collection of tribes. Lastly, they encountered towards the mountains the ancient Numidian race, the Berbers or Kabyles, a race distinct from all the others. This race, driven towards the mountains and the Sahara by all the invading and intrusive races, has yet survived them all. They are in great force in Morocco. They have never been civilized. The Atlas seems to be their cradle or home, yet they are said to have founded Morocco and even Algiers. In remote antiquity they were called Libyans. Into this land of Northern Africa the Negro element never penetrated, and it is said that he cannot live there even now.

The character of the Berber, such as it is now, was drawn by Sallust. They seem to adopt with facility the forms of life of a conquering race, adapting themselves to the new order of things, but relapsing instantly into their primitive life so soon as the dominant race loses the power of coercion. Thus the empire of the Moghreb may pass into the hands of France, but will never become an integral portion of a French empire. The climate, the antipathies of race, the character of the intrusive and aboriginal race, are opposed to such a union, even under the name of the "departments of Alger and of the Moghreb," unless there should appear another Alexander or Cæsar, or Napoleon the Great, who, forewarned by the errors of his great predecessor, may clearly comprehend the distinction between a paltry monarchy and a true empire—a model kingdom after the fashion of a Louis

Quatorze, and an imperial power wielded by a Trajan or
an Antonine, extending to men of all races if not the
unspeakable blessings of true liberty, at least protection
of life and property, and the freedom to follow whatever
form of religious folly they may prefer.

In the view I take of man, race is everything in human
affairs when left to their natural course. The moral and
physical characteristics of nations, as well as of individuals,
depend upon race. Had the illustrious Hungarian Kossuth
studied the nature of the Anglo-Saxon race amongst whom
it was his unhappy fate to be cast in his exile, he might
have saved himself many sufferings and grievous insults;
if he had deeply studied the history of race, he would
never have visited the United States. The friendly reception of Nicholas of Russia, and of all successful, or at
least wealthy tyrants by the Saxon everywhere, ought to
have instructed him as to the character of the Anglo-Saxon
race wherever located, and have warned him of the danger
he incurred in leaving behind him the public treasures of
Hungary, and the crown jewels of the kingdom, when he
fled from his native land. Had he read my work on the
" Races of Man," he would have found therein an outline of
those moral and physical characteristics which he seems
still disposed to ascribe to national influences. Even now
some distinguished men, who I think ought to know better,
persist in tracing to the present government of France
those events which, in an especial and most remarkable
manner, depend on the character of the Gaulish race, by
whatever name you are pleased to call them—French,
Welsh, Caledonian, Irish (for all these are Gaulish); a
race which, as I proved long ago, has never altered its
character since the earliest recorded times. On three
great occasions the centre clan of the race, constituting
the French people, have had its destinies and those of
Europe in its hands, and on every occasion have they
chosen as their form of government a pure unmitigated
despotism, a despotism incompatible with the progress of
the human intellect. M. de Saulcy (to whom I have
already referred), who travelled into Syria during the

short-lived republic of 1848, conversing with an Arab
chief, or sheik, on the nature of that government which
then prevailed in France, and endeavouring to explain to
the Arab the peculiarities of *a republic*, under which form
of government he then lived, was met and silenced at once
by the simple-minded Bedouin, who made to him this
pithy and too true remark, " You cannot go on under such
a form of government; *you must have a sultan*." The
Bedouin could not have read my work on the " Races of
Man,"and yet how true and how prophetic were his words ;
scarcely was the republic constituted when the nation demanded a sultan. No Gaulish man comprehends, as I
proved in that work published many years ago, the meaning of Scandinavian and German institutions. It is in
vain that you endeavour to explain such things to them ;
they have never, under any form of government, been
without passports and battlements, fortified towns, garri-
sons, military shows, pomp and national glory ; it is their
nature. Why abuse them for it ?   We Anglo-Saxons and
Dutch-Saxons have each our oddities also dependant on
our race, furnishing to foreigners and to the matchless pen
of the writers of the " London Charivari " abundant matter
for pleasant abuse. If the French empire be a *sham*, as
many esteem it to be, it is at least as respectable a sham as
the English constitution—an acknowledged sham, even by
ourselves ; and could we believe a portion of the English
press—the boasted American constitution, an Anglo-Saxon
emanation, is something worse.   Would it not be better
to accept of the races of men as nature made them ; study
their history, trace their social history when congregated
into nations, and the modifications it undergoes by civilization ; show them, by good example, the advantages of
modern European civilization, and leave them to govern
themselves ? But all history shows that such an event is
Utopian—a millennium no more to be looked forward to
than that foretold by the Presbyterian rant and prophetic folly, so much the fashion of the times in which
we live ; opposed to its accomplishment stand the antagonism of race to race, the love of *brigandage*, the staple

trade of all nations and races, and the existence in most
nations of the three great classes of men—kings, nobles,
and priests—those three grand curses of humanity.

To understand the past of Africa, as we have just seen,
regard must be had to its physical geography and to its
relations to other continents. A long strip of comparatively fertile land, interrupted by one or two deserts, extends from the Atlantic to the Red Sea. In the southern
portions of this elongated territory runs the Atlas or
Atlaic range of mountains, separating its western portion
from the Sahara, whilst the highlands of Abyssinia in a
similar manner insulate, as it were, Egypt from the more
southern portion of Eastern Africa.

A vast desert—the Sahara—separates to the west and
south these fertile regions from tropical or Central Africa,
cutting off, as it were, the habitable parts of Africa from
the uninhabitable, by Europeans at least. To the east no
such desert as this exists; and thus Egypt communicates
directly with Central Africa by means of the Abyssinian
Mountains and the White Nile. Through this land, in
all probability, the Negro first penetrated into Egypt, and
became known not only to the ancient Egyptians, but to
Europe and the East. On the ancient Egyptian tombs
and monuments to which the illustrious and learned
Lepsius has assigned an antiquity of 4600 years before the
Christian era, or 6400 years to the present day, we find
the Negro race depicted precisely as it now exists, unaltered physically or morally—a fact demonstrable by the
sure testimony of the pictorial and sculptural arts.

To the south of the Sahara and of Egypt is tropical Africa,
the land of the gorilla and of the Negro, of a superabun-
dance of animal and vegetable life. This is the region which
has justly perhaps merited the name of "the white man's
grave," and the statistics presented to the world by the
ablest of all English statisticians, Colonel Tulloch, support
this view. It is a portion of this territory which these
three intrusive European races have oft invaded, but with
no success. The Anglo-Saxon or English, and the Holland-
Saxon or Dutch, redouble their efforts at this moment to

penetrate into the land of the Negro. The Dane or pure
Scandinavian tried it long ago, but failed. We shall return
to this subject presently; in the meantime, it may be remarked that a large portion at least of the central portion
of this intratropical land seems to be composed of vast
lakes and inland freshwater seas, the sources perhaps of
rivers, which, flowing from them, make their way to the
ocean in all directions. The mountains enclosing this vast
basin or succession of basins are not in general lofty; on
the other hand, a parched land of vast desert tracts, inter-
cepted by somewhat lofty mountains, with rivers of no
magnitude, and a few large forests fringed towards the
southern and eastern ocean by a moderately fertile tract,
and separated as it were by the great extent of the Calihari,
or Southern Sahara, from tropical central Africa, constitute
the southern portion of the continent. This is the cradle
seemingly of the Hottentot, or yellow race of Southern
Africa, and of the Caffre nations, much maligned races of
men, who now fight their last battle for existence. Opposed
to them are the strong-armed Anglo-Saxon and Holland-
Saxon, the most celebrated of all filibusters, who proclaim-
ing themselves to be Christian Mensch, and as Saxons the
only true Christian Mensch in the world, now go forth
utterly to exterminate the heathen, and to extirpate the
coloured races from the face of the earth. In this extra-
tropical portion of Southern Africa I travelled and resided
for a long period; the character of the natives and of the
intrusive races is well known to me; the earliest scientific
account of the Caffre race was communicated to the
European world by myself.* No land abounds more in
animal life than this southern land. Here roam the fleet
ostrich, the terrible rhinoceros, the stately giraffe, the
gigantic elephant; antelopes of countless varieties adorn the
karoo and parched lands of these desert countries; the
majestic black-maned lion stalks the desert in the full
blaze of noon. Here it was on the slopes of the Anatolo
and Winterbergen that I first saw, face to face, unmodi-
fied by man, nature's landscape—that landscape so different

* Trans. of the Wernerian Soc., 1821.

in all respects from the cultivated regions of civilized
countries—those trimly-weeded fields which civilized man
mistakes, in the oddest way imaginable, for nature's landscapes and nature's works. The citizen retiring to his
suburban villa, neatly-trimmed garden, Italian terrace,
symmetrical rows of trees, geometrically laid-out walks
and plots of flowers, wherein you may trace all or most of
the figures to be found in the "Elements of Euclid"—talks
of the pleasure of looking at a bit of nature! Could his
gardener explain matters to him, he would soon show him
that there is not a bit of nature in the whole landscape,
and that he never intended there should be; his whole
object being to exclude nature, and to show his master
how perfectly he had done so. On this success depends
the pleasure his employer has in contemplating his work.
The farmer also, when he looks at his well-cultivated
fields, his close even fences, the ripening field of wheat, in
which there is nothing to be seen but wheat, admiring the
perfection of man's handiwork, must, if he reflects on it,
be often amused at the observations of those who mistake
his farm for a natural landscape. To see such go to Africa,
to the wilds of America, and there admire the landscape
fresh from the great Painter's hands. To enjoy this, the
penates you worship (utility and the social arts) must be
left at home: you are in the presence of mysterious nature;
you may guess at her object, but cannot discover it;
admire and worship, but pretend not to unfold her grand
scheme; for of this you must be instinctively aware, that her
plans cannot be yours. Be content with the reflection that
you belong to that mysterious consanguinity, for a time at
least, that ever-renovating, ever-renewed principle which
converted this globe from a lifeless desert into a sphere
teeming with all that is beautiful.

By the banks of the Swarte and White Kei there lay
outstretched before me a portion of the primitive world.
Of human handiwork no vestiges were present. Myriads
of gnoos, hartebeests, bonteboks, zebras, and elands
browsed the plains; the lion was abroad at midday in
troops or single; elephants might be seen in the distance;

also the rhinoceros; nor was the hyena absent, nor the
jackal, so soon as the bright orb of day had descended
behind the distant Sneuwbergen; the wild Bushmen,
children of the desert, peered on us from their rocky
home in the distant mountains—if home it may be called—
as we slowly traversed these plains, hoping by a circuitous
route to circumvent the Caffre nations; whilst overhead
soared the vulture, scanning from his unapproachable
heights the lower world. Into that field civilized man, the
grand antagonist of nature's works, had not then penetrated. To trace his advent and its results forms a leading
part of the lecture; and first of the arrival and progress
in Northern Africa of the intrusive races.

If the Egyptians were an intrusive race, it is not known
for certain whence they came. They seem to have been
the eldest of civilized men. Lepsius assigns to certain of
their architectural monuments an antiquity of about 6100
years. Dunsen hints at a much higher antiquity, whilst
the late researches of M. T. Leonard Horner point to an
antiquity of 11,600 years; such he thinks being the age of
certain indications leading to the belief that at that remote
period a race, possessing some at least of the arts of
civilized life, inhabited the Delta of the Nile. However
this may be—and this is not the place nor the occasion to
weigh the value of these conflicting estimates—we know
from the still existing Egyptian monuments that three
distinct races of men were then in existence in or near
Egypt—the Copt, the Negro, and a fair race of a nature
unknown.

The subsequent conquests of the Egyptians over many
savage nations are mere fables. They knew nothing of
the elephant, though living in close contiguity to Elephantina, the country of the elephants; the camel—and
this is almost incredible—seems to have been equally
unknown to them as to the Greeks or Trojans during the
age of Homer, and, like the same Greeks and Trojans, the
Copt was ignorant of the use of cavalry as an instrument
of war. Their conquests were probably mere fables and

romances, but their monuments remain the wonder of the world.

If we follow the African land westward from Egypt, we find the Libyan desert and the oasis interposed between the Valley of the Nile and that comparatively fertile tract to which I have already alluded as extending from the margin of this desert to the shores of the Atlantic, and from the Mediterranean to that ocean of sand, the great and terrible Sahara. Here on this tract flourished in rapid succession the Carthaginian, Roman of both empires, Vandalic, Saracen, Ottoman forms of civilization; where are they now, and where the races which gave origin to them? All but extinct. The barbarous Moor, the Tibboo, the Bedouin, alone remain. They were there before the arrival of Queen Dido, they are there now; being the aboriginal race, they survive, whilst all intrusive races have become extinct. Thus it ever seems to happen (and history supports this view) with intrusive races; after flourishing for a time, they degenerate and become extinct.

This fact, which I was the first to announce, was much doubted and strongly denied at first, but many able writers have now given in their adhesion to the view.* The United States men themselves would perish and soon become extinct, were the race not continually fed and sustained by fresh blood from Europe. The history of the intrusive races into Northern Africa tells the same tale; all have become extinct in time. And now, after centuries of a terrible barbarism spread over these fine lands by the abhorred Turcoman, an Asiatic race still suffered to occupy some of the richest provinces of Europe, another European race, the Gaulish, once more intrudes itself into Northern Africa. Judging from the past, it seems not difficult to foretel its future extinction. But this is not the question at present. What I propose considering is the comparative progress of the two races who now invade Africa, the Gaulish, namely, and the Saxon and Scandinavian; and to understand the full import of this contest—a question

* Gervinus, in his latest works.

N N

wholly misunderstood by the writers in the *Revue des Deux Mondes*—we must proceed to Southern Africa, the field selected by the Anglo-Saxon and the Dutch-Saxon for the exercise of all that practical energy which stamps him as the prince of filibusters; the race who look on all dark men as mere "niggers," and apply this name to them; the race destined, as they themselves declare, utterly to root out and exterminate the heathen—that is, the "niggers,"— from the face of the earth, or, what in the meantime may be more profitable to them, by reducing them to hopeless slavery, so debase the coloured races as to deprive them for ever of all chance of recovering that inestimable treasure beyond all price or value, freedom of speech, thought, and action; in a word, the rights of man. How has this antagonism of race arisen? The truth is, it has always existed, but it never appeared in its terrible form until the Saxon race began to migrate over the earth, to establish free colonies, as they are called—free to the white man and their own race—dens of horror and of cruelty to the coloured. Look at India; look at the United States of America, and see the antagonism of race to race, carried to the utmost point of virulence. But we need not go beyond Southern Africa to find the characteristic of the Anglo-Saxon and the Holland-Saxon (for they are identical) displayed in full perfection. Watch the proceedings in Australia, and the antipathy of the white race to the coloured, and say, is not this the old antipathy of race to race? During the grandest periods of the Roman empire this antagonism was not suffered to show itself in any great degree; but long prior to that epoch Alexander and all subsequent conquerors, Greek and Roman, were aware of its existence. During the entire period of Roman power, the Romans never came in contact with any nation or race with whom they could not amalgamate or admit into the fellowship of the Roman world. Central Africa, the true Negro land, was as unknown to them as America, and so were the coloured races of Asia; nor was it until the time of Justinian that this great question which now agitates the world was mooted by the Roman

citizen—namely, "Whether it was proper to admit into
the bosom of civilized society a race of savage Negroes."
Here, then, under a Christian emperor was the question
first raised and entertained, whether or not there existed
on the face of the earth a race or races of men who were
not entitled to "the rights of men." Since then, the
European, and more especially the Anglo-Saxon, has extended this objection to all or nearly all coloured races of
men; it has become the question of the day, and for a
time will agitate the civilized world, for everywhere do
we find the grand and seemingly the natural enemy of the
coloured races victorious in the colonizing strife—the
contest for new lands. Spreading over the earth, the race
has seised on Northern America, and now aims at the
Southern half of that continent. India, Australia, Southern
and Central Africa, China, Japan—all are threatened. So
far it is consolatory to think that it is the overflowing of a
race who, when rescued from the ancient despotisms and
the so-called constitutional monarchies of Europe, establish free states, and proclaim the natural rights of man;
the one great drawback is, that they refuse to other races
the rights they claim for themselves.

Into Northern Africa the Romans carried a civilization
seemingly superior to any form that now exists on the
earth: were the same lands to fall under the dominion of
the Anglo-Saxon or Dutch-Saxon, they would become a
den of slavery and wretchedness for the coloured races—a
land of servitude and horrors. What its future may be
under the Celtic sway I may consider towards the close of
the lecture. But it must never be forgotten that the Celt
always and under all circumstances will have "a sultan;"
on the individual character of that sultan will depend the
fortunes of the race. When the Saxon throws off the
serfdom inherited from his ancestors, and repudiates the
sham and imposture of a constitutional monarchy, he
claims for himself "the rights of man." The laws he
proposes to obey, he himself makes; pity it is he cannot
permit to all the human race the enjoyment of those
sacred rights which, after a terrible struggle with the

most dangerous of all despotisms (the English), because
the best masked, he finally established for himself in
Washington.

Let us now turn our attention to South Africa, and,
more properly speaking, to its extra-tropical portion. The
history of the first appearance of the intrusive races of
men into South Africa, long known as the Cape of Good
Hope, must now be familiar to all who read. The land
was first discovered by the Portuguese or Lusitanian race
—a race long since in a state of decadence and decrepitude.
They discovered the Cape, and attempted a settlement at
the mouth of the Rio d'Iufante, better known as the Great
Fish River, whose bushy banks have of late years acquired
an unhappy and melancholy notoriety as the scene of so
many sharp conflicts between the European and Caffre, a
bold and noble race of men, fighting for their lives and
property, and for all that men hold dear. But the Portuguese soon abandoned the territory, on finding that it
afforded neither gold nor Negroes, the two commodities
they were in search of, and the abandoned territory fell
into the hands of Van Riebeck and the Dutch. True
to their nature, that is, to the character of their race, they
massacred and enslaved the feeble Quaiquæ, whom we
call Hottentots, plundering them of their lands and cattle,
wives and children, and shooting them down like wild
beasts; the sad tale may be read in the pages of Barrow
and Phillips, of Burchell and Livingstone, and of nearly
all travellers who have visited that interesting land. As
they, the Dutch, progressed (the Saxons are always progressing at the expense of their neighbours,) eastward and
northward, they soon encountered the dark Caffre nations,
whom they very naturally and as became white Christian
mensch, treated as wild beasts they were bound to exterminate. This laudable enterprise they are still engaged in.
After the Cape fell into the hands of the English, the
Dutch policy, somehow or other, did not much change;
the Caffre wars continued, and they still go on. They are
profitable wars to the colonists, as Dr. Livingstone has
well hinted at. Chief after chief falls, and being tried for

some misdemeanour, is of course found guilty, and transferred to a jail. It is the old Tarquin policy : cut off the
heads of all the tall poppies, the rest are harmless and
may be spared. To comprehend the late doings in respect
of this noble race of men, the Caffre race, you must read
Livingstone, and reflect on what you read; no race ever
possessed nobler qualities than the Caffre, whose degradation, if he be really degraded, is due to his contact with
the intrusive European race. Colonel Graham, who founded
Grahamstown, assured me that when he first came in contact with the Caffre race, they were a mild, amiable, gentle,
and most hospitable race, but that the Europeans had converted them into tigers. For my own part, I found them
to be such as he describes them to have been, and withal
intelligent and disposed to industry. I do not believe
them to be equal to any European race, but they are much
superior to the Negro. The story of their Arabian origin
is simply a fable. In this primitive land, where I first
saw nature's landscape and the unsophisticated aborigines
of the soil, an opportunity also occurred of remarking the
rapidity with which a highly intellectual and energetic
race of Europeans, when long settled in a country remote
from the great stream of European civilization, may
descend in the scale of intelligence. The ignorance of the
Dutch Boers—that is, of the descendants of Europeans
long settled in the country—can scarcely be imagined; but
climate has not modified the race to any great extent, and
instead of becoming shorter in stature, so as to approach
the pigmy Bosjieman in that peculiarity, they, on the contrary, are a tall and still vigorous race. But it is said, on
good authority, that their families are not numerous, and
that, notwithstanding the extraordinary salubrity of the
climate, and the absence of such diseases as fever, dysentery,
and pulmonary consumption, the race would finally, even
in this delightful climate, become extinct, were it not
maintained by fresh imports from Europe.

The primitive races of this land are or were two, the
Hottentot, namely, or yellow race of men, and the Caffre.
No two races differ more from each other than these two

limitrophic races. French travellers speak of other races of a
lower stature even than the pigmy Bushmen and Hottentot,
but their reports have not been confirmed by others. In
front of the strong-armed, rapacious, unprincipled European intrusive race, these two primitive aboriginal races
rapidly disappear. Driven from their native lands, the
Europeans now follow them to the tropics, where both meet
the helpless Negro, doomed, as it would seem, to be a slave
to the rest of mankind. In the meantime, the antagonism
of civilized man to nature is exemplified on its largest
scale, and the landscape of nature fast disappears before
civilization. The aboriginal Fauna and Flora, including
the aboriginal man, will in time become extinct, or nearly
so, and civilized man, with his domestic animals, gardens,
and fields, will, for a season, take their place. The intrusive
race here is the Scandinavian and the German, composed
chiefly of the Anglo and Dutch Saxons, the race supposed
by many to possess the highest qualifications for colonists.
These qualifications, in whatever light they may be viewed,
do not, as M. Montalembert imagines, depend upon their
political institutions, but on their race. On leaving the
monarchy-oppressed atmosphere of Europe, where men
are not acknowledged to have any rights as men, but are
merely permitted to live as the *subjects* of a hereditary
robber, the bold Saxon emigrant, whether Dutch or
English, declares himself a freeman ; his cry is onward ;
he recognises no chief, no king, nor governor, as the
Celtic man ever does, but *the law :* that is his sultan.
The country of his adoption becomes his own ; he ceases
to be an Englishman or Hollander as soon as possible ;
throws off his allegiance to his parent country, and acts up
for himself. This the Celt never does, but clings instinctively to those institutions which suit his nature ; with
him it is always the age of Louis Quatorze, or the grand
epoch of *the* Empire. He looks constantly backwards—
to the past ; the Saxon ever forwards. To this is due his
superiority as a colonist, and not to any great amount of
freedom permitted him by the oligarchical institutions
of his parent state. Now if we apply the doctrine of the

influence of race over the destinies of nations to the present
condition of Africa, we may discover, I think, the elements
for solving the problem as to the probable future of Africa.
The Lusitanian race gradually dies out in tropical Africa
and will disappear; the Celtic race occupying Algiers with
an army of 80,000 men, has not as yet reached the Sahara;
Morocco and Tunis are still in the hands of the savage
Moor, the Arab, and the Turcoman. In the south, on
the contrary, the Anglo-Saxon, preceded by the Dutch
Saxon, has already reached the tropic; before them the
native races vanish. The discovery having been made
that the possession of the country on or near the equator
decides the fate of nearly all that is valuable in Africa,
missionaries and travellers are boldly pushed into Central
Africa as pioneers, to be followed by bales of cotton goods.
These of course require protection; chief after chief,
nation after nation, fall before the strong-armed race;
their aim is the possession of Central Africa, the land of
gold and of the Negro, the master-key to the entire continent. For such an enterprise, Pretorius, with a few
hundred Saxon Boers, is worth a whole army of Celtic
men, though led by the bold soldier who stormed and took
the Malakoff.* The Scandinavian and old Saxon, when

* When I first learned, more than two years ago, that the Government of France had once more turned its attention to the lamentable
failure of Algeria as a colony, and was about to establish, in hopes of
bettering its condition, a system of railways in the province, I was
curious to know in what direction these railways were to run. To my
surprise, I learned that they were to be "coast lines." Happening to
be in communication with a French officer, an ancient friend and most
estimable man, I took the liberty of calling his attention to the remarkable differences in the colonisation plans of the two races now
aiming at the conquest of Africa, pointing out to him that in the hands
of a Saxon race three lines of rails would have long since been laid
down, of which one would lead directly to Fez, another to Tunis, and a
third towards Central Africa. I took occasion also to recommend him
to inquire of the colonial minister for France, if there be such a person,
by what peculiar Celtic management the fine colony of Senegal had
remained in abeyance for nearly two hundred years, profoundly asleep.
In the hands of a few Saxon Boers of the Pretorius' cast, a line of commercial stations would long since have been established between the
River of Senegal and the Niger, and the French flag would now have
floated on Lake Tchad and in Timbuctoo, and the key to the possession
of Africa would long ere this have belonged to France. No notice of
my communication was taken. In the same communication I pointed

they emigrate to a foreign land, unlike the Celts, are sure
to take possession of it, and to identify themselves with it ;
in a word, they forget their fatherland and assume a new
name.

Thus, we have Americans who are only Americans by
accident of birth: Tasmanians, Australians, Africaners,
all intrusive races of one stock into foreign lands—men
who have forgotten, or who will soon forget, their fatherland. So it will be with Africa, unless climate inter-
fere; the Saxon, having now discovered the great strategical point for the subjugation of the continent, pushing
northwards, will take possession of the entire continent,
ousting the Celtic and the other races as they did in
America and India; future Clives, Wellesleys, and Dal-
housies will conquer and annex, until, becoming sufficiently
strong, the colonists may repeat the scenes of Boston and
Bunker's Hill, sending forth a "Declaration of Independence." The rights of men is a phrase for ever in their
mouths; by men we now know they mean white men.
When the day arrives for the flag of independence to be
unfurled on the Zambesi, or the banks of Lake Tchad, or
on the equator as it crosses Central Africa, then woo to
the dark races whom nature placed there. It were better

out to my friend that even their best political writers, such as the
reviewers in the *Revue des Deux Mondes*, seemed to be wholly ignorant
of the geographical relations of Central Africa to the surrounding territory, and thus misunderstood all political, commercial, and strategical
questions connected with that continent. It probably proved offensive
to the bureau. Since then, however, I find that some one must have
thought the advice worth attending to, for an expedition is announced
as about to penetrate from the Senegal to Timbuctoo. It will consist,
no doubt, of soldiers, according to the old-established rule of Celtic
colonization, at the sight of whom the industrious become pale, and
hide themselves; fear seizes the trader, the capitalist escapes from the
land. All this I pointed out to my friend in Paris, but as race never
alters, so I do not for a moment imagine that any system but the one
employed in Algeria will be resorted to in the attempt on Central
Africa from the Senegal. In the meantime, the missionary and the
trader from South Africa are on their march from the Cape, and
will reach Lake Tchad and the southern border of the Sahara long
before the fighting column of Celtic dragoons will have reached the
Niger. Since this was written, my prediction has been verified:
Marshal Pellisier has been named Governor of Algeria, to whom the
task has been assigned of *decentralizing* the colony and bringing forward
the civil power ! !

for them that the feeble Lusitanian or the dreamy Celt,
with his everlasting age of Louis Quatorze, his *gloire
nationale*, his passports, his forts and redoubts, had prevailed.   A noble-minded man[*] has just said to three
European races of men, whom he mistakes for nationalities,
—"Cannot you respect each other, and live at peace?" but
I would rather say, why not embrace within this grand
and truly Christian proposition all the races of men?
Why not say to them, "As nature seems to have made
you antagonists of each other, why not labour by education, by commerce, by mutual forbearance, by respect for
each other's gifts, to overcome the eternal and mysterious
fiat, which stamped on each race moral and physical
qualities admired by their possessors, despised by the
rest of mankind?"   But will a Celtic empire—or rather
monarchy (for it is no empire), supposing the Celtic race
to be successful, or a Saxon republic, in the event of
Africa falling into the hands of a Saxon race, continue to
hold Africa?   That is a question for time and nature to
solve.   If we look to past history, I feel disposed to say,
that such a power can endure only for a limited time, to
become extinct after certain generations, and disappear, as
did the Carthaginian and Roman, Greek and Vandal,
leaving, perhaps, to nature the restoration of her aboriginal
productions; to nature, a never-ceasing force, which,
however bent, will surely return the instant the compressing power is relaxed.   That compressing and antagonistic
force is civilization, which, ceasing to act but for an instant,
permits the wild man, and beast, and plant to re-occupy
the land from which they had been driven.   But all may
not return, for some species may in the meantime have
become extinct.   The wild Bushman, like the Gipsy, if
extinguished as a race, will cease to occupy a place in the
ethnological history of mankind, unless represented picto-
rially or otherwise in the scientific works of the learned;
for from his skeleton remains could never be conjectured
the singular peculiarities of his external forms whilst a
living race.   Thus, whatever fate destines for Africa, it

[*] Kossuth.

seems not difficult to predict its probable future for a period of time. Should it pass into the hands of the noble and chivalrous race who now invade it from the North (an event, to say the least, extremely improbable), and who, unfortunately for the rest of mankind and for the progress of humanity, cannot be made to comprehend the meaning of the term "the rights of man"—in a word, who do not admit men to have any natural rights at all, but only those which the bayonet gives and maintains, then Africa, unhappily, will become the dependency of, or colony of, a grand monarchy, to be ruled, as now, by sabreurs, pure and simple.

But the Celtic race, composing the population of France, deals, it must be admitted, mildly with their darker brethren, and in this respect Africa might gain by passing from the hands of the Turcoman, the Saracen, and the savage Saxon Boer, into the hands of a race and a government to whom the very principles on which an empire must ever be based seem to be wholly unknown; whose minds are wrapt up in the model monarchy of Louis Quatorze; who cannot live without a sultan.

If, on the contrary, the Anglo-Saxon race prevail, and it now, after its usual quiet and seemingly inoffensive way, marches boldly on Central Africa (for this is the land aimed at); sending here a missionary and there a captain of dragoons, now a German doctor, anon a troop of merchants with a government agent and a missionary, merely to look after the interest of the natives in a manner well understood in England, and well explained by Dr. Livingstone, also well known in India and in Australia, but nowhere better than in Caffraria—then woe to the coloured races of men! Their ancient and most implacable enemy is at last on their soil in force, and the United States of Africa may one day achieve for that continent what the race has all but effected in America—the extinction of the aboriginal races of the land. Long ere this, the revolting traffic in slaves would have exhausted Africa also of its native race, but commercial and selfish England, having in the interim lost America and gained India with two

hundred millions of ready-made slaves, and no longer requiring the services of the unhappy Negro, proclaims to
the world that she will not tolerate the African slave
trade. But should Africa come into the possession of tho
Saxon race, England's sham humanity will be of no advantage to that continent, so long as the colonizing, conquering, intrusive race continue to hold for the Negro race that
unconquerable antipathy or antagonism which marks their
intercourse with all the coloured races of men. For Africa
there is but one hope—the establishment of an empire, or
at least of an imperial government, founded, not on the
Napoleonic idea—an aggregation, namely, of petty monarchies, subordinate to a central one—but on the principles
by which Augustus, Trajan, and the Antonines ruled the
then known world. Such empires have long ceased to
exist, and it is questionable if such governments be now
possible; they existed before the antagonism of race had
assumed its present exaggerated character; they existed
before the spread of Christianity and of Mahometanism.
Under an Augustus or an Antonine, man was free to
worship the Deity of his choice or of his belief, to practise
whatever religious folly he preferred; throughout Europe,
at the present time, to cease to be orthodox, to cease to
conform, is to forfeit all, or most of, the privileges of
citizenship.

The future of Africa is, to a certain extent, wrapt up in
the destinies of the two invading or intrusive races,—the
Gaulish, namely, and the descendants of the Jutes, Angles,
and old Saxons. Celtic France may remain stationary in
Algeria, or even retrace her steps without dishonour, abandoning her trans-Mediterranean conquests; for England
there is no such alternative, nor, if there were, would
commercial, energetic England accept of it; she must go
on. In advance of her colonists and armies, rush on the
Saxon-Dutch Boer, committing cruel devastation on the
coloured races of men, and it were as disgraceful as impolitic for England to suffer this much longer. Thus,
she must of necessity advance, such being, as is often said,
" the destiny of the race." If the end resemble her course

in America, India, and Australia, the future of the coloured races of Africa may easily be foretold.

Conclusion.—Thus ascribing to race those events which others ascribe to chance or destiny, I could not but arrive at the conclusion that, as regards progress, the Gaulish race are ill adapted for colonists; and I naturally took a deep interest in the latest attempt of the great Gaulish family to found a colony in Africa. I was curious to know if the race had altered in any way; the hurricane of the first great revolution ostensibly swept off the three grand incubuses, the three destructive and obstructive influences weighing down society, but it had not, and could not bestow new qualities on the race; could not bestow on them the boldness, avarice, practical ability essential to a successful colonist, whilst under the *régime* of the sword, a *régime* they so much prefer, the term citizen can have no meaning. In the absence of that intense labour, stimulated by a desire for accumulation—for gain, I felt convinced that, whether in Africa or America, the Gaul could make no real progress as an intrusive race. Accordingly, after the lapse of thirty years in the case of Algeria, and of three hundred years in that of Surinam, there has not been a single symptom indicative of vitality in the race. In the meantime, writers, journalists of the highest ability, have written about Africa and Algeria—and written well, as they always do.* But in these writings I cannot discover any proofs that the great questions I now consider are even suspected to exist. I am naturally filled with surprise on finding political writers of the first abilities speak of Africa as if it were a hundred years ago, who fail to observe the vastly different relations that continent now bears to the European races to what it did but a very few years ago; who see nothing worthy of note, and draw no inferences respecting the present and the probable future from the discoveries of Galston and Burton, of Speke and Livingstone; who seem to look on these active political partisans as if they were "mere African travellers," and who are evidently wholly unconscious of the true nature of

* The reviewers in the *Revue des Deux Mondes.*

that small and distant cloud, which, scarcely visible from a European point of view, is about to burst on the African soil. Is it that owing to their nature, the Gaul cannot be made to comprehend the possibility of any peaceful conquest? Must he always look to massive battalions and to the sword? Where does he find in history that any true progress was ever made by the mere *sabreur?* What conquest—what advance in civilization, unless the man of peace follow or precede the battalion? What single step in the progress of civilization can be traced to the *class militaire?* Are they not merely the consumers of the labour of others? It must be owing to race, that such circumstances escape the notice of otherwise highly talented men.* And now mark the difference in the mode of action of the two races. On one side battalion after battalion are poured into Africa; on the other, meeting after meeting of shrewd, quiet, political men is held in London and Manchester, Oxford and Cambridge: the Guildhall and the hall of Trinity College are in perfect unison: nobody mistakes the object—no one speaks of it: the aim is Africa. The key giving possession to Central Africa and of all the continent has been discovered, and is now in the possession of England. Political agents, under the form of missionaries, merchants, travellers, boers, captains of dragoons, &c., are marching forward to enter en possession. The commercial man at war with all nations is there; the soldier is at hand, but kept out of view.

On this continent the two great leading European nations now display the essential differences of their race; it is the field-marshal—the *sabreur* pure and simple—who fights not to enrich his nation, but himself, against the bale of cotton and the man of peace; aggressive, fierce—not warlike, but obstinate and courageous in the defence of what he considers to be his right. These two races fought the same battle in America, and are about to try it once more in Africa.

What in the meantime will be the move of the indigenous races? To endeavour to hide themselves, and seek

* The reviewers in the *Revue des Deux Mondes.*

a shelter until the storm blows over. But the intrusive races now follow them up to the cradle of their origin: the savage Dutch Boer is on their *spoor* in Southern Africa; the Anglo-Saxon shoots beyond, and appears on the Zambesi, to be shortly heard of on Lake Tchad and on the Niger. It is the same race which destroyed the Red Indian of America, and who now hold in bondage four millions of Negroes on the American soil. Already the colonists of Natal have petitioned the governor for an enactment, legalizing *enforced labour on the blacks!* Will it end in the scenes lately witnessed in India, or in a repetition of what now exists in the Southern States of the American Union? I lean to this latter opinion for reasons drawn from the history of the United States of America.

In the meantime this new crusade against the heathen, the black man, the Fetiche worshipper, the accursed of Ham, the descendant of the Canaanites, and who, strange to say, were not Negroes as they ought to have been, thrives, and is popular with all classes. It promises new sources of trade, and profitable investment for several influential classes — the military class, the priestly class, the ruling class, the commercial class. The Gaulish race move after their old fashion: to the cry for progress, Government sends them a field-marshal, already well known for his feats of arms in Africa; but it kindly promises a supply of slaves from China, it having been ascertained that to the north of the Sahara the Negro does not thrive.

The name of Albert de Broglie is attached to a well-written article in the *Revue des Deux Mondes* on "Administrative Reform in Africa," meaning, in sober terms, the proper management of the colony of Algeria, which the Gaulish race of France—whether as a monarchy, or a republic, or an empire—have failed to discover. To a man of a Saxon temperament, such a failure at first sight seems almost incredible; and yet it is admitted as a fact by the whole of the French press. The second part of the review, concluding with the author's theories, alone occupies thirty-five closely printed large octavo pages, the essence of

which, with its refutation, it would not be difficult to sum
up in three lines. The Gaulish race, by their nature, cannot be made to believe in the stability or durability of any
government which is not purely military—that is, conducted by a class of men of all men the most hostile to
progress in human affairs—a class which never yet effected
anything for humanity; at the sight of whom men of
peace—the trader, the manufacturer, the agriculturist, the
man of science, philosophy, and art—depart. Thus it is
in Algeria. We have seen the class increase in France
during the reign of Napoleon the Great, until science,
literature, and art became all but extinct. Had that tre-
mendous reign continued but a few years more, all the
genius produced by the glorious revolution of '92 would
have naturally expired, to be replaced by those who have
lived from their earliest years with the naked sabre
at their throats, and to whom all free thought was forbidden.

Under such a *régime* you can only have drill-serjeants
and an armed police. It is a pure absurdity to talk of
citizens, active, intelligent, and enterprising. As this
régime has now returned in France, and recovered all its
pristine Napoleonic vigour, M. Broglie thinks, and no doubt
thinks justly, that from amongst a people so educated,
leaders fit to rule a colony—to forward its interest—to
raise it to the position of a flourishing province, or even a
state equal to its own protection, cannot possibly be found.
The prosperity of English colonies, as compared with those
of France, he ascribes, with much seeming truth, to the
circumstance that in the free parliamentary institution of
England there exists an education calculated to produce a
great many men of expanded ideas—civilians fit to rule
colonies and states. But the whole truth does not lie here;
English colonies thrive, not because they have public-
minded, liberal civilians, statesmen, and gifted men as
governors and secretaries (for it is notorious that the contrary is the truth), but because the colonists are of a laborious, industrious, independent race, who submit for a time,
and most reluctantly, to the ancient military and naval

officers sent to rule them, but are ever ready to throw
them off and to set up for themselves. The cause of failure
in respect of French colonists is the race. But I am free
to admit that with a Clive or Dalhousie as governors,
Algeria must have made some progress, and not proved, as
it has done, a failure. I pointed out to a French officer of
distinction, about three years ago, some of these circumstances,* recommending him to call the attention of the
central government to them, and pointing out the necessity
of doing what Saxon colonists would have done long ago,
namely, of connecting the colony of Senegal with the
Niger and Central Africa, and this latter by direct tram-
ways with Algiers and its southern frontier, sketching to
him all the advantages likely to accrue to France from
such a measure. I learn now, through the public journals,
that the views submitted to my friend have been adopted,
and are about to be acted on. But the scheme will require
to be carried out by other men than mere *sabreurs*, who
simply attend to their own aggrandizement, who measure
the power and status of a nation by the strength of its
army, and who hold in utter contempt the labourer, the
agriculturist, the tradesman, the manufacturer, the man of
peace. I cannot find in the various works on Algiers and
Northern Africa generally any proofs that any of the
writers have correctly understood and appreciated the
great value of modern discoveries in Central Africa, and
seem generally to be wholly unaware that the key to the
possession of Northern and Central Africa lies in the
country stretching from the Senegal to Lake Tchad, and
the sources of the White Nile.

The intruding European race which first gets possession
of this line of country becomes master of the future destinies of Africa. Here exists a Negro population cut off
from the rest of mankind, under governments almost as
odious as the drum-head sovereignties of Europe. In
one respect the unhappy Negro of Central Africa has the
advantage over the European slave, crushed to the earth
by the late Neapolitan, Austrian, Russian, and Spanish

* See note at page 551.

despots. If their bodies are enslaved, their minds are free. The double tyranny is peculiar to Europe.

***

PORTUGUESE IN AFRICA.

After the lapse of about three hundred years the Lusitanian intrusion into Africa approaches a termination. In St. Paul de Loando, the centre of their power, there was, when Dr. Livingstone visited it, one resident Englishman, an official of the English Government; it further contained 12,000 inhabitants, of whom there were

Whites . . . . . 830 {670 males. 160 females.

In Angola there were not more than 1000 whites; in Bengo, 11 whites. The Portuguese never showed any energy in Africa. The elephant abounded, but they could not domesticate it; in fact, they were merely a party of slave-hunting adventurers. Did the race produce no statesman—no man of ability? The Portuguese of Brazil are described by a recent traveller in that country as a race profoundly ignorant, and worthless for any enterprise. Perhaps no European race could meet for any length of time the drain upon its population which the maintenance of a colony in a tropical country necessitates. A European force of 80,000 soldiers is said to be required to maintain British supremacy in India, but it is doubtful if Britain could meet the exigencies of such a force in that country. There is a curious passage in Macaulay's "History of England" respecting the effects on the Celtic race of Ireland when, by the withdrawal of Tyrconnel and the "United Irish," Ireland was drained of its noblest blood. Now they amounted to only 14,000 men, and yet Macaulay thinks that the race never recovered from this loss.

The Celtic, a much more energetic race than the Portuguese, have not been more successful in tropical Africa. The finest position on the western coast of that continent unquestionably is Senegal. It came into the possession of

o o

the French in 1637 ; it possesses a noble river navigable towards the interior for several hundred miles. After more than two centuries of possession, here are the results in 1844.

Population, 18,753.
    Europeans.—Men, 138 ; women, 27=165.
    Indigenès, 6521.—Men, 3198 ; women, 3323.
    Engagées, 801.
    Slaves (here called captives), 10.196.
    Functionaries and Military, 808.

In Jamaica, captured by Cromwell in 1655, the population in 1844 consisted of—

Whites	15,776
Mixed (mulattoes)	68,529
Blacks	293,128
Total	377,433

Jamaica since its conquest has cost England in troops alone 75,000. The death rate is 120 per 1000, instead of 16 as in England. To maintain an armed European effective force (say 5000 men) for the protection of this one colony, would drain of its surplus youth a European population in the mother country of 2,500,000. I speak not of colonizing the island with white blood ; such an effort might prove too much even for England, if the death rate of all ages were found to correspond with that at the military age. Thus to maintain 80,000 men in India fit for military service, would require the surplus youth of a population at least twice as much as that of England, and there arises the momentous political question for the industrious of England, whether or not they find in the military possession of India an adequate return for the loss of so much life and treasure.

CONCLUDING CHAPTER.

THE PRESENT PHASIS OF ETHNOLOGY.

THERE are many, no doubt, who think that Ethnology originated with Blumenbach, and who fondly hope that it terminated with Pritchard. Why so many cling to a delusion of this kind admits of an easy explanation. To most men ethnology is a tabooed subject, forbidden, interdicted, and not to be thought of by the profane. Even scientific men* have blamed me for applying to man the physiological principle regulating all that lives, or that has lived on the globe.

When my " Lectures on the Races of Man" first appeared, it was objected by many that I had introduced into ethnology many questions foreign to it, and amongst these they included man's moral and intellectual nature. But from the very commencement of my inquiries into the history of nature up to the present moment, it had always appeared to me that such questions form of necessity the most important matter of all such inquiries. These qualities I considered to be as unalterable as the more obvious physical ones which, before my time, had exclusively engaged the attention of all ethnologists, and I had but to look at the map of the world at any time in the stream of history to perceive that in all great questions of civilization, religion, national power, or greatness, the element which chiefly influenced these was in reality the element of race. Why go back to ancient times for proofs of the truth of this proposition? Look at Ireland and Austria; America, North and South; at Africa; at India. I was blamed for having first brought forward this dangerous topic, and for placing it so prominently before the reading public; but why conceal the truth? The real

* M. Serres: " Mém. de l'Académie."

o o 2

question for the man of science is, simply truth; whilst I
now write,* the Saxon Government of England refuses to
admit into the medical service of the English army a
native of India, on the ground of his being, to a certain
extent, a coloured man. The Under Secretary of State
denies that the ground of refusal is *colour*; but I know
that it is simply *colour*—that is, race. The hypocrisy of
the Anglo-Saxon tries everywhere to avoid this question,
which meets him in one form or another in every part of
his heterogeneous dominions. He tries to make it appear
that medical men being employed in all climates, a native
of India is not a suitable person to enter the service!
Profound hypocrisy! Dastardly and mean! An insult to
common sense!

No good reason exists for regarding man as a distinct
creation from the living world, whilst as regards the history
and origin of ethnology, I learn from the classic authors
of antiquity, and more especially from the writings of
Hippocrates, that most ethnological questions had been
deeply considered by Greek and Roman writers. The
brilliant sketch of Blumenbach, " *De Varietatibus Humani
Generis*," glanced at, and was indeed based on, an idea
which perhaps originated with Buffon; namely, that the
great continents of the world being centres of creation,
gave origin to those varieties of men which the learned
German declined to call species. But even this idea, that
continents were centres of organic creations, was not new;
neither did it require much philosophy to invent. All
history, as well as the progress of geographical discovery,
showed that, as new continents became known to mankind,
races of men and animals hitherto unknown were found
to occupy these recently-discovered or rediscovered lands;
races which were not to be found on other continents. Of
this fact Buffon happily availed himself, and Blumenbach,
with the tact of a profound naturalist as he was, bestowed
on some of the races of men names derived simply from
their geographical position.

* Case of Dr. Thompson, a native of India, at this moment before
the House of Commons.

Having from my earliest years devoted much attention to the natural history of man, and as the results of my inquiries were opposed to the more generally received opinions, I resolved on the first fitting opportunity to submit these views to the public. Accordingly, as a prelude to a more carefully prepared publication, I delivered several courses of lectures in a considerable number of philosophic institutions, and in most of them with great success.[*] These lectures were afterwards published in a medical journal,[†] and finally collected in a single volume, under the title of "The Races of Men: a Fragment." These lectures preceded nearly all the works on modern ethnology. We are so habituated to view mankind as composed of *nations*, that when I proposed inquiring into their history from this novel point of view, I found but few who could distinctly follow me. The ignorance on this question of race was, as I have proved in the work on the "Races of Men," most profound. The celebrated Dr. Samuel Johnson travelled through Scotland without perceiving that he had come in contact with another race of men, of whom he knew nothing, and the *Times*, a few years ago, sent a special commissioner to Ireland to verify a question of race which could have been decided by a visit to Marylebone and St. Giles'. Thus, for some years I had the whole question to myself, nor was it until the revolutionary epoch of 1848, that the press condescended to admit that *race* had anything to do with human affairs. Since then many brilliant but erroneous articles have appeared in various journals[‡] on this question of race, as was to be expected from those who, finding a new and popular subject of inquiry started by another, proceed in the race much faster than any scientific man can be expected to follow.[§] Without alluding to this further, I may be per-

* In Manchester, Newcastle, Liverpool, Colchester, Sheffield, Chelmsford, Warrington, about fifteen years ago.

† The *Medical Times*.

‡ Especially in the *Times*, whose editor has been in the constant habit of plagiarising all my ideas without acknowledgment.

§ As journalists write for the nonce, they do not stand on scientific trifles.

mitted to remark, that all accustomed to view man as
composed of nations, and to look at his history only from
a national point of view, objected strongly to my theories,
as they were pleased to term them. They could not see
ethnological questions in the present sad condition of
Mexico and the so-called republics of Central and South
America, the past and present attitude of the Gaulish
race in Ireland and in France, the limitation of Pro-
testantism in Europe to the Saxon and Teutonic races
nearly. Day by day the opposition weakens; the great
questions of race are discussed in a calmer and more
philosophic tone, and there is every danger of their
running into the other extreme, and undervaluing those
acquired and artificial qualities strictly the result of
national influences. However this may be, I have the
satisfaction of knowing that these contributions to the
natural theory of man will be much more readily understood than my preceding ones, and that I shall experience
less difficulty in explaining to my readers than formerly to
my audiences, how it is that race influences the civilization
and destinies of nations. Day by day events, sometimes
of a terrible character, occur, proving the correctness of
the view. Whilst I now write, it is admitted that the long-
cherished scheme of amalgamating all the races composing
the Austrian Empire has completely broken down; the German population of Schleswig Holstein refuses to unite with
Scandinavian Denmark; Italy aspires to eject from her
soil all traces of the Goths and Vandals who have so long
misruled her classic land; for hundreds of years every
trace of that numerous and civilized Celtic population,
who built Milan and gave to Northern Italy the name of
Gallia Cisalpina, has long since disappeared, to the great
regret, no doubt, of the gallant armies who won the
battles of Marengo, Magenta, and Solferino. The
hybrids of South America, with the low vitality of all
hybrids, proceed rapidly to the destruction I was the first,
many years ago, to foretel; whilst in Northern America, the
European races, forgetting the land of their origin, have
given themselves new names. But nature disclaims the

deception, and says to them, "You brought with you from
Europe all the characters of race—some Celtic—some
Saxon—some Scandinavian—some German or Teuton—
as such, go where you will, you must for ever remain a
part of the race to which you originally belonged. You
are an intrusive race or races, you and your oxen, horses
and sheep. By avoiding all intermarriage with the aboriginal races of the soil, and with the black race imported
from Africa, you may for a time escape the annihilation of
your races; but a-head of you stands the grand difficulty
—climate and an uncongenial soil—certain in time to
exhaust the vitality of your race, as it has ever done with
all the intrusive." This is one of the checks nature adopts
to preserve her species of living forms, against the universality of one form of life; against man himself; for, inasmuch as *brigandage*, or a desire to plunder other nations
and races, to rob them of their territories, and to reduce
them to a sort of bondage or slavery, is the great aim of all
the nations and races of men, so, long ere this, one strong-
handed, unscrupulous, intellectual race, led by men of
genius, a Cæsar, an Alexander, or a Napoleon, would have
overspread and peopled the earth. But nature's checks ever
and anon upset their policy, arrest their *brigandage*, and
restore the world to what it was. Certain events in
history which seem incomprehensible, admit of a ready
explanation on the theory of race I now advocate. Apply
it, for example, to the Gaulish or Celtic race, whose chief
clan now occupies France; by a singular misnomer the
race are mistaken for Franks or Teutons. Their true name
is Velshes, and their character has never altered since
the remotest historical period, any more than that of any
other race tolerably pure. The Arab chief who, inquiring
of M. De Saulcy the name of the sultan of his nation, was
told by the learned Frenchman that "France was a Republic, and had no sultan," made this reply, "Impossible!
you cannot go on without a sultan." This happened
during the short-lived Republic of 1848. How speedily
was the remark of the Arab chief verified!

Each race, probably from national vanity, the eternal

enemy of all truth, underralues the gifts of other races.
Lowest of all, in the estimation of the other races, stand
the Negro and the Bosjieman. But the Negro is equal
to feats of arms; and, on obtaining their liberty, the blacks
of Hispaniola elected a sultan. This we Saxons esteem as
a great blunder, but we must not think the worse of them
for committing so sad a political error. Some highly civilized races have done the same, or have submitted to be
ruled by maniacs and imbecile dynasties, despicable and
abhorred by other nations; we must not think so meanly
of the Negro. When the Celtic race of France became
once more a republic in 1848, and once more acquired the
natural rights of men, many, not looking to the influence
of *race*, foretold a sublime future for that great country.
I doubted it; nay, I was sure of the contrary. I
rested my doubts on the character of the race, and none
will now venture to say that, in this instance at least, my
theory proved at fault. Races never alter. The war which
the Saxon carried on against the black races some hundred
years ago, he now pursues in Southern Africa. You will
be told the contrary by the interested; I recommend you
to read attentively the travels of the truth-speaking missionary Livingstone; not his speeches at the Guildhall, at
Oxford, and Cambridge, but the words of the traveller
himself, and judge for yourselves.

Ethnology is not a new science, but it starts from a
new basis; and, since the publication of my work on the
"Races of Men," it has entered on a new phasis. Hitherto,
we have been taught to look on mankind merely as
composed of *nations;* I ask you now, and was the first to
do so, to look on them as composed of *races*. M. Agassiz
says, that nature made *nations;* he must mean *races.*
Nations are artificial combinations of men, who may either
be of one race or of several. A moment's reflection on the
history of mankind ought to have proved this to the illustrious Swiss naturalist. Thus, the Germans, or Teutons,
are a race of men, and a most distinguished race too, but
they never formed a nation; the Jews are a race, not a
nation; and so are the Parsees, the Bosjiemen, and the

Gipsies. The Celtic Caledonian and the Kymraig of Wales
are a portion of the great Celtic and Kymraig races, but
they never formed nations, properly so called. But I
admit frankly and at once, that a race, to be entitled to a
page in the history of mankind, must form a nation, and
become, to a certain extent, civilized. Their civilized condition will be deeply influenced by the qualities of *race*,
hence the peculiarities of the civilization of Pekin and of
Paris, which are generally admitted to differ from each
other in some trifling matters; of London and of Madrid;
of Moscow and Naples; of Cairo and Milan. I have been
blamed for asserting that mankind can make no solid progress, more especially under the government of dynasties.
This question I discussed when reviewing the position of
the great American Republic, as compared with the
thoroughly rotten condition of the European populations,
ruled over by dynasties where *heredité* and *feudalité*,
nobles, priests, and kings, have done their best, or their
worst, to degrade mankind, and to say to the millions of
each nation,—" In the great game of life you can take no
part; you have no stake, belong to no class; to a chosen
few belongs the privilege of playing the game with loaded
dice; you have no chance. Nature may have bestowed on
you the highest genius and the greatest practical ability
to make good your position in the nation of which you
form one, but nothing of all this can avail you against
feudalité and *heredité*, against the classes to whom the
patronage of the earth by right belongs."

Under such a dispensation shall I call it? or infliction,
the European races must ever remain nearly as they are.
All dynasties are essentially obstructive; their very existence depends on the successful obstruction they offer to
the progress of intellectual man.

The correctness of my views on the fate of hybrids and
on hybridism has been called in question by some, but
many able inquirers have given their verdict in their
favour, whilst the theory respecting the extinction of intrusive races has met with almost universal support. Some
of my views as to the origin of species or races have been

in part already published.* I am now engaged in a more
extended inquiry into that subject. Ancient cosmogonies
are now on their trial in England; they have been long
set aside in Germany, and even in France, by the thoughtful and the scientifically educated. Zoology has assumed
a new phasis even in this country, or rather zoologists
begin to adopt, cautiously and furtively as it were, the
views of Duffon and Goethe, Oken and Geoffroy St.
Hilaire, Cuvier and De Blainville.† Nevertheless, the
reception so lately given by the Academy of France to
the Memoir of M. Broun, shows significantly that much
remains to be done before the new philosophy of zoology
can fairly be admitted into the temple of science. It was
the observation of Mr. Emerson, I think, and of M.
Guizot, that in no country in the world could they find
such instances of the endurance of customs as in England,
and Mr. Emerson instanced the charity bestowed on all
travellers at the Holy Cross of Winchester in proof—a
charity which had endured for many hundred years. I
could suggest to Mr. Emerson a sufficient reason for the
observance of certain customs in England and elsewhere,
and I feel surprised that the same did not occur to him.
The persistence of customs and beliefs stands on precisely
the same footing,—namely, "the numbers, wealth, and
power of those *interested* in opposing all and every
change."‡ The permanency of any system depends on the
interest taken by a powerful class to resist all change;
remove the interest, and the system ceases. "If you will
secure to me the Bishopric of Rome," said a liberal and
philosophic Pagan, prefect of the city, to a friendly and
urgent Christian, "I shall to-morrow become a Christian."
The metaphysicians of all ages (I do not include Mr.

* In the *Lancet* and *Zoologist*.
† As popularly explained in "The Vestiges of Creation" and in Mr.
Darwin's late work on "The Origin of Species."
‡ Universities and colleges originally founded by papal Rome with
a view to the perpetuation of Roman Catholicism naturally retain, as
an essential character of their constitution, their obstructive nature, re-
sisting to the utmost of their power the real progress of the human
mind. In the place of truth and the laws of evidence they teach logical
formulæ—words for facts.

Hume) have assigned to man a complex intellectual condition, which they have analysed each after his own fashion. But history, which is, or ought to be, an exposition of the practical working of the minds of nations, races, and individuals, when carefully read, disproves this view of humanity, reducing all human actions to a few great and simple principles common to all mankind. Such seems to have been the opinion of Tacitus, Voltaire, Gibbon, Hume, and Niebuhr; I have never seen any grounds for doubting the correctness of their view.

As it is science alone which opposes the spread of fanaticism and human degradation over the earth, scientific men are apt to set too high a value on the influence of science and genius. Arago was one of these persons; yet, even in his own time, Chateaubriand wrote as if no such persons as Cuvier, Laplace, Goethe, and Newton had ever lived. His writings, though opposed to authentic history and to all the truths of science, are in great request in France. Fortunately for science, the demonstrations of Cuvier cannot be classed by any sane mind with the reveries of philosophers; they upset all the ancient cosmogonies; greater than the discoveries of Newton, they reduce all ancient history to a mere fable—a myth. True, he framed many hypotheses, some of which were refuted by De Blainville; but the "Ossemens Fossiles" admit of no refutation. He meddled but little with human history, which yet is the great object of all inquiry. Antagonistic of all nature's works, man creates for himself a world of his own; he is nature's last and most fatal gift to the earth. But he will never succeed in extinguishing all the forms of life she has placed on the globe, although this has been predicated of him. He moves in circles which he mistakes for progress; the arts he invents are looked on by the next generation as mere rubbish; the thoughts and ideas of one generation are laughed at by the succeeding one, and looked on with contempt. The great object of dynastics and dynastic institutions is to arrest, to a certain extent, this grand law of renovated life surging up with each generation. In the attempts to stop nature's laws, lies the great

secret of the downfall of nations, education, the great
arm of the tyrant, being the means employed to paralyse
in the rising generation the influence of renovated life.
In the consolidation and perpetuity of national institutions,
I fancy I see the grave of human intellect, the tombs of
the hopes and progress of the mind of countless generations. Education, the grand arm of the tyrant, stereotypes
certain forms of thought, dwarfing the national mind on
all subjects of importance.* To this, no doubt, may be
traced the degradation of many great empires and races:
—China, India, Egypt, ancient Mexico, bear witness to
the truth of the theory. Hence the alarm at all changes
exhibited by all dynasties and dynastic institutions.

One of the elements which chiefly modify man's history
is the element of race. This natural antagonism of race to
race was first mooted by the subjects of Justinian, who objected to the reception of savage Negro nations into fellowship and union with civilized men. Yet the Abyssinians,
to whom they applied these terms, were not Negroes. And
now the question agitates the entire world; from New
Zealand to the shores of the Baltic, it is a fight of races.
Ireland, Austria, Italy, America, North and South Africa,
India, Syria, are prepared or preparing to fight once more
the battle of race, and to prove of how little avail are moral
and religious codes in modifying the moral and physical
qualities which nature has stamped on the various races
of men. Thus, races of men have their histories as well as
nations—histories lost in the abyss of time; they have
an individualism, and form a family which may be destroyed, but not sensibly modified, by climate. It is this
question of race, and the possible reconstruction of the
map of Europe on the principles of race, which startle and
alarm the gigantic robbers who dismembered Poland and
Sweden, crushed the energies of the Scandinavian race,
and, by maintaining a perpetual conflict in Germany and
Italy, hope to destroy for ever the hopes of the Teuton

* When Napoleon the Great became emperor, he engaged the
venal press of France to write down and calumniate the memory of
Voltaire.

THE PRESENT PHASIS OF ETHNOLOGY. 573

and the Italian, to take their place amongst the great
nations of the earth.

Of the various questions connected with inquiries into
race, the capability of civilization under one form or
another is clearly the most important, civilization being in
fact the great aim of all mankind. Could it be shown
that there exists a race incapable, under any circumstances,
of becoming civilized, who cannot be taught "the laws
that guard the social rights of human kind," then such a
race would unquestionably belong to the untameable
"wilde," and must of necessity be put to the ban of the
world. But on that point the humane may, I think,
take comfort, for no such race exists, or perhaps ever
did exist.

The question next in importance to that of civilization
is the capability of the geographical extension of a race.
On this depends ultimately in some measure the power of
the various races to form communities, nations, empires,
republics, hives derived from the original stock; and we
have seen that this quality is much more limited than is
generally supposed to be. Various races have at different
times overrun the then civilized world; the Arab, for
example; the Mongol; the Turcoman or Tatar; the Greek,
and the Roman—where are they now? Brigandage, or
the attempt to take possession of the lands and property
of foreign nations, is the staple trade of all the races of
men. Hence the importance of tracing these intrusive
outbursts of races and nations into foreign lands, and as
these attempts have been unceasing since the commencement of authentic history, a sufficiency of materials perhaps
exists to trace the effects of this grand system of brigandage
on the destinies of mankind. But these intrusive races are
of necessity exotic; now, exotics seldom thrive, hybrids
never. Of the delusions which beset most races when
formed into powerful nations, one is, the notion that the
earth was made for them alone; another, that all the races
of men may ultimately amalgamate, and so become one; a
third (a very natural delusion) is, that the existing generation is infinitely superior to all that preceded it, conceding

at the same time that, by a continual progress and constant improvement in the *physique* as well as in the *morale*, the human race fast approaches that happy condition called " the perfect."* The solid progress which mankind seems to have made since the commencement of history, is reducible to very narrow limits. A Roman,† who had himself seen and formed a part of the highest civilization to which man can attain, expressed in a few words the history of the progress of humanity; and if Macaulay, adopting and adapting the idea of Sulpicius to modern times, has expressed in more inflated language the same idea, he has coupled with it certain misconceptions and scientific errors which the Roman by a higher generalization avoided. For if, by future New Zealander, Macaulay means a pure and unmixed race, descended from the present savage indigenous race, then all history shows that no such race ever attained any high civilization; if, by future New Zealander,

* There is one race which, having already attained perfection in all things, cannot, to be consistent, admit both theories. That race is the mixed population now occupying England. In proof, I cite the character of the nation as drawn by one of themselves, a popular metropolitan priest, trained no doubt in Oxford or Cambridge, and deeply read in the history of the world. It formed part of a discourse delivered on the 4th of May, 1856, in the church of St. Stephen, Walbrook, by the Reverend Dr. Croly. He is excusing the horrible butcheries committed by the English in India: " England had succeeded to Israel, and had possessed unexampled prosperity as the depository of the true religion. England had the freest constitution in the world; by the gift of God she had the most extensive empire, she had the most exhaustless opulence, she had the most substantial, vigorous, and comprehensive commerce; she had the most productive agriculture; she had the most active manufactures, with the most intelligent artisans, and the wealthiest, best-clothed, best-fed, and manliest peasantry in Europe; she had been gifted with the two great inventions of the age—the steam-engine and the railroad, the greatest inventions in the world; she was the only country in the world where loyalty was a principle, secure while every other throne had been shaken within memory, and the continent was revolutionary at this time; and those exclusive grounds of superiority she acknowledged to be the sole bounty of God as its gifts to the professor of the true faith of the Scriptures." " (The collections for the church to be erected at Constantinople, morning and evening, amounted to 38l. 11s. 7½d.)"

It must, I think, be conceded that nothing more can be said on this subject, and that Condorcet's theory of the advance of mankind towards perfection is wholly inapplicable to the nation spoken of by Dr. Croly, they being already perfect.

† Sulpicius.

he meant a hybrid race, descended from the intrusive
European and autochthonous natives, such a race would
share the fate of all hybrid races—that is, become extinct;
and if, by future New Zealander, he meant a race of pure
European blood, standing their ground for many centuries
in the land of their adoption, then he speculates on what is
most problematical and still to be proved.   Incomparably
superior to the ideas of the hired partisan of a class of
men leagued together for the plunder of Britain and her
colonies, were the views of Gibbon, expressed in sublime
language, worthy the first of historians.   In contrasting
the opposite extremes of savage and civilized life in the
present and past condition of Scotland, in a land in which,
according to St. Jerome, some of the tribes at least in his
days were cannibals, the historian observes: "Such
reflections—the conversion, namely, of the cannibal Scots
into a noble and highly civilized race of men—tend to enlarge the circle of our ideas, and to encourage the pleasing
hope that New Zealand may produce, in some future age,
the Hume of the Southern Hemisphere."[*]   Equally just
in my mind was his view of the progress of humanity,
which in point of fact accords with that of Sulpicius, who
moralized on the fallen cities of Greece and Asia nearly
twenty centuries before the time of Gibbon.   "Since the
first discovery of the arts, wars, commerce, and religious
zeal have diffused among the savages of the old and new
world these inestimable gifts, namely, the use of fire and of
metals; the propagation and service of domestic animals;
the methods of hunting and fishing; the rudiments of navigation; the imperfect cultivation of corn or other nutritive
grain; and the simple practice of the mechanical trades;
these arts can never be lost.   We may, therefore, acquiesce in the pleasing conclusion that every age of the
world has increased, and still increases, the real wealth,
the happiness, the knowledge, and perhaps the virtue of the
human race."   Admitting to the full the correctness of the
great historian's view of human nature, and the extreme

* Of this sublime reflection, Lord Macaulay's celebrated passage is
simply a caricature.

modesty of his claims in favour of the steady progress of
humanity, I still feel disposed to think that there are races
which advance not in civilization ; for the arts enumerated
by him do not constitute civilization, and if lost, would
speedily be rediscovered. Others which, after having worked
out their own civilization—as all races must do and have
ever done—have receded in presence of an intrusive race,
and reverted to a condition unmistakeably barbarous. In
the history of the Arab and the Kabyle, the Jew and Gipsy,
the ancient Peruvians and Mexicans, and in the present
condition of Asia Minor and of the Persian states, we
still find proofs that true civilization is a delicate and
sensitive plant of long and artificial growth, quick to
perish—no matter what the race may be—under the rude
grasp of governments, whose sole objects are spoliation
and robbery of the people. France tells a sad tale, so
also does the history of modern India ; it is about to be
repeated beyond a doubt in Central Africa, for man moves
in circles, of which the last is sometimes the most contracted. A race is a family with strong family likenesses,
moral and physical. What the most Christian people in
the world—indeed, according to their own belief, the only
true Christians on earth—what this wonderful people did
in America and India, they must repeat in Africa, which
they now invade at all points. A new crusade has been
formed, the banners of which are the cross surmounting
a bale of cotton ; Oxford and Manchester combine to push
forward the good work, which, aided by the Armstrong
gun, cannot fail to reduce Africa to the condition we now
so much admire in the United States of America, Australia,
India, etc.—the native races exterminated, or ground to
the earth in the most abject condition humanity can
assume. All this endures for a time. At last nature
resumes her course, and the intrusive race disappears.

But, although this question of the fate of intrusive races
be, after all, the most important in the history of nations,
and even of races, since upon its solution must ever depend
all calculations as to their extension over the earth, their
progress in wealth, in political power, and in the kind of

renown which most men prefer, it yields in certain respects to another, namely, the capability for a high civilization. Hence the history of the civilization of a race, and the progress it has made in the social and fine arts, in literature and science, ought naturally to engage our attention more strongly than mere feats of arms. There is a delusion, which as it flatters the vanity of each successively existing generation, will probably hold its ground for ever. Each generation feels confident that, as being the latest, it must be foremost in all the arts which ornament humanity. They have had the benefit, so they say, of all preceding generations, and of necessity they must be superior. This great delusion probably pervades all the races of men; with the Saxon it is a stereotyped belief; it is organic. Yet there never was a greater delusion nor a deeper misconception of the facts of history. I have called it elsewhere the *pioneer* theory, as based on the idea that the Copts, Assyrians, Hindoo, and Mongols were our pioneers, and as if perfection in art, literature, and science depended on the attempts of successive generations to improve on the practice of their predecessors. But if this were so, how are we to explain the state of Europe during the Middle Ages, occurring so long after the absolutely perfect in art and literature was attained by a race of whom we really know nothing (the antique Greek). For thousands of years after their æra not only did art, literature, and science decline, but even to this day, with the remains of antiquity before us, we cannot approach the ideas of that wonderful race; nor is it going too far to say that many powerful, civilized nations now on the earth cannot even comprehend the meaning of such terms as the absolutely perfect, the true, and the beautiful, in the right conception of which all art, literature, and, perhaps, even science are included. Of the social or mechanical arts I speak not here; they originate in necessity, and after all merit but little consideration in the history of mankind.

The idea of supporting ethnological propositions by the testimony of ancient monuments, originated, I think, with

P P

myself:* in proof I may refer to M. Edwards' letter to
Thierry the historian. The proofs derived from such
monuments are open, I am aware, to many objections.
Some of these I have stated in the observations on the
Coptic race and on other forms of ancient civilization.
Seeing the phasis ethnology has now assumed, its practical
application to human history may be safely left to the
journalists of Europe. In the chapter on the Past, Present,
and Future of Africa, I think I have proved that the element
of race cannot be omitted in solving the great questions
affecting humanity.†

The destinies of civilized nations depend no doubt, to a
certain extent, on the policy of the ruling powers of each ;
but this policy, mainly made up of family connexions
amongst the despots, is being constantly checked and
modified by the element of race. The successors of
Charlemagne divided central Europe amongst them in 843.
Then France became distinct from Germany, and to this
separation and period, historians trace the hatred subsisting between the French and the Germans.‡ But when we
reflect how distinct the Gauls (now called French) have ever
been from the Germans, Scandinavians, Sclavonians and
Italians, it is impossible to refer to a mere political event a
natural antipathy. The true Frankish blood has long disappeared from Gaul and from Italy. For a thousand years
the families in possession of all power have met and remodelled the map of Europe to suit their purposes. In
this remodelling, of which a remarkable one is now in progress, the last thing thought of is the interests of the
people, of the nations. They are no more considered now
than they were in 1815 and in 855. The congresses of

* M. Polsky ascribes the idea to Messrs. Nott and Glidon, but their
observations were made long subsequent to mine.
† I was surprised to observe lately, in a number of the *Times*, that
" Mr. Macaulay had startled the world by ascribing religious differences
to ethnological causes. In no part of Macaulay's works can I find any
reference to such a view, which is indeed contrary to all his theories of
history. It was first proposed in my work on *The Races of Men*.
‡ Voltaire, " Espr. et Mœurs," vol. ii. p. 15.—" Thus was Germany
lost to France." Voltaire ought rather to have said,—" Thus was Gaul
lost to Germany."

the descendants of Charlemagne ended in Europe falling into the hands of a number of petty despots, or barons, and bishops, whose struggles for power and wealth reduced Europe to a state of complete barbarism.

We have seen the Roman or Italian power rise and fall, leaving scarcely a trace of the race in any of the countries it had subdued. If we now trace the barbarous trans-Rhenish and trans-Danubian races over the same grounds we shall find similar results. Vandals and Saxons, Suevi, Alemanni, Goths, in brief, the races whom Rome had not overcome, poured into France, Spain, Africa, Asia Minor, Italy, and held for a time these countries. Nearly every trace of these barbarians has now disappeared, and the primitive races again occupy the land. The Arab, too, arose in his might, and thought to have conquered the earth; they are at present nearly reduced to what they were in the time of Xenophon. The last of the Goths in Spain has been long dead and gone, and the olive races of the Peninsula are now in all probability what they were when Hannibal traversed it on his way to Italy. These Arabs were a superior race to the natives, and but for their *book* were capable of the highest civilization to which an Oriental race is equal.

About the year 812 a race new to Europe appeared on the confines of the Byzantine empire. I allude to the Russ or Muscovite, who now play so important a part in European history. Their great political ruse is to make it appear that in reality they form a portion of the Slavonian race; whilst the Pruss, the first cousin of the Muscovite, strongly desires to be thought a German.

Amongst the European races, as well as amongst others, physical force is the great power which effects everything. As each race poured into civilized Europe, it established its rights by force. In this originated the kingdom of Hungary, peopled by an eastern race; a Tartar race, the same, in fact, who afterwards, under the name of Turks, destroyed the last remains of the Roman Empire in the East.

If we calmly survey the present position of the European races, we may, I think, arrive at the conclusion that little or no improvement can be hoped for so long as they are governed by the present dynasties or families, and educated by the now existing priesthood. It is the interest of these two classes to deny to men their natural rights as men; to perpetuate the rotten institutions of the past, by giving them a new coating of varnish, and so pass them off on mankind as if they were new and in accordance with what they call the spirit of the age. When Malthus, in his anxiety to establish his own theories and refute Condorcet, denied to the human race that principle of progress which the theoretical and ardent mind of the modern Celt desired to bestow on it, arguing, that to the increase of food nature had set certain limits beyond which she could not be compelled to go, and that this limitation in respect to food rendered hopeless and visionary all such theories as that of Condorcet, he might, as I think, have found a better reason for the slow progress in the improvement of mankind, in the institution within whose walls he composed his work on population. Two grand obstacles prevail in Europe, as they have ever done in most countries, to the improvement of the human mind; these are the organized faction or class who enjoy hereditarily the monopoly of the government of a nation and the plunder of the millions; the second is the priesthood, by whose aid have been formed those corporate bodies called Universities, whose aim it is to stereotype for centuries the errors, mistakes, and follies of a bygone age. By these means the progress of the human mind is reduced to its minimum, and so maintained.

It may be asked—How is it that each generation on attaining the force and dignity of manhood, does not shake off these antiquated rottennesses and demand free scope for the human mind? The answer is easy. In each nation there exists a vast conspiracy against the people, united, combined, vigorous, watchful, auspicious. Scarcely any nation can break down such a union. It has been attempted in almost every country, but with little or no success. Whilst it endures, human progress is impossible.

Amongst the various races of Europe it is easy, I think,

to perceive traces of some pre-historic races, of whom we have no account whatever. The Boors, so well represented by Ostade and Teniers, and still to be found in Flanders, seem to me to be the remains of a primitive race spread all over the Low Countries, and extending eastward towards the Black Forest and westward into England. I have been assured that the race still exists in the Black Forest. The Kymri, or Cimbri, still exist in Wales; a few, mingled with the Celts, are to be found in Ireland and Caledonia.

Most writers seem to think that the Belgians are the direct descendants of the Kymri, and the present Welsh (a distinct race of men) have the advantage of being in possession of the name.*

* I subjoin a well-written letter on the subject of the primitive Kymri, written by one who has evidently studied the history of race:—

"Bristol, Dec. 12th, 1868.

"Sir,—I am glad you are going to republish your lectures. I hope you will have each race illustrated with a woodcut; there can be no difficulty in finding individual portraits which would do for types of the several races. With great respect and deference, I also hope you will, more in detail, describe the differences of the subdivisions; for instance, the 'Celtic' is described in your last as one race with general characteristics, whilst in reality there are included in that race subdivisions with the most opposite characteristics; for instance, the Gaelic or Erse is described as having a common character with the Kymric or Welsh, two people differing in blood, language, and religion as much as the true Celt and Saxon; for instance,—

The Kymric	The Erse or Gaelic
Is never witty, always humourous;	Is always witty;
Is always cautious;	Never cautious;
Always makes a good sailor;	Never makes a good sailor, always a good soldier;
Has broad shoulders, high and awkward, waddles as he walks;	Has narrow shoulders, springs as he walks;
Has a receding mouth and prominent chin;	Has a prominent pouting mouth, no chin;
Has a broad, rather a low head, great width between the parietal bones;	Has a high, narrow head;
Is metaphysical and disputative in religion; acknowledges no authority except approved of by his own reasoning;	Never reasons on religion, but likes the showy and sensuous; is by nature made for being priest-ridden;

No facts exist favouring the idea of a Caucasian stock of men, originally appearing in that region, and spreading afterwards over the earth. Wagner, who visited the Caucasus, speaks of the idea as repugnant to history and to common sense. It is sufficiently curious, no doubt, that many distinct races of men have been found to inhabit the Caucasus, but the ancient history of Asia might almost afford an explanation of the circumstance without ascribing it to physical causes. To such a mountainous region, tribes and races would flee from their enemies. As usual, limitrophic races bear no affinity or resemblance to each other, a fact to which I have already called the attention of my readers. The Nogays, for example, show a striking contrast to their nearest neighbour the Circassian, whose nose is aquiline and features noble. The Nogays, on the contrary, have the true Mongol type; small sparkling eyes and projecting cheek bones, exactly resembling those of the Calmuck. "The old men look

The Kymric	The Erse or Gaelic
Never begs, is too proud; wants the Saxon's energy to make money, but has more than the Saxon's caution to take care of it, and so seldom wants; cares not for glory;	Is by nature a beggar, never thinks of the morrow, and so frequently is destitute and a burden to other nations; loves glory;
	When the two races are brought in contact, they always display great antipathy;
Has talent for mathematics (William Price, &c.); Classics (Sir W. Jones, Archdeacon Williams, &c.) Welshmen fill half the Dissenting pulpits of England.	Has talent for mob oratory, with true pathos; for newspaper editing (witness half the newspapers of England); for Government offices (witness the Excise and Customs, &c.)

I could enlarge, but it is unnecessary.

"You are, of course, better acquainted with these matters than the humble writer of this letter. Mr. Propert, of the Benevolent College, is a good specimen of the one race. I should here mention my firm conviction that the Kymri is not the race which inhabited Britain in the time of the Romans, but are the descendants of an invading race which came into the island after the Romans left or when they were about leaving. The Gael is the true ancient Briton. I should mention that, in saying this, I am thoroughly conversant with Kymric literature, and consider it a myth, which proves nothing.

"I remain, sir, yours very respectfully,

"KYMRO."

like satyrs, even uglier and more brutish than the frightful and sensual negroes of the Soudan, met with in
Algeria."*

"I once related," observes Dr. Wagner, "to an
Ossetian, in Tiflis, that amongst the learned in Germany
it is a common opinion that the Germans are of the same
stock as the Ossetians, and that our forefathers formerly
dwelt in the Caucasian mountains. The Ossetian, who
was a very handsome man, with the Circassian aquiline
profile, laughed outright at this, and an educated Russian
who was standing near, agreed with him.

"A Wurtemburg peasant, of the colony of Marienfield,
was just then passing by. The plump figure of this
German, his broad countenance, with its heavy expression,
and his slouching gait, contrasted, certainly, in a striking
manner, with the glorious figure of the Caucasian. 'How
is it possible,' said the Russian, 'that there can be such
fools amongst you as to believe that people of such different types could possibly proceed from the same stock?
No; the ancestors of these two men have no more come
from the same nest than hawks and turkey-cocks. Look
you; this Ossetian and that German carry on the same
business; they plough the field and tend the cattle; let
them send their peasants to the high mountain, and dress
them all in the Caucasian coat, yet you would never make
an Ossetian or Circassian out of them. A thousand years
hence it would be easy to distinguish the posterity of both
a mile off.'"

When we recollect that Hippocrates has placed near
the borders of the Black Sea the former existence of a
race of men called Macrocephali, the whole territory, including the Caucasus and Caspian, becomes of great
interest to the ethnologist. Wagner has treated this
question in a superior manner. On the subject of mixed
marriages he remarks : "The Russ, or Muscovites, are
fond of intermarriage with the women of other races, and
it has been remarked that, whatever be the race of the
woman, the male (Muscovite) influence predominates."

* Wagner.

The Hungarian is a Turk or Tartar, and an intrusive race in Europe. Had he mingled with the Sclavonian, the mixed race might perhaps have stood its ground for a time ; but, as it is, they have probably fought their last national battle in Europe; their only hopes rest in a union with their own race, the Turk, whose expulsion from Europe must, I should think, shortly take place.

The Sclavonian race wants a leader. They are the most intelligent of men, the most intellectual, the most metaphysical, the most original in thought. Kossuth, perhaps, has no equal in the present day. The Bohemians are Sclavonians, not Germans. The Austrians are the descendants of the Gothic race. All these races are now to be found where they were when first they became known to the Romans.

" The features of Oriental women are regular but unimpressive, they want sentiment and soul." The remark strictly applies to the Jewess, who, no doubt, is Asiatic and Oriental.

" The handsomest of the Georgian race are the Imeritians of Colchis."

Some primitive races of men seem to have existed in the vicinity of the Euxine, presenting the form of cranium which in later times has been found to prevail only in America. "The Macrocephali," observes Hippocrates, " were so named by reason of the length of their heads. This disproportion arose at first from a custom, but at present nature concurs also."* " So soon as a child is born they fashion it with their hands, compress it with bandages and other machines adapted to this practice or custom, so that they force it to elongate itself and to take insensibly a spherical form. At first this was merely a custom, but with time, nature was so bent (pliée) that it no longer required to be forced by custom."

He further adds, " If this does not happen amongst these people as formerly, it is that the practice has fallen into disuse by man's negligence."

On reading this passage one is almost tempted to ex-

* P. 72. Coray's edition.

claim, " Is there never to be anything new under the sun ?"
Here is the entire description, theories and all, of those
who have described the same practices as prevailing
amongst the Chenooks.   The coincidence is most remarkable, and leads the cautious, not to say the sceptical, to
entertain the strongest doubts on the subject.

Similar skulls were dug up a few years ago near the
Danube, and were thought to have belonged to the Avars,
a Hungarian race, but were also conjectured by some
to have been the skulls of Peruvians brought to Europe in
the time of Charles V.   They resemble, in fact, the skulls
of the ancient Aztecs.   I have not seen them, and decline
offering any opinion.

Pallas, a distinguished naturalist and original observer,
remarks that " the Tartar mountaineers of the three villages
of Keckenuo, Leimere, and Somans, have a strange
physiognomy, different from that of all the other inhabitants of Crim Tartary.   Faces of an uncommon length,
as well as arched noses, exceedingly long and high heads,
compressed with a view to render them unusually flat, all
contribute to produce diversified caricatures, so that the
greater part of these persons have distorted countenances,
and the least deformed resemble the figures of Satyrs."

" It is further remarkable that the hair and beards of
such mountaineers are almost uniformly light brown,
reddish, or even flaxen, a circumstance seldom occurring in
the Crimea."

In Strabo (xi. 297), I find the following remark bearing
on this question of artificial deformation of the cranium—
" On dit aussi que quelques uns de ces peuples s'étudient
à rendre les têtes de leurs enfans fort longues et à faire en
sorte que leurs fronts saillient au point d'ombrager le
menton."[*]

Thus Pallas borrowed from Scaliger, and he from

---

[*] Pallas' remark may be traced, I think, to Scaliger, who seems to
have disliked the Genoese.   Scaliger, in *Comment. sup. Theophrast. de
Causis Plantarum,* lib. v. p. 287:—" Gennenses cum a Mauris progeni-
toribus accepissent olim morem ut infantibus recens natis tempora com-
primerentur, nunc absque ullo compressu Thersiteo et capite et animo
nascuntur.

Strabo; nevertheless, on Pallas' authority we must believe that there is some foundation in fact for the ill-natured remarks of Scaliger. Pallas resided long in the Crimea.

That the form of the skull might be greatly modified, and even its texture affected by external circumstances, seems to have been a received fact in very ancient times. Thus Herodotus says,* "I saw on the field of battle a very surprising thing, which the inhabitants of the canton pointed out to me. The bones of those who perished on this day (the battle between Cambyses and the Egyptians,) are still dispersed, but separately, so that you see on one side those of the Persians, and on the other those of the Egyptians, in the same places where they were from the beginning. The heads of the Persians are so tender that one may pierce them by striking them merely with a nail (caillou) ; those of the Egyptians, on the contrary, are so hard that one can scarcely break them by striking them with stones. They told me the reason, and easily persuaded me of its truth. The Egyptians, they observed, began at their tenderest age to shave the head ; their skull hardens, by this means exposed to the sun, and they do not become bald ; one sees, in fact, much fewer bald men in Egypt than in any other country. The Persians, on the contrary, have the cranium feeble, because from their youngest years they live in the shade, and have the head always covered with a turban. I remarked at Paprenies something similar in respect of the bones of those who were defeated with Achemenes, son of Darius, by Maros, King of Libya."

Thus early was hypothesis introduced into the great question, involving the very essence of the natural history of man.

I have sometimes felt disposed to view the elongated head as an exaggerated type of cranium, common enough in France and throughout Europe. It is characterized by great length, narrowness, and a depression extending

* *Thalia,* lib. 8, p. 97.

across the vertex nearly from ear to ear. This depression M. Foville regards, erroneously, as I think, as the effect of a mode of swathing or bandaging the head of the new-born infant in some parts of France; but this form of cranium is to be met with frequently enough in Britain where no such practice prevails.

It would seem that amongst European races, there occur from time to time individuals having a form of cranium resembling, to a certain extent, the characteristic forms of other races; but I do not remember ever observing in any European cranium a size of maxillary bones equalling, or even approaching, that of the Negro.

A disfigured or distorted skull is not peculiar to, though most remarkable in, the Chenooks; it affected more or less the whole Carib race. The Aboriginal Peruvians also had the skull distorted, one side of the face being much shorter than the other. This want of symmetry extended to the basis of the skull and involved the maxillary bones.

LINGUISTIC VIEW OF RACE.

I was much pleased to find that so excellent a linguist and observer as the Baron de Dirgkinck Holmfield takes the same view as I have always done in respect of the linguistic question in its bearings on ethnology. In a memoir published in London in 1859, to which my attention was called by my esteemed friend Mr. Somervell, of Hendon, the Baron explains, as I think, clearly, in his theory of the origin of words, why all languages should have certain relations to each other, certain common roots, which in no way, however, proves an identity of race. "Thus when the Jutes call the cow bos, it is far from being derived from the Latin bos, and the theory of affinity among the primitive inhabitants founded on such comparisons is a mere illusion." After the invention of the word from the involuntary expression of striking sensations or impressions, comes their extension by analytical analogy, also common to all men and instinctive. The affinity of lineage between nations must not be rashly supposed on account of a precarious similarity in the forms of

speech, which no more imply a common descent than the
use of similar coverings or dress, and of instruments for
various purposes.* In a word, the affinities of language
do not bear much on the qualities of race, for many reasons
which could be given; their diversities, on the other hand,
prove the existence of different races, each expressing,
after its own fashion, the view it takes of the external
world.

RESUMÉ.

THE object of this *resumé* is to present to the reader desirous of knowing the true bearing of the author's opinions
on the influence of race over human affairs, a brief outline
of these opinions. The inquiries contained in the preceding
pages were first delivered as lectures, and subsequently
collected and published as a work on *The Races of Men*.
To that work he has now added a supplement.

When the author commenced these inquiries, the clever
essay of Blumenbach and its extension by Prichard constituted nearly all that had been written expressly on the
question of race. Historical research speedily satisfied
him that these excellent writers had scarcely touched this
great question; and Court de Gebelin's failure on the
linguistic view of race convinced him that the natural
history of man was not to be arrived at from that point of
view.

All writers on race had, prior to his time, omitted the
history of the *morale* of the race described; an extraordinary omission, seeing that the intellectual character of
the race was a much more important one than the physical.
The causes of this were the vague notions taught in all the
national educational institutions of every civilized nation—
institutions whose object it is to stereotype the human
mind according to their model or pattern and to stop all
intellectual progress. Overcoming this deep-rooted prejudice that the human mind was a *tabula rasa*, and could

* P. 22.

be made to assume by human means any colour, and to
admit and retain any impression; having, in a word, become
convinced that the Hippocratic doctrines were false, and
that it was in reality the quality of race which played the
great part in the modification of human character, there
remained for him but two methods—either to accept of
ancient history as it is, or to endeavour to trace backwards
in time the history of race, starting from the present age,
and pursuing the inquiry until trustworthy documents,
could no longer be found. The first method was wholly
out of the question. The ancient history, accepted by the
men of the last century, had been proved to be utterly
worthless. The Indian, Chinese, and Egyptian records
could not be trusted, and the Jewish chronology had turned
out to be defective in the all-important matter of dates and
circumstances. Its cosmogony was refuted by Cuvier; its
human chronology by Lepsius, Bunsen, and others. There
remained, then, for the author but the second course—
namely, to trace the history of race backwards in time
from the present day, and thus avoid a difficulty which
must for ever prove fatal to all inquiries conducted by the
other method.

A disquisition into the origin of the universe, or even
of the globe itself and what it contains, is scarcely a philosophic inquiry; at all events, it is, for obvious reasons,
not within the bounds of science. It requires no logic of
the schools, but simply common sense, to be convinced that
the human mind cannot penetrate into the origin of things.
For even admitting to the full the philosophy of Goethe and
Lamarck, as popularized by Geoffroy St. Hilaire, and other
modern transcendentalists,* which teaches the transmutation
of forms in time and space, this philosophy (which, be it
observed, is not science) does not explain to us the origin of
life on the globe. The author adopted, therefore, unhesita-
tingly the second method, proceeding from the present to
the past. The materials at first at his command were scanty,
but they increase daily: these materials were, 1st, Anatomical research: 2nd, The artistic remains of ancient and

* The Author of *The Vestiges of Creation*, Darwin, &c.

modern races ; 3rd, History. A few of the leading results
are as follow :—

1. The time and the mode of the introduction of life and
living forms on the globe of the earth are equally uncertain. What is certain is, that the remoteness of the
period surpasses the human imagination. This was demonstrated by Cuvier as regards the so-called lower
animals ; he avoided speaking of man. But, as all living
animal forms have an obvious common *consanguinité*, are
constructed upon one plan, and are physiologically identical
as forming one great chain of being, it is not to the
scientific man a matter of so much moment to determine
man's antiquity on the globe. A fossil man will no doubt
be discovered, together with numerous links in the chain
of being connecting him with the highest of the existing
apes, but now extinct. Between a gorilla and man several
intermediate links have been lost which one day will be
found. The antique or fossil man was no doubt specifically
different from all the now existing races of men. How
specialities arise we know not, but as they constitute the
realizations of nature's great scheme or plan, we must hold
by them ; there being, in fact, no other guide for him in
acquiring a knowledge of the living organic world. Even
were he convinced that there is in reality no such thing as
a distinct species ; that the idea of species is fast leaving
the minds of philosophic observers ; that neither Goethe
nor any of his school ever believed in the doctrine ; still
man, having no other idea to rest on, must hold by this
idea of species, remaining content with the great dogma of
Buffon—species is everything ; is perpetual, and never
alters. The illustrious De Blainville, the greatest anatomist and palæontologist of his day, called the author's
attention, about ten years ago, to the inquiries he was then
engaged on in his cabinet in the Museum. He showed
the author of this *resumé* a series of crania and drawings
of two natural families (the rhinoceros and hippopotamus),
which demonstrate the singular fact, that if you examined
any two of the specimens nearest in anatomical or other
characters, the distinction of species had altogether dis-

appeared, and that it was only by selecting two specimens
remote from each other in the series, that unmistakeable
specific distinctions became apparent. The result was
this: intercalating the palæontological with the living
world, all links were filled up, specific distinctions disappeared. Species then, after all, had no real existence, but
existed solely by this, that the intervening links having
disappeared, differences became apparent and manifest,
which in reality formed no part of nature's plan. What
conclusion, then, did De Blainville draw from these profound researches in which he stood alone? 1. That there
was but one creation; and that specific differences, as they
seem to us, were caused by time and circumstances. But
in truth this was Goethe's view, although the author felt
unwilling to point this out to his illustrious friend—namely,
that there never could have been any creation, life being
eternal and co-existing with matter; that all forms may
spring from all, and that all forms are possible within
certain limits. This is the philosophy of the present day.
It was first presented to the public in a popular manner
by Baron Holbach,* and, after a hundred years, it returns
to us again, slightly modified by the facts of modern
science. Thus all things move in a circle; and history,
instead of never repeating itself, represents the revolutions
of a wheel, which, as it revolves, presents to you the same
aspects, making allowance for time and circumstances.

2. Men are of different races palpably distinct. These
races are entitled to the name of species. These species,
though distinct in themselves, form groups so as to constitute one or more natural families. As in animals, so
in man, who also is one. The affiliated races, although
strongly resembling each other, yet differ remarkably, as
well physically as morally, in a way wholly inexplicable,
but on the principle that essentially they are not of distinct
species or races, however originating. This difference in
moral and physical qualities so remarkably distinguishing
even the European races (mostly formed into nations) is
best seen by referring to their various forms of civilization,

* Système de la Nature.

to their religious follies or belief, their antagonism to each
other, and, generally, to the view they each take of the
external world, which constitutes or gives a tone, as we
say, to the character of their civilization. By this the author
simply means their progress in literature, science, and art,
which together constitute civilization. Confining his observations at first to races frequently mixed and many strongly
affiliated by nature, he would venture to point out that,
as regards modern times, the Celtic race has never altered
or been modified in any way by climate or conquest.
Settled for about 200 years by the banks of the St. Lawrence and in the forests of le bas Canada, they retain the
character, institutions, religion, and habits of their forefathers who emigrated from *La belle France* in the age of
Louis Quatorze.* For at least 700 years the Irish Celt has
never altered, nor the Caledonian for twice that period.
France is Volshes, not Teuton. The author borrows the
phrase from Voltaire. Look at her armies and her present
attitude towards the world. M. de Montalembert complains bitterly that his countrymen had disappointed him
and the world: had he read *The Races of Men,* or the
lectures which preceded that work by some years, he
would therein have found that all was foretold, and that
no race could ever disappoint the author of that work
in respect of what we might expect them to do. Had he
cast aside his Utopian notions of the power and influence
of education, religion, government, and other circumstances,
and studied deeply the *Decline and Fall* of the immortal
Gibbon, or, still better, the *Esprit et Mœurs des Nations*
of his immortal countryman, he would never have experienced any difficulty in predicting how the various races
of men would act under various circumstances. This
unalterability, by climate or other accidental circumstances,
is not confined to the Gaul; it appears equally strong in
the Teutonic, Scandinavian, Gothic, and Sclavonian races.

---

* The minds of the Gaulish race in Canada have been so degraded by
their educational institutions (priesthood) that they benefited neither
by the American nor French Revolutions. In two hundred years they
have not produced a single superior mind.

They may mingle, but they do not give rise to hybrid races ; the original elements being as distinct in Britain, France, Spain, and elsewhere as they ever were. The hybrid races of Central and South America will perish in time.

3. Out of this question of the influence of race arise several others ; such as, what may be the antiquity of some at least of these races, and what the result of a commingling of two or more races ? If we appeal to the present and past conditions of men, we find that races seldom unite ; that when mingled together they gradually separate into their original elements, and that the product is never a hybrid race ; that what more frequently occurs is the extinction of one or other of the races. For many hundred years Italy has been more or less overrun by the Gothic and Celtic races ; all northern Italy was Celtic or Gaulish for more than a thousand years before the time of Augustus. There is no Celtic blood there now ; and this unpleasant fact has been twice made manifest to France in late times on two great occasions ; that is, after the battles of Marongo and Solferino. The "furious Frank and fiery Hun" fought for possession of Italy ; but the Italian race said, "We will have neither of you here any longer." This was in Milan, a Gaulish city built by the Gauls of France. If ever race was to show its sympathies it was surely here ; but, in truth, the Gaulish race, once so powerful in Northern Italy, was long extinct. To this day, all the European races occupy as nearly as may be the localities they were found in by the intrusive Romans, and they are still quite distinct, physically and morally, as proved by the varied forms of their civilization. No hybrid races exist anywhere. Intrusive races constantly perish or disappear in time ; for either the climate so tells on their vitality as to lead to their extinction, or this process is hastened by commingling with the aboriginal race. If this aboriginal race differ widely from the intrusive (as the Negro, for example, and European, or the native American with a race from Europe), the product is a hybrid, which ultimately dies out. Of the morale and physique of such a hybrid population the author need say nothing. In the

Q Q

present condition of Mexico and the States of Central and
South America we have the results foretold in the work on
"The Races of Men" more than twenty years ago, these results originating in the existence of a hybrid population,
and, as hybrid, devoid of every principle. It is fortunate for
humanity that such populations die out in time, returning
generally to the original coloured race. This is the only
theory or view by which the present condition of such
States as are alluded to can be explained, and even historians * begin to admit the truth of the theory.

4. Palæontological research will lead some day to the discovery of man's antiquity on the globe; the antiquity of
race, the author thinks, may be shown to be very great.
He means races as they now are, being still of the opinion
of Cuvier, that species do not alter or become metamorphosed into other forms so long as the existing order of
things continues; but should this be altered, then a new
organic world may appear, not wholly new to man, but new
specifically; and this is what man must ever look to. If
all the young of all the species of an extended natural
family represent the adult forms of all the species com-
prising that natural family, then the young of every species
is a generic animal, having a form so modifiable by altered
circumstances as to assume under these alterations a distinct specific adult form.† The species thus produced is new
to the earth; is to man a *new species;* nevertheless it is the
immediate and direct descendant of the preceding organic
world. Distinct epochs or acts of creation imply a miracle,
and miracles are impossible. The philosophy of Goethe,
adopted by Geoffroy St. Hilaire, Oken, and some popular
writers,‡ is most probably the correct one; but the really
scientific men do not as yet look on the theory as established
on a strictly scientific basis. The candid Broun, backed
by the French Academy, denies it *in toto.* Returning to
man, the author of this work, many years ago, fancied that

---

* Gervinus, in his latest works.
† See " Enquiries into the Natural History of the Salmonidæ," in the
Lancet and *Zoologist.*
‡ The Author of *The Vestiges of Creation,* Mr. Darwin, &c.

the antiquity of certain races at least might be tested by
an appeal to their artistic remains. Accordingly, he traced
and pointed out to many friends the appearance of at least
three races on the tombs of ancient Egypt. What, then,
was the age of these monuments? The lowest date assigned to them is about 7000 years, counting backwards
from the present day. Thus crumbled into ruins the
Mosaic chronology: his six days' cosmogony had been
destroyed by Cuvier.* Niebuhr, the greatest of all critics
in matters of history, has recorded his solemn opinion and
conviction that the Jewish history of mankind is simply a
fable or myth, and is beneath the notice of any historian.
The author of this *resumé* would be glad to see the theologians handle these opinions of Niebuhr in a fair spirit:
they show symptoms of great distress at the publication of
a few harmless essays and reviews, forgetting that Voltaire
and Gibbon, Niebuhr and Gesenius, Hume, Milman, and
Middleton, remain unanswered.

5. Each race on becoming a nation creates its own form
of civilization: what they borrow from others they modify
and adapt to their own nature. Of the elements of civilization the social arts stand lowest; they may indeed exist to a
very great extent without entitling the race to be called civilized. These social arts are human inventions, originating
in the necessities of man, and, consequently, are in relation
to these necessities, to his wealth and to his wants. As they
are not *in nature* no standard of taste is applicable to them,
each generation neglecting and despising the inventions or
discoveries, as they are rather facetiously called, of the
preceding generation. All races are equal to such inventions, however low they may be in intelligence. The
Chinese seem to carry away the palm even from the
Hindoo; then comes the Arab. The strong-armed utilitarian barbarians of Europe followed these slowly and after
a long interval.† It is otherwise with literature and the

* The theologian now endeavours to show that these six days were
vast periods of time: but, in this case, what becomes of the seventh day;
was that a period too?
† In Holland—Flanders first; following, of course, the progress of
commerce and wealth.

fine arts. To excel in these requires that the races possess
that quality of the mind which is not to be found in any
Oriental race—namely, an innate love of truth, of fine
forms, of the perfect, and of the beautiful. These qualities
were innate only in the antique Greek race, the race which
produced Homer and Pindar, Xenophon and Thucydides,
Plato and Socrates, Aristotle and Euclid ; who built the
Parthenon, carved the Venus, and fought the battle of
Marathon ; a matchless race, to whom the world is indebted
for all that is lofty and true in civilization. As we turn
from the contemplation of a Grecian temple, but, still
more, from that of a Grecian statue, to examine the follies
and extravagances of the European workmen (for they
were not artists) of the Middle Ages, and even of the
present day, it is impossible to avoid reflecting on the low
condition to which human intellect had fallen from an
innate contempt for truth, a condition which would have
continued till now, but for the disinterment of the remains
of ancient Greek art. Thus, with the author of this work,
the quality of race is everything in human affairs, and, to
a certain extent, it sways the destinies of nations. Great
conquerors have trodden down *nationalities*, but they
could not so easily extinguish the qualities of race. De-
tach a portion of a race from its cradle and force it into
contact with another, under circumstances to which it must
bend, they may soon lose their language, manners, and
customs, mingling with the mass around ; but provided
they become not extinct, their physical characters and
moral nature remain long after has been effaced the modification which social man receives from his government,
his education, and his laws ; for beneath this superficial
varnish there lies the quality of race, which, like a
smouldering fire, awaits but a spark to rekindle into a
fierce and devouring flame.

6. With the extinction for a time of nationalities and of
the conflicts arising out of the antagonism of race, conse-
quent to the universality of the Roman power, there occurs also the decline of courage and of genius, and the
rapid degeneracy of all the races whose political existence

had been extinguished by Rome: nor was it until Rome fell that life and vigour returned, as it were, to the subjugated races of Europe, Asia, and Africa. The natural antagonism of race to race productive of so much misery, but at the same time of so much activity, had ceased, or at least was not permitted to show itself anywhere between the wall of Antoninus and the Euphrates, between the Rhine and Danube and the borders of the Sahara. Rome was the aim of all; one language alone claimed every respect, and not to be a Roman citizen was not to exist. As the modern phrase is, "Order reigned throughout the world;" freedom of thought, as of action, was incompatible with that "order." Genius and the energy of thought and language could no more exist in the reign of Adrian or Vespasian, than under Cromwell or Napoleon the Great. Hence all the nations composing that vast empire had become, as it were, a compound of well-to-do pigmies "when the fierce giants of the North broke in and reanimated the puny breed." They enabled the ancient races to recover their individual existence; their natural antagonism and the power to show that the Procrustean bed of Roman civilization had ceased to satisfy the minds of men. It must not be supposed that this antagonism of race had ceased: it merely could not exhibit itself. On the dissolution of the central power of Rome it recovered all its ancient vigour.

From the shores of the Baltic and the icy promontories of Norway to the Great Wall of China, the barbarous races of this large zone of the earth quickly perceived that the restraining barrier had become weakened and might be forced. Accordingly it was soon overthrown, and the European races recovered ultimately to a certain extent the power to modify their form of civilization according to the character of the race. They assumed naturally national characters, characteristic in some measure of their race, and falling into the hands of despots, gradually subsided into the present condition of States ruled by despots, who base their government on the sword. Ever ready to assist each other against the peoples, there remains but one hope for the recovery of the rights of men—the continuance and growth of the United States of America.

The experiment had been tried which was to determine the possibility of ruling many races by one power, compelling them to take the same view of the external world, and, in a word, to adopt for civilization a livery of thought impressed on them by the tyranny of the sword. It failed in the hands of the Romans. Since then it has been often repeated on a smaller scale, as by the drumhead governments of Prussia and Austria, but with no better success. Now if with strongly affiliated races the question of antagonism of race cannot be extinguished, analogy leads us to suppose that it must be still more difficult to overcome in respect of races remotely affiliated. The result of the experiment to destroy the antagonism of the Spanish and native American races is before the world, and of this the Author has already spoken. It will come to the same results in India, whilst of its failure in Northern Africa there cannot be a doubt.

Now this leads the author of this resumé to a question of great difficulty. What is the exact standing of the savage races on the earth? and are there races of men, who by reason of their savage nature can never assume any true civilization? To this class of men seems to him to belong most of the coloured races of men, and even others but slightly tinged. The Moor, or Kabyle, is a true savage; just as he was in the time of Marius and Jugurtha, he is still. Under the Roman empire he became, as it were, highly civilized, and affected to be a Christian! It proved a mere varnish simply skin deep. The race, as is said, is still to be found tolerably pure in the island of Sardinia— a country as yet in a barbarous condition; and in the physiognomy of the gallant King of Italy may be traced some slight remains of an Altaic descent. The native American race, or races, are still savages, and so are the New Zealanders; the Hottentot and Caffres will remain as they are. Between the true savage and the civilized man there is, as has ever been, an antagonism not to be overcome. Even England, with all her professions of humanity and

RESUME.

philanthropy, cannot afford to admit within the pale of her society any coloured, that is, savage race ; cannot afford to admit any coloured man to the rights of civil and military freedom ; in other words, no coloured man can attain in England the full enjoyment of the rights of a citizen.* But this is not all. The fall of the Roman empire decided another great question—the question of acclimatation. At one time Southern and Western Europe, and Northern Africa and Western Asia, Syria, to the Euphrates and beyond, were peopled by Roman citizens of the Italian race: now and for many centuries not a vestige of such a race could be pointed out in any of these countries.

It is not merely savage races, properly so called, which seem incapable of civilization; the Oriental races have made no progress since the time of Alexander the Great. The ultimate cause of this, no doubt, is race. One circumstance peculiarly worthy of note is, that from the earliest period of history all their educational institutions were stereotyped, so that all minds ultimately sank to the same level. As a consequence they ever confounded fable with truth, and myths they mistook for history. True science based on an unalterable love of truth they could not comprehend, and thus the *true light* never penetrated the hazy realms of the Oriental mind. By science I do not mean mathematical science; the Hindoo calculated eclipses in the time of Alexander, but still his mind was not open to a physical truth.

7. The power of man to colonize or to live in other zones of the earth than that of which he was the native, has been tested in a great variety of ways from the earliest period. It is interwoven, though not necessarily, with other questions of which the most prominent is, the origin of man from a single stock, and the influence of climate so to alter his constitution without necessarily destroying his

* Decided by Sir C. Lewis, in a question of the half-caste native of Hindostan, who was refused admission to a civil employment in the English army, and in the refusal by Lord Panmure, when Secretary at War, to admit any coloured man of Canadian origin into the English army.

vitality, as to enable him to continue viable and productive
under numerous adverse circumstances.

On this point it is sufficient here to observe, that all
history is against the hypothesis of Hippocrates.   Certain
races only can exist in certain zones of the earth, whilst
over the *morale* of a race climate exercises little or no
influence.*

* At the recent meeting of the British Association at Manchester,
my friend, Dr. Hunt, the Honorary Secretary of the Ethnological
Society, submitted to the meeting statistical proofs of the accuracy of
this view, in an enquiry in which, for the first time, the great question
of the acclimatisation of man has been treated scientifically in this
country.

www.ingramcontent.com/pod-product-compliance
Lightning Source LLC
Chambersburg PA
CBHW021933110726
47901CB00003B/824